YOU DON'T KNOW WHAT LOVE IS

Contemporary American
Love Stories

compiled by
Ron Hansen

Ontario Review Press / Princeton

Library of Congress Cataloging-in-Publication Data

You don't know what love is.

    1. Love stories, American. 2. Short stories, American
I. Hansen, Ron, 1947–
PS648.L6Y68 1987   813'.085'08   87-15219
ISBN 0-86538-060-0

Distributed by George Braziller, Inc.
171 Madison Ave.
New York, NY 10016

"The Man from Mars" by Margaret Atwood. Copyright © 1977, 1982 by O.W. Toad, Ltd. Reprinted from *Dancing Girls and Other Stories* by Margaret Atwood, by permission of Simon & Schuster, Inc.

"My Man Bovanne" by Toni Cade Bambara. Copyright © 1971 by Toni Cade Bambara. Reprinted from *Gorilla, My Love* by Toni Cade Bambara, by permission of Random House, Inc.

"Horace and Margaret's Fifty-Second" by Charles Baxter. Copyright © 1984 by Charles Baxter. Reprinted from *Harmony of the World* by Charles Baxter, by permission of the University of Missouri Press.

"I Dated Jane Austen" by T. Coraghessan Boyle. Copyright © 1979 by T. Coraghessan Boyle. Originally appeared in *The Georgia Review*. Reprinted by permission of the author.

"Feathers" by Raymond Carver. Copyright © 1981, 1982, 1983 by Raymond Carver. Reprinted from *Cathedral* by Raymond Carver, by permission of Alfred A. Knopf, Inc.

"The Consolation of Philosophy" by Nicholas Delbanco. Copyright © 1979, 1983 by Nicholas Delbanco. Reprinted from *About My Table* by Nicholas Delbanco, by permission of William Morrow & Company, Inc.

"A Father's Story" by Andre Dubus. Copyright © 1983 by Andre Dubus. Reprinted from *The Times Are Never So Bad* by Andre Dubus, by permission of David R. Godine, Publisher, Inc.

"Hopeless Acts Performed Properly, with Grace" by Robert Dunn. Copyright © 1979 by Robert Dunn. Originally appeared in *Redbook*. Reprinted by permission of the author.

"True Romance" by Ron Hansen. Copyright © 1984 by Ron Hansen. Originally appeared in *Esquire*. Reprinted by permission of the author.

"In the Cemetery Where Al Jolson Is Buried" by Amy Hempel. Copyright © 1985 by Amy Hempel. Reprinted from *Reasons To Live* by Amy Hempel, by permission of Alfred A. Knopf, Inc.

CONTENTS

Preface

I HAVE APPROPRIATED the title *You Don't Know What Love Is* from a poem by Raymond Carver in his book *At Night the Salmon Move.* About an evening with Charles Bukowski the poem opens with these lines: "You don't know what love is Bukowski said / I'm 51 years old look at me / I'm in love with this young broad / I got it bad but she's hung up too / so it's all right man that's the way it should be . . ."

Although it's customary for some of us to exempt ourselves from saying so, we all presume ourselves expert in some aspect of love which often puts us at odds with another's conception. Like Charles Bukowski, we contentiously think of ourselves as superior in our insights or senior in our experience. We're even given to penitential rites in which one-sided expressions of misery give rise to corresponding advice about dumping the creep or some other prompt and serious action, and it all boils down to wising up some other person, getting him or her to be less of a sap.

In the same way, the stories in this book can be read as squint-eyed replies to a philosophy of love that is wanting in its accuracy or completeness. We can easily imagine the storyteller listening patiently and oh-so-sympathetically, but then, with some exasperation, saying, "You call that love? *I'll* tell you what love is." And what follows is one of these tales of ecstasy and despair, appreciation and resentment, friendship and jealousy, loss and redemption.

Everyone who has loved deeply knows that the pleasures of romance are accompanied by pessimism, sadness, anxiety, and pain—indeed, we typically measure a paramount love by the supreme torment it caused us, even raising the shirt of discretion to display our once-upon-a-time passion like the pink and wicked scar of an appendectomy. The *Lettres portugaises* that were thought to have been written by Sister Mariana Alcoforado tell the story of a seventeenth-century French officer on duty in Portugal who seduced the spirited young nun in her convent and then, in horror of the consequences, scurried away, on rat's feet, to France. Even though she was anguished by her great sin and dismayed by his betrayal, Mariana could write the Chevalier de C—: "I thank you from the bottom of my heart for the desperation you cause me, and I detest the tranquility in which I lived before I knew you."

A good half of the stories in *You Don't Know What Love Is* could have used that as an epigraph. We appear to seek out the spice of desperation and quickly put tranquility up on the shelf with the corn flakes.

The scope of this story collection is limited to sundry perspectives on love, and its ever-present companion hope, in order to give a comprehensive picture of the great variety of possible artistic responses to one general topic. And perhaps the relentlessness and psychic heat of the book's theme was my own reaction to so much in our society that is inchoate, neutral, and temporary, and so much in contemporary American fiction that is passive, indifferent, and suave. I have preferred stories of emotional persistence over those of that hyperactivity and be-still-my-heart emotional seizure we feel whenever we fall in love, but I have not preferred any one narrative approach over another. Stories of high moral seriousness may be neighbored by stories of tender comedy, psychological realism, anarchic sport and parody, wise-cracking elegy, or pathos, but the stories have in common spirit, shrewdness, percipience, and a cause or pursuit that matters.

In his book review of Denis de Rougemont's *Love Declared*, John Updike took the author to task for his complaint that in Western literature "happy love has no history" by pointing out that "the essence of a story is conflict—obstruction in [de Rougemont's] term. Happy love, unobstructed love, is the possibility that animates all romances; their plots turn on obstructions because they are plots. One might as well complain that 'easy success has no history.'"

So it is with these stories. *Eros*, or physical love, is interrupted, misunderstood, postponed, spoiled, or sundered in such stories as Margaret Atwood's "The Man from Mars," Tobias Wolff's "Desert Breakdown, 1968," Jim Shepard's "Piano Starts Here," "Manslaughter" by Joyce Carol Oates, and "The Priest's Wife" by John L'Heureux. *Agape*, the easier but no less bittersweet path of spiritual love and friendship, is the underlying theme in Jeanne Schinto's "The Friendships of Girls Unpopular Together," John Updike's "The Happiest I've Been," Amy Hempel's "In the Cemetery Where Al Jolson Is Buried," and John Irving's "Weary Kingdom," stories of affections and conciliations that are complicated by disillusionment, misinterpretation, premature death, or the simple fact that we all finally grow up. José Ortega y Gasset has written that "in most 'love affairs' there is a little of everything except that which strictly speaking deserves to be called love." Lorrie Moore's "How to Be an Other Woman" and Nicholas

Delbanco's "The Consolation of Philosophy" make the philosopher's meaning plain; while Jonathan Penner's "Frankenstein Meets the Ant People," David Leavitt's "Territory," "Death Apples" by Mary Morris, and "A Father's Story" by Andre Dubus beautifully illustrate the complex love relationships between parents and children. According to the German theologian Thomas à Kempis, "There is no living in love without suffering," an idea amply documented on many of these pages.

The book's contents are arranged in rough chronology, in accordance with the ages of the protagonists. Thus, a boy with an ant farm gives way to a teenaged girl and she, in turn, to a college sophomore at Harvard, and so on through Toni Cade Bambara's hussy and her nice ole gent Bovanne to Charles Baxter's cranky couple on their fifty-second wedding anniversary. However, the book need not be read from first page to last to have a significant impact, for in each of its twenty-four episodes, human depths are explored and interpreted with mastery and insight, intelligence and grace.

RON HANSEN

You Don't Know What Love Is

Frankenstein Meets the Ant People

JONATHAN PENNER

T HEY LAY CURLED in their chaise longues; the ocean foamed at the island dunes like milk. Perry and his wife were sharing a cottage with another couple. On the darkest nights, when the island seemed to slip its moorings, he sometimes liked to tell about his father and Jasmine.

He had been twelve, he could remember this distinctly. His father had come home on a Friday, impatiently fingered through the mail, lit a burner under the waiting potatoes that Mrs. Lawrence always peeled and sliced, mixed mayonnaise into the carrots that Mrs. Lawrence invariably shredded, and asked—he'd been a widower since Perry was two—"What would you think of my getting married?"

But the question was how Perry, a shrimp with an old man's cane and built-up shoe, no brother or sister, no money or lawyer, no understanding of guns, could prevent it. The woman would share his father's bedroom, where Perry would have to knock before entering. He could foresee the complete loss of his own privacy, and a shortage of closet space. In his own closet were collections and toys not touched for years, things that would seem babyish today, lifted out into the light.

"Who to," he asked.

For a long time his father had dated a woman like those in movie previews—that was how Perry still thought of them, because the movies themselves, his father had said, would be dull as hell for them both. The woman was thin, with huge mobile eyes, the whites too large for the irises, the irises too small for the pupils. Her perfume was stupefying, and she gave Perry stale sticks of gum from her purse when his father wasn't looking. When his father took him to baseball games she often came too, cheered at the wrong times, and incited Perry to plead for a cupped slush both of them loved, one that (his father shouted) destroyed the teeth, then the jaw.

But the woman whose name his father now pronounced, as neutrally as the time of day—"Jasmine Cook"—a partner in his architectural firm, didn't chew gum and couldn't possibly have ever cheered at anything. Her eyes were dead as marbles. All her expression was in her dark abundant hair, on which she must have spent half her life, transforming herself every day or two: poodles and ponytails, bunches and bangs, severe parts and sumptuous waves.

Vanity? Boredom? An architect's hobby? You'd see her head chained in braids, which it seemed to burst overnight, appearing the next morning in shock waves of fluff. For years, Perry hadn't understood that her manifestations were all of one person. She looked built to the scale of his father, the biggest guy in line at any ticket window. Her skin was so unblemished that it seemed to have just come from the store. Except for her unpredictable hair, she might have been a newly bought refrigerator, and it was that, her seeming not human, that always made Perry feel creepy after he had seen her.

"I don't know," he said.

Now his father was sprinkling paprika on the four chicken breasts, eaten five nights a week and endlessly reincarnated, that Mrs. Lawrence eternally skinned. In two minutes his father would turn on the radio for five minutes of six o'clock news. Then they would both sit at the kitchen table, reading, eating applesauce, while the potatoes boiled and the chicken filled the house with its sharpening aroma. Nothing would be the same: Perry felt a suffocating rage.

"I don't think you should," he said. Then he turned his chair around, away from the table, and sat squeezing both his soft upper arms. He knew that his father knew he was crying, but that they could continue the conversation as long as his father didn't see his face. If that happened he would find himself swinging through the air onto his father's lap, held between his father's arms and beating chest, inhaling the smell of his father's clothes and body; and if *that* happened he wouldn't be sure why he was crying, or whether he could stop.

His trouble, he would say in years to come, out for napoleons after the movies, masked and perspiring at Halloween parties—his trouble, he explained at poolside barbecues, standing chest-deep with a can of beer (he barely swam but loved the weightlessness)—his trouble had been that he never had a plan, because even thinking about Jasmine hurt so much he had to stop.

The Saturday after his father told him, Jasmine came over so they could all (said his father) discuss it reasonably. But none of them discussed anything. His father mowed the lawn at furious speed while Jasmine, her hair back in a kerchief, edged and swept the walks. Perry sat on the grass with his cane and radio and canteen of grape juice, now and then pulling weeds from the flowerbed border, feeling the house and lawn shift their loyalty from himself to her. When the mail came he hurried to get it—he didn't think he could even touch it if Jasmine touched it first. His father stopped and straightened, pressing both hands into the small of his back, arching so that his belly protruded in a way Perry found disgusting, then wrung out his sweatband and asked, "Anything good?"

And there was. The brown-wrapped box was marked KEEP FROM EXTREMES OF HEAT AND COLD. Perry took it inside and opened it at the kitchen table.

This was one of those times when the world surprised him with its fairness. It was months before that he'd ordered an Ant City from an illustrated ad in *Boy's Life* magazine, the drawing a closeup of two huge ants conversing in a cross-sectioned tunnel. Please Allow Six Weeks For Delivery—that seemed excessive, shameless, and he'd been pessimistic from the start, drawing less hope from the "Please" each time he reread the clipping. He came to sense the ant merchant's sneering triumph: here was a crippled twelve-year-old whose father didn't want ants anyway, the kind of kid you could do anything you wanted to.

But here was the package, and inside a manual—*Enjoying Your Ants* —and what looked like a little double windowpane, the space between its two glass panels halfway filled with sand—and a thumb-sized cardboard tube marked "LIVE ANTS!" His father and Jasmine had come into the kitchen behind him. "Lemonade?" his father asked, rattling ice from a tray of cubes. Jasmine pulled up a chair next to Perry's. He could smell her unfamiliar sweat, sweeter than his father's, somehow damper.

"How fascinating," she said.

Sweeping a dripping hand an inch above the swimming pool's surface, or, supine on webbed plaid plastic, thoughtfully patting his baking belly, Perry would try to convey to his listeners exactly how Jasmine talked. "How fascinating"—as though it were boring, and elementary, and sad. That was her only tone of voice, the pitch of defeated wisdom. No matter what she was saying, she said endurance was all there was.

She was turning rapidly through *Enjoying Your Ants*—even his father couldn't read that fast, and Perry guessed she was faking. "First drip some water into the city," she said. "May I help?" She brought the thing shaped like a double windowpane over to the sink, then back to the table. "Why don't I hold it," she said, "and you be the one to put them in."

"I'm not a four-year-old," said Perry.

"What?"

He began peeling off the tape that secured the cap of the tube. Of all times, he wished she were not here now, but with his father looming up at his other side, glugging and sighing at a tall glass of lemonade, there was nothing he could say. He pulled off the cap and peered inside—a slowly churning tangle of black. Excited, he gently began tapping them from the tube down into their waiting city.

There were far fewer than he had expected, no more than fifteen or twenty, but they were enormous ones, and Perry could see that this was going to be wonderful. They would always be in sight: their city was sliced so thin that their tunnels and rooms would have walls of glass. When the tube was empty he told Jasmine, "Put the top on." She reached to close the city. Then she made a peculiar sound, as though she had been suddenly squeezed.

A single ant had somehow not gone in and was clinging to the top rim of the city, its antennae twiddling the air. "*Wait,*" said Perry. But she was already coming down, her face averted as though the ant might jump at her. She caught him between the city and its top, and he hung out by one leg, his other legs working furiously. Perry grabbed the city, freed the ant, and dropped him in. The trapped leg detached itself and fell to the kitchen table.

"Hate them," Jasmine said, backing slowly away from the table, her hands spread like pitchforks against her thighs. Her face was still expressionless. Perry's father, wetting a fingertip, picked up the severed leg at once and took it outside, from where came the clang of the garbage can lid. "If you marry her," Perry screamed into the wall, but ended in humiliating silence—what could he even threaten?—stopped as suddenly as though his canetip had entered a crevasse.

"I want you at the wedding," said his father.

The ants milled slowly, apparently helpless, atop their sandwich of sand, and when Perry went to bed that night he expected to find them dead in the morning. But again, to his surprise and somehow his worry, the world was working as advertised. The little guys had gotten themselves organized and made a start on tunnel construction, piling what they excavated, so that the building went up as well as down.

"I want you at the wedding," said his father.

After that they did a lot of their work in the daytime, and Perry watched as the network of tunnels grew brilliantly, stupidly, intricate. The ants seemed to have no sense of how constricted they were, or how few. Did they think they could raise their young in those tunnels? *Enjoying Your Ants* said all of them were workers—shipping queens was against the law. How did they expect to reproduce, or what else were they building for? He fed them a cornflake every day, watered them, and waited for the first deaths: the dead, said *Enjoying Your Ants*, would be buried in a graveyard at the top of the city. But even Fiveleg—the only one Perry could identify—was hauling his grains of sand with what seemed inexhaustible vigor.

"I want you at the wedding," said his father. "Have some faith in me." He crossed his legs on the footrest of his reclining chair. "I've known her a long time. We work well together."

"Do you—" Perry attempted a knowing expression that a moment later he felt was ridiculous. Do you love her, he had thought he would ask, but the words seemed too silly.

Nevertheless his father understood. "Not like I love you. This is different."

"You haven't justified it, Dad."

His father looked at him closely. "I want you to be my best man." Then his father stared down at his huge slippered feet, pinching his cheeks with one hand so that his lips protruded. Finally he said, with an anger that startled Perry, "If it's a mistake I can *make* a mistake."

Perry felt unfairly beaten. How could you argue with something like that? "I won't live here," he said. Suddenly his life with his father seemed laminated into the past—even right now, stretched on the carpet next to the big chair, doing homework while his father rustled and snapped through newspapers, the smell of his father's socks coming through his cracked black slippers: strange! He wished he could tell his father what it was like—remembering the present.

("That's obscure," his wife would remind him years later, hearing the story again, with friends in a bar about to close—"Get to the car horns," she would tell him, stranded in a foreign airport.)

"I want you to be my best man," said his father. Perry saw himself in the wedding procession, walking alone in his great shoe, tilting over his cane. "I want you to hand me the ring."

Later, Jasmine came to his room, to see the ants, she said. Perry pointed to where their city stood on his dresser, next to his clock and Jacques Cousteau bathyscaphe. The bathyscaphe was a masterpiece— the only survivor from his years of building models. Now, seeing Jasmine's eyes flick past it, he knew he would throw it out as soon as she left the room.

"They're amazing," she said. "Why don't those tunnels collapse?" It sounded as though she wished they would.

"This is my room," said Perry.

Jasmine had begun to lower herself to the floor, but now she stood up straight, huger than ever next to Perry's little dresser, near his child-sized desk and chair. Her hair was styled like a helmet, as though she'd come from another planet. "Why don't you like me?" she asked, expressionless.

He would never be able to bear her as long as he lived, that was all he knew, no more than Jacques Cousteau could swim free of his brilliant chamber. "Because you're ugly."

"That's so." She seemed relieved, as though something hard had turned out to be simple. "When I was little, everyone thought so." And to Perry's amazement she began to clap her hands above her head, sidestepping around him in a little circle, while he rotated to watch her as she chanted: "Jasmine is a friend of mine, She resembles Franken-stein, I forget the something line, She resembles Frankenstein."

("Of course," said the girl who would soon become Perry's wife, as they lay through summer weekends in her vacationing parents' bed —"Of course," she said, stroking the hair back from his forehead, or kissing his foot that had never fully formed, "you knew it was yielding your father that you hated, not that poor lady." Jasmine had been something he loathed, not hated—a disfiguring illness—and though his heart was now quiet, the mark was there. Perry didn't reply, because he badly needed this girl. And in a minute she held his head against her breasts, or sat up in bed cross-legged, or brought fresh ice cubes for their coffee cups of wine, and asked him to tell her again.)

The morning of the wedding, while his father was out getting his hair cut, Perry stuffed some clothes into his school briefcase and caught a bus downtown. He had emptied his bank account the day before.

But at the Greyhound station, nauseous with diesel fumes, the throb of engines muttering from its tiled walls, all he did was sit on a bench ornate with obscenities, watching people depart and arrive. And it was as though Jasmine had infected everyone, because none of them looked human to him. Even children younger than himself—aliens in plastic skins.

Every few minutes a new bus delivered more, and others left. On one wall was a Greyhound route map like a vast anthill seen in cross-section. Perry saw how it was. The world was crawling with them.

He walked all the way home. The sun was high by the time he arrived. He wanted to be so tired he wouldn't think, but what he felt was only his regular walking pain and a terrible thirst.

At first he thought he'd mistaken the house. There were strange cars and a van in front. Inside, he found people in uniform: a fat woman in the kitchen, two waitresses setting out trays of half-dollar-sized sandwiches, and a white-jacketed bartender who quickly gave him a ginger ale. "Nice home," the bartender told him. "Those your ants? Pretty nifty setup."

"Your father was *sick*," said the fat woman, watching him gulp his ginger ale.

"Sick?"

"Just *sick*. I told him this is *his* day. Do you know he almost called it *off*? I told him absolutely *not*."

She bowled away back to the kitchen. The bartender, looking after her, made one hand into a flapping, quacking jaw. Then he fixed another ginger ale, this time with cherries. Burping, Perry took it to his room. But now the room hardly seemed his, he'd thrown out so many things he couldn't bear for Jasmine to see—books with print that was childishly large, walky-talkies with dead batteries, board games missing most of their cards, old snapshots of himself: in a sandbox, in a crib, riding on his father's back.

In later years a time came when Perry had to enter the hospital. He was to have tests for cancer, possibly an operation. While he was waiting to find out, his wife sat with him every day. Their friends from the city came, friends from the shore, until the room was like a florist's shop, and the nurses' aides laughed and brought more chairs, and people had to leave so new ones could sit, chewing each other's chocolates.

The man who shared his hospital room had no visitors at all. He could not speak; the doctors had taken his larynx. The cancer was still active in him. After visiting hours, when Perry's wife and friends had gone in a flurry of careful hugs, the mute loved for the curtains between their beds to be drawn back, and for Perry to talk. He lay on his side, listening, bright-eyed. It helped him go longer without his shot.

Perry told him the story of his father and Jasmine—how on the day of their wedding he had almost run away. How, coming home, he lay on his bed with the tingle of ginger ale in his nostrils, and realized, when he saw something move, that it was time to get rid of them, too.

He brought their city to his bed. Stretched on his stomach, his eyes inches from the glass, he watched their mindless scramble and rush. They couldn't know he existed, or even that they themselves did. And this, *Enjoying Your Ants* had claimed, was educational for the entire family. The ants knew nothing, Perry tried to explain—only what the whole world knew, the same imperative that held the oceans in their beds and hurled apart the stars. The mute, his cheek flat against his sheet, gave a horizontal nod. He was beginning to sweat.

At the end of the most remote tunnel an ant was lying still, and lay still as Perry continued to watch, even when he shook the city slightly. It was Fiveleg, apparently dead. Contrary to what *Enjoying Your Ants* had promised, he had not been removed to a cemetery. The other ants were just letting him lie there.

Perry had been expecting death—how long could these creatures continue?—and wasn't surprised that Fiveleg was the first to go. It was actually a relief. He got a tweezers from the bathroom and reached into the city, collapsing Fiveleg's tunnel, to pull him out and flush him away. Reaching into the air between the high hospital beds, he pantomimed the operation of tweezers, while the man with no larynx stared and nodded.

But Perry saw with horror that now, crushed in the grip of the tweezers, Fiveleg was spasmodically moving. "Reflex action," he explained to the mute, who crinkled his eyes in doubt. And in fact Perry wasn't sure that he hadn't killed Fiveleg himself, or even that the ant had been finally dead. He got rid of him in the toilet, then washed the tweezers and scrubbed his hands until they hurt.

Back at the city, he felt better to see that several others looked feeble. It was obviously time for them to go. He carried the city out to the back yard, to a spot that was mostly bare dirt, and dumped them. They wandered blindly, lost.

Church bells, he told the mute—who was now sopping with sweat, his hand wandering toward his call button in swimming gestures—the sudden pealing of bells was probably an invention of memory. But something had made him wonder whether he still had time to get to the church and hand his father the thin gold ring. He knew where the church was. He felt certain he could walk that far.

But he was still there in the back yard, retying his shoelaces, brushing dirt from the knees and seat of his pants, cleaning his hands and face at the garden hose and slicking down his hair, when he heard (to hear it again was why he liked to tell this story) the approaching joyous clamor of many cars blowing their horns.

The Friendships of Girls Unpopular Together

JEANNE SCHINTO

T HE FRIENDSHIPS OF GIRLS unpopular together are particularly sorry. One hopes for the best from these friendships, but it rarely comes.

I don't remember who my first pen pal was, but I do remember my last one. Her name was Mary Jane Dunphy and she lived in Bridgeport, Connecticut.

We were matched up as a service of the Beatles International Fan Club. I gave them various statistics about myself, and they gave me Mary Jane's address. In turn they gave her mine, but I was the first one to write. I waited and waited for a response. Ten days passed.

It was May, and at school we'd rehearsed all month for the procession to honor the Mother Mary. Early on the morning of her Flower Feast, I snipped an armful of purple bearded iris, ironed my pastel-colored dress, and walked uptown to the church.

The nuns roughly took us each by the shoulders, their black, berry-sized beads clicking as they worked, shoving boy, then girl, then boy into the long, hard golden oak pews. Some boys, in order to be kept still, needed an even greater separation from each other. In these rows were put two girls, then a boy, then two girls—handmaids of the most trustworthy kind, who rarely spoke or laughed with either gender; shy in and out of church. I was one.

While our straining voices blended, near the end of the first hymn, as always I saw Mary's statue smile, and I cried a little. I had grown worried throughout the month, because this statue was a new one—muted, putty-colored with vague, modern lines, unholy, unsentimental. Not like the old one, clad in blue and white, with realistic crimson lips and chaste, ivory teeth.

When the priest began to say the Mass, I prayed for the souls in Purgatory, particularly those who were there for impure thoughts and had at least a thousand years to go and had no one here on earth any longer to pray for them. By the time the first Communion bell rang, I felt I had earned myself a prayer: I asked for a letter from Mary Jane, and for a trip to Liverpool. The trip to England was the prize being offered to the winner of a Beatles jingle contest. A radio station in Boston was the sponsor. I had tuned in the station one clear night and heard the announcement from so many miles north; I told Mary that I understood that this was a sign, sure proof that God, her Son, Jesus Christ wanted me to enter, wanted me to help myself, wanted me to win. I had already sent in twenty postcards or more, finding among my stamp collection, stamps that did not look cancelled, and affixing them to three-by-five cards.

We were given a half-day off from school in order to go home and have lunch to break our long Communion fast, and there Mary Jane's letter sat on the kitchen counter! To "Miss" Estelle Otthouse! In a careful ink-pen script on sophisticated, bumpy blue stationery! The letter began with a short apology for having taken so long to write back. And then some talk about the Beatles, and her school, and her family. "You're Catholic, so you *couldn't* marry John, even if he *got* a divorce," she wrote in a postscript. I was forced to agree. I went upstairs and lay across my bed to write her a long response.

That summer I became a haunter of stationers. I visited my favorite one so often, the proprietor came to suspect me of something irregular. He assigned a clerk to watch and follow me every time I entered the store. I did not often buy paper—not as often as I would have liked to, anyway. Usually I just browsed, planning what I might buy if I ever had a pen pal who required a daily tome. Mary Jane, like the many others before her, was never as prompt a correspondent as I, and I resisted the impulse to write to her out of turn. What if our letters crossed? That would confuse everything. Besides, there was nothing for me to respond to, without a letter in hand. When I wanted to write blind and cold, I took down my diary.

It was Mary Jane's idea that we meet. Bridgeport wasn't too far away. I think now she was merely too lazy to write as the summer wore on. I asked so many questions, and perhaps she imagined that many of them might be answered with the proper facial expression instead of three or four paragraphs of her beautiful script. We exchanged school pictures, and I took the bus up to Bridgeport.

Flesh is so much realer than words, and Mary Jane had a lot of it. She was not fat; just very, very tall—perhaps even close to six feet; she loped camel-like towards me when we picked each other out of the crowd. She was smiling, and she had not been smiling in the school picture, so I could see her crooked teeth poking out from beneath her upper lip. I thought she should have told me about the teeth, just as she had about her height. I took it almost as a lie that she had not been smiling in the picture.

Girls such as I was do not shake hands, but Mary Jane did. She gave me a limp rag of a handshake, and bobbed her head down low to me in a kind of bowing gesture, half mock. Then she seemed unsure of where to put her gangling arms. She tried resting one on her hip, the other on top of her hat. She was wearing a black John Lennon cap as we had prearranged. I wore a madras Ringo cap, the better for her to recognize me. I was about to take the hat off—it made me feel foolish, even though I considered it almost a religious garment—but then came rushing towards us out of the newsstand a man as tall as, or taller than, Mary Jane: her father. Mr. Dunphy's hair was black and oily as the hair of boys at school, and was combed into a curl that hung down into his face. He kept thrusting it aside with a flip of his neck. He flipped and smiled, rushing towards me, he, too, with an outstretched palm. So I shook hands twice in two minutes, probably for the first time without jesting, without saying, "Shakespeare, kick in the rear!" and delivering the kick in the behind. Mr. Dunphy and I exchanged some niceties, he all the while surveying me very carefully—me, the little return addressee in the corner of my envelopes now come alive. Then he led the way to the car.

As we drove, Mr. Dunphy pointed out to me the murky sights of Bridgeport. Mary Jane and he were in the front seat; I sat in the back. Mr. Dunphy kept turning around to be sure to look at me while he spoke. I saw he was very much younger than my parents; he reminded me of boyfriends of my sister—overly polite and so sincere: I felt a little sorry for him and didn't know why. Mary Jane did not speak and seemed bored, and until she found a good song flipped the radio dial back and forth, which made a noise that to me sounded like someone falling down a flight of stairs.

Mrs. Dunphy, a lofty tree of a woman, met us at the kitchen door. She wore a white apron, and had lunch all ready: steaming bowls of chicken-noodle soup, slabs of homemade bread spread with butter softened just enough, and big wedges of homemade apple pie and speckled vanilla ice cream for dessert. We said no grace. Throughout the meal, Mr. Dunphy talked, while Mrs. Dunphy ran from stove to table, whispering softly, continually, like a big tree stirring, "Mary Jane, Mary Jane," with behavioral suggestions. I made a vow in my head at once that when I grew up and married a Beatle and had children I would be a mother exactly like Mrs. Dunphy, and my Beatle husband would be exactly like Mary Jane's father. He'd be living incognito of course as, possibly, a university administrator, which is what Mr. Dunphy was.

After lunch we went to Mary Jane's bedroom, a frilly, pink place.

"Do you want to see your letters?" she asked, looking around the room as if she could think of nothing else to do with me.

"Yes!" What a wonderful suggestion. "I always wish I could see where my envelopes end up, with the postmarks and everything."

"I didn't save the envelopes," Mary Jane mumbled as she reached a long arm underneath her bed and pulled out a shoebox.

"Oh, well," I said, hiding my disappointment. "My mother told me never to write in a letter what I wouldn't want printed in the newspaper. This way, with only the signature, they won't be able to trace me."

"Do you save my envelopes?" Mary Jane asked warily.

I nodded guiltily, wishing for once that I were able to bring myself to lie.

"Better get rid of them when you get home."

I said meekly that I would.

I read through a few of my letters, but grew uncomfortable. Reading them over was like catching a glimpse of myself in an unexpected mirror. This was me, each signature testified, but I still could not quite believe it. In my mind's eye I always pictured myself in my pastel-colored dress, looking pretty. These letters had been written by a lonely little girl. Had I really suggested to Mary Jane that we invite our favorite Beatles to the States? My plan was to have them over for the weekend, at her house or mine; we could cook them dinner, watch TV; on Sunday, take them to church. If that ended up in the newspaper, I'd die a thousand deaths, and go to Hell, for denying it—every single word.

Mary Jane's father drove us to the college stadium that evening. Mary Jane had gotten us tickets to a Herman's Hermits concert. She asked her father to leave us off quite a distance away from the main gate, so that we might walk in unassisted, so to speak, like the other young people moving along in great droves.

We sat in the bleachers between happy couples, who crawled over, under and around us to get to their seats, then out of their seats again, to visit with friends. Girls hung onto boys, kissing them, and vice versa. I saw Mary Jane alternately stare at the couples, then look embarrassedly away. How did one learn to kiss people? I had practiced on mirrors, but it hadn't instilled the kind of confidence I needed to actually try it. I squeezed my hands between my knees, very glum.

When Herman and his band ran rollicking out onto the field, my mood did not improve. The matchbox stage was so far away, I could not keep myself reminded that the boys were real. They reminded me of a trained flea circus I had seen once at a carnival. Also, I liked better the renditions of their songs that they had recorded. Whenever they deviated, to my ear, it sounded like a wrong note struck. And of course they weren't the Beatles. I had to be an appreciative guest, though. I didn't mention what I was thinking to Mary Jane, but I wished that the concert would soon be over, that the whole weekend would. Impulsively, I told myself I would not write to Mary Jane again.

When the concert ended, we walked to the spot where Mary Jane had told her father to pick us up. On the drive home, she flipped the radio dial as she had done on the way back from the bus station, and this time I was grateful for the noise. I could not hear what her father was saying in his cheery sing-song voice, so I did not have to respond. He did not often ask a question, I noticed. He simply made observations that he himself found poignant or amusing. He had a way of smoothing over everything, making everything seem nice. Things weren't all nice—didn't he see? There were very many things which were bad. Should I point them out to him? The couples walking home together . . . ? Should I shout or start crying and surprise him? Him and Mary Jane both? I did nothing but sit quietly, picking out the sights of Bridgeport by myself, having begun to recognize them from the morning, even though now it was as dark as moonless nights can get. Besides, when Mary Jane turned her head, to catch a final glimpse of a couple walking arm-in-arm, I saw that she looked just the way I felt.

"Mary Jane, Mary Jane." Mrs. Dunphy shook our shoulders to awaken us. This was the morning that I was to leave. We dressed and ate toast and thick black raspberry jam for breakfast, and dragged ourselves to the car without speaking. Even Mr. Dunphy said nothing as all four of us drove to the home of Mr. Dunphy's boss at the university.

The Dean of Faculty, thin, pale, and timid as a balding third-grader, with a priest-like edge of authority to his small voice, made the towering Mr. Dunphy hunch. The Dean's wife, very big, sweetly scented, too sweetly for this early in the morning—like certain unpleasant flowers—commanded Mrs. Dunphy's attention with a piece of gossip that curled her lips as she delivered it. Then she and her husband got into the car.

The couple was about to embark on a transatlantic voyage. The Dunphys would see them off. I would be dropped off at home on their way back through my town, and none too soon. Mary Jane and I had had to squeeze into the station wagon's back compartment with the luggage, like a couple of children. Mary Jane, her legs folded foal-like under her, sulked heartily. Neither of us was any too happy about cuddling up with each other. After the concert, when we got home, we had started to sour and snap at each other. This morning, we slept, or pretended to, until we heard Mr. Dunphy cry out to God at the early-morning spectacle of New York harbor.

We parked the car and found the ship—it looked like the side of a building. It looked in no mood to be going anywhere, but would nonetheless in a few hours be wrenched from this side of the ocean and made to find its way to the other. I began to grow excited about this bon voyage. There was an excitement here. I felt somehow a part of this crowd, this time, moving towards the ship, speaking many languages. I hurried. I could hardly wait, for what I did not know. I looked to see if Mary Jane felt it, too, but I couldn't tell if she did. She was walking in her same loping steps. She seemed to have allied herself with her mother now; she walked along beside her, though her mother paid no attention to her. Mrs. Dunphy's job today was to listen to the boss's wife, her head turned slightly so that the Mrs. Dean might see Mrs. Dunphy's implacable grin as she listened enraptured. "I'm like one of those big ships myself now," the Dean's wife was saying. "I take a day to stop, a day to reverse direction, a day to get going in the opposite direction again."

The ship did not rock, at least we did not feel it, no more than we felt the movement of the earth spinning on its axis as we had long ago learned in school that it did. But the ship did tilt off at a definite angle, creating a fun-house effect that made me feel mildly reckless.

A steward showed us to a lower level. The sailors and other stewards we passed winked at us two girls. The young men all wore uniform hats and pants that made them look like schoolboys, innocent and slightly unreal—or like circus people, theatre types heading for the nearest stage. All of them seemed to have bright red lips, which looked painted.

A waiter brought a tray of canapes to the stateroom of the Dean and his wife. They were devoured, largely by me, while Mrs. Dunphy

eyed me. Then Mr. Dunphy suggested we girls go take a look around
the corner, around the corridors of the ship by ourselves. The
stateroom was after all no place for six, and perhaps he was just a
little embarrassed by me. I had sat down on the Dean's bed, elbows
back, swinging my legs.

Mary Jane had to be coaxed into going with me. She preferred to
stay with the adults. I would have been just as happy to go exploring
by myself. I was thinking of stowing away. Never mind the Beatles
jingle contest. I would write to my parents when I got there. And to
Mary Jane, too, I supposed, reneging on my vow to forget her.

The walls of the corridors were a dingy yellow—the color of
nicotine-stained teeth—shined as best they could be, but dulled all
the same. In our nostrils was the smell of frogs and toads and other
amphibious things, mold and mustiness, boys' gym lockers—girls'
gym lockers, too. Then we turned a corner and began to walk downhill, the smells getting stronger all the while. We took iron stairs down
to another level; then we met a door.

We entered a large pool room.

"You girls aren't rich by any chance, are you?"

Addressing us in a French accent was a short, pudgy, kind-faced
man, who stood near the edge of the pool in a stretchy blue bathing
suit that looked completely dry. Waves of light reflected off the water
onto him, the walls, the ceiling. Swimming around in the pool
haphazardly were two young men. The Frenchman explained to us
that the swimmers were his friends who came over when the ship
was in port and their office was slow. "They are hoping to meet a
millionaire," he laughed. "They always threaten not to leave the ship
on time unless I produce one."

"Jean-Claude knows lots of millionaires," one of the swimmers
said in an American accent. "But he won't share them with us. Will
you, J.-C.?"

"It's my job to keep people like you away from them," Jean-Claude
said good-naturedly, shrugging like a boy.

The other swimmer said something to the one who had spoken.
I could not make out the words, but I could hear that he was an
American, too. They laughed. The one who had spoken first swam
over to the side, none too expertly. He draped his thick elbows over
the pool's rim. I could see he was heavy-breasted and hairless. He
reminded me of a boy in my class, big and goofy and permanently
embarrassed, whose blood ran clear when he cut himself falling down
in the schoolyard. The other one, a much better swimmer, thin and

dark, moved like a snake in the water, making almost no splashes. Treading water invisibly, he said to us: "Come on in."

"You come out," Mary Jane giggled.

I noticed that Mary Jane's posture had changed. One shoulder was flung back; one dipped forward. She no longer slouched. And I could guess that she was trying to catch the attention of the dark one, who now was swimming over to the ladder at the end of the pool where the diving board was. Mary Jane watched as he reached the ladder, pulled himself up, then fell backwards back into the pool, making a blue explosion of water. He did the backstroke over to the other side of the deep end, swam until he was under the diving board, then made a leap for it, and hung onto that with his long, brown arms. The reflection of the water made his face look ghoulishly blue.

I looked around to see where Jean-Claude was; he was getting dressed into a steward's uniform that was all laid out on a wooden bench.

"Yes, come out," Jean-Claude said politely, stepping into his pants. "It's time for everyone to come out now. The bell will ring very soon."

The dark one ignored Jean-Claude, swimming over to Mary Jane; the heavier one ignored him, too, and began to eye me. I could add two and two just as well as anyone, and I saw I was paired with him.

I took off my Ringo cap and ran my fingers through my unwashed hair. Where was I getting my nerve? I was not one bit frightened. The presence of Jean-Claude seemed to make it all right, somehow. His cheeks glowed rosy and bright, and he, all dressed now, from shoes to cap, looked especially fine. Almost as authoritative as a policeman, but without the harshness of the gun and the stick and the badge and the squawking radio.

Jean-Claude paced at the side of the pool. "You know what will happen! You know! You know!" Suddenly nervous now. "I will lose my job! You know this! If you don't leave here on time. And I wish you girls would leave, too. Go back to your staterooms."

"We don't have any staterooms," Mary Jane said haughtily.

Jean-Claude slapped his head.

The heavier one must have been the more considerate of the two, for he was swimming to the side; I'm sure he was preparing to haul himself out of the pool even as the other one swam into the center and Jean-Claude began shouting in French: *"Fiche le camp! Fiche le camp—!"* So the dark one swam back to the side, grabbed Jean-Claude by the leg, and pulled him in.

The water closed over Jean-Claude's head. And his hands fluttered like leaves on the surface, then sank beneath the surface, and the water was calm around him.

The heavier one and the dark one both scrambled, fighting over the ladder, to be the first one out of the pool. Mary Jane put a finger to her cheek. "Oh, dear," she said, like a heroine; she did not move. And neither did I. I watched the spot where Jean-Claude had disappeared, and waited for his head to bob up; silently I was rooting for him to recover with aplomb.

When Jean-Claude's head finally did appear again, his mouth was large and open and making a strange, inward gushing noise. His hands made a fluttering again, as if they were trying to lift him into the air. His elbows were working, too, but looked as if they were weighted down, like a marionette's elbows, pulled down by gravity.

I tried to read his face. He seemed unaware of everything but the water. There was no anger in his eyes, only wonder and terror at the water. Then his apple cheeks disappeared again, as if something were pulling him under, pulling him down by the legs.

The two young men were out of the pool now, watching, standing naked, having kicked off and away their bathing suits.

"What do you know? The bastard can't swim!" said the dark one.

They pulled on their clothes.

The men walked quickly, did not run, to the exit, their shoes in their hands, smoothing their heads like men running to a train, more important matters to attend to. They didn't look back, not even when Mary Jane called after them. Then she turned to me.

We both watched Jean-Claude pull himself along the edge of the pool to the ladder. His gaze was as sure and constant as steel. He was seeing something very clearly. I suddenly became frightened.

Mary Jane and I ran to the exit, ran out into the corridor. We fell into step with the gathering crowd, and moved along with them, men and women all together. A bell sounded over our heads. We kept close, arms touching, in step in the disorderly procession. We did not speak a word, but we kept close. And we must have seemed to have been huddled, as if for protection from something.

The Happiest I've Been

JOHN UPDIKE

NEIL HOVEY came for me wearing a good suit. He parked his father's blue Chrysler on the dirt ramp by our barn and got out and stood by the open car door in a double-breasted tan gabardine suit, his hands in his pockets and his hair combed with water, squinting up at a lightning rod an old hurricane had knocked crooked.

We were driving to Chicago, so I had dressed in worn-out slacks and an outgrown corduroy shirt. But Neil was the friend I had always been most relaxed with, so I wasn't very disturbed. My parents and I walked out from the house, across the low stretch of lawn that was mostly mud after the thaw that had come on Christmas Day, and my grandmother, though I had kissed her good-bye inside the house, came out onto the porch, stooped and rather angry-looking, her head haloed by wild old woman's white hair and the hand more severely afflicted by arthritis waggling at her breast in a worried way. It was growing dark and my grandfather had gone to bed. "Nev-er trust the man who wears the red necktie and parts his hair in the middle," had been his final advice to me.

We had expected Neil since middle afternoon. Nineteen almost twenty, I was a college sophomore home on vacation; that fall I had met in a fine arts course a girl I had fallen in love with, and she had invited me to the New Year's party her parents always gave and to stay at her house a few nights. She lived in Chicago and so did Neil now, though he had gone to our high school. His father did something—sell steel was my impression, a huge man opening a briefcase and saying "The I-beams are very good this year"—that required him to be always on the move, so that at about thirteen Neil had been boarded with Mrs. Hovey's parents, the Lancasters. They had lived in Olinger since the town was incorporated. Indeed, old Jesse Lancaster, whose sick larynx whistled when he breathed to us boys his shocking and uproarious thoughts on the girls that walked past his porch all day long, had twice been burgess. Meanwhile Neil's father got a stationary job, but he let Neil stay to graduate; after the night he graduated, Neil drove throughout the next day to join his parents. From Chicago to this part of Pennsylvania was seventeen hours. In the twenty months he had been gone Neil had come east fairly often; he loved driving and Olinger was the one thing he had that was close to a childhood home. In Chicago he was working in a garage and getting his teeth straightened by the Army so they could draft him. Korea was on. He had to go back, and I wanted to go, so it was a happy arrangement. "You're all dressed up," I accused him immediately.

"I've been saying good-bye." The knot of his necktie was loose and the corners of his mouth were rubbed with pink. Years later my mother recalled how that evening his breath to her stank so strongly of beer she was frightened to let me go with him. "*Your* grandfather always thought *his* grandfather was a very dubious character," she said then.

My father and Neil put my suitcases into the trunk; they contained all the clothes I had brought, for the girl and I were going to go back to college on the train together, and I would not see my home again until spring.

"Well, good-bye, boys," my mother said. "I think you're both very brave." In regard to me she meant the girl as much as the roads.

"Don't you worry, Mrs. Nordholm," Neil told her quickly. "He'll be safer than in his bed. I bet he sleeps from here to Indiana." He looked at me with an irritating imitation of her own fond gaze. When they shook hands good-bye it was with an equality established on the base of my helplessness. His being so slick startled me, but then you can have a friend for years and never see how he operates with adults.

I embraced my mother and over her shoulder with the camera of my head tried to take a snapshot I could keep of the house, the woods behind it and the sunset behind them, the bench beneath the walnut tree where my grandfather cut apples into skinless bits and fed them to himself, and the ruts in the soft lawn the bakery truck had made that morning.

We started down the half-mile of dirt road to the highway that, one way, went through Olinger to the city of Alton and, the other way, led through farmland to the Turnpike. It was luxurious, after the stress of farewell, to two-finger a cigarette out of the pack in my shirt pocket. My family knew I smoked but I didn't do it in front of them; we were all too sensitive to bear the awkwardness. I lit mine and held the match for Hovey. It was a relaxed friendship. We were about the same height and had the same degree of athletic incompetence and the same curious lack of whatever force it was that aroused loyalty and compliance in beautiful girls. There was his bad teeth and my skin allergy; these were being remedied now, when they mattered less. But it seemed to me the most important thing—about both our friendship and our failures to become, for all the love we felt for women, actual lovers—was that he and I lived with grandparents. This improved both our backward and forward vistas; we knew about the bedside commodes and midnight coughing fits that awaited most men, and we had a sense of childhoods before 1900, when the farmer ruled the land and America faced west. We had gained a humane dimension that made us gentle and humorous among peers but diffident at dances and hesitant in cars. Girls hate boys' doubts: they amount to insults. Gentleness is for married women to appreciate. (This is my thinking then.) A girl who has received out of nowhere a gift worth all Africa's ivory and Asia's gold wants more than just humanity to bestow it on.

Coming onto the highway, Neil turned right toward Olinger instead of left toward the Turnpike. My reaction was to twist and assure myself through the rear window that, though a pink triangle of sandstone stared through the bare treetops, nobody at my house could possibly see.

When he was again in third gear, Neil asked, "Are you in a hurry?"

"No. Not especially."

"Schuman's having his New Year's party two days early so we can go. I thought we'd go for a couple hours and miss the Friday night stuff on the Pike." His mouth moved and closed carefully over the dull, silver, painful braces.

"Sure," I said. "I don't care." In everything that followed there was this sensation of my being picked up and carried.

It was four miles from the farm to Olinger; we entered by Buchanan Road, driving past the tall white brick house I had lived in until I was fifteen. My grandfather had bought it before I was born and his stocks became bad, which had happened in the same year. The new owners had strung colored bulbs all along the front door frame and the edges of the porch roof. Downtown the cardboard Santa Claus still nodded in the drugstore window but the loudspeaker on the undertaker's lawn had stopped broadcasting carols. It was quite dark now, so the arches of red and green lights above Grand Avenue seemed miracles of lift; in daylight you saw the bulbs were just hung from a straight cable by cords of different lengths. Larry Schuman lived on the other side of town, the newer side. Lights ran all the way up the front edges of his house and across the rain gutter. The next-door neighbor had a plywood reindeer-and-sleigh floodlit on his front lawn and a snowman of papier-mâché leaning tipsily (his eyes were x's) against the corner of his house. No real snow had fallen yet that winter. The air this evening, though, hinted that harder weather was coming.

The Schumans' living room felt warm. In one corner a blue spruce drenched with tinsel reached to the ceiling; around its pot surged a drift of wrapping paper and ribbon and boxes, a few still containing presents, gloves and diaries and other small properties that hadn't yet been absorbed into the mainstream of affluence. The ornamental balls were big as baseballs and all either crimson or indigo; the tree was so well-dressed I felt self-conscious in the same room with it, without a coat or tie and wearing an old green shirt too short in the sleeves. Everyone else was dressed for a party. Then Mr. Schuman stamped in comfortingly, crushing us all into one underneath his welcome, Neil and I and the three other boys who had showed up so far. He was dressed to go out on the town, in a vanilla topcoat and silvery silk muffler, smoking a cigar with the band still on. You could see in Mr. Schuman where Larry got the red hair and white eyelashes and the self-confidence, but what in the son was smirking and pushy was in the father shrewd and masterful. What the one used to make you nervous the other used to put you at ease. While Mr. was jollying us, Zoe Loessner, Larry's probable fiancée and the only other girl at the party so far, was talking nicely to Mrs., nodding with her entire neck and fingering her Kresge pearls and blowing cigarette smoke through the corners of her mouth, to keep it away from the middle-aged woman's face. Each time Zoe spat out a plume, the shelf of honey hair overhanging her temple bobbed. Mrs. Schuman beamed serenely above her mink coat and rhinestone pocketbook. It was odd to see her dressed in the trappings of the prosperity that usually supported her good nature invisibly, like a firm mattress under a bright homely quilt. Everybody loved her. She was a prime product of the county, a Pennsylvania Dutch woman with sons, who loved feeding her sons and who imagined that the entire world, like her life, was going well. I never saw her not smile, except at her husband. At last she moved him into the outdoors. He turned at the threshold and did a trick with his knees and called in to us, "Be good and if you can't be good, be careful."

With them out of the way, the next item was getting liquor. It was a familiar business. Did anybody have a forged driver's license? If not, who would dare to forge theirs? Larry could provide India ink. Then again, Larry's older brother Dale might be home and would go if it didn't take too much time. However, on weekends he often went straight from work to his fiancée's apartment and stayed until Sunday. If worse came to worse, Larry knew an illegal place in Alton, but they really soaked you. The problem was solved strangely. More people were arriving all the time and one of them, Cookie Behn, who had been held back one year and hence was deposited in our grade, announced that last November he had become in honest fact twenty-one. I at least gave Cookie my share of the money feeling a little queasy, vice had become so handy.

The party was the party I had been going to all my life, beginning with Ann Mahlon's first Hallowe'en party, that I attended as a hot, lumbering, breathless, and blind Donald Duck. My mother had made the costume, and the eyes kept slipping, and were further apart than my eyes, so that even when the clouds of gauze parted, it was to reveal the frustrating depthless world seen with one eye. Ann, who because her mother loved her so much as a child had remained some-what childish, and I and another boy and girl who were not involved in any romantic crisis went down into Schuman's basement to play circular ping-pong. Armed with paddles, we stood each at a side of the table and when the ball was stroked ran around it counter-clockwise, slapping the ball and screaming. To run better the girls took off their heels and ruined their stockings on the cement floor. Their faces and arms and shoulder sections became flushed, and when a girl lunged forward toward the net the stiff neckline of her semi-formal dress dropped away and the white arcs of her brassiere could be glimpsed cupping fat, and when she reached high her shaved armpit gleamed like a bit of chicken skin. An earring of Ann's flew off and the two connected rhinestones skidded to lie near the wall, among the Schumans' power mower and badminton poles and empty bronze motor-oil cans twice punctured by triangles. All these images were immediately lost in the whirl of our running; we were dizzy before we stopped. Ann leaned on me getting back into her shoes.

When we pushed it open the door leading down into the cellar banged against the newel post of the carpeted stairs going to the second floor; a third of the way up these, a couple sat discussing. The girl, Jacky Iselin, cried without emotion—the tears and nothing else, like water flowing over wood. Some people were in the kitchen mixing drinks and making noise. In the living room others danced to records: 78s then, stiff discs stacked in a ponderous leaning cylinder on the spindle of the Schumans' console. Every three minutes with a click and a crash another dropped and the mood abruptly changed. One moment it would be "Stay As Sweet As You Are": Clarence Lang with the absolute expression of an idiot standing and rocking monotonously with June Kaufmann's boneless sad brown hand trapped in his and their faces, staring in the same direction, pasted together like the facets of an idol. The music stopped; when they parted, a big squarish dark patch stained the cheek of each. Then the next moment it would be Goodman's "Loch Lomond" or "Cherokee" and nobody but Margaret Lento wanted to jitterbug. Mad, she danced by herself, swinging her head recklessly and snapping her backside; a corner of her skirt flipped a Christmas ball onto the rug, where it collapsed into a hundred convex reflectors. Female shoes were scattered in innocent pairs about the room. Some were flats, resting under the sofa shyly toed in; others were high heels lying cockeyed, the spike of one thrust into its mate. Sitting alone and ignored in a great armchair, I experienced within a warm keen dishevelment, as if there were real tears in my eyes. Had things been less unchanged they would have seemed less tragic. But the girls who had stepped out of these shoes were with few exceptions the ones who had attended my life's party. The alterations were so small: a haircut, an engagement ring, a franker plumpness. While they wheeled above me I sometimes caught from their faces an unfamiliar glint, off of a hardness I did not remember, as if beneath their skins these girls were growing more dense. The brutality added to the features of the boys I knew seemed a more willed effect, more desired and so less grievous. Considering that there was a war, surprisingly many were present, 4-F or at college or simply waiting to be called. Shortly before midnight the door rattled and there, under the porchlight, looking forlorn and chilled in their brief athletic jackets, stood three members of the class ahead of ours who in the old days always tried to crash Schuman's parties. At Olinger High they had been sports stars, and they still stood with that well-coördinated looseness, a look of dangling from strings. The three of them had enrolled together at Melanchthon, a small Lutheran college on the edge of Alton, and in this season played on the Melanchthon basketball team. That is, two did; the third hadn't been good enough. Schuman, out of cowardice more than mercy, let them in, and they hid without hesitation in the basement, and didn't bother us, having brought their own bottle.

There was one novel awkwardness, Darryl Bechtel had married Emmy Johnson and the couple came. Darryl had worked in his father's greenhouse and was considered dull; it was Emmy that we knew. At first no one danced with her, and Darryl didn't know how, but then Schuman, perhaps as host, dared. Others followed, but Schuman had her in his arms most often, and at midnight, when we were pretending the new year began, he kissed her; a wave of kissing swept the room now, and everyone struggled to kiss Emmy. Even I did. There was something about her being married that made it extraordinary. Her cheeks in flame, she kept glancing around for rescue, but Darryl, embarrassed to see his wife dance, had gone into old man Schuman's den, where Neil sat brooding, sunk in mysterious sorrow.

When the kissing subsided and Darryl emerged, I went in to see Neil. He was holding his face in his hands and tapping his foot to a record playing on Mr. Schuman's private phonograph: Krupa's "Dark Eyes." The arrangement was droning and circular and Neil had kept the record going for hours. He loved saxophones; I guess all of us children of that Depression vintage did. I asked him, "Do you think the traffic on the Turnpike has died down by now?"

He took down the tall glass off the cabinet beside him and took a convincing swallow. His face from the side seemed lean and somewhat blue. "Maybe," he said, staring at the ice cubes submerged in the ochre liquid. "The girl in Chicago's expecting you?"

"Well, yeah, but we can call and let her know, once *we* know."

"You think she'll spoil?"

"How do you mean?"

"I mean, won't you be seeing her all the time after we get there? Aren't you going to marry her?"

"I have no idea. I might."

"Well then: you'll have the rest of Kingdom Come to see her." He looked directly at me, and it was plain in the blur of his eyes that he was sick-drunk. "The trouble with you guys that have all the luck," he said slowly, "is that you don't give a fuck about us that don't have any." Such melodramatic rudeness coming from Neil surprised me, as had his blarney with my mother hours before. In trying to evade his wounded stare, I discovered there was another person in the room: a girl sitting with her shoes on, reading *Holiday*. Though she held the magazine in front of her face I knew from her clothes and her unfamiliar legs that she was the girlfriend Margaret Lento had brought. Margaret didn't come from Olinger but from Riverside, a section of Alton, not a suburb. She had met Larry Schuman at a summer job in a restaurant and for the rest of high school they had more or less gone together. Since then, though, it had dawned on Mr. and Mrs. Schuman that even in a democracy distinctions exist, probably welcome news to Larry. In the cruellest and most stretched-out way he could manage he had been breaking off with her throughout the year now nearly ended. I had been surprised to find her at this party. Obviously she had felt shaky about attending and had brought the friend as the only kind of protection she could afford. The other girl was acting just like a hired guard.

There being no answer to Neil, I went into the living room, where Margaret, insanely drunk, was throwing herself around as if wanting to break a bone. Somewhat in time to the music she would run a few steps, then snap her body like a whip, her chin striking her chest and her hands flying backward, fingers fanned, as her shoulders pitched forward. In her state her body was childishly plastic; unharmed, she would bounce back from this jolt and begin to clap and kick and hum. Schuman stayed away from her. Margaret was small, not more than 5'3", with the smallness ripeness comes to early. She had bleached a section of her black hair platinum, cropped her head all over, and trained the stubble into short hyacinthine curls like those on antique statues of boys. Her face seemed quite coarse from the front, so her profile was classical unexpectedly. She might have been Portia. When she was not putting on her savage pointless dance she was in the bathroom being sick. The pity and the vulgarity of her exhibition made everyone who was sober uncomfortable; our common guilt in witnessing this girl's rites brought us so close together in that room that it seemed never, not in all time, could we be parted. I myself was perfectly sober. I had the impression then that people only drank to stop being unhappy and I nearly always felt at least fairly happy.

Luckily, Margaret was in a sick phase around one o'clock, when the elder Schumans came home. They looked in at us briefly. It was a pleasant joke to see in their smiles that, however corrupt and unwinking we felt, to them we looked young and sleepy: Larry's friends. Things quieted after they went up the stairs. In half an hour people began coming out of the kitchen balancing cups of coffee. By two o'clock four girls stood in aprons at Mrs. Schuman's sink, and others were padding back and forth carrying glasses and ashtrays. Another blameless racket pierced the clatter in the kitchen. Out on the cold grass the three Melanchthon athletes had set up the badminton net and in the faint glow given off by the house were playing. The bird, ascending and descending through uneven bars of light, glimmered like a firefly. Now that the party was dying Neil's apathy seemed deliberately exasperating, even vindictive. For at least another hour he persisted in hearing "Dark Eyes" over and over again, holding his head and tapping his foot. The entire scene in the den had developed a fixity that was uncanny; the girl remained in the chair and read magazines, *Holiday* and *Esquire*, one after another. In the meantime, cars came and went and raced their motors out front; Schuman took Ann Mahlon off and didn't come back; and the athletes carried the neighbor's artificial snowman into the center of the street and disappeared. Somehow in the arrangements shuffled together at the end, Neil had contracted to drive Margaret and the other girl home. Margaret convalesced in the downstairs bathroom for most of that hour. I unlocked a little glass bookcase ornamenting a desk in the dark dining room and removed a volume of Thackeray's Works. It turned out to be Volume II of *Henry Esmond*. I began it, rather than break another book out of the set, which had been squeezed in there so long the bindings had sort of interpenetrated.

Henry was going off to war again when Neil appeared in the archway and said, "O.K., Norseman. Let's go to Chicago." "Norseman" was a variant of my name he used only when feeling special affection.

We turned off all the lamps and left the hall bulb burning against Larry's return. Margaret Lento seemed chastened. Neil gave her his arm and led her into the back seat of his father's car; I stood aside to let the other girl get in with her, but Neil indicated that I should. I supposed he realized this left only the mute den-girl to go up front with him. She sat well over on her side, was all I noticed. Neil backed into the street and with unusual care steered past the snowman. Our headlights made vivid the fact that the snowman's back was a hollow right-angled gash; he had been built up against the corner of a house.

From Olinger, Riverside was diagonally across Alton. The city was sleeping as we drove through it. Most of the stoplights were blinking green. Among cities Alton had a bad reputation; its graft and gambling and easy juries and bawdy houses were supposedly notorious throughout the Middle Atlantic states. But to me it always presented an innocent face; row after row of houses built of a local dusty-red brick the shade of flowerpots, each house fortified with a tiny, intimate, balustraded porch, and nothing but the wealth of movie houses and beer signs along its main street to suggest that its citizens loved pleasure more than the run of mankind. Indeed, as we moved at moderate speed down these hushed streets bordered with parked cars, a limestone church bulking at every corner and the hooded street lamps keeping watch from above, Alton seemed less the ultimate center of an urban region than itself a suburb of some vast mythical metropolis, like Pandemonium or Paradise. I was conscious of ever-green wreaths on door after door and of fanlights of stained glass in which the house number was embedded. I was also conscious that every block was one block further from the Turnpike.

Riverside, fitted into the bends of the Schuylkill, was not so regu-larly laid out. Margaret's house was one of a short row, composition-shingled, which we approached from the rear, down a tiny cement alley speckled with drains. The porches were a few inches higher than the alley. Margaret asked us if we wanted to come in for a cup of coffee, since we were going to Chicago; Neil accepted by getting out of the car and slamming his door. The noise filled the alley, alarming me. I wondered at the easy social life that evidently existed among my friends at three-thirty in the morning. Margaret did, how-ever, lead us in stealthily, and she turned on only the kitchen switch. The kitchen was divided from the living room by a large sofa, which faced into littered gloom where distant light from beyond the alley spilled over the window sill and across the spines of a radiator. In one corner the glass of a television set showed; the screen would seem absurdly small now, but then it seemed disproportionately ele-gant. The shabbiness everywhere would not have struck me so defi-nitely if I hadn't just come from Schuman's place. Neil and the other girl sat on the sofa: Margaret held a match to a gas burner and, as the blue flame licked an old kettle, doled instant coffee into four flowered cups.

Some man who had once lived in this house had built by the kitchen's one window a breakfast nook, nothing more than a booth, a table between two high-backed benches. I sat in it and read all the words I could see: "Salt," "Pepper," "Have Some Lumps," "Decem-ber," "Mohn's Milk Inc.—A Very Merry Christmas and Joyous New Year—Mohn's Milk is *Safe* Milk—'Mommy, Make It Mohn's!,'" "Matches," "Hotpoint," "press," "Magee Stove Federal & Furnace Corp.," "God Is In This House," "Ave Maria Gratia Plena," "Shred-ded Wheat Benefits Exciting New Pattern Kungsholm." After serving the two on the sofa, Margaret came to me with coffee and sat down opposite me in the booth. Fatigue had raised two blue welts beneath her eyes.

"Well," I asked her, "did you have a good time?"

She smiled and glanced down and made the small sound "Ch," vestigial of "Jesus." With absent-minded delicacy she stirred her coffee, lifting and replacing the spoon without a ripple.

"Rather odd at the end," I said, "not even the host there."

"He took Ann Mahlon home."

"I know." I was surprised that she knew, having been sick in the bathroom for that hour.

"You sound jealous," she added.

"Who does? I do? I don't."

"You like her, John, don't you?" Her using my first name and the quality of the question did not, although discounting parties we had just met, seem forward, considering the hour and that she had brought me coffee. There is very little further to go with a girl who has brought you coffee.

"Oh, I like everybody," I told her, "and the longer I've known them the more I like them, because the more they're me. The only people I like better are ones I've just met. Now Ann Mahlon I've known since kindergarten. Every day her mother used to bring her to the edge of the schoolyard for months after all the other mothers had stopped." I wanted to cut a figure in Margaret's eyes, but they were too dark. Stoically she had gotten on top of her weariness, but it was growing bigger under her.

"Did you like her then?"

"I felt sorry for her being embarrassed by her mother."

She asked me, "What was Larry like when he was little?"

"Oh, bright. Kind of mean."

"Was he mean?"

"I'd say so. Yes. In some grade or other he and I began to play chess together. I always won until secretly he took lessons from a man his parents knew and read strategy books."

Margaret laughed, genuinely pleased. "Then did he win?"

"Once. After that I really tried, and after *that* he decided chess was kid stuff. Besides, I was used up. He'd have these runs on people where you'd be down at his house every afternoon, then in a couple months he'd get a new pet and that'd be that."

"He's funny," she said. "He has a kind of cold mind. He decides on what he wants, then he does what he has to do, you know, and nothing anybody says can change him."

"He does tend to get what he wants," I admitted guardedly, realizing that to her this meant her. Poor bruised little girl, in her mind he was all the time cleaving with rare cunning through his parents' objections straight to her.

My coffee was nearly gone, so I glanced toward the sofa in the other room. Neil and the girl had sunk out of sight behind its back. Before this it had honestly not occurred to me that they had a relationship, but now that I saw, it seemed plausible and, at this time of night, good news, though it meant we would not be going to Chicago yet.

So I talked to Margaret about Larry, and she responded, showing really quite an acute sense of him. To me, considering so seriously the personality of a childhood friend, as if overnight he had become a factor in the world, seemed absurd; I couldn't deeply believe that even in her world he mattered much. Larry Schuman, in little more than a year, had become nothing to me. The important thing, rather than the subject, was the conversation itself, the quick agreements, the slow nods, the weave of different memories; it was like one of those Panama baskets shaped underwater around a worthless stone.

She offered me more coffee. When she returned with it, she sat down, not opposite, but beside me, lifting me to such a pitch of gratitude and affection the only way I could think to express it was by *not* kissing her, as if a kiss were another piece of abuse women suffered. She said, "Cold. Cheap bastard turns the thermostat down to sixty," meaning her father. She drew my arm around her shoulders and folded my hand around her bare forearm, to warm it. The back of my thumb fitted against the curve of one breast. Her head went into the hollow where my arm and chest joined; she was terribly small, measured against your own body. Perhaps she weighed a hundred pounds. Her lids lowered and I kissed her two beautiful eyebrows and then the spaces of skin between the rough curls, some black and some bleached, that fringed her forehead. Other than this I tried to keep as still as a bed would be. It *had* grown cold. A shiver starting on the side away from her would twitch my shoulders when I tried to repress it; she would frown and unconsciously draw my arm tighter. No one had switched the kitchen light off. On Margaret's foreshortened upper lip there seemed to be two pencil marks; the length of wrist my badly fitting sleeve exposed looked pale and naked against the spiralling down of the smaller arm held beneath it.

Outside on the street the house faced there was no motion. Only once did a car go by: around five o'clock, with twin mufflers, the radio on and a boy yelling. Neil and the girl murmured together incessantly; some of what they said I could overhear.

"No. Which?" she asked.

"I don't care."

"Wouldn't you want a boy?"

"I'd be happy whatever I got."

"I know, but which would you *rather* have? Don't men want boys?"

"I don't care. You."

Somewhat later, Mohn's truck passed on the other side of the street. The milkman, well-bundled, sat behind headlights in a warm orange volume the size of a phone booth, steering one-handed and smoking a cigar that he set on the edge of the dashboard when, his wire carrier vibrant, he ran out of the truck with bottles. His passing led Neil to decide the time had come. Margaret woke up frightened of her father; we hissed our farewells and thanks to her quickly. Neil dropped the other girl off at her house a few blocks away; he knew where it was. Sometime during that night I must have seen this girl's face, but I have no memory of it. She is always behind a magazine or in the dark or with her back turned. Neil married her years later, I know, but after we arrived in Chicago I never saw him again either.

Red dawn light touched the clouds above the black slate roofs as, with a few other cars, we drove through Alton. The moon-sized clock of a beer billboard said ten after six. Olinger was deathly still. The air brightened as we moved along the highway; the glowing wall of my home hung above the woods as we rounded the long curve by the Mennonite dairy. With a .22 I could have had a pane of my parents' bedroom window, and they were dreaming I was in Indiana. My grandfather would be up, stamping around in the kitchen for my grandmother to make him breakfast, or outside, walking to see if any ice had formed on the brook. For an instant I genuinely feared he might hail me from the peak of the barn roof. Then trees interceded and we were safe in a landscape where no one cared.

At the entrance to the Turnpike Neil did a strange thing, stopped the car and had me take the wheel. He had never trusted me to drive his father's car before; he had believed my not knowing where the crankshaft and fuel pump were handicapped my competence to steer. But now he was quite complacent. He hunched under an old mackinaw and leaned his head against the metal of the window frame and soon was asleep. We crossed the Susquehanna on a long smooth bridge below Harrisburg, then began climbing toward the Alleghenies. In the mountains there was snow, a dry dusting like sand, that waved back and forth on the road surface. Further along there had been a fresh fall that night, about two inches, and the plows had not yet cleared all the lanes. I was passing a Sunoco truck on a high curve when without warning the scraped section gave out and I realized I might skid into the fence if not over the edge. The radio was singing "Carpets of clover, I'll lay right at your feet," and the speedometer said 85. Nothing happened; the car stayed firm in the snow and Neil slept through the danger, his face turned skyward and his breath struggling in his nose. It was the first time I heard a contemporary of mine snore.

When we came into tunnel country the flicker and hollow amplification stirred Neil awake. He sat up, the mackinaw dropping to his lap, and lit a cigarette. A second after the scratch of his match occurred the moment of which each following moment was a slight diminution, as we made the long irregular descent toward Pittsburgh. There were many reasons for my feeling so happy. We were on our way. I had seen a dawn. This far, Neil could appreciate, I had brought us safely. Ahead, a girl waited who, if I asked, would marry me, but first there was a vast trip: many hours and towns interceded between me and that encounter. There was the quality of the 10 A.M. sunlight as it existed in the air ahead of the windshield, filtered by the thin overcast, blessing irresponsibility—you felt you could slice forever through such a cool pure element—and springing, by implying how high these hills had become, a widespreading pride: Pennsylvania, your state—as if you had made your life. And there was knowing that twice since midnight a person had trusted me enough to fall asleep beside me.

The Man from Mars

MARGARET ATWOOD

A LONG TIME AGO Christine was walking through the park. She was still wearing her tennis dress; she hadn't had time to shower and change, and her hair was held back with an elastic band. Her chunky reddish face, exposed with no softening fringe, looked like a Russian peasant's, but without the elastic band the hair got in her eyes. The afternoon was too hot for April; the indoor courts had been steaming, her skin felt poached.

The sun had brought the old men out from wherever they spent the winter: she had read a story recently about one who lived for three years in a manhole. They sat weedishly on the benches or lay on the grass with their heads on squares of used newspaper. As she passed, their wrinkled toadstool faces drifted towards her, drawn by the movement of her body, then floated away again, uninterested.

The squirrels were out too, foraging; two or three of them moved towards her in darts and pauses, eyes fixed on her expectantly, mouths with the rat-like receding chins open to show the yellowed front teeth. Christine walked faster, she had nothing to give them. People shouldn't feed them, she thought, it makes them anxious and they get mangy.

Halfway across the park she stopped to take off her cardigan. As she bent over to pick up her tennis racquet again someone touched her on her freshly bared arm. Christine seldom screamed; she straightened up suddenly, gripping the handle of her racquet. It was not one of the old men, however: it was a dark-haired boy of twelve or so.

"Excuse me," he said, "I search for Economics Building. It is there?" He motioned towards the west.

Christine looked at him more closely. She had been mistaken: he was not young, just short. He came a little above her shoulder, but then, she was above the average height; "statuesque," her mother called it when she was straining. He was also what was referred to

in their family as "a person from another culture": oriental without
a doubt, though perhaps not Chinese. Christine judged he must be
a foreign student and gave him her official welcoming smile. In high
school she had been President of the United Nations Club; that year
her school had been picked to represent the Egyptian delegation at
the Mock Assembly. It had been an unpopular assignment—nobody
wanted to be the Arabs—but she had seen it through. She had made
rather a good speech about the Palestinian refugees.

"Yes," she said, "that's it over there. The one with the flat roof.
See it?"

The man had been smiling nervously at her the whole time. He
was wearing glasses with transparent plastic rims, through which his
eyes bulged up at her as though through a goldfish bowl. He had
not followed where she was pointing. Instead he thrust towards her
a small pad of green paper and a ballpoint pen.

"You make map," he said.

Christine set down her tennis racquet and drew a careful map.
"We are here," she said, pronouncing distinctly. "You go this way.
The building is here." She indicated the route with a dotted line and
an X. The man leaned close to her, watching the progress of the map
attentively; he smelled of cooked cauliflower and an unfamiliar brand
of hair grease. When she had finished Christine handed the paper
and pen back to him with a terminal smile.

"Wait," the man said. He tore the piece of paper with the map off
the pad, folded it carefully and put it in his jacket pocket; the jacket
sleeves came down over his wrists and had threads at the edges. He
began to write something; she noticed with a slight feeling of revulsion
that his nails and the ends of his fingertips were so badly bitten they
seemed almost deformed. Several of his fingers were blue from the
leaky ballpoint.

"Here is my name," he said, holding the pad out to her.

Christine read an odd assemblage of G's, Y's and N's, neatly printed
in block letters. "Thank you," she said.

"You now write *your* name," he said, extending the pen.

Christine hesitated. If this had been a person from her own culture
she would have thought he was trying to pick her up. But then,
people from her own culture never tried to pick her up: she was too
big. The only one who had made the attempt was the Moroccan waiter
at the beer parlour where they sometimes went after meetings, and
he had been direct. He had just intercepted her on the way to the
Ladies' Room and asked and she said no; that had been that. This

man was not a waiter though but a student; she didn't want to offend him. In his culture, whatever it was, this exchange of names on pieces of paper was probably a formal politeness, like saying Thank You. She took the pen from him.

"That is a very pleasant name," he said. He folded the paper and placed it in his jacket pocket with the map.

Christine felt she had done her duty. "Well, goodbye," she said. "It was nice to have met you." She bent for her tennis racquet but he had already stooped and retrieved it and was holding it with both hands in front of him, like a captured banner.

"I carry this for you."

"Oh no, please. Don't bother, I am in a hurry," she said, articulating clearly. Deprived of her tennis racquet she felt weaponless. He started to saunter along the path; he was not nervous at all now, he seemed completely at ease.

"Vous parlez français?" he asked conversationally.

"Oui, un petit peu," she said. "Not very well." How am I going to get my racquet away from him without being rude? she was wondering.

"Mais vous avez un bel accent." His eyes goggled at her through the glasses: was he being flirtatious? She was well aware that her accent was wretched.

"Look," she said, for the first time letting her impatience show, "I really have to go. Give me my racquet, please."

He quickened his pace but gave no sign of returning the racquet. "Where you are going?"

"Home," she said. "My house."

"I go with you now," he said hopefully.

"*No*," she said: she would have to be firm with him. She made a lunge and got a grip on her racquet; after a brief tug of war it came free.

"Goodbye," she said, turning away from his puzzled face and setting off at what she hoped was a discouraging jog-trot. It was like walking away from a growling dog, you shouldn't let on you were frightened. Why should she be frightened anyway? He was only half her size and she had the tennis racquet, there was nothing he could do to her.

Although she did not look back she could tell he was still following. Let there be a streetcar, she thought, and there was one, but it was far down the line, stuck behind a red light. He appeared at her side, breathing audibly, a moment after she reached the stop. She gazed ahead, rigid.

"You are my friend," he said tentatively.

Christine relented: he hadn't been trying to pick her up after all, he was a stranger, he just wanted to meet some of the local people; in his place she would have wanted the same thing.

"Yes," she said, doling him out a smile.

"That is good," he said. "My country is very far."

Christine couldn't think of an apt reply. "That's interesting," she said. "Très interessant." The streetcar was coming at last; she opened her purse and got out a ticket.

"I go with you now," he said. His hand clamped on her arm above the elbow.

"You . . . stay . . . *here,*" Christine said, resisting the impulse to shout but pausing between each word as though for a deaf person. She detached his hand—his hold was quite feeble and could not compete with her tennis biceps—and leapt off the curb and up the streetcar steps, hearing with relief the doors grind shut behind her. Inside the car and a block away she permitted herself a glance out a side window. He was standing where she had left him; he seemed to be writing something on his little pad of paper.

When she reached home she had only time for a snack, and even then she was almost late for the Debating Society. The topic was, "Resolved: That War Is Obsolete." Her team took the affirmative, and won.

Christine came out of her last examination feeling depressed. It was not the exam that depressed her but the fact that it was the last one: it meant the end of the school year. She dropped into the coffee shop as usual, then went home early because there didn't seem to be anything else to do.

"Is that you, dear?" her mother called from the living room. She must have heard the front door close. Christine went in and flopped on the sofa, disturbing the neat pattern of the cushions.

"How was your exam, dear?" her mother asked.

"Fine," said Christine flatly. It had been fine, she had passed. She was not a brilliant student, she knew that, but she was conscientious. Her professors always wrote things like "A serious attempt" and "Well thought out but perhaps lacking in *élan*" on her term papers; they gave her B's, the occasional B + . She was taking Political Science and Economics, and hoped for a job with the Government after she graduated; with her father's connections she had a good chance.

"That's nice."

Christine felt, resentfully, that her mother had only a hazy idea of what an exam was. She was arranging gladioli in a vase; she had rubber gloves on to protect her hands as she always did when engaged in what she called "housework." As far as Christine could tell her housework consisted of arranging flowers in vases: daffodils and tulips and hyacinths through gladioli, iris and roses, all the way to asters and mums. Sometimes she cooked, elegantly and with chafing dishes, but she thought of it as a hobby. The girl did everything else. Christine thought it faintly sinful to have a girl. The only ones available now were either foreign or pregnant; their expressions usually suggested they were being taken advantage of somehow. But her mother asked what they would do otherwise, they'd either have to go into a Home or stay in their own countries, and Christine had to agree this was probably true. It was hard anyway to argue with her mother, she was so delicate, so preserved-looking, a harsh breath would scratch the finish.

"An interesting young man phoned today," her mother said. She had finished the gladioli and was taking off her rubber gloves. "He asked to speak with you and when I said you weren't in we had quite a little chat. You didn't tell me about him, dear." She put on the glasses which she wore on a decorative chain around her neck, a signal that she was in her modern, intelligent mood rather than her old-fashioned whimsical one.

"Did he leave his name?" Christine asked. She knew a lot of young men but they didn't often call her, they conducted their business with her in the coffee shop or after meetings.

"He's a person from another culture. He said he would call back later."

Christine had to think a moment. She was vaguely acquainted with several people from other cultures, Britain mostly; they belonged to the Debating Society.

"He's studying Philosophy in Montreal," her mother prompted. "He sounded French."

Christine began to remember the man in the park. "I don't think he's French, exactly," she said.

Her mother had taken off her glasses again and was poking absent-mindedly at a bent gladiolus. "Well, he sounded French." She meditated, flowery sceptre in hand. "I think it would be nice if you had him to tea."

Christine's mother did her best. She had two other daughters, both of whom took after her. They were beautiful, one was well married already and the other would clearly have no trouble. Her friends consoled her about Christine by saying, "She's not fat, she's just big-boned, it's the father's side," and "Christine is so healthy." Her other daughters had never gotten involved in activities when they were at school, but since Christine could not possibly ever be beautiful even if she took off weight, it was just as well she was so athletic and political, it was a good thing she had interests. Christine's mother tried to encourage her interests whenever possible. Christine could tell when she was making an extra effort, there was a reproachful edge to her voice.

She knew her mother expected enthusiasm but she could not supply it. "I don't know, I'll have to see," she said dubiously.

"You look tired, darling," said her mother. "Perhaps you'd like a glass of milk."

Christine was in the bathtub when the phone rang. She was not prone to fantasy but when she was in the bathtub she often pretended she was a dolphin, a game left over from one of the girls who used to bathe her when she was small. Her mother was being bell-voiced and gracious in the hall; then there was a tap at the door.

"It's that nice young French student, Christine," her mother said.

"Tell him I'm in the bathtub," Christine said, louder than necessary. "He isn't French."

She could hear her mother frowning. "That wouldn't be very polite, Christine. I don't think he'd understand."

"Oh all right," Christine said. She heaved herself out of the bathtub, swathed her pink bulk in a towel and splattered to the phone.

"Hello," she said gruffly. At a distance he was not pathetic, he was a nuisance. She could not imagine how he had tracked her down: most likely he went through the phone book, calling all the numbers with her last name until he hit on the right one.

"It is your friend."

"I know," she said. "How are you?"

"I am very fine." There was a long pause, during which Christine had a vicious urge to say, "Well, goodbye then," and hang up; but she was aware of her mother poised figurine-like in her bedroom doorway. Then he said, "I hope you also are very fine."

"Yes," said Christine. She wasn't going to participate.

"I come to tea," he said.

This took Christine by surprise. "You do?"

"Your pleasant mother ask me. I come Thursday, four o'clock."

"Oh," Christine said, ungraciously.

"See you then," he said, with the conscious pride of one who has mastered a difficult idiom.

Christine set down the phone and went along the hall. Her mother was in her study, sitting innocently at her writing desk.

"Did you ask him to tea on Thursday?"

"Not exactly, dear," her mother said. "I did mention he might come round to tea *some*time, though."

"Well, he's coming Thursday. Four o'clock."

"What's wrong with that?" her mother said serenely. "I think it's a very nice gesture for us to make. I do think you might try to be a little more co-operative." She was pleased with herself.

"Since you invited him," said Christine, "you can bloody well stick around and help me entertain him. I don't want to be left making nice gestures all by myself."

"Christine *dear*," her mother said, above being shocked. "You ought to put on your dressing gown, you'll catch a chill."

After sulking for an hour Christine tried to think of the tea as a cross between an examination and an executive meeting: not enjoyable, certainly, but to be got through as tactfully as possible. And it *was* a nice gesture. When the cakes her mother had ordered arrived from *The Patisserie* on Thursday morning she began to feel slightly festive; she even resolved to put on a dress, a good one, instead of a skirt and blouse. After all, she had nothing against him, except the memory of the way he had grabbed her tennis racquet and then her arm. She suppressed a quick impossible vision of herself pursued around the living room, fending him off with thrown sofa cushions and vases of gladioli; nevertheless she told the girl they would have tea in the garden. It would be a treat for him, and there was more space outdoors.

She had suspected her mother would dodge the tea, would contrive to be going out just as he was arriving: that way she could size him up and then leave them alone together. She had done things like that to Christine before; the excuse this time was the Symphony Committee. Sure enough, her mother carefully mislaid her gloves and located them with a faked murmur of joy when the doorbell rang. Christine relished for weeks afterwards the image of her mother's dropped jaw and flawless recovery when he was introduced: he wasn't quite the foreign potentate her optimistic, veil-fragile mind had concocted.

He was prepared for celebration. He had slicked on so much hair cream that his head seemed to be covered with a tight black patent-leather cap, and he had cut the threads off his jacket sleeves. His orange tie was overpoweringly splendid. Christine noticed however as he shook her mother's suddenly braced white glove that the ballpoint ink on his fingers was indelible. His face had broken out, possibly in anticipation of the delights in store for him; he had a tiny camera slung over his shoulder and was smoking an exotic-smelling cigarette.

Christine led him through the cool flowery softly padded living room and out by the French doors into the garden. "You sit here," she said. "I will have the girl bring tea."

This girl was from the West Indies: Christine's parents had been enraptured with her when they were down at Christmas and had brought her back with them. Since that time she had become pregnant, but Christine's mother had not dismissed her. She said she was slightly disappointed but what could you expect, and she didn't see any real difference between a girl who was pregnant before you hired her and one who got that way afterwards. She prided herself on her tolerance; also there was a scarcity of girls. Stangely enough, the girl became progressively less easy to get along with. Either she did not share Christine's mother's view of her own generosity, or she felt she had gotten away with something and was therefore free to indulge in contempt. At first Christine had tried to treat her as an equal. "Don't call me 'Miss Christine,'" she had said with an imitation of light, comradely laughter. "What you want me to call you then?" the girl had said, scowling. They had begun to have brief, surly arguments in the kitchen, which Christine decided were like the arguments between one servant and another: her mother's attitude towards each of them was similar, they were not altogether satisfactory but they would have to do.

The cakes, glossy with icing, were set out on a plate and the teapot was standing ready; on the counter the electric kettle boiled. Christine headed for it, but the girl, till then sitting with her elbows on the kitchen table and watching her expressionlessly, made a dash and intercepted her. Christine waited until she had poured the water into the pot. Then, "I'll carry it out, Elvira," she said. She had just decided she didn't want the girl to see her visitor's orange tie; already, she knew, her position in the girl's eyes had suffered because no one had yet attempted to get *her* pregnant.

"What you think they pay me for, Miss Christine?" the girl said insolently. She swung towards the garden with the tray; Christine trailed her, feeling lumpish and awkward. The girl was at least as big as she was but she was big in a different way.

"Thank you, Elvira," Christine said when the tray was in place. The girl departed without a word, casting a disdainful backward glance at the frayed jacket sleeves, the stained fingers. Christine was now determined to be especially kind to him.

"You are very rich," he said.

"No," Christine protested, shaking her head; "we're not." She had never thought of her family as rich, it was one of her father's sayings that nobody made any money with the Government.

"Yes," he repeated, "you are very rich." He sat back in his lawn chair, gazing about him as though dazed.

Christine set his cup of tea in front of him. She wasn't in the habit of paying much attention to the house or the garden; they were nothing special, far from being the largest on the street; other people took care of them. But now she looked where he was looking, seeing it all as though from a different height: the long expanses, the border flowers blazing in the early-summer sunlight, the flagged patio and walks, the high walls and the silence.

He came back to her face, sighing a little. "My English is not good," he said, "but I improve."

"You do," Christine said, nodding encouragement.

He took sips of his tea, quickly and tenderly as though afraid of injuring the cup. "I like to stay here."

Christine passed him the cakes. He took only one, making a slight face as he ate it; but he had several more cups of tea while she finished the cakes. She managed to find out from him that he had come over on a Church fellowship—she could not decode the denomination—and was studying Philosophy or Theology, or possibly both. She was feeling well-disposed towards him: he had behaved himself, he had caused her no inconvenience.

The teapot was at last empty. He sat up straight in his chair, as though alerted by a soundless gong. "You look this way, please," he said. Christine saw that he had placed his miniature camera on the stone sundial her mother had shipped back from England two years before: he wanted to take her picture. She was flattered, and settled herself to pose, smiling evenly.

He took off his glasses and laid them beside his plate. For a moment she saw his myopic, unprotected eyes turned towards her, with something tremulous and confiding in them she wanted to close herself off from knowing about. Then he went over and did something to the camera, his back to her. The next instant he was crouched beside her, his arm around her waist as far as it could reach, his other hand covering her own hands which she had folded in her lap, his cheek jammed up against hers. She was too startled to move. The camera clicked.

He stood up at once and replaced his glasses, which glittered now with a sad triumph. "Thank you, Miss," he said to her. "I go now." He slung the camera back over his shoulder, keeping his hand on it as though to hold the lid on and prevent escape. "I send to my family; they will like."

He was out the gate and gone before Christine had recovered; then she laughed. She had been afraid he would attack her, she could admit it now, and he had; but not in the usual way. He had raped, *rapeo, rapere, rapui, to seize and carry off*, not herself but her celluloid image, and incidently that of the silver tea service, which glinted mockingly at her as the girl bore it away, carrying it regally, the insignia, the official jewels.

Christine spent the summer as she had for the past three years: she was the sailing instructress at an expensive all-girls camp near Algonquin Park. She had been a camper there, everything was familiar to her; she sailed almost better than she played tennis.

The second week she got a letter from him, postmarked Montreal and forwarded from her home address. It was printed in block letters on a piece of green paper, two or three sentences. It began, "I hope you are well," then described the weather in monosyllables and ended, "I am fine." It was signed "Your friend." Each week she got another of these letters, more or less identical. In one of them a colour print was enclosed: himself, slightly cross-eyed and grinning hilariously, even more spindly than she remembered him against her billowing draperies, flowers exploding around them like firecrackers, one of his hands an equivocal blur in her lap, the other other out of sight; on her own face, astonishment and outrage, as though he was sticking her in the behind with his hidden thumb.

She answered the first letter, but after that the seniors were in training for the races. At the end of the summer, packing to go home, she threw all the letters away.

When she had been back for several weeks she received another of the green letters. This time there was a return address printed at the top which Christine noted with foreboding was in her own city. Every day she waited for the phone to ring; she was so certain his first attempt at contact would be a disembodied voice that when he came upon her abruptly in mid-campus she was unprepared.

"How are you?"

His smile was the same, but everything else about him had deteriorated. He was, if possible, thinner; his jacket sleeves had sprouted a lush new crop of threads, as though to conceal hands now so badly bitten they appeared to have been gnawed by rodents. His hair fell over his eyes, uncut, ungreased; his eyes in the hollowed face, a delicate triangle of skin stretched on bone, jumped behind his glasses like hooked fish. He had the end of a cigarette in the corner of his mouth and as they walked he lit a new one from it.

"I'm fine," Christine said. She was thinking, I'm not going to get involved again, enough is enough, I've done my bit for internationalism. "How are you?"

"I live here now," he said. "Maybe I study Economics."

"That's nice." He didn't sound as though he was enrolled anywhere.

"I come to see you."

Christine didn't know whether he meant he had left Montreal in order to be near her or just wanted to visit her at her house as he had done in the spring; either way she refused to be implicated. They were outside the Political Science building. "I have a class here," she said. "Goodbye." She was being callous, she realized that, but a quick chop was more merciful in the long run, that was what her beautiful sisters used to say.

Afterwards she decided it had been stupid of her to let him find out where her class was. Though a timetable was posted in each of the colleges: all he had to do was look her up and record her every probable movement in block letters on his green notepad. After that day he never left her alone.

Initially he waited outside the lecture rooms for her to come out. She said Hello to him curtly at first and kept on going, but this didn't work; he followed her at a distance, smiling his changeless smile. Then she stopped speaking altogether and pretended to ignore him, but it made no difference, he followed her anyway. The fact that she was in some way afraid of him—or was it just embarrassment?—seemed only to encourage him. Her friends started to notice, asking her who he was and why he was tagging along behind her; she could hardly answer because she hardly knew.

As the weekdays passed and he showed no signs of letting up, she began to jog-trot between classes, finally to run. He was tireless, and had an amazing wind for one who smoked so heavily: he would speed along behind her, keeping the distance between them the same, as though he was a pull-toy attached to her by a string. She was aware of the ridiculous spectacle they must make, galloping across campus, something out of a cartoon short, a lumbering elephant stampeded by a smiling, emaciated mouse, both of them locked in the classic pattern of comic pursuit and flight; but she found that to race made her less nervous than to walk sedately, the skin on the back of her neck crawling with the feel of his eyes on it. At least she could use her muscles. She worked out routines, escapes: she would dash in the front door of the Ladies' Room in the coffee shop and out the back door, and he would lose the trail, until he discovered the other entrance. She would try to shake him by detours through baffling archways and corridors, but he seemed as familiar with the architectural mazes as she was herself. As a last refuge she could head for the women's dormitory and watch from safety as he was skidded to a halt by the receptionist's austere voice: men were not allowed past the entrance.

Lunch became difficult. She would be sitting, usually with other members of the Debating Society, just digging nicely into a sandwich, when he would appear suddenly as though he'd come up through an unseen manhole. She then had the choice of barging out through the crowded cafeteria, sandwich half-eaten, or finishing her lunch with him standing behind her chair, everyone at the table acutely aware of him, the conversation stilting and dwindling. Her friends learned to spot him from a distance; they posted lookouts. "Here he comes," they would whisper, helping her collect her belongings for the sprint they knew would follow.

Several times she got tired of running and turned to confront him. "What do you want?" she would ask, glowering belligerently down at him, almost clenching her fists; she felt like shaking him, hitting him.

"I wish to talk with you."

"Well, here I am," she would say. "What do you want to talk about?"

But he would say nothing; he would stand in front of her, shifting his feet, smiling perhaps apologetically (though she could never pinpoint the exact tone of that smile, chewed lips stretched apart over the nicotine-yellowed teeth, rising at the corners, flesh held stiffly in place for an invisible photographer), his eyes jerking from one part of her face to another as though he saw her in fragments.

Annoying and tedious though it was, his pursuit of her had an odd result: mysterious in itself, it rendered her equally mysterious.

No-one had ever found Christine mysterious before. To her parents she was a beefy heavyweight, a plodder, lacking in flair, ordinary as bread. To her sisters she was the plain one, treated with an indulgence they did not give to each other: they did not fear her as a rival. To her male friends she was the one who could be relied on. She was helpful and a hard worker, always good for a game of tennis with the athletes among them. They invited her along to drink beer with them so they could get into the cleaner, more desirable Ladies and Escorts side of the beer parlour, taking it for granted she would buy her share of the rounds. In moments of stress they confided to her their problems with women. There was nothing devious about her and nothing interesting.

Christine had always agreed with these estimates of herself. In childhood she had identified with the False Bride or the ugly sister; whenever a story had begun, "Once there was a maiden as beautiful as she was good," she had known it wasn't her. That was just how it was, but it wasn't so bad. Her parents never expected her to be a brilliant social success and weren't overly disappointed when she wasn't. She was spared the maneuvering and anxiety she witnessed among others her age, and she even had a kind of special position among men: she was an exception, she fitted none of the categories they commonly used when talking about girls, she wasn't a cock-teaser, a cold fish, an easy lay or a snarky bitch; she was an honorary person. She had grown to share their contempt for most women.

Now however there was something about her that could not be explained. A man was chasing her, a peculiar sort of man, granted, but still a man, and he was without doubt attracted to her, he couldn't leave her alone. Other men examined her more closely than they ever had, appraising her, trying to find out what it was those twitching bespectacled eyes saw in her. They started to ask her out, though they returned from these excursions with their curiosity unsatisfied, the secret of her charm still intact. Her opaque dumpling face, her solid bear-shaped body became for them parts of a riddle no-one could solve. Christine knew this and began to use it. In the bathtub she no longer imagined she was a dolphin; instead she imagined she was an elusive water-nixie, or sometimes, in moments of audacity, Marilyn Monroe. The daily chase was becoming a habit; she even looked forward to it. In addition to its other benefits she was losing weight.

All those weeks he had never phoned her or turned up at the house. He must have decided however that his tactics were not having the desired result, or perhaps he sensed she was becoming bored.

The phone began to ring in the early morning or late at night when he could be sure she would be there. Sometimes he would simply breathe (she could recognize, or thought she could, the quality of his breathing), in which case she would hang up. Occasionally he would say again that he wanted to talk to her, but even when she gave him lots of time nothing else would follow. Then he extended his range: she would see him on her streetcar, smiling at her silently from a seat never closer than three away; she could feel him tracking her down her own street, though when she would break her resolve to pay no attention and would glance back he would be invisible or in the act of hiding behind a tree or hedge.

Among crowds of people and in daylight she had not really been afraid of him; she was stronger than he was and he had made no recent attempt to touch her. But the days were growing shorter and colder, it was almost November, often she was arriving home in twilight or a darkness broken only by the feeble orange streetlamps. She brooded over the possibility of razors, knives, guns; by acquiring a weapon he could quickly turn the odds against her. She avoided wearing scarves, remembering the newspaper stories about girls who had been strangled by them. Putting on her nylons in the morning gave her a funny feeling. Her body seemed to have diminished, to have become smaller than his.

Was he deranged, was he a sex maniac? He seemed so harmless, yet it was that kind who often went berserk in the end. She pictured those ragged fingers at her throat, tearing at her clothes, though she could not think of herself as screaming. Parked cars, the shrubberies near her house, the driveways on either side of it, changed as she passed them from unnoticed background to sinisterly shadowed foreground, every detail distinct and harsh: they were places a man might crouch, leap out from. Yet every time she saw him in the clear light of morning or afternoon (for he still continued his old methods of pursuit), his aging jacket and jittery eyes convinced her that it was she herself who was the tormentor, the persecutor. She was in some sense responsible; from the folds and crevices of the body she had treated for so long as a reliable machine was emanating, against her will, some potent invisible odour, like a dog's in heat or a female moth's, that made him unable to stop following her.

Her mother, who had been too preoccupied with the unavoidable fall entertaining to pay much attention to the number of phone calls Christine was getting or to the hired girl's complaints of a man who hung up without speaking, announced that she was flying down to

New York for the weekend; her father decided to go too. Christine panicked: she saw herself in the bathtub with her throat slit, the blood drooling out of her neck and running in a little spiral down the drain (for by this time she believed he could walk through walls, could be everywhere at once). The girl would do nothing to help; she might even stand in the bathroom door with her arms folded, watching. Christine arranged to spend the weekend at her married sister's.

When she arrived back Sunday evening she found the girl close to hysterics. She said that on Saturday she had gone to pull the curtains across the French doors at dusk and had found a strangely contorted face, a man's face, pressed against the glass, staring in at her from the garden. She claimed she had fainted and had almost had her baby a month too early right there on the living-room carpet. Then she called the police. He was gone by the time they got there but she had recognized him from the afternoon of the tea; she had informed them he was a friend of Christine's.

They called Monday evening to investigate, two of them; they were very polite, they knew who Christine's father was. Her father greeted them heartily; her mother hovered in the background, fidgeting with her porcelain hands, letting them see how frail and worried she was. She didn't like having them in the living room but they were necessary.

Christine had to admit he'd been following her around. She was relieved he'd been discovered, relieved also that she hadn't been the one to tell, though if he'd been a citizen of the country she would have called the police a long time ago. She insisted he was not dangerous, he had never hurt her.

"That kind don't hurt you," one of the policemen said. "They just kill you. You're lucky you aren't dead."

"Nut cases," the other one said.

Her mother volunteered that the thing about people from another culture was that you could never tell whether they were insane or not because their ways were so different. The policeman agreed with her, deferential but also condescending, as though she was a royal halfwit who had to be humoured.

"You know where he lives?" the first policeman asked. Christine had long ago torn up the letter with his address on it; she shook her head.

"We'll have to pick him up tomorrow then," he said. "Think you can keep him talking outside your class if he's waiting for you?"

After questioning her they held a murmured conversation with her father in the front hall. The girl, clearing away the coffee cups, said if they didn't lock him up she was leaving, she wasn't going to be scared half out of her skin like that again.

Next day when Christine came out of her Modern History lecture he was there, right on schedule. He seemed puzzled when she did not begin to run. She approached him, her heart thumping with treachery and the prospect of freedom. Her body was back to its usual size: she felt herself a giantess, self-controlled, invulnerable.

"How are you?" she asked, smiling brightly.

He looked at her with distrust.

"How have you been?" she ventured again. His own perennial smile faded; he took a step back from her.

"This the one?" said the policeman, popping out from behind a notice board like a Keystone Cop and laying a competent hand on the worn jacket shoulder. The other policeman lounged in the background; force would not be required.

"Don't *do* anything to him," she pleaded as they took him away. They nodded and grinned, respectful, scornful. He seemed to know perfectly well who they were and what they wanted.

The first policeman phoned that evening to make his report. Her father talked with him, jovial and managing. She herself was now out of the picture; she had been protected, her function was over.

"What did they *do* to him?" she asked anxiously as he came back into the living room. She was not sure what went on in police stations.

"They didn't do anything to him," he said, amused by her concern. "They could have booked him for Watching and Besetting, they wanted to know if I'd like to press charges. But it's not worth a court case: he's got a visa that says he's only allowed in the country as long as he studies in Montreal, so I told them to just ship him up there. If he turns up here again they'll deport him. They went around to his rooming house, his rent's two weeks overdue; the landlady said she was on the point of kicking him out. He seems happy enough to be getting his back rent paid and a free train ticket to Montreal." He paused. "They couldn't get anything out of him though."

"*Out* of him?" Christine asked.

"They tried to find out why he was doing it; following you, I mean." Her father's eyes swept her as though it was a riddle to him also. "They said when they asked him about that he just clammed up. Pretended he didn't understand English. He understood well enough, but he wasn't answering."

Christine thought it was the end, but somehow between his arrest and the departure of the train he managed to elude his escort long enough for one more phone call.

"I see you again," he said. He didn't wait for her to hang up.

Now that he was no longer an embarrassing present reality he could be talked about, he could become an amusing story. In fact he was the only amusing story Christine had to tell, and telling it preserved both for herself and for others the aura of her strange allure. Her friends and the men who continued to ask her out speculated about his motives. One suggested he had wanted to marry her so he could remain in the country; another said that oriental men were fond of well-built women: "It's your Rubens quality."

Christine thought about him a lot. She had not been attracted to him, rather the reverse, but as an idea only he was a romantic figure, the one man who had found her irresistible; though she often wondered, inspecting her unchanged pink face and hefty body in her full-length mirror, just what it was about her that had done it. She avoided whenever it was proposed the theory of his insanity: it was only that there was more than one way of being sane.

But a new acquaintance, hearing the story for the first time, had a different explanation. "So he got you too," he said, laughing. "That has to be the same guy who was hanging around our day camp a year ago this summer. He followed all the girls like that. A short guy, Japanese or something, glasses, smiling all the time."

"Maybe it was another one," Christine said.

"There couldn't be two of them, everything fits. This was a pretty weird guy."

"What . . . *kind* of girls did he follow?" Christine asked.

"Oh, just anyone who happened to be around. But if they paid any attention to him at first, if they were nice to him or anything, he was unshakeable. He was a bit of a pest, but harmless."

Christine ceased to tell her amusing story. She had been one among many, then. She went back to playing tennis, she had been neglecting her game.

A few months later the policeman who had been in charge of the case telephoned her again.

"Like you to know, Miss, that fellow you were having the trouble with was sent back to his own country. Deported."

"What for?" Christine asked. "Did he try to come back here?"

Maybe she had been special after all, maybe he had dared everything for her.

"Nothing like it," the policeman said. "He was up to the same tricks in Montreal but he really picked the wrong woman this time—a Mother Superior of a convent. They don't stand for things like that in Quebec—had him out of here before he knew what happened. I guess he'll be better off in his own place."

"How old was she?" Christine asked, after a silence.

"Oh, around sixty, I guess."

"Thank you very much for letting me know," Christine said in her best official manner. "It's such a relief." She wondered if the policeman had called to make fun of her.

She was almost crying when she put down the phone. What *had* he wanted from her then? A Mother Superior. Did she really look sixty, did she look like a mother? What did convents mean? Comfort, charity? Refuge? Was it that something had happened to him, some intolerable strain just from being in this country; her tennis dress and exposed legs too much for him, flesh and money seemingly available everywhere but withheld from him wherever he turned, the nun the symbol of some final distortion, the robe and the veil reminiscent to his nearsighted eyes of the women of his homeland, the ones he was able to understand? But he was back in his own country, remote from her as another planet; she would never know.

He hadn't forgotten her though. In the spring she got a postcard with a foreign stamp and the familiar block-letter writing. On the front was a picture of a temple. He was fine, he hoped she was fine also, he was her friend. A month later another print of the picture he had taken in the garden arrived, in a sealed manila envelope otherwise empty.

Christine's aura of mystery soon faded away: anyway, she herself no longer believed in it. Life became again what she had always expected. She graduated with mediocre grades and went into the Department of Health and Welfare; she did a good job, and was seldom discriminated against for being a woman because nobody thought of her as one. She could afford a pleasant-sized apartment, though she did not put much energy into decorating it. She played less and less tennis; what had been muscle with a light coating of fat turned gradually to fat with a thin substratum of muscle. She began to get headaches.

As the years were used up and the war began to fill the newspapers and magazines, she realized which Eastern country he had actually been from. She had known the name but it hadn't registered at the time, it was such a minor place; she could never keep them separate in her mind.

But though she tried, she couldn't remember the name of the city, and the postcard was long gone—had he been from the North or the South, was he near the battle zone or safely from it? Obsessively she bought the magazines and poured over the available photographs, dead villagers, soldiers on the march, colour blow-ups of frightened or angry faces, spies being executed; she studied maps, she watched the late-night newscasts, the distant country and terrain becoming almost more familiar to her than her own. Once or twice she thought she could recognize him but it was no use, they all looked like him.

Finally, she had to stop looking at the pictures. It bothered her too much, it was bad for her; she was beginning to have nightmares in which he was coming through the French doors of her mother's house in his shabby jacket, carrying a packsack and a rifle and a huge bouquet of richly coloured flowers. He was smiling in the same way but with blood streaked over his face, partly blotting out the features. She gave her television set away and took to reading nineteenth century novels instead; Trollope and Galsworthy were her favourites. When, despite herself, she would think about him, she would tell herself that he had been crafty and agile-minded enough to survive, more or less, in her country, so surely he would be able to do it in his own, where he knew the language. She could not see him in the army, on either side; he wasn't the type, and to her knowledge he had not believed in any particular ideology. He would be something nondescript, something in the background, like herself; perhaps he had become an interpreter.

I Dated Jane Austen

T. CORAGHESSAN BOYLE

HER HANDS WERE COLD. She held them out for me as I stepped into the parlor. "Mr. Boyle," announced the maid, and Jane was rising to greet me, her cold white hands like an offering. I took them, said my good evenings, and nodded at each of the pairs of eyes ranged round the room. There were brothers, smallish and large of head, whose names I didn't quite catch; there was her father, the Reverend, and her sister, the spinster. They stared at me like sharks on the verge of a feeding frenzy. I was wearing my pink boots, 'Great Disasters' T-shirt and my Tiki medallion. My shoulders slumped under the scrutiny. My wit evaporated.

"Have a seat, son," said the Reverend, and I backed onto a settee between two brothers. Jane retreated to an armchair on the far side of the room. Cassandra, the spinster, plucked up her knitting. One of the brothers sighed. I could see it coming, with the certainty and illogic of an aboriginal courtship rite: a round of polite chit-chat.

The Reverend cleared his throat. "So what do you think of Mrs. Radcliffe's new book?"

I balanced a glass of sherry on my knee. The Reverend, Cassandra and the brothers revolved tiny spoons around the rims of teacups. Jane nibbled at a croissant and focused her huge unblinking eyes on the side of my face. One of the brothers had just made a devastating witticism at the expense of the *Lyrical Ballads* and was still tittering over it. Somewhere cats were purring and clocks ticking. I glanced at my watch: only seventeen minutes since I'd stepped in the door.

I stood. "Well Reverend," I said, "I think it's time Jane and I hit the road."

He looked up at the doomed Hindenburg blazing across my chest and smacked his lips. "But you've only just arrived."

There really wasn't much room for Cassandra in the Alfa Romeo, but the Reverend and his troop of sons insisted that she come along. She hefted her skirts, wedged herself into the rear compartment and flared her parasol, while Jane pulled a white cap down over her curls and attempted a joke about Phaetons and the winds of Aeolus. The Reverend stood at the curb and watched my fingers as I helped Jane fasten her seatbelt, and then we were off with a crunch of gravel and a billow of exhaust.

The film was Italian, in black and white, full of social acuity and steamy sex. I sat between the two sisters with a bucket of buttered popcorn. Jane's lips were parted and her eyes glowed. I offered her some popcorn. "I do not think that I care for any just now, thank you," she said. Cassandra sat stiff and erect, tireless and silent, like a mileage marker beside a country lane. She was not interested in popcorn either.

The story concerned the seduction of a long-legged village girl by a mustachioed adventurer who afterward refuses to marry her on the grounds that she is impure. The girl, swollen with child, bursts in upon the nuptials of her seducer and the daughter of a wealthy merchant, and demands her due. She is turned out into the street. But late that night, as the newlyweds thrash about in the bridal bed—

It was at this point that Jane took hold of my arm and whispered that she wanted to leave. What could I do? I fumbled for her wrap, people hissed at us, great nude thighs slashed across the screen, and we headed for the glowing EXIT sign.

I proposed a club. "Oh do let's walk!" Jane said. "The air is so frightfully delicious after that close, odious theatre—don't you think?" Pigeons flapped and cooed. A panhandler leaned against the fender of a car and drooled into the gutter. I took Jane's arm. Cassandra took mine.

At *The Mooncalf* we had our wrists stamped with luminescent ink and then found a table near the dance floor. The waitress' fingernails were green daggers. She wore a butch haircut and three-inch heels. Jane wanted punch, Cassandra tea. I ordered three margaritas.

The band was recreating the fall of the Third Reich amid clouds of green smoke and flashing lights. We gazed out at the dancers in their

jumpsuits and platform shoes as they bumped bums, heads and geni-
tals in time to the music. I thought of Catherine Morland at Bath and
decided to ask Jane for a dance. I leaned across the table. "Want to
dance?" I shouted.

"Beg your pardon?" Jane said, leaning over her margarita.

"Dance," I shouted, miming the action of holding her in my arms.

"No, I'm very sorry," she said. "I'm afraid not."

Cassandra tapped my arm. "I'd love to," she giggled.

Jane removed her cap and fingered out her curls as Cassandra and
I got up from the table. She grinned and waved as we receded into
the crowd. Over the heads of the dancers I watched her sniff suspi-
ciously at her drink and then sit back to ogle the crowd with her black
satiric eyes.

Then I turned to Cassandra. She curtsied, grabbed me in a fox trot
sort of way and began to promenade round the floor. For so small a
woman (her nose kept poking at the moribund Titanic listing across
my lower ribcage), I was amazed at her energy. We pranced through
the hustlers and bumpers like kiddies round a Maypole. I was even
beginning to enjoy myself when I glanced over at our table and saw
that a man in fierce black sideburns and mustache had joined Jane.
He was dressed in a ruffled shirt, antique tie and coattails that hung
to the floor as he sat. At that moment a fellow terpsichorean flung
his partner into the air, caught her by wrist and ankle and twirled
her like a toreador's cape. When I looked up again Jane was sitting
alone, her eyes fixed on mine through the welter of heads.

The band concluded with a crunching metallic shriek and Cassandra
and I made our way back to the table. "Who was that?" I asked Jane.

"Who was whom?"

"That mustachioed murderer's apprentice you were sitting with."

"Oh," she said. "Him."

I realized that Cassandra was still clutching my hand.

"Just an acquaintance."

As we pulled into the drive at Steventon, I observed a horse tethered
to one of the palings. The horse lifted its tail, then dropped it. Jane
seemed suddenly animated. She made a clucking sound and called
to the horse by name. The horse flicked its ears. I asked her if she
liked horses. "Hm?" she said, already looking off toward the silhou-
ettes that played across the parlor curtains. "Oh yes, yes. Very much

so," she said, and then she released the seatbelt, flung back the door and tripped up the stairs into the house. I killed the engine and stepped out into the dark drive. Crickets sawed their legs together in the bushes. Cassandra held out her hand.

Cassandra led me into the parlor where I was startled to see the mustachioed ne'er-do-well from *The Mooncalf*. He held a teacup in his hand. His boots shone as if they'd been razor-stropped. He was talking with Jane.

"Well, well," said the Reverend, stepping out of the shadows. "Enjoy yourselves?"

"Oh, immensely, father," said Cassandra.

Jane was grinning at me again. "Mr. Boyle," she said. "Have you met Mr. Crawford?" The brothers, with their fine bones and disproportionate heads, gathered round. Crawford's sideburns reached nearly to the line of his jaw. His mustache was smooth and black. I held out my hand. He shifted the teacup and gave me a firm handshake. "Delighted," he said.

We found seats (Crawford shoved in next to Jane on the love seat; I wound up on the settee between Cassandra and a brother in naval uniform), and the maid served tea and cakes. Something was wrong— of that I was sure. The brothers were not their usual witty selves, the Reverend floundered in the midst of a critique of Coleridge's cult of artifice, Cassandra dropped a stitch. In the corner, Crawford was holding a whispered colloquy with Jane. Her cheeks, which tended toward the flaccid, were now positively bloated, and flushed with color. It was then that it came to me. "Crawford," I said, getting to my feet. "*Henry* Crawford?"

He sprang up like a gunfighter summoned to the OK Corral. "That's right," he leered. His eyes were deep and cold as crevasses. He looked pretty formidable—until I realized that he couldn't have been more than five-three or -four, give or take an inch for his heels.

Suddenly I had hold of his elbow. The Tiki medallion trembled at my throat. "I'd like a word with you outside," I said. "In the garden."

The brothers were on their feet. The Reverend spilled his tea. Crawford jerked his arm out of my grasp and stalked through the door that gave onto the garden. Nightsounds grated in my ears, the brothers murmured at my back, and Jane, as I pulled the door closed, grinned at me as if I'd just told the joke of the century.

*   *   *

Crawford was waiting for me in the ragged shadows of the trees, turned to face me like a bayed animal. I felt a surge of power. I wanted to call him a son of a bitch, but, in keeping with the times, I settled for cad. "You cad," I said, shoving him back a step, "how dare you come sniffing around her after what you did to Maria Bertram in *Mansfield Park*? It's people like you—corrupt, arbitrary, egocentric— that foment all the lust and heartbreak of the world and challenge the very possibility of happy endings."

"Hah!" he said. Then he stepped forward and the moon fell across his face. His eyes were like the birth of evil. In his hand, a riding glove. He slapped my face with it. "Tomorrow morning, at dawn," he hissed. "Beneath the bridge."

"Okay, wiseguy," I said, "okay," but I could feel the Titanic sinking into my belt.

A moment later the night was filled with the clatter of hoofs.

I was greeted by silence in the parlor. They stared at me, sated, as I stepped through the door. Except for Cassandra, who mooned at me from behind her knitting, and Jane, who was bent over a notebook, scribbling away like a court recorder. The Reverend cleared his throat and Jane looked up. She scratched off another line or two and then rose to show me out. She led me through the parlor and down the hall to the front entrance. We paused at the door.

"I've had a memorable evening," she said, and then glanced back to where Cassandra had appeared at the parlor door. "Do come again." And then she held out her hands.

Her hands were cold.

Desert Breakdown, 1968

TOBIAS WOLFF

K RYSTAL WAS ASLEEP when they crossed the Colorado. Mark had promised to stop for some pictures, but when the moment came he looked over at her and drove on. Krystal's face was puffy from the heat blowing into the car. Her hair, cut short for summer, hung damp against her forehead. Only a few strands lifted in the breeze. She had her hands folded over her belly and that made her look even more pregnant than she was.

The tires sang on the metal grillwork of the bridge. The river stretched away on both sides, blue as the empty sky. Mark saw the shadow of the bridge on the water with the car running through the girders, and the glint of water under the grillwork. Then the tires went silent. *California*, Mark thought, and for a time he felt almost as good as he had expected to feel.

But it soon passed. He had broken his word, and he was going to hear about it when Krystal woke up. He almost turned the car around. But he didn't want to have to stop, and hoist Hans up on his shoulders, and watch Krystal point that camera at him again. By now Krystal had hundreds of pictures of Mark, Mark with Hans on his shoulders standing in front of canyons and waterfalls and monumental trees and the three automobiles they'd owned since coming Stateside.

Mark did not photograph well. For some reason he always looked discouraged. But those pictures gave the wrong idea. An old platoon sergeant of Mark's had an expression he liked to use—"free, white, and twenty-one." Well, that was an exact description of Mark. Everything was in front of him. All he needed was an opening.

Two hawks wheeled overhead, their shadows immense on the baking gray sand. A spinning funnel of dust moved across the road and disappeared behind a billboard. The billboard had a picture of Eugene McCarthy on it. McCarthy's hair was blowing around his head. He was grinning. The caption below said, "A Breath of Fresh Air." You could tell this was California because in Arizona a McCarthy billboard would last about five minutes. This one had bullet holes in

it, but in Arizona someone would have burned it down or blown it
up. The people there were just incredibly backward.

In the distance the mountains were bare and blue. Mark passed
exit signs for a town called Blythe. He considered stopping for some
gas, but there was still half a tank and he did not want to risk waking
Krystal or Hans. He drove on into the desert.

They would make Los Angeles by dinnertime. Mark had an army
buddy there who'd offered to put them up for as long as they wanted
to stay. There was plenty of room, his buddy had said. He was house-
sitting for his parents while they made up their minds whether to get
divorced or not.

Mark was sure he'd find something interesting in Los Angeles.
Something in the entertainment field. He had been in plays all through
high school and could sing pretty well. But his big talent was impersonation. He could mimic anybody. In Germany he had mimicked a
Southern fellow in his company so accurately that after a couple of
weeks of it the boy asked to be transferred to another unit. Mark
knew he'd gone overboard. He laid off and in the end the boy with-
drew his request for transfer.

His best impersonation was his father, Dutch. Sometimes, just for
fun, Mark called his mother and talked to her in Dutch's slow, heavy
voice, rolling every word along on treads, like a tank. She always fell
for it. Mark would go on until he got bored, then say something like,
"By the way, Dottie, we're bankrupt." Then she would catch on and
laugh. Unlike Dutch, she had a sense of humor.

A truck hurtled past. The sound of the engine woke Hans, but
Mark reached into the back and rubbed the satin edge of the baby
blanket against Hans's cheek. Hans put his thumb in his mouth. Then
he stuck his rear end in the air and went back to sleep.

The road shimmered. It seemed to float above the desert floor.
Mark sang along with the radio, which he had been turning up as
the signal grew weaker. Suddenly it blared. He turned it down, but
he was too late. Hans woke up again and started fussing. Mark rubbed
his cheek with the blanket. Hans pushed Mark's arm away and said,
"No!" It was the only word he knew. Mark glanced back at him. He'd
been sleeping on a toy car and the wheels had left four red dents on
the side of his face. Mark stroked his cheek. "Pretty soon," he said,
"pretty soon, Hansy," not meaning anything in particular but wanting
to sound confident, upbeat.

Krystal was awake now too. For a moment she didn't move or say
anything. Then she shook her head rapidly from side to side. "So

hot," she said. She held up the locket-watch around her neck and looked at Mark. He kept his eyes on the road. "Back from the dead," he said. "Boy, you were really out."

"The pictures," she said. "Mark, the pictures."

"There wasn't any place to stop," he said.

"But you promised."

Mark looked at her, then back at the road. "I'm sorry," he said. "There'll be other rivers."

"I wanted that one," Krystal said, and turned away. Mark could tell that she was close to tears. It made him feel tired. "All right," he said. "Do you want me to go back?" He slowed the car to prove he meant it. "If that's what you want just say the word."

She shook her head.

Mark sped up.

Hans began to kick the back of the seat. Mark didn't say anything. At least it was keeping Hans busy and quiet. "Hey, gang," Mark said. "Listen up. I've got ten big ones that say we'll be diving into Rick's pool by six o'clock."

Hans gave the seat a kick that Mark felt clear through to his ribs. "Ten big ones," Mark said. "Any takers?" He looked over at Krystal and saw that her lips were trembling. He patted the seat beside him. She hesitated, then slid over and leaned against him, as he knew she would. Krystal was not one to hold a grudge. He put his arm around her shoulder.

"So much desert," she said.

"It's something, all right."

"No trees," she said. "At home I could never imagine."

Hans stopped kicking. Then, without warning, he grabbed Mark's ears. Krystal laughed and pulled him over the seat onto her lap. He immediately arched his back and slid down to the floor, where he began to tug at the gear shift.

"I have to stop," Krystal said. She patted her belly. "This one likes to sit just so, here, on my bladder."

Mark nodded. Krystal knew the English words for what Dottie had always been content to call her plumbing, and when she was pregnant she liked to describe in pretty close detail what went on in there. It made Mark queasy.

"Next chance we get," he said. "We're low anyway."

Mark turned off at an exit with one sign that said GAS. There was no mention of a town.

The road went north over bleached hardpan crazed with fissures. It seemed to be leading them toward a solitary mountain far away that looked to Mark like a colossal sinking ship. Phantom water glistened in the desert. Rabbits darted back and forth across the road. Finally they came to the gas station, an unpainted cement-block building with some pickup trucks parked in front. Mark pulled in.

There were four men sitting on a bench in the shade of the building. They watched the car come toward them.

"Cowboys," Krystal said. "Look, Hans, cowboys!"

Hans stood on Krystal's legs and looked out the window.

Krystal still thought that everyone who wore a cowboy hat was a cowboy. Mark had tried to explain that it was a style, but she refused to understand. He drove up to a pump and turned off the engine.

The four men stared at them. Their faces were dark under the wide brims of their hats. They looked as if they had been there forever. One of the men got up from the bench and walked over. He was tall and carried a paunch that seemed out of place on his bony frame. He bent down and looked inside the car. He had little black eyes with no eyebrows. His face was red, as if he were angry about something.

"Regular, please," Mark said. "All she'll take."

The man stared openly at Krystal's belly. He straightened up and walked away, past the men on the bench, up to the open door of the building. He stuck his head inside and yelled. Then he sat on the bench again. The man next to him looked down and mumbled something. The others laughed.

Somebody else in a cowboy hat came out of the building and went around to the back of the car. "Mark," Krystal said.

"I know," Mark said. "The bathroom." He got out of the car. The heat took him by surprise; he could feel it coming down like rain. The person pumping gas said, "You need oil or anything?" and that was when Mark realized it was a woman. She was looking down at the nozzle, so he couldn't see her face, only the top of her hat. Her hands were black with grease. "My wife would like to use your bathroom," he said.

She nodded. When the tank was full she thumped on the roof of the car. "Okay," she said, and walked toward the building.

Krystal opened the door. She swung her legs out, then rocked forward and pushed herself up into the light. She stood for a moment, blinking. The four men looked at her. So did Mark. He made allowances for the fact that Krystal was pregnant, but she was still too heavy. Her bare arms were flushed from the heat. So was her face. She looked like one of those stein-slinging waitresses in the *Biergarten* where she and Mark used to drink. He wished that these fellows could have seen the way Krystal looked wearing that black dress of hers, with her hair long, when they'd first started going out together.

Krystal shaded her eyes with one hand. With the other hand she pulled her blouse away from where it stuck to her skin. "More desert," she said. She lifted Hans out of the car and began to carry him toward the building, but he kicked free and ran over to the bench. He stood there in front of the men, naked except for his diaper.

"Come here," Krystal said. When he didn't obey she started toward him, then looked at the men and stopped. Mark went over. "Let's go Hansy," he said. He picked Hans up, and felt a sudden tenderness that vanished when Hans began to struggle.

The woman took Krystal and Hans inside the building, then came out and sat on the pile of scrap lumber beside the door. "Hans," she said. "That's a funny name for a little boy."

"It was her father's name," Mark said, and so it was. The original Hans had died shortly before the baby was born. Otherwise Mark never would have agreed. Even Germans didn't name their kids Hans anymore.

One of the men flicked a cigarette butt toward Mark's car. It fell just short and lay there, smoldering. Mark took it as a judgment on the car. It was a good car, a 1958 Bonneville he'd bought two weeks ago when the Ford started to smoke, but a previous owner had put a lot of extra chrome on it and right now it was gleaming every which way. It looked foolish next to these dented pickups with their gun racks and dull blistering paint. Mark wished he'd tanked up in Blythe.

Krystal came outside again, carrying Hans. She had brushed her hair and looked better.

Mark smiled at her. "All set?"

She nodded. "Thank you," she said to the woman.

Mark would have liked to use the bathroom too, but he wanted to get out of there. He started toward the car, Krystal behind him. She laughed deep in her throat. "You should have seen," she said. "They have a motorcycle in their bedroom." Krystal probably thought she was whispering but to Mark every word was like a shout.

He didn't say anything. He adjusted the visor while Krystal settled Hans on the back seat. "Wait," she told Mark, and got out of the car again. She had the camera.

"Krystal," Mark said.

She aimed the camera at the four men. When she snapped the shutter their heads jerked up. Krystal advanced the film, then aimed the camera again.

Mark said, "Krystal, get in!"

"Yes," Krystal said, but she was still aiming, braced on the open door of the car, her knees bent slightly. She snapped another picture and slid onto the seat. "Good," she said. "Cowboys for Reiner."

Reiner was Krystal's brother. He had seen *Shane* more than a hundred times.

Mark didn't dare look toward the bench. He put the key in the ignition and glanced up and down the road. He turned the key. Nothing happened.

Mark took a deep breath and waited for a moment. Then he tried again. Still nothing happened. The ignition went *tick tick tick tick*, and that was all. Mark turned it off and the three of them sat there. Even Hans was quiet. Mark felt the men watching him. That was why he did not lower his head to the wheel and give way to tears. But they were in his eyes, blurring the line of the horizon, the shape of the building, the dark forms of the trucks and the figure coming toward them over the white earth.

It was the woman. She bent down. "Okay," she said. "What's the trouble?" The smell of whiskey filled the car.

For almost half an hour the woman messed with the engine. She had Mark turn the key while she watched, then turn it some more while she did various things under the hood. At last she decided that the trouble was in the alternator. She couldn't fix it, and she had no parts on hand. Mark would have to get one in Indio or Blythe or maybe as far away as Palm Springs. It wasn't going to be easy, finding an alternator for a ten-year-old car. But she said she'd call around for him.

Mark waited in the car. He tried to act as if everything were all right, but when Krystal looked at him she made a sympathetic noise and squeezed his arm. Hans was asleep in her lap. "Everything will be fine," Krystal said.

Mark nodded.

The woman came back toward the car, and Mark got out to meet her.

"Aren't you the lucky one," she said. She gave Mark a piece of paper with an address written on it. "There wasn't anything in Indio," she said, "but this fellow in Blythe can fix you up. I'll need two dollars for the calls."

Mark opened his wallet and gave her the two dollars. He had sixty-five dollars left, all that remained of his army severance pay. "How much will the alternator cost?" he asked.

She closed the hood of the car. "Fifty-eight ninety-nine, I think it was."

"Jesus," Mark said.

The woman shrugged. "You're lucky they had one."

"I suppose so," Mark said. "It just seems like a lot of money. Can you jump-start me?"

"If you've got cables. Mine are lent out."

"I don't have any," Mark said. He squinted against the sun. Though he had not looked directly at the men on the bench, he knew that they had been watching him. He was sure that they had heard everything. He was also sure that they had jumper cables. People who drove trucks always carried stuff like that.

But if they didn't want to help, he wasn't going to ask.

"I guess I could walk up to the highway and hitch a ride," Mark said, more loudly than he meant to.

"I guess you could," the woman said.

Mark looked back at Krystal. "Is it okay if my wife stays here?"

"I guess she'll have to," the woman said. She took off her hat and wiped her brow with the back of her sleeve. Her hair was pure yellow, gathered in a loose bun that glowed in the light. Her eyes were black. She put her hat back on and told Mark how to get to the parts store. She made him repeat the directions. Then he went back to the car.

Krystal looked straight ahead and bit her lip while Mark explained the situation. "Here?" she said. "You are going to leave us here?"

Hans was awake again. He had pulled the volume knob off the radio and was banging it on the dashboard.

"Just for a couple of hours," Mark said, though he knew it would take twice as long, maybe longer.

Krystal wouldn't look at him.

"There's no choice," he said.

The woman had been standing next to Mark. She moved him aside and opened the door. "You come with me," she said. "You and the little one." She held out her arms. Hans went to her immediately and peered over her shoulder at the men on the bench. Krystal hesitated, then got out of the car, ignoring Mark's hand when he reached down to help her.

"It won't take long," he said. He smiled at Hans. "Pretty soon, Hansy," he said, and turned and began to walk toward the road.

*   *   *

The woman went inside with Hans. Krystal stood beside the car and watched Mark move farther and farther away, until the line of his body started to waver in the heat and then vanished altogether. This happened suddenly. It was like seeing someone slip below the surface of a lake.

The men stared at Krystal as she walked toward the building. She felt heavy, and vaguely ashamed.

The woman had all the shades pulled down. It was like evening inside: dim, peaceful, cool. Krystal could make out the shapes of things but not their colors. There were two rooms. One had a bed and a motorcycle. The second, big room had a sofa and chairs on one side and on the other a refrigerator and stove and table.

Krystal sat at the table with Hans in her lap while the woman poured Pepsi from a big bottle into three tumblers full of ice. She had taken her hat off, and the weak light shining from the open door of the refrigerator made a halo around her face and hair. Usually Krystal measured herself against other women, but this one she watched with innocent, almost animal curiosity.

The woman took another, smaller bottle down from the top of the refrigerator. She wiggled it by the neck. "You wouldn't want any of this," she said. Krystal shook her head. The woman poured some of the liquor into her glass and pushed the other two glasses across the table. Hans took a drink, then began to make motorboat noises.

"That boy," the woman said.

"His name is Hans."

"Not this one," the woman said. "The other one."

"Oh," Krystal said. "Mark. Mark is my husband."

The woman nodded and took a drink. She leaned back in her chair. "Where are you people headed?"

Krystal told her about Los Angeles, about Mark finding work in the entertainment field. The woman smiled, and Krystal wondered if she had expressed herself correctly. In school she had done well in English, and the American boys she talked to always complimented her, but during those weeks with Mark's parents in Phoenix she had lost her confidence. Dutch and Dottie always looked bewildered when she spoke, and she herself understood almost nothing of what was said around her though she pretended that she did.

The woman kept smiling, but there was a tightness to her mouth that made the smile look painful somehow. She took another drink. "What does he do?" she asked.

Krystal tried to think of a way to explain what Mark did. When she first saw him, he had been sitting on the floor at a party and everyone around him was laughing. She had laughed too, though she didn't know why. It was a gift he had. But it was difficult to put into words. "Mark is a singer," she said.

"A singer," the woman said. She closed her eyes and leaned her head back and began to sing. Hans stopped fidgeting and watched her.

When the woman was through, Krystal said, "Good, good," and nodded, though she hadn't been able to follow the song and hated the style, which sounded to her like yodeling.

"My husband always liked to hear me sing," the woman said. "I suppose I could have been a singer if I'd wanted." She finished her drink and looked at the empty glass.

From outside Krystal heard the voices of the men on the bench, low and steady. One of them laughed.

"We had Del Ray to sing at our prom," the woman said.

The door banged. The man who'd stared at Krystal's belly stomped into the kitchen and stared at her again. The woman smiled at him. The tightness left her mouth and her lips parted slightly, as if she were about to say something. He turned and started pulling bottles of Pepsi out of the refrigerator. "Webb, what do you think?" the woman said. "This girl's husband's a singer." She reached out and ran one hand up and down his back. "We'll need something for supper," she said, "unless you want rabbit again."

He kicked the refrigerator door shut with his foot and started out of the kitchen, bottles clinking against each other. Hans slid to the floor and ran after him.

"Hans," Krystal said.

The man stopped and looked down at him. "That's right," he said. "You come with me."

It was the first time Krystal had heard him speak. His voice was thin and dry. He went back outside with Hans behind him.

The shoes Mark had on were old and loose, comfortable in the car, but his feet started to burn after a few minutes of walking in them. His eyes burned too, from sweat and the bright sun shining into his face.

For a while he sang songs, but after a couple of numbers his throat cracked with dryness so he gave it up. Anyway it made him feel stupid singing about Camelot in this desert, stupid and a little afraid because his voice sounded so small. He walked on.

The road was sticky underfoot. Mark's shoes made little sucking noises at every step. He considered walking beside the road instead of on it but he was afraid that a snake would bite him.

He wanted to stay cheerful, but he kept thinking that now they would never get to Los Angeles in time for dinner. They'd pull in late like they always did, stuff spilling out of the car, Mark humping the whole mess inside while Krystal stood by looking dazed in the glare of the headlights, Hans draped over her shoulder. Mark's buddy would be in his bathrobe. They'd try to joke but Mark would be too preoccupied. After they made up a bed for Krystal and put the crib together for Hans, which would take forever because half the screws were missing, Mark and his buddy would go down to the kitchen and drink a beer. They'd try to talk but they would end up yawning in each other's faces. Then they would go to bed.

Mark could see the whole thing. Whatever they did, it always turned out like this. Nothing ever worked.

A truck went past going the other way. There were two men inside wearing cowboy hats. They glanced at Mark, then looked straight ahead again. He stopped and watched the truck disappear into the heat.

He turned and kept walking. Broken glass glittered along the roadside.

If Mark lived here and happened to be driving down this road and saw some person walking all by himself, he would stop and ask if there was anything wrong. He believed in helping people.

But he didn't need them. He would manage without them, just as he'd manage without Dutch and Dottie. He would do it alone, and someday they would wish they'd helped. He would be in some place like Las Vegas, performing at one of the big clubs. Then, at the end of his booking, he would fly Dutch and Dottie out for his last big show—the finale. He'd fly them first class and put them up in the best hotel, the Sands or whatever, and he'd get them front row seats. And when the show was over, when the people were going crazy, whistling and stamping on the floor and everything, he would call Dutch and Dottie up to the stage. He would stand between them, holding their hands, and then, when all the clapping and yelling trailed off and everybody was quiet, smiling at him from the tables, he would raise Dutch and Dottie's hands above his head and say, Folks, I just wanted you to meet my parents and tell you what they did for me. He would stop for a second and get this really serious look on his face. It's impossible to tell you what they did for me, he would say, pausing for effect—because they didn't do *anything* for me! They didn't do *squat* for me!

Then he would drop their hands and jump off the stage and leave them there.

Mark walked faster, leaning forward, eyes narrowed against the light. His hands flicked back and forth as he walked.

No, he wouldn't do that. People might take it wrong. A stunt like that could ruin his career. He would do something even better. He would stand up there and tell the whole world that without the encouragement and support the two of them had given him, the faith and love, et cetera, he would have thrown in the towel a long time ago.

And the great part was, *it wouldn't be true!* Because Dutch and Dottie wouldn't do a thing for him unless he stayed in Phoenix and got a "real job"—like selling houses. But nobody would know that except Dutch and Dottie. They would stand up on the stage listening to all those lies, and the more he complimented them the more they would see the kind of parents they could have been and weren't, and the more ashamed they would feel, and the more grateful to Mark for not exposing them.

He could hear a faint rushing sound in the hot air, a sound like applause. He walked faster still. He hardly felt the burning of his feet. The rushing sound grew louder, and Mark looked up. Ahead of him, no more than a hundred yards off, he saw the highway—not the road itself, but a long convoy of trucks moving across the desert, floating westward through a blue haze of exhaust.

The woman told Krystal that her name was Hope.

"Hope," Krystal said. "How lovely."

They were in the bedroom. Hope was working on the motorcycle. Krystal lay on the bed, propped up with pillows, watching Hope's long fingers move here and there over the machine and through the parts on the floor, back to the sweating glass at her side. Hans was outside with the men.

Hope took a drink. She swirled the ice around and said, "I don't know, Krystal."

Krystal felt the baby move in her. She folded her hands across her belly and waited for the bump to come again.

All the lights were off except for a lamp on the floor beside Hope. There were engine parts scattered around her, and the air smelled of oil. She picked up a part and looked at it, then began to wipe it down with a cloth. "I told you we had Del Ray to our prom," she said. "I don't know if you ever heard of Del Ray where you came from, but us girls were flat crazy about him. I had a Del Ray pillow I slept on. Then he showed up and it turned out he was only about yay high." Hope held her hand a few inches above the floor. "Personally," she said, "I wouldn't look twice at a man that couldn't stand up for me if it came to the point. No offense," she added.

Krystal didn't understand what Hope had said, so she smiled.

"You take Webb," Hope said. "Webb would kill for me. He almost did, once. He beat a man to an inch of his life."

Krystal understood this. She felt sure it was true. She ran her tongue over her dry lips. "Who?" she asked. "Who did he beat?"

Hope looked up from the part she was cleaning. She smiled at Krystal in such a way that Krystal had to smile back.

"My husband," Hope said. She looked down again, still smiling.

Krystal waited, uncertain whether she had heard Hope right.

"Webb and me were hot," Hope said. "We were an item. When we weren't together, which was most of the time, we were checking up on each other. Webb used to drive past my house at all hours and follow me everywhere. Sometimes he'd follow me places with his wife in the car next to him." She laughed. "It was a situation."

The baby was pressing against Krystal's spine. She shifted slightly.

Hope looked up at her. "It's a long story."

"Tell me."

"I need some mouthwash," Hope said. She got up and went out to the kitchen. Krystal heard the crack of an ice tray. It was pleasant to lie here in this dark, cool room.

Hope came back and settled on the floor. "Don't get me going," she said. She took a drink. "The long and the short is, Webb lost his senses. It happened at the movie theater in front of half the town. Webb was sitting behind us and saw my husband put his arm around me. He came right over the chairs." She shook her head. "I can tell you we did some fancy footwork after that. Had to. My husband had six brothers and two of them in the police. We got out of there and I mean we *got*. Nothing but the clothes we had on. Never gone back since. Never will, either."

"Never," Krystal said. She admired the sound of the word. It was like Beethoven shaking his fist at the heavens.

Hope picked up the rag again. But she didn't do anything with it. She leaned against the wall, out of the little circle of light the lamp made.

"Did you have children?" Krystal asked.

Hope nodded. She held up two fingers.

"It must be hard, not to see them."

"Sometimes. Not all that much. The thing about kids, they don't leave you any room. They crowd you out of your own life. You know what I mean."

Krystal nodded.

"They'll do all right," Hope said. "They're both boys." She ran her fingers over the floor, found the part she'd been cleaning, and without looking at it began to wipe it down again.

"I couldn't leave Hans," Krystal said.

"Sure you could," Hope said. The motion of her arms slowed. She grew still. "I remember when I fell for Webb. We'd known him for years, but this one day he came into our station on his Harley. It was cold. His cheeks were red and his hair was all blown back. I remember it like it was yesterday."

Hope sat there with her hands in her lap. Her breathing got deep and slow, and Krystal, peering through the gloom, saw that her eyes were closed. She was asleep, or just dreaming—maybe of that man out there riding over the desert on this machine, his hair pushed back in the way that was special to her.

Krystal settled herself on her side. The baby was quiet now.

The air conditioner went off abruptly. Krystal lay in the dark and listened to the sounds it had covered, the dry whirr of insects, the low voices of the men, Hope's soft snoring. Krystal closed her eyes. She felt herself drifting, and as she drifted she remembered Hans. *Hans,* she thought. Then she slept.

Mark had assumed that when he reached the highway someone would immediately pick him up. But car after car went by, and the few drivers who looked at him scowled as if they were angry with him for needing a ride and putting them on the spot.

Mark's face burned, and his throat was so dry it hurt to swallow. Twice he had to leave the road to stand in the shade of a billboard. Cars passed him by for more than an hour, cars from Wisconsin and Utah and Georgia and just about everywhere. Mark felt like the whole country had turned its back on him. The thought came to him that he could die out here.

Finally a car stopped. It was a hearse. Mark hesitated, then ran toward it.

There were three people in the front seat, a man between two women. There was no rear seat. The space in back was full of electrical equipment. Mark pushed some wires out of his way and sat cross-legged on the floor. He felt the breeze from the air conditioner; it was like a stream of cold water running over him.

The driver pulled back onto the road.

"Welcome to the stiffmobile," said the man beside her. He turned around. His head was shaved except for one bristling stripe of hair down the center. It was the first Mohawk haircut Mark had ever seen. The man's eyebrows were the same carroty color as his hair. He had freckles. The freckles covered his entire face and even the shaved parts of his skull.

"Stiffmobile, cliffmobile," said the woman driving. "Riffmobile."

"Bet you thought you'd be riding with a cold one," the man said.

Mark shrugged. "I'd rather ride with a cold one than a hot one."

The man laughed and pounded on the back of the seat.

The two women also laughed. The one not driving turned around and smiled at Mark. She had a round, soft-looking face. Her lips were full. She wore a small gold earring in one side of her nose. "Hi," she said.

"Speaking of cold ones," the man said, "there's a case of them right behind you."

Mark fished four cans of beer out of the cooler and passed three of them up front. He took a long swallow, head back, eyes closed. When he opened his eyes again the man with the Mohawk was watching him. They introduced themselves, all but the woman driving. She never looked at Mark or spoke, except to herself. The man with the Mohawk was Barney. The girl with the earring was Nance. They joked back and forth, and Mark discovered that Nance had a terrific sense of humor. She picked up on almost everything he said. After a while the earring in her nose ceased to bother him.

When Barney heard that Mark had been in the army he shook his head. "Pass on that," he said. "No bang-bang for Barney. I can't stand the sight of my own brains."

"Trains," the driver said. "Cranes, lanes, stains."

"Smoothe out," Barney told her. He turned back to Mark. "So what was it like over there?"

Mark realized that Barney meant Vietnam. Mark had not been to Vietnam. He'd had orders to go, but the orders were killed just before he left and never reissued. He didn't know why. It was too complicated to explain, so he just said, "Pretty bad," and left it at that.

"Wrong question," Barney said. "That subject is strictly underwater. Scout's honor." He held up three fingers.

The mention of Vietnam broke the good feeling between them. They drank their beers and looked at the desert passing by. Then Barney crumpled his can and threw it out the window. Hot air blew into Mark's face. He remembered what it was like out there, and felt glad to be right where he was.

"I could get behind another beer," Nance said.

"Right," Barney said. He turned around and told Mark to pop some more frosties. While Mark was getting the cans out of the cooler Barney watched him, playing his fingers over the top of the seat as if it were a keyboard. "So what's in Blythe?" he said.

"Smythe," the driver said. "Smythe's in Blythe."

"Be cool," Nance said to her.

"I need a part," Mark said. He handed out the beers. "An alternator. My car's on the fritz."

"Where's your car?" Barney said.

Mark jerked his thumb over his shoulder. "Back there. I don't know the name of the place. It's just this gas station off the highway." Nance was looking at him. He smiled. She kept watching him.

"Hey," she said. "What if you didn't stop smiling? What if you just kept smiling and never stopped?"

Barney looked at her. Then he looked back at Mark. "To me," he said, "there are places you go and places you don't go. You don't go to Rochester. You don't go to Blythe."

"You definitely don't go to Blythe," Nance said.

"Right," Barney said. Then he listed some of the places where, in his opinion, you do go. They were going to one of them now, San Lucas, up in the mountains above Santa Fe. They were part of a film crew shooting a Western there. They had shot another movie in the same place a year ago and this was the sequel. Barney was a sound man. Nance did make-up. They didn't say anything about the driver.

"The place is unbelievable," Barney said. He paused and shook his head. Mark was waiting for him to describe San Lucas, but Barney just shook his head again and said, "The place is completely unbelievable."

"Really," Nance said.

It turned out that the star of the picture was Nita Damon. This was a real coincidence, because Mark had seen Nita Damon about six months ago in a show in Germany, a Bob Hope Christmas Special.

"That's amazing," Nance said. She and Barney looked at each other. "You should scratch Blythe," Barney said.

Mark grinned.

Nance was staring at him. "Marco," she said. "You're not a Mark, you're a Marco."

"You should sign on with us," Barney said. "Ride the stiffmobile express."

"You should," Nance said. "San Lucas is just incredible."

"Partyville," Barney said.

"Jesus," Mark said. "No. I couldn't."

"Sure you could," Barney said. "Lincoln freed the slaves, didn't he? Get your car later."

Mark was laughing. "Come on," he said. "What would I do up there?"

Barney said, "You mean like work?"

Mark nodded.

"No problem," Barney said. He told Mark that there was always something to do. People didn't show up, people quit, people got sick—there was always a call out for warm bodies. Once you found a tasty spot, you just settled in.

"You mean I'd be working on the movie? On the film crew?"

"Absitively," Barney said. "I guarantee."

"Jesus," Mark said. He took a breath. He looked at Barney and Nance. "I don't know," he said.

"That's all right," Barney said. "I know."

"Barney knows," Nance said.

"What have you got to lose?" Barney said.

Mark didn't say anything. He took another breath.

Barney watched him. "Marco," he said. "Don't tell me—you've got a little something else back there besides the car, right?" When Mark didn't answer, Barney laughed. "That's mellow," he said. "You're among friends. Anything goes."

"I have to think," Mark said.

"Okay," Barney said. "Think. You've got till Blythe." He turned around. "Don't disappoint me," he said.

Nance smiled. Then she turned around too. The top of her head was just visible over the high seat-back.

The desert went past the window, always the same. The road had an oily look. Mark felt rushed, a little wild.

His first idea was to get the directions to San Lucas, then drive up with Krystal and Hans after the car was fixed. But that wouldn't work. He wouldn't have enough money left for the gas, let alone food and motels and a place to live once they got there. He'd miss his chance.

Because that's what this was—a chance.

There was no point in fooling himself. He could go to Los Angeles and walk the streets for months, years maybe, without ever getting anywhere. He could stand outside closed doors and suck up to nobodies and sit in plastic chairs half his life without ever coming close to where he was right now, on his way to a guaranteed job in Partyville.

Los Angeles wasn't going to work. Mark could see that. He'd borrow money from his friend and start hustling and he wouldn't get the time of day from anyone, because he was hungry, and nobody ever had time for hungry people. Hungry people got written off. It was like Dutch said—them as has, gets.

He would run himself ragged and the money would disappear, the way all his other money had disappeared. Krystal would get worried and sad. After a couple of weeks Mark and his buddy wouldn't have anything to say to each other, and his buddy would get tired of living with a guy he didn't really know that well and a yelling kid and a sad, pregnant woman. He would tell Mark some lie to get rid of them—his girl was moving in, his parents had decided to stay together after all. By then Mark would be broke again. Krystal would have a fit and probably go into labor.

What if that happened? What then?

Mark knew what. Crawl home to Dutch and Dottie.

No. No sir. The only way he was going back to Phoenix was in a coffin.

The driver started talking to herself. Barney rapped her on top of the head with his knuckles. "Do you want me to drive?" he said. It sounded like a threat. She quieted down. "All right," he said. Without looking back he said, "Five miles to Blythe."

Mark looked out the window. He couldn't get it out of his mind that here he had exactly what he needed. A chance to show what he was made of. He'd have fun, sure, but he'd also be at work on time in the morning. He would do what he was told and do it right. He would keep his eyes open and his mouth shut and after a while people would start to notice him. He wouldn't push too hard, but now and then he might do a song at one of the parties, or impersonate some of the actors. He could just hear Nita Damon laughing and saying, "Stop it, Mark! Stop it!"

What he could do, Mark thought, was to call Krystal and arrange to meet up with her at his buddy's house in a month or two, after they'd shot the film. Mark would have something going then. He'd be on his way. But that wouldn't work, either. He didn't know how to call her. She had no money. And she wouldn't agree.

Mark wasn't going to fool himself. If he left Krystal and Hans back there, she would never forgive him. If he left them, he left them for good.

I can't do that, Mark thought. But he knew this wasn't true. He had decided not to fool himself, and that meant being honest about everything. He could leave them. People left one another, and got left, every day. It was a terrible thing. But it happened and people survived, as they survived worse things. Krystal and Hans would survive, too. When she understood what had happened she would call Dutch. Dutch would hit the roof, but in the end he would come through for them. He didn't have any choice. And in four or five years what happened today would be nothing but a bad memory.

Krystal would do well for herself. Men liked her. Even Dutch liked her, though he'd been dead set against the marriage. She would meet a good man someday, a man who could take care of her. She and Hans and the new baby would be able to go to sleep at night without wondering what would happen to them when they woke up. They didn't need Mark. Without him they would have a better life than if he and Krystal stayed together.

This was a new thought for Mark, and when he had it he felt aggrieved. It hurt him to see how unimportant he really was to Krystal. Before now he had always assumed that their coming together had somehow been ordained, and that in marrying Krystal he had filled some need of the universe. But if they could live without each other, and do better without each other, then this could not be true and must never have been true.

They did not need each other. There was no particular reason for them to be together. Then what was it all about? If he couldn't make her happy, then what was the point? They were dragging each other down like two people who couldn't swim. If they were lucky, they might keep at it long enough to grow old in the same house.

That was what they had to look forward to if they were lucky.

It wasn't right. She deserved better, and so did he.

Mark felt that he had been deceived, played with. Not by Krystal, she would never do that, but by everyone who had ever been married and knew the truth about it and went on acting as if it were something good. The truth was different. The truth was that when you got married you had to give up one thing after another. It never ended.

You had to give up your life—the special one that you were meant to have—and lead some middle kind of life that went where neither of you had ever thought of going, or wanted to go. And you never knew what was happening. You gave up your life and didn't even know it.

"Blythe," Barney said.

Mark looked at the town, what he could see of it from the road. Lines of heat quivered above the rooftops.

"Blythe," Barney said again. "Going, going, gone."

When Krystal came up from sleep she expected to open her eyes on the sight of water, the great Colorado River. She had been dreaming that she was in the car with Mark and Hans, that it was still morning and this day had not happened yet. She blinked in the gloom. In a moment she knew where she was.

"Hans," she whispered.

"He's outside," Hope said. Hope was standing over the lamp, feeding shells into a shotgun. Her shadow swayed back and forth against the wall. "I'm going to get us some dinner," she said. "You just lie here and rest up. The boy will be fine." She finished loading the gun and pushed a few more shells into the pockets of her jeans. "Be right back," she said.

Krystal lay on the bed, restless and thirsty, but feeling too heavy to rise. Outside the men had a radio on. One of those whiny songs was playing, like Hope had sung in the kitchen. Krystal had heard no good music for two months now, since the day she left home. A warm day in late spring—lieder playing on the radio, sunlight flickering through the trees along the road. On the bridge leading out of town her mother had stopped the car to watch a swan paddling upstream with two cygnets behind her.

"Ah, God," Krystal said.

She pushed herself up. She lifted the shade of the window and looked out. There was the desert, and the mountains. And there was Hope, walking into the desert with her shotgun. The light was softer than before, still white but not so sharp. The tops of the mountains were touched with pink.

Krystal stared out the window. How could anyone live in such a place? There was nothing, nothing at all. Through all those days in Phoenix, Krystal had felt a great emptiness around her where she would count for no more than a rock or a spiny tree; now she was there.

Krystal thought she might cry, but she gave the idea up. It didn't interest her.

She closed her eyes and leaned her forehead against the glass.

I will say a poem, Krystal thought, and when I am finished he will be here. At first silently, because she had promised to speak only English now, then in a whisper, and at last plainly, Krystal recited a poem the nuns had made her learn at school long ago, the only poem she remembered. She repeated it twice, then opened her eyes. Mark was not there. As if she had really believed he would be there, Krystal kicked the wall with her bare foot. The pain gave an edge of absolute clarity to what she'd been pretending not to know: that of course he wouldn't be there, because he had never really been there and was never going to be there in any way that mattered.

The window was hot under Krystal's forehead. She watched Hope move farther and farther away. Then Hope stopped. She raised her gun. A moment later Krystal heard the boom, and felt the glass shudder against her skin.

A few miles past Blythe the driver began to talk to herself again. Her voice was flat. Mark looked out the window and tried to ignore it but after a time he found himself listening, trying to make sense of the things she said. There wasn't any reason to her words. Every possibility of meaning ended in the beginning of another possibility. It was frustrating to Mark. He became uncomfortable.

Then he noticed that the hearse was moving at great speed, really racing. The driver passed every car they came upon. She changed lanes without any purpose.

Mark tried to find a break between her words to say something, just a note of caution, something about how tough the police were around here, but no break came. The car was going faster and faster. He hoped that Barney would tell her to shut up and slow down, maybe even take over himself for a while, but Barney wasn't saying anything and neither was Nance. She had disappeared completely and all Mark could see of Barney were the bristles of his hair.

"Hey," Mark said. "What's the hurry?"

The driver seemed not to hear him. She passed three more cars and went on talking to herself. Then Mark saw that she had only one hand on the steering wheel, her left hand. She was gripping the wheel so tightly that her hand had turned white. He could see the bones of her fingers.

"Better slow down," Mark said.

"Blue horse sells kisses," she said, then repeated the words.

"Jesus," Mark said. He bent forward and leaned over the top of the seat to get a look at the speedometer. Then he saw what was going on up there and sat back. He had never seen anything like that before. It took the wind out of him. He felt far, far away from himself. Then the hearse started to shimmy. The driver was making what sounded like animal noises in the jungle. Nance giggled.

"Stop the car," Mark said.

"Stop the war," the driver said.

"Stop the car," Mark said again.

"Hey," Barney said. "What's the problem?" His voice was soft, remote.

"I want out," Mark said.

Nance giggled again. The tires began to whine.

"Everything's sweet," Barney said. "Just settle into it, Marco. You decided, remember?"

Mark didn't know what to say. It was hard to talk to someone he couldn't see.

He heard Nance whispering. Then Barney said, "Hey—Marco. Come on up here."

"Midnight phone book," the driver said.

"Come on," Barney said. "You're with us now."

"Stop the car," Mark said. He reached over the seat and began to rap on the driver's head, softly at first, then hard. He could hear the knocking of his knuckles against her skull. She turned and smiled at him. Her face was white. That was all he saw, the whiteness of her face, before she turned again. She stopped the hearse in the middle of the road. Mark looked back. There was a car bearing down on them. It swerved into the other lane and went past with its horn wailing.

"Okay, Marco," Barney said. "Ciao. You blew it."

Mark scrambled over equipment and cords and let himself out the back. When he closed the gate the driver pulled away, fast. Mark crossed the road and watched the hearse until it disappeared. The road was empty. He turned and walked back toward Blythe.

A few minutes later an old man stopped for him. He took a liking to Mark and drove him all the way to the parts store. They were closing up when he arrived, but after Mark explained his situation the boss let him inside and found the alternator for him. With tax, the price came to seventy-one dollars.

"I thought it was fifty-eight," Mark said.

"Seventy-one," the boss said.

Mark showed him the figures that the woman had written down, but it did no good. "Jesus," Mark said. He stared at the alternator. "I've only got sixty-five."

"I'm sorry," the boss said. He put his hands on the counter and waited.

"Look," Mark said. "I just got back from Vietnam. Me and my wife are on our way to Los Angeles. Once we get there I can send you the other six. I'll put it in the mail tomorrow morning. I swear."

The boss looked at him. Mark could see that he was hesitating.

"I've got a job waiting," Mark said.

"What kind of job?"

"I'm a sound man," Mark said.

"Sound man." The boss nodded. "I'm sorry," he said. "You think you'll send the money but you won't."

Mark argued for a while but without heat, because he knew that the man was right—he would never send the money. He gave up and went outside again. The parts store adjoined a salvage yard filled with crumpled cars. Across the street there was a U-Haul depot and a gas station. Mark began to walk toward the gas station. A black dog appeared on the other side of the salvage yard fence and kept pace with Mark. When Mark looked at him, the dog silently bared his fangs and gave Mark such a fright that he crossed the street.

He was hot and tired. He could smell himself. He remembered the coolness of the hearse and thought, *I blew it.*

There was a pay phone outside the gas station. Mark got a handful of change and shut himself in. He wanted to call his buddy in Los Angeles and figure something out, but he had left the address book in the car and it turned out that the number was unlisted. He tried to explain things to the operator but she refused to listen. She hung up on him.

Mark looked out at the street. The dog was still at the fence, watching him. The only thing he could do, Mark decided, was to keep calling Los Angeles information until he got a human being on the other end. There had to be somebody sympathetic out there.

But first he was going to call Phoenix and give Dutch and Dottie a little something to sleep on. He would put on his official voice and tell them that he was Sergeant Smith—no, *Smythe*—Sergeant Smythe of the highway patrol, calling to report an accident. A head-on collision just outside of Palm Springs. It was his duty, he was sorry to say—his voice would crack—there were no survivors. No, ma'am, not one. Yes, ma'am, he was sure. He'd been at the scene. The one good thing he could tell her was that nobody had suffered. It was over just like *that*, and here Mark would snap his fingers into the receiver.

He closed his eyes and listened to the phone ring through the cool, quiet house. He saw Dottie where she sat in her avocado kitchen, drinking coffee and making a list, saw her rise and gather her cigarettes and lighter and ashtray. He heard her shoes tapping on the tile floor as she came toward the phone.

But it was Dutch who answered. "Strick here," he said.

Mark took a breath.

"Hello," Dutch said.

"It's me," Mark said. "Dad, it's me—Mark."

Krystal was washing her face when she heard the gun go off again. She paused, water running through her fingers, then finished up and left the bedroom. She wanted to find Hans. He should have been changed long before now, and it was almost time for him to eat. She missed him.

Picking her way through the parts on the floor, she went into the main room. It was almost completely dark. Krystal felt her way along the wall to the light switch. She turned the light on and stood there with her hand against the wall.

Everything was red. The carpet was red. The lamp shades were red, and had little red tassels hanging down from them. The chairs and the couch were red. The pillows on the couch were shaped like hearts and covered in a satiny material that looked wet under the light, so that for a moment they had the appearance of real organs.

Krystal stared at the room. In a novel she'd once read she had come upon the expression "love nest," and after considering it for a moment imagined light-washed walls, tall pines reaching to the balcony outside, an old bed with spiraling posts and a hunting scene carved across the headboard. But this, she thought, looking at the room, this was a love nest. It was horrible, horrible.

Krystal moved over to the door and opened it a crack. Someone was lying on the front seat of the car, his bare feet sticking out the window, his boots on the ground below with yellow socks hanging from the tops. She could not see the men on the bench but one of them was saying something, the same word again and again. Krystal couldn't make it out. Then she heard Hans repeat the word, and the men laughed.

She opened the door wider. Still standing inside, she said, "Hans, come here."

She waited. She heard someone whisper.

"Hans," she said.

He came to the door. There was dirt all over his face but he looked happy. "Come in," she said.

Hans looked over his shoulder and smiled, then turned back to Krystal.

"Come, Hans," she said.

He stood there. "Bitch," he said.

Krystal stepped backwards. She shook her head. "No," she said. "No no no. Don't say that. Come, sweet boy." She held out her arms.

"Bitch," he said again.

"Oh!" Krystal said. Her hand went up to her mouth. Then she pushed open the door and walked up to Hans and slapped him across the face, something she had never done before. She slapped him hard. He sat down and looked up at her. Krystal took a flat board from the pile of scrap and turned toward the three men on the bench. They were watching her from under their big hats. "Who did that?" she said. "Who taught him that word?" When they didn't answer she started toward the bench, reviling them in German, using words she had never used before. They stood and backed away from her. Hans began to cry. Krystal turned on him. "Be quiet!" she said. He whimpered once and was still.

Krystal turned back to the men. "Who taught him that word?"

"It wasn't me," one of them said.

The other two just stood there.

"Shame," Krystal said. She looked at them, then walked over to the car. She kicked the boots aside. Holding the board with both hands, she swung it as hard as she could across the bare feet sticking out of the window. The man inside screamed. Krystal hit his feet again and he pulled them back.

"Get out," she said. "Out, out, out!"

The man who'd been sleeping inside, the one called Webb, scrambled out the other door and hopped from foot to foot toward the building. He had left his hat in the car. As he danced over the hot sand his hair flapped up and down like a wing. He stopped in the shade and looked back, still shifting from foot to foot. He kept his eyes on Krystal. So did Hans, sitting by the door. So did the men near the bench. They were all watching to see what she would do next.

So, Krystal thought. She flung the board away, and one of the men flinched. Krystal almost smiled. She thought, How angry I must look, how angry I am, and then her anger left her. She tried to keep it, but it was gone the moment she knew it was there.

She shaded her eyes and looked around her. The distant mountains cast long shadows into the desert. The desert was empty and still. Nothing moved but Hope, walking toward them with the gun over her shoulder. As she drew near Krystal waved, and Hope raised her arms. A rabbit hung from each hand, swinging by its ears.

In the Cemetery Where
Al Jolson Is Buried

AMY HEMPEL

"TELL ME THINGS I won't mind forgetting," she said. "Make it useless stuff or skip it."

I began. I told her insects fly through rain missing every drop, never getting wet. I told her no one in America owned a tape recorder before Bing Crosby did. I told her the shape of the moon is like a banana—you see it looking full, you're seeing it end-on.

The camera made me self-conscious and I stopped. It was trained on us from a ceiling mount—the kind of camera banks use to photograph robbers. It played us to the nurses down the hall in Intensive Care.

"Go on, girl," she said. "You get used to it."

I had my audience. I went on. Did she know that Tammy Wynette had changed her tune? Really. That now she sings "Stand By Your Friends"? That Paul Anka did it too, I said. Does "You're Having *Our* Baby." That he got sick of all that feminist bitching.

"What else?" she said. "Have you got something else?"

Oh, yes.

For her I would always have something else.

"Did you know that when they taught the first chimp to talk, it lied? That when they asked her who did it on the desk, she signed back Max, the janitor. And that when they pressed her, she said she was sorry, that it was really the project director. But she was a mother, so I guess she had her reasons."

"Oh, that's good," she said. "A parable."

"There's more about the chimp," I said. "But it will break your heart."

"No, thanks," she says, and scratches at her mask.

*   *   *

We look like good-guy outlaws. Good or bad, I am not used to the mask yet. I keep touching the warm spot where my breath, thank God, comes out. She is used to hers. She only ties the strings on top. The other ones—a pro by now—she lets hang loose.

We call this place the Marcus Welby Hospital. It's the white one with the palm trees under the opening credits of all those shows. A Hollywood hospital, though in fact it is several miles west. Off camera, there is a beach across the street.

She introduces me to a nurse as the Best Friend. The impersonal article is more intimate. It tells me that *they* are intimate, the nurse and my friend.

"I was telling her we used to drink Canada Dry ginger ale and pretend we were in Canada."

"That's how dumb *we* were," I say.

"You could be sisters," the nurse says.

So how come, I'll bet they are wondering, it took me so long to get to such a glamorous place? But do they ask?

They do not ask.

Two months, and how long is the drive?

The best I can explain it is this—I have a friend who worked one summer in a mortuary. He used to tell me stories. The one that really got to me was not the grisliest, but it's the one that did. A man wrecked his car on 101 going south. He did not lose consciousness. But his arm was taken down to the wet bone—and when he looked at it—it scared him to death.

I mean, he died.

So I hadn't dared to look any closer. But now I'm doing it—and hoping that I will live through it.

She shakes out a summer-weight blanket, showing a leg you did not want to see. Except for that, you look at her and understand the law that requires two people to be with the body at all times.

"I thought of something," she says. "I thought of it last night. I think there is a real and present need here. You know," she says, "like for someone to do it for you when you can't do it yourself. You call them up whenever you want—like when push comes to shove."

She grabs the bedside phone and loops the cord around her neck.

"Hey," she says, "the end o' the line."

She keeps on, giddy with something. But I don't know with what.

"I can't remember," she says. "What does Kübler-Ross say comes after Denial?"

It seems to me Anger must be next. Then Bargaining, Depression, and so on and so forth. But I keep my guesses to myself.

"The only thing is," she says, "is where's Resurrection? God knows, I want to do it by the book. But she left out Resurrection."

She laughs, and I cling to the sound the way someone dangling above a ravine holds fast to the thrown rope.

"Tell me," she says, "about that chimp with the talking hands. What do they do when the thing ends and the chimp says, 'I don't want to go back to the zoo'?"

When I don't say anything, she says, "Okay—then tell me another animal story. I like animal stories. But not a sick one—I don't want to know about all the seeing-eye dogs going blind."

No, I would not tell her a sick one.

"How about the hearing-ear dogs?" I say. "They're not going deaf, but they are getting very judgmental. For instance, there's this golden retriever in New Jersey, he wakes up the deaf mother and drags her into the daughter's room because the kid has got a flashlight and is reading under the covers."

"Oh, you're killing me," she says. "Yes, you're definitely killing me."

"They say the smart dog obeys, but the smarter dog knows when to disobey."

"Yes," she says, "the smarter anything knows when to disobey. Now, for example."

She is flirting with the Good Doctor, who has just appeared. Unlike the Bad Doctor, who checks the I.V. drip before saying good morning, the Good Doctor says things like "God didn't give epileptics a fair shake." The Good Doctor awards himself points for the cripples he could have hit in the parking lot. Because the Good Doctor is a little in love with her, he says maybe a year. He pulls a chair up to her bed and suggests I might like to spend an hour on the beach.

"Bring me something back," she says. "Anything from the beach. Or the gift shop. Taste is no object."

He draws the curtain around her bed.

"Wait!" she cries.

I look in at her.

"Anything," she says, "except a magazine subscription."

The doctor turns away.

I watch her mouth laugh.

What seems dangerous often is not—black snakes, for example, or clear-air turbulence. While things that just lie there, like this beach, are loaded with jeopardy. A yellow dust rising from the ground, the heat that ripens melons overnight—this is earthquake weather. You can sit here braiding the fringe on your towel and the sand will all of a sudden suck down like an hourglass. The air roars. In the cheap apartments on-shore, bathtubs fill themselves and gardens roll up and over like green waves. If nothing happens, the dust will drift and the heat deepen till fear turns to desire. Nerves like that are only bought off by catastrophe.

"It never happens when you're thinking about it," she once observed. "Earthquake, earthquake, earthquake," she said.

"Earthquake, earthquake, earthquake," I said.

Like the aviaphobe who keeps the plane aloft with prayer, we kept it up until an aftershock cracked the ceiling.

That was after the big one in '72. We were in college; our dormitory was five miles from the epicenter. When the ride was over and my jabbering pulse began to slow, she served five parts champagne to one part orange juice, and joked about living in Ocean View, Kansas. I offered to drive her to Hawaii on the new world psychics predicted would surface the next time, or the next.

I could not say that now—next.

Whose next? she could ask.

Was I the only one who noticed that the experts had stopped saying *if* and now spoke of *when*? Of course not; the fearful ran to thousands. We watched the traffic of Japanese beetles for deviation. Deviation might mean more natural violence.

I wanted her to be afraid with me. But she said, "I don't know. I'm just not."

She was afraid of nothing, not even of flying.

I have this dream before a flight where we buckle in and the plane moves down the runway. It takes off at thirty-five miles an hour, and then we're airborne, skimming the tree tops. Still, we arrive in New York on time.

It is so pleasant.

One night I flew to Moscow this way.

She flew with me once. That time she flew with me she ate macadamia nuts while the wings bounced. She knows the wing tips can bend thirty feet up and thirty feet down without coming off. She believes it. She trusts the laws of aerodynamics. My mind stampedes. I can almost accept that a battleship floats when everybody knows steel sinks.

I see fear in her now, and am not going to try to talk her out of it. She is right to be afraid.

After a quake, the six o'clock news airs a film clip of first-graders yelling at the broken playground per their teacher's instructions.

"*Bad* earth!" they shout, because anger is stronger than fear.

But the beach is standing still today. Everyone on it is tranquilized, numb, or asleep. Teenaged girls rub coconut oil on each other's hard-to-reach places. They smell like macaroons. They pry open compacts like clamshells; mirrors catch the sun and throw a spray of white rays across glazed shoulders. The girls arrange their wet hair with silk flowers the way they learned in *Seventeen*. They pose.

A formation of low-riders pulls over to watch with a six-pack. They get vocal when the girls check their tan lines. When the beer is gone, so are they—flexing their cars on up the boulevard.

Above this aggressive health are the twin wrought-iron terraces, painted flamingo pink, of the Palm Royale. Someone dies there every time the sheets are changed. There's an ambulance in the driveway, so the remaining residents line the balconies, rocking and not talking, one-upped.

The ocean they stare at is dangerous, and not just the undertow. You can almost see the slapping tails of sand sharks keeping cruising bodies alive.

If she looked, she could see this, some of it, from her window. She would be the first to say how little it takes to make a thing all wrong.

*   *   *

There was a second bed in the room when I got back to it!

For two beats I didn't get it. Then it hit me like an open coffin.

She wants every minute, I thought. She wants my life.

"You missed Gussie," she said.

Gussie is her parents' three-hundred-pound narcoleptic maid. Her attacks often come at the ironing board. The pillowcases in that family are all bordered with scorch.

"It's a hard trip for her," I said. "How is she?"

"Well, she didn't fall asleep, if that's what you mean. Gussie's great—you know what she said? She said, 'Darlin, stop this worriation. Just keep prayin, down on your knees'—me, who can't even get out of bed."

She shrugged. "What am I missing?"

"It's earthquake weather," I told her.

"The best thing to do about earthquakes," she said, "is not to live in California."

"That's useful," I said. "You sound like Reverend Ike—'The best thing to do for the poor is not be one of them.'"

We're crazy about Reverend Ike.

I noticed her face was bloated.

"You know," she said, "I feel like hell. I'm about to stop having fun."

"The ancients have a saying," I said. "'There are times when the wolves are silent; there are times when the moon howls.'"

"What's that, Navajo?"

"Palm Royale lobby graffiti," I said. "I bought a paper there. I'll read you something."

"Even though I care about nothing?"

I turned to the page with the trivia column. I said, "Did you know the more shrimp flamingo birds eat, the pinker their feathers get?" I said, "Did you know that Eskimos need refrigerators? Do you know *why* Eskimos need refrigerators? Did you know that Eskimos need refrigerators because how else would they keep their food from freezing?"

I turned to page three, to a UPI filler datelined Mexico City. I read her "Man Robs Bank with Chicken," about a man who bought a barbecued chicken at a stand down the block from a bank. Passing the bank, he got the idea. He walked in and approached a teller. He pointed the brown paper bag at her and she handed over the day's receipts. It was the smell of barbecue sauce that eventually led to his capture.

* * *

The story had made her hungry, she said—so I took the elevator down six floors to the cafeteria, and brought back all the ice cream she wanted. We lay side by side, adjustable beds cranked up for optimal TV-viewing, littering the sheets with Good Humor wrappers, picking toasted almonds out of the gauze. We were Lucy and Ethel, Mary and Rhoda in extremis. The blinds were closed to keep light off the screen.

We watched a movie starring men we used to think we wanted to sleep with. Hers was a tough cop out to stop mine, a vicious rapist who went after cocktail waitresses.

"This is a good movie," she said when snipers felled them both.

I missed her already.

A Filipino nurse tiptoed in and gave her an injection. The nurse removed the pile of popsicle sticks from the nightstand—enough to splint a small animal.

The injection made us both sleepy. We slept.

I dreamed she was a decorator, come to furnish my house. She worked in secret, singing to herself. When she finished, she guided me proudly to the door. "How do you like it?" she asked, easing me inside.

Every beam and sill and shelf and knob was draped in gay bunting, with streamers of pastel crepe looped around bright mirrors.

"I have to go home," I said when she woke up.

She thought I meant home to her house in the Canyon, and I had to say No, *home* home. I twisted my hands in the time-honored fashion of people in pain. I was supposed to offer something. The Best Friend. I could not even offer to come back.

I felt weak and small and failed.

Also exhilarated.

I had a convertible in the parking lot. Once out of that room, I would drive it too fast down the Coast highway through the crab-smelling air. A stop in Malibu for sangria. The music in the place would be sexy and loud. They'd serve papaya and shrimp and water-melon ice. After dinner I would shimmer with lust, buzz with heat, vibrate with life, and stay up all night.

*   *   *

Without a word, she yanked off her mask and threw it on the floor. She kicked at the blankets and moved to the door. She must have hated having to pause for breath and balance before slamming out of Isolation, and out of the second room, the one where you scrub and tie on the white masks.

A voice shouted her name in alarm, and people ran down the corridor. The Good Doctor was paged over the intercom. I opened the door and the nurses at the station stared hard, as if this flight had been my idea.

"Where is she?" I asked, and they nodded to the supply closet.

I looked in. Two nurses were kneeling beside her on the floor, talking to her in low voices. One held a mask over her nose and mouth, the other rubbed her back in slow circles. The nurses glanced up to see if I was the doctor—and when I wasn't, they went back to what they were doing.

"There, there, honey," they cooed.

On the morning she was moved to the cemetery, the one where Al Jolson is buried, I enrolled in a Fear of Flying class. "What is your worst fear?" the instructor asked, and I answered, "That I will finish this course and still be afraid."

I sleep with a glass of water on the nightstand so I can see by its level if the coastal earth is trembling or if the shaking is still me.

What do I remember?

I remember only the useless things I hear—that Bob Dylan's mother invented Wite-out, that twenty-three people must be in a room before there is a fifty-fifty chance two will have the same birthdate. Who cares whether or not it's true? In my head there are bath towels swaddling this stuff. Nothing else seeps through.

I review those things that will figure in the re-telling: a kiss through surgical gauze, the pale hand correcting the position of the wig. I noted these gestures as they happened, not in any retrospect—though

I do not know why looking back should show us more than looking *at*.
  It is just possible I will say I stayed the night.
  And who is there that can say that I did not?

  I think of the chimp, the one with the talking hands.
  In the course of the experiment, that chimp had a baby. Imagine how her trainers must have thrilled when the mother, without prompting, began to sign to her newborn.
  Baby, drink milk.
  Baby, play ball.
  And when the baby died, the mother stood over the body, her wrinkled hands moving with animal grace, forming again and again the words, Baby, come hug, Baby, come hug, fluent now in the language of grief.

for Jessica Wolfson

Territory

DAVID LEAVITT

N EIL'S MOTHER, Mrs. Campbell, sits on her lawn chair behind a card table outside the food co-op. Every few minutes, as the sun shifts, she moves the chair and table several inches back so as to remain in the shade. It is a hundred degrees outside, and bright white. Each time someone goes in or out of the co-op a gust of air-conditioning flies out of the automatic doors, raising dust from the cement.

Neil stands just inside, poised over a water fountain, and watches her. She has on a sun hat, and a sweatshirt over her tennis dress; her legs are bare, and shiny with cocoa butter. In front of her, propped against the table, a sign proclaims: MOTHERS, FIGHT FOR YOUR CHILDREN'S RIGHTS—SUPPORT A NON-NUCLEAR FUTURE. Women dressed exactly like her pass by, notice the sign, listen to her brief spiel, finger pamphlets, sign petitions or don't sign petitions, never give money. Her weary eyes are masked by dark glasses. In the age of Reagan, she has declared, keeping up the causes of peace and justice is a futile, tiresome, and unrewarding effort; it is therefore an effort fit only for mothers to keep up. The sun bounces off the window glass through which Neil watches her. His own reflection lines up with her profile.

Later that afternoon, Neil spreads himself out alongside the pool and imagines he is being watched by the shirtless Chicano gardener. But the gardener, concentrating on his pruning, is neither seductive nor seducible. On the lawn, his mother's large Airedales—Abigail, Lucille, Fern—amble, sniff, urinate. Occasionally, they accost the gardener, who yells at them in Spanish.

After two years' absence, Neil reasons, he should feel nostalgia, regret, gladness upon returning home. He closes his eyes and tries to muster the proper background music for the cinematic scene of return. His rhapsody, however, is interrupted by the noises of his mother's trio—the scratchy cello, whining violin, stumbling piano—as she and Lillian Havalard and Charlotte Feder plunge through Mozart.

The tune is cheery, in a Germanic sort of way, and utterly inappropriate to what Neil is trying to feel. Yet it *is* the music of his adolescence; they have played it for years, bent over the notes, their heads bobbing in silent time to the metronome.

It is getting darker. Every few minutes, he must move his towel so as to remain within the narrowing patch of sunlight. In four hours, Wayne, his lover of ten months and the only person he has ever imagined he could spend his life with, will be in this house, where no lover of his has ever set foot. The thought fills him with a sense of grand terror and curiosity. He stretches, tries to feel seductive, desirable. The gardener's shears whack at the ferns; the music above him rushes to a loud, premature conclusion. The women laugh and applaud themselves as they give up for the day. He hears Charlotte Feder's full nasal twang, the voice of a fat woman in a pink pants suit—odd, since she is a scrawny, arthritic old bird, rarely clad in anything other than tennis shorts and a blouse. Lillian is the fat woman in the pink pants suit; her voice is thin and warped by too much crying. Drink in hand, she calls out from the porch, "Hot enough!" and waves. He lifts himself up and nods to her.

The women sit on the porch and chatter; their voices blend with the clink of ice in glasses. They belong to a small circle of ladies all of whom, with the exception of Neil's mother, are widows and divorcées. Lillian's husband left her twenty-two years ago, and sends her a check every month to live on; Charlotte has been divorced twice as long as she was married, and has a daughter serving a long sentence for terrorist acts committed when she was nineteen. Only Neil's mother has a husband, a distant sort of husband, away often on business. He is away on business now. All of them feel betrayed—by husbands, by children, by history.

Neil closes his eyes, tries to hear the words only as sounds. Soon, a new noise accosts him: his mother arguing with the gardener in Spanish. He leans on his elbows and watches them; the syllables are loud, heated, and compressed, and seem on the verge of explosion. But the argument ends happily; they shake hands. The gardener collects his check and walks out the gate without so much as looking at Neil.

He does not know the gardener's name; as his mother has reminded him, he does not know most of what has gone on since he moved away. Her life has gone on, unaffected by his absence. He flinches at his own egoism, the egoism of sons.

"Neil! Did you call the airport to make sure the plane's coming in on time?"

"Yes," he shouts to her. "It is."

"Good. Well, I'll have dinner ready when you get back."

"Mom—"

"What?" The word comes out in a weary wail that is more of an answer than a question.

"What's wrong?" he says, forgetting his original question.

"Nothing's wrong," she declares in a tone that indicates that everything is wrong. "The dogs have to be fed, dinner has to be made, and I've got people here. Nothing's wrong."

"I hope things will be as comfortable as possible when Wayne gets here."

"Is that a request or a threat?"

"Mom—"

Behind her sunglasses, her eyes are inscrutable. "I'm tired," she says. "It's been a long day. I . . . I'm anxious to meet Wayne. I'm sure he'll be wonderful, and we'll all have a wonderful, wonderful time. I'm sorry. I'm just tired."

She heads up the stairs. He suddenly feels an urge to cover himself; his body embarrasses him, as it has in her presence since the day she saw him shirtless and said with delight, "Neil! You're growing hair under your arms!"

Before he can get up, the dogs gather round him and begin to sniff and lick at him. He wriggles to get away from them, but Abigail, the largest and stupidest, straddles his stomach and nuzzles his mouth. He splutters and, laughing, throws her off. "Get away from me, you goddamn dogs," he shouts, and swats at them. They are new dogs, not the dog of his childhood, not dogs he trusts.

He stands, and the dogs circle him, looking up at his face expectantly. He feels renewed terror at the thought that Wayne will be here soon: Will they sleep in the same room? Will they make love? He has never had sex in his parents' house. How can he be expected to be a lover here, in this place of his childhood, of his earliest shame, in this household of mothers and dogs?

"Dinnertime! Abbylucyferny, Abbylucyferny, dinnertime!" His mother's litany disperses the dogs, and they run for the door.

"Do you realize," he shouts to her, "that no matter how much those dogs love you they'd probably kill you for the leg of lamb in the freezer?"

*   *   *

Neil was twelve the first time he recognized in himself something like sexuality. He was lying outside, on the grass, when Rasputin—the dog, long dead, of his childhood—began licking his face. He felt a tingle e did not recognize, pulled off his shirt to give the dog access to more of him. Rasputin's tongue tickled coolly. A wet nose started to sniff down his body, toward his bathing suit. What he felt frightened him, but he couldn't bring himself to push the dog away. Then his mother called out, "Dinner," and Rasputin was gone, more interested in food than in him.

It was the day after Rasputin was put to sleep, years later, that Neil finally stood in the kitchen, his back turned to his parents, and said, with unexpected ease, "I'm a homosexual." The words seemed insufficient, reductive. For years, he had believed his sexuality to be detachable from the essential him, but now he realized that it was part of him. He had the sudden, despairing sensation that though the words had been easy to say, the fact of their having been aired was incurably damning. Only then, for the first time, did he admit they were true, and he shook and wept in regret for what he would not be for his mother, for having failed her. His father hung back, silent; he was absent for that moment as he was mostly absent—a strong absence. Neil always thought of him sitting on the edge of the bed in his underwear, captivated by something on television. He said, "It's O.K., Neil." But his mother was resolute; her lower lip didn't quaver. She had enormous reserves of strength to which she only gained access at moments like this one. She hugged him from behind, wrapped him in the childhood smells of perfume and brownies, and whispered, "It's O.K., honey." For once, her words seemed as inadequate as his. Neil felt himself shrunk to an embarrassed adolescent, hating her sympathy, not wanting her to touch him. It was the way he would feel from then on whenever he was in her presence—even now, at twenty-three, bringing home his lover to meet her.

All through his childhood, she had packed only the most nutritious lunches, had served on the PTA, had volunteered at the children's library and at his school, had organized a successful campaign to ban a racist history textbook. The day after he told her, she located and got in touch with an organization called the Coalition of Parents of Lesbians and Gays. Within a year, she was president of it. On weekends, she and the other mothers drove their station wagons to San Francisco, set up their card tables in front of the Bulldog Baths, the Liberty Baths, passed out literature to men in leather and denim who were loath to admit they even had mothers. These men, who would habitually do violence to each other, were strangely cowed by the suburban ladies with their informational booklets, and bent their heads. Neil was a sophomore in college then, and lived in San Francisco. She brought him pamphlets detailing the dangers of bathhouses and back rooms, enemas and poppers, wordless sex in alleyways. His excursion into that world had been brief and lamentable, and was over. He winced at the thought that she knew all his sexual secrets, and vowed to move to the East Coast to escape her. It was not very different from the days when she had campaigned for a better playground, or tutored the Hispanic children in the audiovisual room. Those days, as well, he had run away from her concern. Even today, perched in front of the co-op, collecting signatures for nuclear disarmament, she was quintessentially a mother. And if the lot of mothers was to expect nothing in return, was the lot of sons to return nothing?

Driving across the Dumbarton Bridge on his way to the airport, Neil thinks, I have returned nothing; I have simply returned. He wonders if she would have given birth to him had she known what he would grow up to be.

Then he berates himself: Why should he assume himself to be the cause of her sorrow? She has told him that her life is full of secrets. She has changed since he left home—grown thinner, more rigid, harder to hug. She has given up baking, taken up tennis; her skin has browned and tightened. She is no longer the woman who hugged him and kissed him, who said, "As long as you're happy, that's all that's important to us."

The flats spread out around him; the bridge floats on purple and green silt, and spongy bay fill, not water at all. Only ten miles north, a whole city has been built on gunk dredged up from the bay.

He arrives at the airport ten minutes early, to discover that the plane has landed twenty minutes early. His first view of Wayne is from behind, by the baggage belt. Wayne looks as he always looks—slightly windblown—and is wearing the ratty leather jacket he was wearing the night they met. Neil sneaks up on him and puts his hands on his shoulders; when Wayne turns around, he looks relieved to see him.

They hug like brothers; only in the safety of Neil's mother's car do they dare to kiss. They recognize each other's smells, and grow comfortable again. "I never imagined I'd actually see you out here." Neil says, "but you're exactly the same here as there."

"It's only been a week."

They kiss again. Neil wants to go to a motel, but Wayne insists on being pragmatic. "We'll be there soon. Don't worry."

"We could go to one of the bathhouses in the city and take a room for a couple of aeons," Neil says. "Christ, I'm hard up. I don't even know if we're going to be in the same bedroom."

"Well, if we're not," Wayne says, "we'll sneak around. It'll be romantic."

They cling to each other for a few more minutes, until they realize that people are looking in the car window. Reluctantly, they pull apart. Neil reminds himself that he loves this man, that there is a reason for him to bring this man home.

He takes the scenic route on the way back. The car careers over foothills, through forests, along white four-lane highways high in the mountains. Wayne tells Neil that he sat next to a woman on the plane who was once Marilyn Monroe's psychiatrist's nurse. He slips his foot out of his shoe and nudges Neil's ankle, pulling Neil's sock down with his toe.

"I have to drive," Neil says. "I'm very glad you're here."

There is a comfort in the privacy of the car. They have a common fear of walking hand in hand, of publicly showing physical affection, even in the permissive West Seventies of New York—a fear that they have admitted only to one another. They slip through a pass between two hills, and are suddenly in residential Northern California, the land of expensive ranch-style houses.

As they pull into Neil's mother's driveway, the dogs run barking toward the car. When Wayne opens the door, they jump and lap at him, and he tries to close it again. "Don't worry. Abbylucyferny! Get in the house, damn it!"

His mother descends from the porch. She has changed into a blue flower-print dress, which Neil doesn't recognize. He gets out of the car and halfheartedly chastises the dogs. Crickets chirp in the trees. His mother looks radiant, even beautiful, illuminated by the head-lights, surrounded by the now quiet dogs, like a Circe with her slaves. When she walks over to Wayne, offering her hand, and says, "Wayne, I'm Barbara," Neil forgets that she is his mother.

"Good to meet you, Barbara," Wayne says, and reaches out his hand. Craftier than she, he whirls her around to kiss her cheek.

Barbara! He is calling his mother Barbara! Then he remembers that Wayne is five years older than he is. They chat by the open car door, and Neil shrinks back—the embarrassed adolescent, uncomfortable, unwanted.

So the dreaded moment passes and he might as well not have been there. At dinner, Wayne keeps the conversation smooth, like a cap-tivated courtier seeking Neil's mother's hand. A faggot son's sodomist—such words spit into Neil's head. She has prepared tiny meatballs with fresh coriander, fettucine with pesto. Wayne talks about the street people in New York; El Salvador is a tragedy; if only Sadat had lived; Phyllis Schlafly—what can you do?

"It's a losing battle," she tells him. "Every day I'm out there with my card table, me and the other mothers, but I tell you, Wayne, it's a losing battle. Sometimes I think us old ladies are the only ones with enough patience to fight."

Occasionally, Neil says something, but his comments seem stupid and clumsy. Wayne continues to call her Barbara. No one under forty has ever called her Barbara as long as Neil can remember. They drink wine; he does not.

Now is the time for drastic action. He contemplates taking Wayne's hand, then checks himself. He has never done anything in her pres-ence to indicate that the sexuality he confessed to five years ago was a reality and not an invention. Even now, he and Wayne might as well be friends, college roommates. Then Wayne, his savior, with a single, sweeping gesture, reaches for his hand, and clasps it, in the midst of a joke he is telling about Saudi Arabians. By the time he is laughing, their hands are joined. Neil's throat contracts; his heart begins to beat violently. He notices his mother's eyes flicker, glance downward; she never breaks the stride of her sentence. The dinner goes on, and every taboo nurtured since childhood falls quietly away.

She removes the dishes. Their hands grow sticky; he cannot tell which fingers are his and which Wayne's. She clears the rest of the table and rounds up the dogs.

"Well, boys, I'm very tired, and I've got a long day ahead of me tomorrow, so I think I'll hit the sack. There are extra towels for you in Neil's bathroom, Wayne. Sleep well."

"Good night, Barbara," Wayne calls out. "It's been wonderful meeting you."

They are alone. Now they can disentangle their hands.

"No problem about where we sleep, is there?"

"No," Neil says. "I just can't imagine sleeping with someone in this house."

His leg shakes violently. Wayne takes Neil's hand in a firm grasp and hauls him up.

Later that night, they lie outside, under redwood trees, listening to the hysteria of the crickets, the hum of the pool cleaning itself.

Redwood leaves prick their skin. They fell in love in bars and apartments, and this is the first time that they have made love outdoors.
Neil is not sure he has enjoyed the experience. He kept sensing eyes,
imagined that the neighborhood cats were staring at them from behind
a fence of brambles. He remembers he once hid in this spot when he
and some of the children from the neighborhood were playing sar-
dines, remembers the intoxication of small bodies packed together,
the warm breath of suppressed laughter on his neck. "The loser had
to go through the spanking machine," he tells Wayne.

"Did you lose often?"

"Most of the time. The spanking machine never really hurt—just
a whirl of hands. If you moved fast enough, no one could actually
get you. Sometimes, though, late in the afternoon, we'd get naughty.
We'd chase each other and pull each other's pants down. That was
all. Boys and girls together!"

"Listen to the insects," Wayne says, and closes his eyes.

Neil turns to examine Wayne's face, notices a single, small pimple.
Their lovemaking usually begins in a wrestle, a struggle for domi-
nance, and ends with a somewhat confusing loss of identity—as now,
when Neil sees a foot on the grass, resting against his leg, and tries
to determine if it is his own or Wayne's.

From inside the house, the dogs begin to bark. Their yelps grow
into alarmed falsettos. Neil lifts himself up. "I wonder if they smell
something," he says.

"Probably just us," says Wayne.

"My mother will wake up. She hates getting waked up."

Lights go on in the house; the door to the porch opens.

"What's wrong, Abby? What's wrong?" his mother's voice calls
softly.

Wayne clamps his hand over Neil's mouth. "Don't say anything,"
he whispers.

"I can't just—" Neil begins to say, but Wayne's hand closes over
his mouth again. He bites it, and Wayne starts laughing.

"What was that?" Her voice projects into the garden. "Hello?" she
says.

The dogs yelp louder. "Abbylucyferny, it's O.K., it's O.K." Her
voice is soft and panicked. "Is anyone there?" she asks loudly.

The brambles shake. She takes a flashlight, shines it around the
garden. Wayne and Neil duck down; the light lands on them and
hovers for a few seconds. Then it clicks off and they are in the dark—a
new dark, a darker dark, which their eyes must readjust to.

"Let's go to bed, Abbylucyferny," she says gently. Neil and Wayne hear her pad into the house. The dogs whimper as they follow her, and the lights go off.

Once before, Neil and his mother had stared at each other in the glare of bright lights. Four years ago, they stood in the arena created by the headlights of her car, waiting for the train. He was on his way back to San Francisco, where he was marching in a Gay Pride Parade the next day. The train station was next door to the food co-op and shared its parking lot. The co-op, familiar and boring by day, took on a certain mystery in the night. Neil recognized the spot where he had skidded on his bicycle and broken his leg. Through the glass doors, the brightly lit interior of the store glowed, its rows and rows of cans and boxes forming their own horizon, each can illuminated so that even from outside Neil could read the labels. All that was missing was the ladies in tennis dresses and sweatshirts, pushing their carts past bins of nuts and dried fruits.

"Your train is late," his mother said. Her hair fell loosely on her shoulders, and her legs were tanned. Neil looked at her and tried to imagine her in labor with him—bucking and struggling with his birth. He felt then the strange, sexless love for women which through his whole adolescence he had mistaken for heterosexual desire.

A single bright light approached them; it preceded the low, haunting sound of the whistle. Neil kissed his mother, and waved goodbye as he ran to meet the train. It was an old train, with windows tinted a sort of horrible lemon-lime. It stopped only long enough for him to hoist himself on board, and then it was moving again. He hurried to a window, hoping to see her drive off, but the tint of the window made it possible for him to make out only vague patches of light—street lamps, cars, the co-op.

He sank into the hard, green seat. The train was almost entirely empty; the only other passenger was a dark-skinned man wearing bluejeans and a leather jacket. He sat directly across the aisle from Neil, next to the window. He had rough skin and a thick mustache. Neil discovered that by pretending to look out the window he could study the man's reflection in the lemon-lime glass. It was only slightly hazy—the quality of a bad photograph. Neil felt his mouth open, felt sleep closing in on him. Hazy red and gold flashes through the glass pulsed in the face of the man in the window, giving the curious impression of muscle spasms. It took Neil a few minutes to realize that the man was staring at him, or rather, staring at the back of his head—staring at his staring. The man smiled as though to say, I know exactly what you're staring at, and Neil felt the sickening sensation of desire rise in his throat.

Right before they reached the city, the man stood up and sat down in the seat next to Neil's. The man's thigh brushed deliberately against his own. Neil's eyes were watering; he felt sick to his stomach. Taking Neil's hand, the man said, "Why so nervous, honey? Relax."

Neil woke up the next morning with the taste of ashes in his mouth. He was lying on the floor, without blankets or sheets or pillows. Instinctively, he reached for his pants, and as he pulled them on came face to face with the man from the train. His name was Luis; he turned out to be a dog groomer. His apartment smelled of dog.

"Why such a hurry?" Luis said.

"The parade. The Gay Pride Parade. I'm meeting some friends to march."

"I'll come with you," Luis said. "I think I'm too old for these things, but why not?"

Neil did not want Luis to come with him, but he found it impossible to say so. Luis looked older by day, more likely to carry diseases. He dressed again in a torn T-shirt, leather jacket, bluejeans. "It's my everyday apparel," he said, and laughed. Neil buttoned his pants, aware that they had been washed by his mother the day before. Luis possessed the peculiar combination of hypermasculinity and effeminacy which exemplifies faggotry. Neil wanted to be rid of him, but Luis's mark was on him, he could see that much. They would become lovers whether Neil liked it or not.

They joined the parade midway. Neil hoped he wouldn't meet anyone he knew; he did not want to have to explain Luis, who clung to him. The parade was full of shirtless men with oiled, muscular shoulders. Neil's back ached. There were floats carrying garishly dressed prom queens and cheerleaders, some with beards, some actually looking like women. Luis said, "It makes me proud, makes me glad to be what I am." Neil supposed that by darting into the crowd ahead of him he might be able to lose Luis forever, but he found it difficult to let him go; the prospect of being alone seemed unbearable.

Neil was startled to see his mother watching the parade, holding up a sign. She was with the Coalition of Parents of Lesbians and Gays; they had posted a huge banner on the wall behind them proclaiming: OUR SONS AND DAUGHTERS, WE ARE PROUD OF YOU. She spotted him; she waved, and jumped up and down.

"Who's that woman?" Luis asked.

"My mother. I should go say hello to her."

"O.K.," Luis said. He followed Neil to the side of the parade. Neil kissed his mother. Luis took off his shirt, wiped his face with it, smiled.

"I'm glad you came," Neil said.

"I wouldn't have missed it, Neil. I wanted to show you I cared."

He smiled, and kissed her again. He showed no intention of introducing Luis, so Luis introduced himself.

"Hello, Luis," Mrs. Campbell said. Neil looked away. Luis shook her hand, and Neil wanted to warn his mother to wash it, warned himself to check with a V.D. clinic first thing Monday.

"Neil, this is Carmen Bologna, another one of the mothers," Mrs. Campbell said. She introduced him to a fat Italian woman with flushed cheeks, and hair arranged in the shape of a clamshell.

"Good to meet you, Neil, good to meet you," said Carmen Bologna. "You know my son, Michael? I'm so proud of Michael! He's doing so well now. I'm proud of him, proud to be his mother I am, and your mother's proud, too!"

The woman smiled at him, and Neil could think of nothing to say but "Thank you." He looked uncomfortably toward his mother, who stood listening to Luis. It occurred to him that the worst period of his life was probably about to begin and he had no way to stop it.

A group of drag queens ambled over to where the mothers were standing. "Michael! Michael!" shouted Carmen Bologna, and embraced a sticklike man wrapped in green satin. Michael's eyes were heavily dosed with green eyeshadow, and his lips were painted pink.

Neil turned and saw his mother staring, her mouth open. He marched over to where Luis was standing, and they moved back into the parade. He turned and waved to her. She waved back; he saw pain in her face, and then, briefly, regret. That day, he felt she would have traded him for any other son. Later, she said to him, "Carmen Bologna really was proud, and speaking as a mother, let me tell you, you have to be brave to feel such pride."

Neil was never proud. It took him a year to dump Luis, another year to leave California. The sick taste of ashes was still in his mouth. On the plane, he envisioned his mother sitting alone in the dark, smoking. She did not leave his mind until he was circling New York, staring down at the dawn rising over Queens. The song playing in his earphones would remain hovering on the edges of his memory, always associated with her absence. After collecting his baggage, he took a bus into the city. Boys were selling newspapers in the middle of highways, through the windows of stopped cars. It was seven in the morning when he reached Manhattan. He stood for ten minutes on East Thirty-fourth Street, breathed the cold air, and felt bubbles rising in his blood.

Neil got a job as a paralegal—a temporary job, he told himself. When he met Wayne a year later, the sensations of that first morning returned to him. They'd been up all night, and at six they walked across the park to Wayne's apartment with the nervous, deliberate gait of people aching to make love for the first time. Joggers ran by with their dogs. None of them knew what Wayne and he were about to do, and the secrecy excited him. His mother came to mind, and the song, and the whirling vision of Queens coming alive below him. His breath solidified into clouds, and he felt happier than he had ever felt before in his life.

The second day of Wayne's visit, he and Neil go with Mrs. Campbell to pick up the dogs at the dog parlor. The grooming establishment is decorated with pink ribbons and photographs of the owner's champion pit bulls. A fat, middle-aged woman appears from the back, leading the newly trimmed and fluffed Abigail, Lucille, and Fern by three leashes. The dogs struggle frantically when they see Neil's mother, tangling the woman up in their leashes. "Ladies, behave!" Mrs. Campbell commands, and collects the dogs. She gives Fern to Neil and Abigail to Wayne. In the car on the way back, Abigail begins pawing to get on Wayne's lap.

"Just push her off," Mrs. Campbell says. "She knows she's not supposed to do that."

"You never groomed Rasputin," Neil complains.

"Rasputin was a mutt."

"Rasputin was a beautiful dog, even if he did smell."

"Do you remember when you were a little kid, Neil, you used to make Rasputin dance with you? Once you tried to dress him up in one of my blouses."

"I don't remember that," Neil says.

"Yes. I remember," says Mrs. Campbell. "Then you tried to organize a dog beauty contest in the neighborhood. You wanted to have runners-up—everything."

"A dog beauty contest?" Wayne says.

"Mother, do we have to—"

"I think it's a mother's privilege to embarrass her son," Mrs. Campbell says, and smiles.

When they are about to pull into the driveway, Wayne starts screaming, and pushes Abigail off his lap. "Oh, my God!" he says.

"The dog just pissed all over me."

Neil turns around and sees a puddle seeping into Wayne's slacks. He suppresses his laughter, and Mrs. Campbell hands him a rag.

"I'm sorry, Wayne," she says. "It goes with the territory."

"This is really disgusting," Wayne says, swatting at himself with the rag.

Neil keeps his eyes on his own reflection in the rearview mirror and smiles.

At home, while Wayne cleans himself in the bathroom, Neil watches his mother cook lunch—Japanese noodles in soup. "When you went off to college," she says, "I went to the grocery store. I was going to buy ramen noodles, and I suddenly realized you weren't going to be around to eat them. I started crying right then, blubbering like an idiot."

Neil clenches his fists inside his pockets. She has a way of telling him little sad stories when he doesn't want to hear them—stories of dolls broken by her brothers, lunches stolen by neighborhood boys on the way to school. Now he has joined the ranks of male children who have made her cry.

"Mama, I'm sorry," he says.

She is bent over the noodles, which steam in her face. "I didn't want to say anything in front of Wayne, but I wish you had answered me last night. I was very frightened—and worried."

"I'm sorry," he says, but it's not convincing. His fingers prickle. He senses a great sorrow about to be born.

"I lead a quiet life," she says. "I don't want to be a disciplinarian. I just don't have the energy for these—shenanigans. Please don't frighten me that way again."

"If you were so upset, why didn't you say something?"

"I'd rather not discuss it. I lead a quiet life. I'm not used to getting woken up late at night. I'm not used—"

"To my having a lover?"

"No, I'm not used to having other people around, that's all. Wayne is charming. A wonderful young man."

"He likes you, too."

"I'm sure we'll get along fine."

She scoops the steaming noodles into ceramic bowls. Wayne returns, wearing shorts. His white, hairy legs are a shocking contrast to hers, which are brown and sleek.

"I'll wash those pants, Wayne," Mrs. Campbell says. "I have a special detergent that'll take out the stain."

She gives Neil a look to indicate that the subject should be dropped.

He looks at Wayne, looks at his mother; his initial embarrassment gives way to a fierce pride—the arrogance of mastery. He is glad his mother knows that he is desired, glad it makes her flinch.

Later, he steps into the back yard; the gardener is back, whacking at the bushes with his shears. Neil walks by him in his bathing suit, imagining he is on parade.

That afternoon, he finds his mother's daily list on the kitchen table:

TUESDAY

7:00—breakfast
Take dogs to groomer
Groceries (?)

Campaign against Draft—4-7

Buy underwear
Trios—2:00
Spaghetti
Fruit
Asparagus if sale
Peanuts
Milk

Doctor's Appointment (make)
Write Cranston/Hayakawa
re disarmament

Handi-Wraps
Mozart
Abigail
Top Ramen
Pedro

Her desk and trash can are full of such lists; he remembers them from the earliest days of his childhood. He had learned to read from them. In his own life, too, there have been endless lists—covered with check marks and arrows, at least one item always spilling over onto the next day's agenda. From September to November, "Buy plane ticket for Christmas" floated from list to list to list."

The last item puzzles him: Pedro. Pedro must be the gardener. He observes the accretion of names, the arbitrary specifics that give a sense of his mother's life. He could make a list of his own selves: the child, the adolescent, the promiscuous faggot son, and finally the good son, settled, relatively successful. But the divisions wouldn't work; he is today and will always be the child being licked by the dog, the boy on the floor with Luis; he will still be everything he is ashamed of. The other lists—the lists of things done and undone—tell their own truth: that his life is measured more properly in objects than in stages. He knows himself as "jump rope," "book," "sunglasses," "underwear."

"Tell me about your family, Wayne," Mrs. Campbell says that night, as they drive toward town. They are going to see an Esther Williams movie at the local revival house: an underwater musical, populated by mermaids, underwater Rockettes.

"My father was a lawyer," Wayne says. "He had an office in Queens, with a neon sign. I think he's probably the only lawyer in the world who had a neon sign. Anyway, he died when I was ten. My mother never remarried. She lives in Queens. Her great claim to fame is that when she was twenty-two she went on 'The $64,000 Question.' Her category was mystery novels. She made it to sixteen thousand before she got tripped up."

"When I was about ten, I wanted you to go on 'Jeopardy,'" Neil says to his mother. "You really should have, you know. You would have won."

"You certainly loved 'Jeopardy,'" Mrs. Campbell says. "You used to watch it during dinner. Wayne, does your mother work?"

"No," he says. "She lives off investments."

"You're both only children," Mrs. Campbell says. Neil wonders if she is ruminating on the possible connection between that coincidence and their "alternative life style."

The movie theater is nearly empty. Neil sits between Wayne and his mother. There are pillows on the floor at the front of the theater, and a cat is prowling over them. It casts a monstrous shadow every now and then on the screen, disturbing the sedative effect of water ballet. Like a teen-ager, Neil cautiously reaches his arm around Wayne's shoulder. Wayne takes his hand immediately. Next to them, Neil's mother breathes in, out, in, out. Neil timorously moves his other arm and lifts it behind his mother's neck. He does not look at her, but he can tell from her breathing that she senses what he is doing. Slowly, carefully, he lets his hand drop on her shoulder; it twitches spasmodically, and he jumps, as if he had received an electric shock. His mother's quiet breathing is broken by a gasp; even Wayne notices. A sudden brightness on the screen illuminates the panic in her eyes, Neil's arm frozen above her, about to fall again. Slowly, he lowers his arm until his fingertips touch her skin, the fabric of her dress. He has gone too far to go back now; they are all too far.

Wayne and Mrs. Campbell sink into their seats, but Neil remains stiff, holding up his arms, which rest on nothing. The movie ends, and they go on sitting just like that.

"I'm old," Mrs. Campbell says later, as they drive back home. "I remember when those films were new. Your father and I went to one on our first date. I loved them, because I could pretend that those women underwater were flying—they were so graceful. They really took advantage of Technicolor in those days. Color was something to appreciate. You can't know what it was like to see a color movie for the first time, after years of black-and-white. It's like trying to explain the surprise of snow to an East Coaster. Very little is new anymore, I fear."

Neil would like to tell her about his own nostalgia, but how can he explain that all of it revolves around her? The idea of her life before he was born pleases him. "Tell Wayne how you used to look like Esther Williams," he asks her.

She blushes. "I was told I looked like Esther Williams, but really more like Gene Tierney," she says. "Not beautiful, but interesting. I like to think I had a certain magnetism."

"You still do," Wayne says, and instantly recognizes the wrongness of his comment. Silence and a nervous laugh indicate that he has not yet mastered the family vocabulary.

When they get home, the night is once again full of the sound of crickets. Mrs. Campbell picks up a flashlight and calls the dogs. "Abbylucyferny, Abbylucyferny," she shouts, and the dogs amble from their various corners. She pushes them out the door to the back yard and follows them. Neil follows her. Wayne follows Neil, but hovers on the porch. Neil walks behind her as she tramps through the garden. She holds out her flashlight, and snails slide from behind bushes, from under rocks, to where she stands. When the snails become visible, she crushes them underfoot. They make a wet, cracking noise, like eggs being broken.

"Nights like this," she says, "I think of children without pants on, in hot South American countries. I have nightmares about tanks rolling down our street."

"The weather's never like this in New York," Neil says. "When it's hot, it's humid and sticky. You don't want to go outdoors."

"I could never live anywhere else but here. I think I'd die. I'm too used to the climate."

"Don't be silly."

"No, I mean it," she says. "I have adjusted too well to the weather."

The dogs bark and howl by the fence. "A cat, I suspect," she says. She aims her flashlight at a rock, and more snails emerge—uncountable numbers, too stupid to have learned not to trust light.

"I know what you were doing at the movie," she says.

"What?"

"I know what you were doing."

"What? I put my arm around you."

"I'm sorry, Neil," she says. "I can only take so much. Just so much."

"What do you mean?" he says. "I was only trying to show affection."

"Oh, affection—I know about affection."

He looks up at the porch, sees Wayne moving toward the door, trying not to listen.

"What do you mean?" Neil says to her.

She puts down the flashlight and wraps her arms around herself. "I remember when you were a little boy," she says. "I remember, and I have to stop remembering. I wanted you to grow up happy. And I'm very tolerant, very understanding. But I can only take so much."

His heart seems to have risen into his throat. "Mother," he says, "I think you know my life isn't your fault. But for God's sake, don't say that your life is my fault."

"It's not a question of fault," she says. She extracts a Kleenex from her pocket and blows her nose. "I'm sorry, Neil. I guess I'm just an old woman with too much on her mind and not enough to do." She laughs halfheartedly. "Don't worry. Don't say anything," she says. "Abbylucyferny, Abbylucyferny, time for bed!"

He watches her as she walks toward the porch, silent and regal. There is the pad of feet, the clinking of dog tags as the dogs run for the house.

He was twelve the first time she saw him march in a parade. He played the tuba, and as his elementary-school band lumbered down the streets of their then small town she stood on the sidelines and waved. Afterward, she had taken him out for ice cream. He spilled some on his red uniform, and she swiped at it with a napkin. She had been there for him that day, as well as years later, at that more memorable parade; she had been there for him every day.

Somewhere over Iowa, a week later, Neil remembers this scene, remembers other days, when he would find her sitting in the dark, crying. She had to take time out of her own private sorrow to appease his anxiety. "It was part of it," she told him later. "Part of being a mother."

"The scariest thing in the world is the thought that you could unknowingly ruin someone's life," Neil tells Wayne. "Or even change someone's life. I hate the thought of having such control. I'd make a rotten mother."

"You're crazy," Wayne says. "You have this great mother, and all you do is complain. I know people whose mothers have disowned them."

"Guilt goes with the territory," Neil says.

"Why?" Wayne asks, perfectly seriously.

Neil doesn't answer. He lies back in his seat, closes his eyes, imagines he grew up in a house in the mountains of Colorado, surrounded by snow—endless white snow on hills. No flat places, and no trees; just white hills. Every time he has flown away, she has come into his mind, usually sitting alone in the dark, smoking. Today she is outside at dusk, skimming leaves from the pool.

"I want to get a dog," Neil says.

Wayne laughs. "In the city? It'd suffocate."

The hum of the airplane is druglike, dazing. "I want to stay with you a long time," Neil says.

"I know." Imperceptibly, Wayne takes his hand.

"It's very hot there in the summer, too. You know, I'm not thinking about my mother now."

"It's O.K."

For a moment, Neil wonders what the stewardess or the old woman on the way to the bathroom will think, but then he laughs and relaxes.

Later, the plane makes a slow circle over New York City, and on it two men hold hands, eyes closed, and breathe in unison.

Hopeless Acts Performed Properly, with Grace

ROBERT DUNN

W HEN HE WAS YOUNG, Peter Dreyer collected baseball cards voraciously but put them away when he was fifteen in a cardboard shoebox, grouped by teams, with a fat rubber band around each group. The box is at his parents' house in Los Angeles, three thousand miles away. Sometimes he gets the urge to riffle a stack, pull out a card and flip it against the wainscoting. When he moved across the country to New York he had his parents ship him a box of his college books, but he doesn't think they would understand why he wants his baseball cards. Peter doesn't understand either. He cares little for organized sports and prides himself on having no idea which team is first in the National Football League or what it means that Doctor J. has left the Nets. He thinks this complete disinterest in sports is one of his attractive features. No woman he ever lives with—Diane? the woman next door, whom he loves—will have to put up with a feet-on-the-sofa, beer-can-in-hand intoxication with TV sports. She'll have him to talk with her, to comment with interest on her *salade niçoise*, to take long walks through the park with her. She won't go to her job and complain about her husband or friend or roommate like the secretaries who sit outside his office. Peter is certain he'll always be solicitous of this woman when he finds her. At times he aches with the desire to care for her.

Peter gets some comfort from an article in *The New York Times* about changing demographic trends. More and more people are living alone, he reads; people are forsaking marriage, even ceasing to live together. He reads about a woman in Washington, a Congressional assistant, who told the reporter she enjoyed living alone. She had more time to herself, she could do the things she wanted to do, her life was her own. Peter also has time for himself, he does only the things he wants to do, his life *is* his own. The Congressional assistant was happy. Peter reads the article over a pastrami sandwich at a nearby delicatessen. It cheers him up. Although the streets are icy with frozen snow, he takes a walk before going home. He passes a long-haired couple with their hands in each other's coats and it doesn't bother him; he doesn't think of Diane. Later he reads an article by Mimi Sheraton, the *Times* restaurant critic, in which she mentions some criteria to judge a person's self-respect. They are: (1) having no holes in your socks, (2) making your bed each morning even if no company is expected and (3) taking the time to prepare good food even if you are dining alone. Peter's orlon socks look like fishnet around the toes and are completely bare on the heel. The sleeping bag and two blankets on his mattress on the floor are tangled and only half cover the fitted sheet. And even though he hates himself for doing it, dinner that night is, as usual, a can of chunky-style soup, a small package of oven-ready buttermilk biscuits, coleslaw out of a plastic tub and a glass of milk.

Peter's college friend David Halstrom writes from graduate school at the University of Michigan: "Your letter was good for me because it made me see that I'm not the only sad and dispossessed man in North America, and because it provided a model for enduring and getting on with things. What can these women want? Your Diane has put you through a wringer, yet I think you're doing all you can. Sometimes you have to wait for events to reveal themselves. Herrigel says in *Zen in the Art of Archery:* 'You must learn to wait properly.' It's always going to be like this: people like you and me are going to be waiting all our lives (for the right woman, the right idea, the right work, the right appreciation). So we should try to perform this hopeless act properly, with grace."

Peter writes back: "Diane and I still aren't talking. I haven't seen her in a week, though I heard her moving around furniture Tuesday. Sometimes I hear her alarm clock go off. That upsets me for the rest of the day. I don't know if she's avoiding me or not. I try not to think of her and sometimes I don't, but trying to forget her usually brings her to mind. You're right, I guess—I'll just have to wait. But it's not easy. I need a vacation, a long boat trip or a sunny stretch of beach in Spain.

"Everything else? The proofreading job is slow. Spring, I'm told, will come. It was never this cold in Los Angeles. How are you in Ann Arbor? . . ."

Peter meets Diane at the trash chute. She's carrying a black plastic bag with an orange twist top. Peter's holding a brown supermarket bag with dark, oily stains. Diane smiles, not at him but past him. Peter doesn't know what to do. She's wearing her Bennington sweat shirt and bell-bottom denim jeans. She's barefoot. Her blond hair is pinned up. Peter looks at her, sees the gentle curve of her nose, remembers running his finger over it and feels a sharp pain in his chest. He turns away. Trying to pretend she's not there, he waits. She says nothing. His hands are shaking and a soup can falls out of the bag. As he picks it up he hears her door shut.

Peter thinks it's both a curse and a blessing that he never slept with Diane. Bad because if he had, there might be more between them now. He might feel he had more of a right to confront her. Good because he mostly misses the idea of her, the possibility of Diane as his lover. If he had slept with her, he'd miss the real person more, and that could only be worse. If she weren't next door, he's sure he'd forget her. As it is, he waits—for her to come to him or for her to move away or back in with her husband.

Peter didn't know Diane was married until after he'd fallen in love with her. Even then he didn't think it mattered. She rarely saw Ralph, and Peter was certain he never spent the night at Diane's apartment. But she wouldn't spend the night with Peter either. The subject had become endlessly tiresome, but it was unavoidable. The last time it had come up was in a Greenwich Village coffeehouse where they had gone after a Truffaut movie at the Bleecker Street Cinema.

"I don't feel right about it," Diane had said. "I'm still confused."

Peter wanted to say, "I love you." He had always thought there was a magic to the words that would disarm resistance. But each time he used the phrase, Diane got nervous. Her fingernails would click against the table. Once she spilled a glass of wine. That was when these discussions took place in her apartment. Weeks ago she stopped letting him come over in the evenings. His beseeching threatened direct action, and she said she'd see him only in a public place. That's when they started going out to movies and coffeehouses.

"You have me coming and going," Peter said. He was smoking cigarettes again, and banged the filter of one against the table. "I don't know what to do."

"Wait," she said. She took his hand and her finger ran over the curve between his thumb and pointer finger. "I have to straighten everything out."

"What do you want?"

"I'm not ready yet. I want you to be close. I want to know that I can count on you, that you're steady, that you'll wait."

Peter was angry. "That's a lot," he said. He took his hand away from hers. He needed a minute alone and got up to go to the toilet. There was a pay meter on the door and he fished through his change for a dime. Finally he broke a dollar with a waiter. When he got back to the table he had a speech set.

"I can't win. I'm damned if I do and now I'm damned if I don't. What you want is unjust. You want me *not* to love you and yet continue to love you. You show me no consideration. I want you— what's wrong with that? You have me feeling guilty for desiring you. That's a terrible thing."

"Don't be angry," Diane said. Peter said nothing. He waited, but she didn't move or say anything else. He stood up and dropped two dollars on the table.

"I'm not angry," he said. "I needed to say some final words and that was it. Can you get home all right by yourself?"

Diane nodded. Peter left.

He decided he'd wait up until two for Diane to return, figuring that she'd come to him or she wouldn't come back at all, that she'd be so upset by his speech that she'd go stay with Ralph. He wanted her to be that upset. So he was surprised when he heard her door open and close five minutes after he got home. He was even more surprised when she passed him in the hall the next day without speaking, and when she didn't acknowledge the African violet plant he left outside her door that evening.

Peter faces another Saturday. It stretches before him like a wide superhighway shooting straight through the desert, with few turnoffs and little of passing interest. There are a few bright spots—one, at eight P.M., when reruns of *The Mary Tyler Moore Show* come on TV. Even this pleasure is compromised, though, by the thought that there are thousands of women, many of whom he'd like, many of whom would like him, watching the same TV show and thinking the same thoughts. At ten-thirty Peter goes out for the *Times* and at eleven-thirty watches *Saturday Night Live* while reading the *Times* Book Review during the commercials. Fortunately his sleep is untroubled.

This Saturday, Peter decides to go out. It's the first warm weekend since November. The winter, everyone says, has been extraordinarily cold. It is his first winter out of southern California, so he has nothing to judge it by. Still, it kept him indoors too much. When he first came to New York, last July, his greatest pleasure was taking long walks. On free days he'd strike out in an arbitrary direction. Always he'd see something of interest—a wind quintet playing Telemann in the park; a building he'd heard of, like the Dakota Apartments, where people said they'd filmed *Rosemary's Baby*. Now he's pleased it's so warm that his breath doesn't mist before him. He walks into the park.

Peter is actively looking for a new girl friend, but he's doing a poor job of it. The affair with Diane has sapped his confidence, which was never too full, and he's much shyer than at other times. It's hard not knowing anyone well here in New York. He waits for someone to invite him to a dinner party and introduce him to an aspiring actress. He expects a dancer will bump into him in the market where he buys his soup, take pity on his lean purchases and invite him home for dinner. So far, nothing like this has happened.

There's a dark-haired woman in a green ski parka throwing a stick to a German shepherd, who, after fetching it, coyly prances around the woman for a minute before she can coax the stick away from him. Peter sits on a wooden bench and watches. He hopes she'll throw the stick by mistake toward him so he can return it and talk with her. Although she's pretty, Peter doesn't really care for the way she looks; yet he does want to meet her. He's become a great and indiscriminate believer in fate. He hardly knows what he wants any more, so he awaits signs that will tell him. Maybe the girl with the stick is the mate destiny has planned for him. Peter supposes that if she lost a little weight, he could get along with her. Probably he could get used to her too-thick eyebrows and weak chin. The dog is slavering onto the wet grass and the woman is retying a calico scarf over her head. She throws the stick again, but the dog is uninterested. "All right, George," she calls to him. "We can go home now." The dog runs up to her and then dashes down the path toward the place where Peter sits. The girl follows. The dog stops before Peter and then leaps up at him. Peter holds him back with two hands. The dog licks Peter. "George, down!" the girls says. "Sorry," she says to Peter. She unrolls a leather leash and clips it onto the dog's collar. "George, come!" she says. It's clear she's not going to stop. Her brown hair flounces beneath her scarf as she walks away.

Peter wakes up and wonders if he should go to work. He has a sore spot way back in his throat. A while back he read an article in *Esquire* about "Lonely Guys." Lonely guys, the article said, have colds all the time. They get strep throat and always have bronchitis. This makes being a lonely guy worse because there is no one to care for him. Peter's throat is definitely raw. He has trouble swallowing. When he was young he could get out of going to school if his father okayed it. He'd take a flashlight and peer into Peter's throat. If he saw an inflammation, Peter could stay home. Peter doesn't have a regular flashlight but he does have a penlight. He stands before the bathroom mirror, twisting his face around so he can see the light shining on the back of his throat. He finally gets everything aligned and his throat does look red, but he's not sure if it's red enough. He goes to work anyway.

Peter hasn't heard a sound from Diane's apartment for four days. At first he was worried that she might have fallen or got sick, or something, but after thinking about it he decides that she is probably just out, and that going to her would be pointless if not inappropriate. He has good reason to stay away from her. The last time they talked it went badly. They were riding up in the elevator together.

"I want to have a talk with you," he said. He couldn't look at her or anything else. "I have to get some things straight."

"I'd be much happier if you didn't bother me," Diane said. She wasn't smiling, but she wasn't not smiling. There was no rancor; she sounded friendly, but without interest in him. The elevator stopped and a woman got in. Peter said nothing. Diane's indifference disarmed him. He was prepared to argue with her, even throw himself before her if she spurned him, but he was not ready for her pleasant, curt response. It had no feeling. He thought she cared something for him, but now it seemed she didn't.

The elevator opened onto their floor. Peter followed Diane out.

"Diane—" he said.

She turned; her blond hair flipped. She looked straight at him.

"Sorry," she said.

Later Peter decided that her look expressed nothing but deep pity for him. He didn't move until she'd gone into her apartment; then he slunk into his own.

After this Peter knew that approaching her would be humiliating. He was willing to humiliate himself except that he knew it wouldn't do any good and that she'd despise him for it. So he ignores her too. On the fifth day his worry gets the best of him and he knocks on her door. There is no answer. He stops himself before he goes to ask the super to let him in. Two days later he hears her door shut and a Linda Ronstadt record play loudly from her stereo.

Peter likes going to movies alone. He sees what he wants to see; he gives the movie his full attention. He's about to go to a double bill of Robert Altman films when his phone rings. It's Diane; she asks him if he'd like to go to Avery Fisher Hall to hear the New York Philharmonic. She says a friend gave her two tickets. Peter is speechless. Diane's voice is sunny; it's as if there has been no strain between them. A touch of pride makes him pause and think to answer that he's busy, but he doesn't. It is Diane on the phone. "Sure," he tells her. "I'll be over in a minute."

Peter keeps his distance from Diane on the subway and even in the orchestra seat next to her. It's an all-Mozart performance: The Masonic Funeral Music, an early divertimento, and the "Haffner" symphony. Diane is enjoying herself. She is smiling; occasionally her head bobs and her gold, pagoda-shaped earrings jangle. Peter hardly hears the music. Though Diane is not wearing perfume, something rises off her that Peter is extraordinarily sensitive to. Perhaps it's her body warmth. He tries not to look at her, but does constantly. She's wearing an apricot-colored blouse with a Peter Pan collar. Her neck is white and smooth. Peter wipes his wet hands on his pants leg; then he sets his right hand on the armrest. Diane's hand falls onto his forearm. He thinks she gives it a squeeze but he's not sure. She doesn't look at him.

After the symphony Peter can hardly speak. As they wait for the bus Diane prattles on about a tennis game she played last weekend. Peter, who couldn't care less about tennis, listens attentively. The bus comes and they find seats. Diane's talking now about Easter with her family in Larchmont. Her younger brother said he was going to leave college and her father beat him. Diane was terribly upset. Peter wonders how she can be so calm now. All he can do is nod his head and mumble that it's all very interesting.

Diane stops talking when they're in the elevator going up to their floor. She smiles widely at him, and even winks. Peter doesn't know what's going on. She's getting ready to do something, though, something unexpected. For a second Peter thinks she might shoot him. He waits for her hand to go into her purse. The elevator stops and Peter pulls the handle to open it. They stand apart, looking at each other.

"Do you mind if I come in?" Diane asks.

Peter waits to answer. He feels his blood course through his body. Two fingers seem to be pressing against his temples.

"Please," he says.

Inside, Peter apologizes for the mess. Diane says it looks fine to her. She picks up a guitar he bought in Mexico seven years before. It has only five strings and is hopelessly out of tune. She runs a long fingernail down the strings and says, "So, how have you been?"

Peter's decided he's much too nervous to be direct with Diane, and he answers, "Fine, though it's been a cold winter. I've been okay. How have you been?"

"Oh, all right."

"I haven't seen you much lately."

"Oh, I've been busy."

"Doing what?"

"Things . . ."

"I've been busy too," Peter says. He doesn't know why the conversation goes so poorly, and wants to do something about it.

Diane sets the guitar down, tilting it against an end table, and lies back on the couch, propping up her head with two pillows. Her fingers play with a loose curl of hair; her eyelids seem to flutter. This makes Peter jump up and pace across the oval throw rug in front of the couch. He looks at Diane, who seems very comfortable, very much at home there, but also untouchable, like a Chinese vase that's had a place in the family for generations. He's fidgeting with a cigarette and trying to think what to say next when she speaks.

"Peter, do you mind if I stay here with you tonight?"

Peter is startled. He stops moving and looks at her. What can this mean? Does she mean sleep with him?

"Why?" Peter asks, but he swallows the word so it comes out like a cough.

"Excuse me?" Diane says. She's still smiling. Not a line of doubt seems to crease her wide forehead.

"May I ask why?" Peter says.

"I've missed you."

"Why have you been ignoring me, then?"

"I haven't been ignoring you," Diane says. She extends her hand toward Peter. Her fingers wiggle. "I've been busy."

"Diane . . ." he says, but what he meant to say—"Why are you doing this to me? Why are you so capricious?"—is choked off and lost in a quake of uncertainty. "Can I get you something to drink?" he says instead. He shuffles off to the tiny kitchen.

"Please, a glass of white wine."

In the kitchen he pauses. He looks at a wall calendar that Diane gave him for Christmas, with bushels of wheat and ears of corn around the dates, but can't focus on it. He should be happy. But he's just confused. He has an open bottle of Rhine wine in the refrigerator, and he pours two glasses. Back in the other room, Diane beckons him to the couch. He still doesn't know what to expect.

"Why do you want to spend the night here?" he asks. He sits next to her and hands her the teardrop-shaped glass.

Diane gives him a quizzical look, as if he were a dim child. She smiles with the corner of her mouth.

"Do you want to sleep with me?" Peter asks.

"Yes," Diane says. The word comes short and with little breath. Though both of them hold their wineglasses before them, neither thinks to make a toast.

Peter aches with desire. The questions he's been afraid to ask for months come to his mind and mix with the desire: Why *has* Diane ignored him? Does she care at all for him? Does she think of him as he thinks of her? Did she ever? Is she seeing Ralph regularly? Is she going to move back with him? Is she seeing anyone else? And now, why is she here? He sits beside her and tries not to think, to drive these questions away. At points later in the evening, glasses tinkle against each other, pillows are rearranged, the heels of Diane's boots drop with a thud against the floor.

Four days later Diane meets Peter for lunch at a Szechwan Chinese restaurant and tells him she doesn't want to see him any longer. Peter's been expecting something like this. Although they spent two more nights together after the first (though not the night before), Peter was never able to relax or feel certain of Diane's moods. One night they had dinner at Diane's, and then sat talking. Diane went on happily about a veal dish she had learned to make at her French cooking class, and then they talked about a D.H. Lawrence novel she was reading. She left him to do the dishes, and when she got back her mood had changed. She turned on the TV and sat impassively beside him. Peter draped an arm over her shoulders and hugged her to him, but she didn't react and moved like a dead weight. He became nervous, but kept his arm over her shoulder until it started to go dead, and then he was too self-conscious to move it. He didn't know where she had slipped away to, and felt too uncomfortable to ask. After twenty minutes she livened up, and they were able to get through the night.

Now Diane is looking at Peter and asking if their separation is all right with him. The hot-and-sour soup comes and he waits for the waiter to leave. He still wants her and his heart is breaking, but he doesn't know what to say. He knows he can't talk her into loving him, so what good would argument do?

His nods languidly and agrees. Through the meal they make only small talk.

The rest of the day is hell. When he gets home from work there's a letter from David. Peter reads: "I've become involved in a semisecret affair with the wife of a lecturer in Russian. She's pretty and brilliant, twenty-six, bored with her husband but still attached to him. The affair has been marvelous and important to me because it offsets to some degree my theory of my own personality, one that has been growing like a cancer inside of me for a long time: viz., that I was a dark, cold and empty person, a human black hole, an eccentric for whom there was no place in normal human relations. Of course, it may be argued that sleeping with the wives of other men hardly describes normal human relations. But still, it's something a dead star couldn't do, and I'm a little encouraged by it. While I don't think there's any danger that I'll ever become a decent and generally acceptable human being, there is now tangible proof that I'm not Caliban either."

Peter waits a week and then writes back: "I'm glad things go well for you. I'm on a teeter-totter here, worse than usual. Last week Diane and I were together for three days. It was very, very good. Then, for no clear reason, we stopped seeing each other and now we avoid each other again. I don't understand it. I think she's seeing her husband. I can hear his key in her door when he comes over late in the evening. Maybe she'll go back to him and get out of my life.

"I need a change. Almost everything seems stale to me, even spring. I'm told I won't get a vacation until September. I've been trying to go see John Rubinstein in New Haven, but he's involved with a big project and has no free time. If I simply want to get out of Manhattan for a day, he says, I can come visit, but he can't do any more than have dinner with me. I don't see any point to it, and continue to waste away here. . . ."

In the hallway outside his apartment Peter bumps into Ralph. Peter's met him before, and they shake hands. Ralph is wearing a polo shirt and tennis shorts. A blue-and-white-striped headband rises above his forehead. Ralph is in a good mood—he swings his right arm back and forth as if he were practicing his forehand and backhand. Peter has just bought a ten-speed bicycle in honor of spring, and he asks Ralph to hold it upright while he unlocks his door. Diane comes into the hallway, carrying a tennis racket and a can of tennis balls. She greets Peter, who looks back at her over his shoulder. The situation should be awkward, but Peter seems to be the only one who thinks it is. He inhales deeply and then says, "Have a good game."

"Thanks," Ralph says.

Peter takes the bicycle from him and wheels it into his vestibule. He hears each link of the bike chain click as it falls into the sprocket. The elevator opens and closes. He leans the bicycle against the wall and cringes at the thought of the impossibility of his situation.

Peter has got a stack of train timetables from Pennsylvania Station. He stretches out on his couch, turns the floor lamp on and looks through them. A professor of his who once taught a year in Japan told him that the Japanese regularly pass the time by reading train schedules. It simulates trips they can't take; it carries them away from their problems. Peter picks at random the flyer for the Southwest Limited. His eyes run over the list of cities:

> 6 10p New York (Penn. Station)
> 6 25p Newark (Penn. Station)
> 7 05p Trenton
> 7 33p North Philadelphia
> 9 38p Harrisburg
> 3 24a Pittsburgh (Penn. Station)
> 8 05a Columbus . . .

He reaches back and adjusts the pillow behind his head. He imagines the clack of steel wheels roaring over the rails. For quite a while he lies there, absorbed. "This is Santa Fe," he says quietly to himself. "The next stop is Albuquerque."

A week later Peter takes a train from Grand Central to see John Rubinstein in New Haven. John's still too busy to see him but Peter doesn't care; he has to get away. At night he dreams of Diane and hears her moving around next door even when she's not there.

At Grand Central, Peter buys a weekend *Post* and on the train desultorily leafs through it. Nothing catches his interest. He shoves it under the seat and stares out the window at the parking lots, back yards, glimpses of brackish-looking bay and the backs of factories that surround Bridgeport. The train's half full, and Peter sees the crowns of people's heads pop above the seats in front of him. Fewer people are parting their hair on the left, he notices. Many have no parts at all. Two rows in front of him and across the aisle is a woman with blond hair the shade and cut of Diane's. Could it be she? His fingers beat against the dusty window glass. He tucks his traveling bag out of sight in the seat well, leaves his coat on his seat and walks toward the front of the train. He's too uneasy to turn and look at her, so he goes three cars forward to the club car, buys a soda and heads back. The woman has a fat, blue-covered paperback held up close to her eyes, so Peter can't see her too clearly, but he's sure it's not Diane. The blond woman looks enough like her, though, to attract him. No one's sitting next to her; the seat doesn't even have a book bag or coat on it. Peter slows as he passes her, but she doesn't look up. For a second he wants to stop and talk to her, but doesn't and retakes his seat.

Is he crazy? he wonders. Peter sees her hand—a small, graceful hand with a jade ring on her ring finger—rise above the seat back and stroke her hair. She has beautiful hair. Should he talk to her? Peter recently read the book the woman is reading—a biography of Samuel Johnson—and he could ask her what she thinks of it. Peter continues thinking back and forth about whether he should talk to her until all rational reasons for either case fall away and it's a simple question of whether he has the courage to approach her. A few minutes after the train conductor swings through the car announcing, "Milford, next stop is Milford," he does.

How to Be an Other Woman

LORRIE MOORE

MEET IN EXPENSIVE BEIGE RAINCOATS, on a pea-soupy night. Like a detective movie. First, stand in front of Florsheim's Fifty-seventh Street window, press your face close to the glass, watch the fake velvet Hummels inside revolving around the wing tips; some white shoes, like your father wears, are propped up with garlands on a small mound of chemical snow. All the stores have closed. You can see your breath on the glass. Draw a peace sign. You are waiting for a bus.

He emerges from nowhere, looks like Robert Culp, the fog rolling, then parting, then sort of closing up again behind him. He asks you for a light and you jump a bit, startled, but you give him your "Lucky's Lounge—Where Leisure Is a Suit" matches. He has a nice chuckle, nice fingernails. He lights the cigarette, cupping his hands around the end, and drags deeply, like a starving man. He smiles as he exhales, returns you the matches, looks at your face, says: "Thanks."

He then stands not far from you, waiting. Perhaps for the same bus. The two of you glance furtively at each other, shifting feet. Pretend to contemplate the chemical snow. You are two spies glancing quickly at watches, necks disappearing in the hunch of your shoulders, collars upturned and slowly razoring the cab and store-lit fog like sharkfins. You begin to circle, gauging each other in primordial sniffs, eyeing, sidling, keen as Basil Rathbone.

A bus arrives. It is crowded, everyone looking laughlessly into one another's underarms. A blonde woman in barrettes steps off, holding her shoes in one hand.

You climb on together, grab adjacent chrome posts, and when the bus hisses and rumbles forward, you take out a book. A minute goes by and he asks what you're reading. It is *Madame Bovary* in a Doris Day biography jacket. Try to explain about binding warpage. He smiles, interested.

Return to your book. Emma is opening her window, thinking of Rouen.

"What weather," you hear him sigh, faintly British or uppercrust Delaware.

Glance up. Say: "It is fit for neither beast nor vegetable."

It sounds dumb. It makes no sense.

But it is how you meet.

At the movies he is tender, caressing your hand beneath the seat.

At concerts he is sweet and attentive, buying cocktails, locating the ladies' lounge when you can't find it.

At museums he is wise and loving, leading you slowly through the Etruscan cinerary urns with affectionate gestures and an art history minor from Columbia. He is kind; he laughs at your jokes.

After four movies, three concerts, and two-and-a-half museums, you sleep with him. It seems the right number of cultural events. On the stereo you play your favorite harp and oboe music. He tells you his wife's name. It is Patricia. She is an intellectual property lawyer. He tells you he likes you a lot. You lie on your stomach, naked and still too warm. When he says, "How do you feel about that?" don't say "Ridiculous" or "Get the hell out of my apartment." Prop your head up with one hand and say: "It depends. What is intellectual property law?"

He grins. "Oh, you know. Where leisure is a suit."

Give him a tight, wiry little smile.

"I just don't want you to feel uncomfortable about this," he says.

Say: "Hey. I am a very cool person. I am tough." Show him your bicep.

When you were six you thought *mistress* meant to put your shoes on the wrong feet. Now you are older and know it can mean many things, but essentially it means to put your shoes on the wrong feet.

You walk differently. In store windows you don't recognize yourself; you are another woman, some crazy interior display lady in glasses stumbling frantic and preoccupied through the mannequins. In public restrooms you sit dangerously flat against the toilet seat, a strange flesh sundae of despair and exhilaration, murmuring into your bluing thighs: "Hello, I'm Charlene. I'm a mistress."

It is like having a book out from the library.

It is like constantly having a book out from the library.

You meet frequently for dinner, after work, split whole liters of the house red, then wamble the two blocks east, twenty blocks south to your apartment and lie sprawled on the living room floor with your expensive beige raincoats still on.

He is a systems analyst—you have already exhausted this joke—but what he really wants to be, he reveals to you, is an actor.

"Well, how did you become a systems analyst?" you ask, funny you.

"The same way anyone becomes anything," he muses. "I took courses and sent out resumes." Pause. "Patricia helped me work up a great resume. Too great."

"Oh." Wonder about mistress courses, certification, resumes. Perhaps you are not really qualified.

"But I'm not good at systems work," he says, staring through and beyond, way beyond, the cracked ceiling. "Figuring out the cost-effectiveness of two hundred people shuffling five hundred pages back and forth across a new four-and-a-half-by-three-foot desk. I'm not an organized person, like Patricia, for instance. She's just incredibly organized. She makes lists for everything. It's pretty impressive."

Say flatly, dully: "What?"

"That she makes lists."

"That she makes lists? You like that?"

"Well, yes. You know, what she's going to do, what she has to buy, names of clients she has to see, et cetera."

"Lists?" you murmur hopelessly, listlessly, your expensive beige raincoat still on. There is a long, tired silence. Lists? You stand up, brush off your coat, ask him what he would like to drink, then stump off to the kitchen without waiting for the answer.

At one-thirty, he gets up noiselessly except for the soft rustle of his dressing. He leaves before you have even quite fallen asleep, but before he does, he bends over you in his expensive beige raincoat and kisses the ends of your hair. Ah, he kisses your hair.

CLIENTS TO SEE
Birthday snapshots
Scotch tape
Letters to TD and Mom

Technically, you are still a secretary for Karma-Kola, but you wear your Phi Beta Kappa key around your neck on a cheap gold chain, hoping someone will spot you for a promotion. Unfortunately, you have lost the respect of all but one of your co-workers and many of your

superiors as well, who are working in order to send their daughters
to universities so they won't have to be secretaries, and who, therefore,
hold you in contempt for having a degree and being a failure anyway.
It is like having a degree in failure. Hilda, however, likes you. You
are young and remind her of her sister, the professional skater.

"But I hate to skate," you say.

And Hilda smiles, nodding, "Yup, that's exactly what my sister
says sometimes and in that same way."

"What way?"

"Oh, I don't know," says Hilda. "Your bangs parted on the side
or something."

Ask Hilda if she will go to lunch with you. Over Reuben sandwiches
ask her if she's ever had an affair with a married man. As she attempts,
mid-bite, to complete the choreography of her chomp, Russian
dressing spurts out onto her hands.

"Once," she says. "That was the last lover I had. That was over
two years ago."

Say: "Oh my god," as if it were horrible and tragic, then try to
mitigate that rudeness by clearing your throat and saying, "Well,
actually, I guess that's not so bad."

"No," she sighs good-naturedly. "His wife had Hodgkin's disease,
or so everyone thought. When they came up with the correct diag-
nosis, something that wasn't nearly so awful, he went back to her.
Does that make sense to you?"

"I suppose," say doubtfully.

"Yeah, maybe you're right." Hilda is still cleaning Reuben off the
backs of her hands with a napkin. "At any rate, who are you involved
with?"

"Someone who has a wife that makes lists. She has List-maker's
disease."

"What are you going to do?"

"I don't know."

"Yeah," says Hilda. "That's typical."

CLIENTS TO SEE
Tomatoes, canned
Health food toothpaste
Health food deodorant

Vit. C on sale, Rexall
Check re: other shoemaker, 32nd St.

*   *   *

"Patricia's really had quite an interesting life," he says, smoking a cigarette.

"Oh, really?" you say, stabbing one out in the ashtray.

Make a list of all the lovers you've ever had.

    Warren Lasher
    Ed "Rubberhead" Catapano
    Charles Deats or Keats
    Alfonse

Tuck it in your pocket. Leave it lying around, conspicuously. Somehow you lose it. Make "mislaid" jokes to yourself. Make another list.

Whisper, "Don't go yet," as he glides out of your bed before sunrise and you lie there on your back cooling, naked between the sheets and smelling of musky, oniony sweat. Feel gray, like an abandoned locker room towel. Watch him as he again pulls on his pants, his sweater, his socks and shoes. Reach out and hold his thigh as he leans over and kisses you quickly, telling you not to get up, that he'll lock the door when he leaves. In the smoky darkness, you see him smile weakly, guiltily, and attempt a false, jaunty wave from the doorway. Turn on your side, toward the wall, so you don't have to watch the door close. You hear it thud nonetheless, the jangle of keys and snap of the bolt lock, the footsteps loud, then fading down the staircase, the clunk of the street door, then nothing, all his sounds blending with the city, his face passing namelessly uptown in a bus or a badly heated cab, the room, the whole building you live in, shuddering at the windows as a truck roars by toward the Queensboro Bridge.

Wonder who you are.

"Hi, this is Attila," he says in a false deep voice when you pick up your office phone.

Giggle. Like an idiot. Say: "Oh. Hi, Hun."

Hilda turns to look at you with a what's-with-you look on her face. Shrug your shoulders.

"Can you meet me for lunch?"

Say: "Meet? I'm sorry, I don't eat meat."

"Cute, you're cute," he says, not laughing, and at lunch he gives you his tomatoes.

Drink two huge glasses of wine and smile at all his office and mother-in-law stories. It makes his eyes sparkle and crinkle at the corners, his face pleased and shining. When the waitress clears the plates away, there is a silence where the two of you look down then back up again.

"You get more beautiful every day," he says to you, as you hold your wine glass over your nose, burgundy rushing down your throat. Put your glass down. Redden. Smile. Fiddle with your Phi Beta Kappa key.

When you get up to leave, take deep breaths. In front of the restaurant, where you will stride off in different directions, don't give him a kiss in the noontime throng. Patricia's office is nearby and she likes to go to the bank right around now; his back will stiffen and his eyes dart around like a crazy person's. Instead, do a quick shuffle-ball-chain like you saw Barbra Streisand do in a movie once. Wave gigantically and say: "Till we eat again."

In your office building the elevator is slow and packed and you forget to get off at the tenth floor and have to ride all the way back down again from the nineteenth. Five minutes after you arrive dizzily back at your desk, the phone rings.

"Meet me tomorrow at seven," he says, "in front of Florsheim's and I'll carry you off to my castle. Patricia is going to a copyright convention."

Wait freezing in front of Florsheim's until seven-twenty. He finally dashes up, gasping apologies (he just now got back from the airport), his coat flying open, and he takes you in tow quickly uptown toward the art museums. He lives near art museums. Ask him what a copyright convention is.

"Where leisure is a suit *and* a suite," he drawls, long and smiling, quickening his pace and yours. He kisses your temple, brushes hair off your face.

You arrive at his building in twenty minutes.

"So, this is it?" The castle doorman's fly is undone. Smile politely. In the elevator, say: "The unexamined fly is not worth zipping."

The elevator has a peculiar rattle, for all eight floors, like someone obsessively clearing her throat.

When he finally gets the apartment door unlocked, he shows you into an L-shaped living room bursting with plants and gold-framed posters announcing exhibitions you are too late for by six years. The kitchen is off to one side—tiny, digital, spare, with a small army of chrome utensils hanging belligerent and clean as blades on the wall. Walk nervously around like a dog sniffing out the place. Peek into the bedroom: in the center, like a giant bloom, is a queen-sized bed with a Pennsylvania Dutch spread. A small photo of a woman in ski garb is propped on a nightstand. It frightens you.

Back in the living room, he mixes drinks with Scotch in them. "So, this is it," you say again with a forced grin and an odd heaving in your rib cage. Light up one of his cigarettes.

"Can I take your coat?"

Be strange and awkward. Say: "I like beige. I think it is practical."

"What's wrong with you?" he says, handing you your drink.

Try to decide what you should do:

1. rip open the front of your coat, sending the buttons torpedoing across the room in a series of pops into the asparagus fern;

2. go into the bathroom and gargle with hot tap water;

3. go downstairs and wave down a cab for home.

He puts his mouth on your neck. Put your arms timidly around him. Whisper into his ear: "There's a woman, uh, another woman in your room."

When he is fast asleep upon you, in the middle of the night, send your left arm out slowly toward the nightstand like a mechanical limb programmed for a secret intelligence mission, and bring the ski garb picture back close to your face in the dark and try to study the features over his shoulder. She seems to have a pretty smile, short hair, no eyebrows, tough flaring nostrils, body indecipherably ensconced in nylon and down and wool.

Slip carefully out, like a shoe horn, from beneath his sleeping body—he grunts groggily—and go to the closet. Open it with a minimum of squeaking and stare at her clothes. A few suits. Looks like beige blouses and a lot of brown things. Turn on the closet light. Look at the shoes. They are all lined up in neat, married pairs on the closet floor. Black pumps, blue sneakers, brown moccasins, brown T-straps. They have been to an expensive college, say, in Massachusetts. Gaze into her shoes. Her feet are much larger than yours. They are like small cruise missiles.

Inside the caves of those shoes, eyes form and open their lids, stare up at you, regard you, wink at you from the insoles. They are half-friendly, conspiratorial, amused at this reconnaissance of yours, like little smiling men from the open hatches of a fleet of military submarines. Turn off the light and shut the door quickly, before they start talking or dancing or something. Scurry back to the bed and hide your face in his armpit.

In the morning he makes you breakfast. Something with eggs and mushrooms and hot sauce.

Use his toothbrush. The red one. Gaze into the mirror at a face that looks too puffy to be yours. Imagine using her toothbrush by mistake. Imagine a wife and a mistress sharing the same toothbrush forever and ever, never knowing. Look into the medicine cabinet:

Midol
dental floss
Tylenol
Merthiolate
package of eight emory boards
razors and cartridges
two squeezed in the middle toothpaste tubes: Crest *and* Sensodyne
Band-Aids
hand lotion
rubbing alcohol
three small bars of Cashmere Bouquet stolen from a hotel

On the street, all over, you think you see her, the boring hotel-soap stealer. Every woman is her. You smell Cashmere Bouquet all over the place. That's her. Someone waiting near you for the downtown express: yup, that's her. A woman waiting behind you in a deli near Marine Midland who has smooth, hand-lotioned hands and looks like she skis: good god, what if that is her. Break out in cold sweats. Stare into every pair of flared nostrils with clinical curiosity and unbridled terror. Scrutinize feet. Glance sidelong at pumps. Then look quickly away, like a woman, some other woman, who is losing her mind.

Alone on lunch hours or after work, continue to look every female over the age of twelve straight in the nose and straight in the shoes. Feel your face aquiver and twice bolt out of Bergdorf's irrationally when you are sure it is her at the skirt sale rack choosing brown again, a Tylenol bottle peeking out from the corner of her purse. Sit on a granite wall in the GM plaza and catch your breath. Listen to an old man singing "Frosty the Snowman." Lose track of time.

"You're late," Hilda turns and whispers at you. "Carlyle's been back here twice already asking where you were and if the market survey report has been typed up yet."

Mutter: "Shit." You are only on the T's: Tennessee Karma-Kola consumption per square dollar-mile of investment market. Figures for July 1980–October 1981.

Texas—Fiscal Year 1980
Texas—Fiscal Year 1981
Utah.

It is like typing a telephone directory. Get tears in your eyes.

CLIENTS TO SEE
1. Fallen in love(?) Out of control. Who is this? Who am I? And who is this wife with the skis and the nostrils and the Tylenol and does she have orgasms?
2. Reclaim yourself. Pieces have fluttered away.
3. Everything you do is a masochistic act. Why?
4. Don't you like yourself? Don't you deserve better than all of this?
5. Need: something to lift you from your boots out into the sky, something to make you like little things again, to whirl around the curves of your ears and muss up your hair and call you every single day.
6. A drug.
7. A man.
8. A religion.
9. A good job. Revise and send out resumes.
10. Remember what Mrs. Kloosterman told the class in second grade: Just be glad you have legs.

"What are you going to do for Christmas?" he says, lying supine on your couch.

"Oh. I don't know. See my parents in New Jersey, I guess." Pause. "Wanna come? Meet my folks?"

A kind, fatherly, indulgent smile. "Charlene," he purrs, sitting up to pat your hand, your silly ridiculous little hand.

He gives you a pair of leather slippers. They were what you wanted. You give him a book about cars.

*   *   *

"Ma, open the red one first. The other package goes with it."

"A coffee grinder, why thank you, dear." She kisses you wetly on the cheek, a Christmas mist in her eyes. She thinks you're wonderful. She's truly your greatest fan. She is aging and menopausal. She stubbornly thinks you're an assistant department head at Karma-Kola. She wants so badly, so earnestly, to be you.

"And this bag is some exotic Colombian bean, and this is a chocolate-flavored decaf."

Your father fidgets in the corner, looking at his watch, worrying that your mom should be checking the crown roast.

"Decaf bean," he says. "That's for me?"

Say: "Yeah, Dad. That's for you."

"Who is he?" says your mom, later, in the kitchen after you've washed the dishes.

"He's a systems analyst."

"What do they do?"

"Oh . . . they get married a lot. They're usually always married."

"Charlene, are you having an affair with a married man?"

"Ma, do you have to put it that way?"

"You are asking for big trouble," she says, slowly, and resumes polishing silver with a vehement energy.

Wonder why she always polishes the silver *after* meals.

Lean against the refrigerator and play with the magnets.

Say, softly, carefully: "I know, Mother, it's not something you would do."

She looks up at you, her mouth trembling, pieces of her brown-gray hair dangling in her salty eyes, pink silverware cream caking onto her hands, onto her wedding ring. She stops, puts a spoon down, looks away and then hopelessly back at you, like a very young girl, and, shaking her head, bursts into tears.

"I missed you," he practically shouts, ebullient and adolescent, pacing about the living room with a sort of bounce, like a child who is up way past his bedtime and wants to ask a question. "What did you do at home?" He rubs your neck.

"Oh, the usual holiday stuff with my parents. On New Year's Eve I went to a disco in Morristown with my cousin Denise, but I dressed wrong. I wore the turtleneck and plaid skirt my mother gave me, because I wanted her to feel good, and my slip kept showing."

He grins and kisses your cheek, thinking this sweet.

Continue: "There were three guys, all in purple shirts and paper hats, who kept coming over and asking me to dance. I don't think they were together or brothers or anything. But I danced, and on 'New York City Girl,' that song about how jaded and competent urban women are, I went crazy dancing and my slip dropped to the floor. I tried to pick it up, but finally just had to step out of it and jam it into my purse. At the stroke of midnight, I cried."

"I'll bet you suffered terribly," he says, clasping you around the small of your back.

Say: "Yes, I did."

I'm thinking of telling Patricia about us."

Be skeptical. Ask: "What will you say?"

He proceeds confidently: "I'll go, 'Dear, there's something I have to tell you.'"

"And she'll look over at you from her briefcase full of memoranda and say: 'Hmmmmmmmm?'"

"And I'll say, 'Dear, I think I'm falling in love with another woman, and I *know* I'm having sex with her.'"

"And she'll say, 'Oh my god, what did you say?'"

"And I'll say: 'Sex.'"

"And she'll start weeping inconsolably and *then* what will you do?

There is a silence, still as the moon. He shifts his legs, seems confused. "I'll . . . tell her I was just kidding." He squeezes your hand.

Shave your legs in the bathroom sink. Philosophize: you are a mistress, part of a great hysterical you mean historical tradition. Wives are like cockroaches. Also part of a great historical tradition. They will survive you after a nuclear attack—they are tough and hardy and travel in packs—but right now they're not having any fun. And when you look in the bathroom mirror, you spot them scurrying, up out of reach behind you.

An hour of gimlets after work, a quick browse through Barnes and Noble, and he looks at his watch, gives you a peck, and says: "Good night. I'll call you soon."

Walk out with him. Stand there, shivering, but do not pout. Say: "Call you 'later' would sound better than 'soon.' 'Soon' always means just the opposite."

He smiles feebly. "I'll phone you in a few days."

And when he is off, hurrying up Third Avenue, look down at your feet, kick at a dirty cigarette butt, and in your best juvenile mumble, say: "Fuck you, jack."

Some nights he says he'll try to make it over, but there's no guarantee. Those nights, just in case, spend two hours showering, dressing, applying makeup unrecognizably, like someone in drag, and then, as it is late, and you have to work the next day, climb onto your bed like that, wearing perfume and an embarrassing, long, flowing, lacy bathrobe that is really not a bathrobe at all, but a "hostess loungecoat." With the glassed candle by your bed lit and burning away, doze off and on, arranged with excruciating care on top of the covers, the window lamp on in the living room, the door unlocked for him in case he arrives in a passionate flurry, forgetting his key. Six blocks from Fourteenth Street: you are risking your life for him, spread out like a ridiculous cake on the bed, waiting with the door unlocked, thinking you hear him on the stairs, but no. You should have a corsage, you think to yourself. You should have a goddamned orchid pinned to the chest of your long flowing hostess coat, then you would be appropriately absurd. Think: What has happened to me? Why am I lying like this on top of my covers with too much Jontue and mascara and jewelry, pretending casually that this is how I always go to bed, while a pervert with six new steak knives is about to sneak through my unlocked door. Remember: at Blakely Falls High, Willis Holmes would have done anything to be with you. You don't have to put up with this: you were second runner-up at the Junior Prom.

A truck roars by.

Some deaf and dumb kids, probably let out from a dance at the school nearby, are gathered downstairs below your window, hooting and howling, making unearthly sounds. You guess they are laughing and having fun, but they can't hear themselves, and at night the noises are scary, animal-like.

Your clock-radio reads 1:45.

Wonder if you are getting old, desperate. Believe that you have really turned into another woman:

your maiden aunt Phyllis;

some vaporish cocktail waitress;

a glittery transvestite who has wandered, lost, up from the Village.

* * *

When seven consecutive days go by that you do not hear from him, send witty little postcards to all your friends from college. On the eighth day, when finally he calls you at the office, murmuring lascivious things in German, remain laconic. Say: "*Ja . . . nein . . . ja.*"

At lunch regard your cream of cauliflower soup with a pinched mouth and ask what on earth he and his wife *do* together. Sound irritated. He shrugs and says, "Dust, eat, bicker about the shower curtain. Why do you ask?"

Say: "Gee, I don't know. What an outrageous question, huh?"

He gives you a look of sympathy that could bring a dead cat back to life. "You're upset because I didn't call you." He reaches across the table to touch your fingers. Pull your hand away. Say: "Don't flatter yourself." Look slightly off to one side. Put your hand over your eyes like you have a headache. Say: "God, I'm sorry."

"It's okay," he says.

And you think: Something is backward here. Reversed. Wrong. Like the something that is wrong in "What is wrong with this picture?" in kids' magazines in dentists' offices. Toothaches. Stomachaches. God, the soup. Excuse yourself and hurry toward the women's room. Slam the stall door shut. Lean back against it. Stare into the throat of the toilet.

Hilda is worried about you and wants to fix you up with a cousin of hers from Brooklyn.

Ask wearily: "What's his name?"

She looks at you, frowning. "Mark. He's a banker. And what the hell kind of attitude is that?"

Mark orders you a beer in a Greek coffee shop near the movie theater.

"So, you're a secretary."

Squirm and quip: "More like a sedentary," and look at him in surprise and horror when he guffaws and snorts way too loudly.

Say: "Actually, what I really should have been is a dancer. Everybody has always said that."

Mark smiles. He likes the idea of you being a dancer.

Look at him coldly. Say: "No, nobody has ever said that. I just made it up."

All through the movie you forget to read the subtitles, thinking instead about whether you should sleep with Mark the banker. Glance at him out of the corner of your eye. In the dark, his profile seems important and mysterious. Sort of. He catches you looking at him and turns and winks at you. Good god. He seems to be investing something in all of this. Bankers. Sigh. Stare straight ahead. Decide you just don't have the energy, the interest.

"I saw somebody else."
"Oh?"
"A banker. We went to a Godard movie."
"Well . . . good."
"Good?"
"I mean for you, Charlene. You should be doing things like that once in a while."
"Yeah. He's real rich."
"Did you have fun?"
"No."
"Did you sleep with him?"
"No."
He kisses you, almost gratefully, on the ear. Fidget. Twitch. Lie. Say: "I mean, yes."
He nods. Looks away. Says nothing.

Cut up an old calendar into week-long strips. Place them around your kitchen floor, a sort of bar graph on the linoleum, representing the number of weeks you have been a mistress: thirteen. Put X's through all the national holidays.

Go out for a walk in the cold. Three little girls hanging out on the stoop are laughing and calling to strange men on the street. "Hi! Hi, Mister!" Step around them. Think: They have never had orgasms.

A blonde woman in barrettes passes you in stockinged feet, holding her shoes.

There are things you have to tell him.

CLIENTS TO SEE
1. This affair is demeaning.
2. Violates decency. Am I just some scampish tart, some tartish scamp?
3. No emotional support here.
4. Why do you never say "I love you" or "Stay in my arms forever my little tadpole" or "Your eyes set me on fire my sweet nubkin"?

*   *   *

The next time he phones, he says: "I was having a dream about you and suddenly I woke up with a jerk and felt very uneasy."

Say: "Yeah, I hate to wake up with jerks."

He laughs, smooth, beautiful, and tenor, making you feel warm inside of your bones. And it hits you; maybe it all boils down to this: people will do anything, anything, for a really nice laugh.

Don't lose your resolve. Fumble for your list. Sputter things out as convincingly as possible.

Say: "I suffer indignities at your hands. And agonies of duh feet. I don't know why I joke. I hurt."

"That is why."

"What?"

"That is why."

"But you don't really care." Wince. It sounds pitiful.

"But I do."

For some reason this leaves you dumbfounded.

He continues: "You know my situation . . . or maybe you don't." Pause. "What can I do, Charlene? Stand on my goddamned head?"

Whisper: "Please. Stand on your goddamned head."

"It is ten o'clock," he says. "I'm coming over. We need to talk."

What he has to tell you is that Patricia is not his wife. He is separated from his wife; her name is Carrie. You think of a joke you heard once: What do you call a woman who marries a man with no arms and no legs? Carrie. Patricia is the woman he lives with.

"You mean, I'm just another one of the fucking gang?"

He looks at you, puzzled. "Charlene, what I've always admired about you, right from when I first met you, is your strength, your independence."

Say: "That line is old as boots."

Tell him not to smoke in your apartment. Tell him to get out.

At first he protests. But slowly, slowly, he leaves, pulling up the collar on his expensive beige raincoat, like an old and haggard Robert Culp.

Slam the door like Bette Davis.

Love drains from you, takes with it much of your blood sugar and water weight. You are like a house slowly losing its electricity, the fans slowing, the lights dimming and flickering; the clocks stop and go and stop.

At Karma-Kola the days are peg-legged and aimless, collapsing into one another with the comic tedium of old clowns, nowhere fast.

In April you get a raise. Celebrate by taking Hilda to lunch at the Plaza.

Write for applications to graduate schools.

Send Mark the banker a birthday card.

Take long walks at night in the cold. The blonde in barrettes scuttles timelessly by you, still carrying her shoes. She has cut her hair.

He calls you occasionally at the office to ask how you are. You doodle numbers and curlicues on the corners of the Rolodex cards. Fiddle with your Phi Beta Kappa key. Stare out the window. You always, always, say: "Fine."

Piano Starts Here

JIM SHEPARD

W E WERE TRYING to see a dog that could've been dead already and we weren't getting anywhere, Susan said. We were standing outside her veterinarian's office in a four a.m. drizzle. My hair felt like wet old clothes on my neck. Susan's breath ghosted the glass. She had asked to be let in, and the boy inside had not yet responded. He gazed at us uncertainly, his mop handle teetering, running water shifting and realigning his image on the pane. Susan spread a hand across it, as if to push through. She had twice explained that her dog was in there and that the doctor had given her permission to come down so late. The boy seemed to have trouble focusing.

Doppleresque trucks rushed and whined on the interstate in the distance. The boy palmed the handle of the door with an appealing gentleness. He puffed his cheeks like a bugler, and turned the latch, and the door shivered and swung outward.

"Audrey," Susan said, once inside. "A beagle mix. She hasn't come out of the anaesthetic."

The boy did not respond. He led us through a second door. Susan's boots made amphibious sounds on the tile.

Audrey was still on the table. She had been brought in earlier unable to stand on her hind legs, and cortizone had been no help. The decision had been made to operate and they had found a lesion impinging on the spinal cord. The recommendation was to let her go. That was the veterinarian's phrase. Susan was taking the night to think it over.

Audrey had not revived from the anaesthetic and was not a good bet to do so. She lay on her side with her midsection and rear shaved and bandaged. One paw hung from the table.

"I come in and checked earlier," the boy said, "but she don't move."

Susan smiled wanly. "Audie-feeber," she said. "Old Audrey-feen." She sounded like the loser on a quiz show. "Here we got our big numbers tomorrow and where will you be?"

Our recital in Adult Music was the next afternoon at three.

We had signed up together eleven weeks previous. Susan had kept her distance from me, and that was something I hoped to change. Friends scoffed and remained casual about the possibilities, musical or romantic. They allowed that they themselves rarely did that which was in their best interests, whether because of the kids or work or general laziness; around me they seemed distracted, skeptical, as if always aware of neglected parallel tracks of richer possibility.

Susan and I showed zero aptitude for the instrument. I had no ability. Susan flustered and grew frustrated and banged the keys like someone losing an argument. For us the keyboards stretched limitless in each direction and the keys lay in quiet and narrow rows as individual as grains of rice. We had both, it turned out (Susan saw nothing interesting in the coincidence), abandoned the instruments in childhood, spurning the loneliness of solitary application to music, I theorized, for yet another sort. We had sat imprisoned with stereotypic piano teachers in dark parlors, reinventing simple exercises, sweating and hesitant, imagining a world of joy and laughter beyond our windows while our hands produced a series of remorseless sounds.

The patterns returned to our adult lives in the singsong cadences of nonachievement: *Every Good Boy Deserves Favor. All Cows Eat Grass. Big Dogs Fight All Cats.* We behaved as true believers trusting that refusing to confront the catastrophe might yet reverse it.

Susan and Audrey arrived at the North Adams Congregational Church hall that first day in my company, though she specified for the benefit of our instructor that we were not attached. She taught fourth and fifth level high school history, she said, and for what? Her last groups' PSATs were so low, she said, she'd recommended to one kid, when he had asked where he should go to school, The University of Mars. She was getting burnt out, in other words.

"Well, let's see what happens," she said, and cracked her knuckles theatrically. Audrey laid a chin on the piano bench.

We stood ready at that point to commit ourselves to eleven weeks of Adult Music and become part of a group seemingly already dispirited by a lack of adults. Mrs. Proekopp, our instructor, assured us she'd add younger people if necessary to fill out the class. She gestured as evidence towards a tiny child waiting wide-eyed with her mother by the front door.

The church hall had been rented for the occasion, and Mrs. Proekopp had not put herself out. Upright pianos were arranged back to back on the maroon linoleum, and the effect was that of a half-realized and dismal Busby Berkeley number.

Mrs. Proekopp had speculated right off the bat that the dog would naturally be a disruption and in the future would be better off and no doubt happier at home, and Susan had suggested that she would be the judge of that, thank you, and when the dog disturbed anyone they would let her know. Audrey had yawned.

The few other students had looked on with interest. Susan believed in serious rudeness when people in her opinion refused to see or speak clearly.

"We need something, I guess," she allowed that first day.

"You never know what you can do until you try," I said, settling into the piano beside hers. Audrey shot me a look.

"Then you do," Susan said. "That's the problem." She lifted the index card with her name pencilled on it from the fallboard. "Makes me feel like a kid again," she said, and played four notes, *plink plank plonk plunk*, and squinted at the music sheet.

I watched her hands rehearsing and re-rehearsing their intended patterns above the keyboard, her brow furrowed in puzzlement. She stared at the music like someone facing crisis in an exotic land trying to read the instructions on the emergency gear.

Her problem, she said, was that she didn't like what she'd done with herself and she didn't like what she was doing. "*One* problem, anyway," she added. The situation demanded change.

There on the first day of Getting Acquainted with our instruments even basic techniques remained blandly elusive. The exercises drifted serenely around my attempts to order them. Susan at one point compared the effect to that of a system created by random generation. We did not improve. Audrey lay under the piano bench, dreamily twitching.

The second day the tiny girl in the doorway, Mary Alice, was admitted to the group, and Susan told her by way of explaining me, "He thinks he's in love with me." Mary Alice looked uncertain as to how to process the information, and regarded me unsympathetically. I suggested by my expression that I didn't at that point need the sympathy of children.

At the break we sniffed coffee in styrofoam cups and lingered near the donuts. Mrs. Proekopp kept a wary eye on Audrey, who nosed the air around the tray experimentally.

"There's a difference between believing in things and refusing to see," Susan said. "You've got that love-at-first-sight thing in your head now; I can see it. Forget it. You and me, we're not made for each other. We're just not."

I suggested it wasn't something that needed deciding right then.
"It's *been* decided," Susan said. "Smell the coffee, pal."

"It isn't a wholly rational process," I said. She made a squeaking
noise with her lips.

"You're something," she said. "Your mouth's writing checks your
behind can't cash." We were back at the pianos and donut residue
left filmy fingerprints on the ebony keys.

Between sessions we met coincidentally in a garage. Her tired
orange Opel hatchback balked in the cold, she reported. Desmond,
her mechanic, tells her now to just leave the checkbook.

Dog dishes spotted the cement floor. "For the rats," she explained.
"This place is Rat Motel." I pulled up my feet.

In the Pan Tree across the street she cupped both her hands around
her cup of Constant Comment and watched Desmond poke disinter-
estedly at the insides of her car. Audrey remained upright and stoic
in the back seat, resembling at that distance the mysterious figures
in the windows of suspense movies.

"You don't know me," she said. "We never dated. I have B.O. I'm
always pissed off at something. I'm not your dream girl." She looked
away, and I was encouraged. "All this interest is sad."

I asked about a piece of hers in the *Advocate* entitled "Jazz Giants
Snub the Berkshires." Her thesis had been that they had no place to
play, and it was inevitable. We talked about the older greats: Jelly
Roll Morton, Art Tatum, Fatha Hines, and Willie the Lion Smith. I
was frequently pretending to appreciations I didn't have. She tried
to make comprehensible Tatum's sixteenth note runs at uptempo. We
considered ways of improving articulation. We had very little idea
what we were talking about.

Garage lights shone across the street. Desmond clanked something
against what seemed to be the bumper, with a sound audible at that
distance, through glass. "Want to go to the Blind Pig?" I asked. "For
a drink."

"I don't know," Susan sighed. "What am I doing? What are you
doing?"

"You're teaching, and writing for the *Advocate*," I said. "That could
be exciting."

She nodded, her eyes on the Opel and the shadow of Audrey.
"They got me covering a guy who does gun rack art," she said.

I folded and straightened the paper around my pumpkin muffins.
I asked if she remembered the little girl, Amanda, from our first
meeting, at the Fourth of July fireworks. Amanda had stood near us

petting Audrey while the huge flower-like colors boomed and popped in the sky. Her mouth had been open and the lights had warmed our faces. Susan spoke quietly with her. Someone took us for a family. Amanda leaned back, her palm leaving Audrey and patting air. Look at the noise! she said. Look at the noise! Susan had lifted her up, as if for a closer look. I thought then that we were both happy. I thought, *she's usually unhappy, and I'm usually unhappy.* I called her after that, tried to shop where she shopped.

"I remember her," Susan said. "Beautiful girl."

The car still wasn't ready when we finished so we walked the strip to the Artery Arcade. From the benches in front of the Zayres we could see over the Motor Vehicle Bureau to Mount Greylock. Susan rubbed her eyes industriously with her fingertips. She said, "I'm thirty-three already. Billy DeBerg was sixteen years ago."

"Billy DeBerg?" I asked. She did not elaborate.

There was an immense and distant crash, as though someone had dropped a carton of bedpans.

"Fat," she said sadly, as if that followed.

"You're very beautiful," I said. This kind of talk did not come easily to me and I tried to list specifics.

"Right here," she said. With two fingers and a thumb she pinched her hip and twisted it. "Miss Cushions."

I brought up Audrey, who was scratching herself. She told of how the dog ate the spines of books, and at the age of eleven still urinated with joy when Susan came back from school.

"*Don't* you?" she asked. Audrey's tail thumped. We sat with her unperturbed silence as our model. The world seemed to be rewarding restraint only incrementally, but I refused on my part to push things. I had the patience of a coral reef.

Mrs. Proekopp informed us two weeks later that she wasn't pleased with our progress, and could not believe, after hearing my hands skitter like frightened crabs across the keyboard, that I had been diligent in my practicing.

"Come now," she said, looking over her glasses at me. "Do you think you would sound like that if you practiced?"

I looked helplessly at my hands.

"Listen," she said. "Mary Alice, play the piece." Mary Alice straightened up and her tiny frame hunched forward. She peered at the music and began. Her version was not very good, but it was a resounding improvement. She appeared to be five to seven years old.

Mrs. Proekopp was not one to tread lightly on a point. "Did yours sound like that?" she asked, unnecessarily. "Class? Did his sound like that?" Around me neutral murmurs, blank looks. "Susan," she said. "Has he been practicing?"

"It doesn't sound like it," Susan said.

"Class," Mrs. Proekopp concluded with an excess of elan, "we are not going to get anywhere"—she thumped my shoulder for emphasis—"not anywhere, if we do not p-r-a-c-t-i-c-e."

On the chalkboard as we entered the hall every afternoon were separate lists for each student which our instructor had entitled WHAT WE NEED TO WORK ON. Susan and I by week three were not on the board. We attributed this to a lack of space.

"Have you thought there might be other girls out there looking for you?" she said during one session, looking at her hands.

"I like *you*," I said. She bared her teeth at the music book.

"I don't know what to do with you two," Mrs. Proekopp said. Mrs. Bunteen, an elderly widow from Adams, looks on with the lights glazing her glasses. "Neither of you seems able to accomplish the smallest things with a keyboard."

"You're being too hard," I said, in Susan's defense.

"Prove it," she said. She believed herself to be, she confided, a whiz at motivation.

The room was silent. I realized I had the opportunity at that point to play for the two of us, to redeem weeks of performance with one flourish and show up the instructor. I began without taking a breath and my fingers spilled around with a palsied urgency. Mrs. Proekopp granted me a short grace period and then walked around the piano to bring an ear closer to the atrocities. Slowly and clearly she called out the missed notes like a public autopsy: B flat. G flat. B flat. B flat. At a tricky bridge I stopped, some fingers still trembling. I imagined for my hands the most grotesque punishments.

Mrs. Proekopp had by that time been reduced to grim little noises. Susan and I had been doing daily violence to the Minuet in G for two weeks. Mrs. Bunteen had begun to master the piece in six days. Mary Alice in three. Mrs. Proekopp crossed to the donut table and from her satchel pulled a sheaf of dittoed pages, which she divided between Susan and myself.

"Here," she said. "Take these home."

Susan leafed through the first few, pale. Centered on the page before her was a small cartoon figure of a smiling quarter note. *Hi there*, he was saying. *I'm B flat.*

She agreed to dinner, at her place, after practice—circling the wagons, she called it. We sat on the living-room sofa, Audrey snoring on one end, and looked out on the erratically shingled roof next door. We had a lot of California wine. *Mr. Smith Goes to Washington* was on cable. On the jacket of an album I pulled from behind her Radio Shack stereo Art Tatum was making a thumbs-up sign and grinning, under the title *Piano Starts Here.*

She apologized for the cork in the wine and said we should have more because of it. She laughed at the movie and made fun of a woman in a commercial who worried about feminine protection. During a Miller Lite ad she asked unexpectedly about football pads. "I never figured out where the pads went, exactly," she said. The knees, I said. The thighs, the hips, the tail bone. She made a face and said I wasn't being too specific.

So I traced the outline of a kneepad around her knee. I traced the broader shape of the thigh pad. I showed her where on the hips.

She was looking at me, serious. My hands described around her head the narrowed globe of the helmet, my fingers outlining the full cage of the face mask.

Audrey sighed and turned onto her back. The commercial ended. Susan put her glass down and her legs flexed and resettled like beautiful animals. She relaxed, a little sadder, I thought. A frazzled Jimmy Stewart filibustered on the floor of the Senate. His head was lowered in close-up and he examined letters in his hand. He mentioned lost causes. Claude Rains, sitting nearby, looked uncomfortable.

I woke in the darkness disoriented. I was on the sofa. Susan poked a coverlet beneath my chin like a bib, her frizzed hair silhouetted against the lamplight from her bedroom. I could hear Audrey lapping water faintly in the distance.

"My Boy Senator," she said. "We sure bring a lot to the party, don't we."

Around week eight of our lessons Audrey began to have difficulty rising after any time at all off her feet and Susan worried and speculated on her getting old and stiffening up. Mrs. Proekopp posted her recital decisions. I was paired with Mary Alice—five-year-old Mary Alice—in a duet. If it was an effort to hide me it could only have been spectacularly unsuccessful.

Mary Alice was no happier with the arrangement and in fact claimed equal humiliation. We resolved to make the best of it and huddled in one corner of the hall to schedule extra practice sessions, miserable Mary Alice in her MOZART sweatshirt trying distractedly to remember which days her mother could provide a ride, which days her father could pick her up. On the third emergency meeting she pounded the keys with startling force, crying "No No No No No *No*," and asked herself, as though I wasn't there, "What am I gonna *do*?"

Things got worse. Susan's improvement was imperceptible and my fingers moved like sinkers as we hurtled towards our recital. She called and said something was wrong, Audrey wasn't getting up, she couldn't reach the vet, and when I went over, there was Audrey pained and sheepish over her inability to rise, pulling herself slightly this way and that in the hopes of alleviating Susan's distress. The operation was authorized. Audrey was passed from arm to arm in the veterinarian's office and seemed bemused when I last saw her, before the doors shut us out.

We stood at the Greylock Animal Hospital before Audrey packaged like an animal coming apart and the boy with the mop said he had a lot of cleaning to do, and turned away. The four a.m. stillness amplified sounds. He went through the cabinets and poured Janitor in a Drum quietly into a clean yellow bucket, hushing the sound by easing the liquid down the tilted edge as though drawing a beer. The smell filled the air around us. On the far side of the room the animals in their holding cages were quiet. Their nails made occasional and light sounds on the metal screens of the doors.

The boy's mop slid across the floor in even strokes, renewing the shine. The tiles gleamed in streaks. We were all listening to Audrey breathing. The boy worked the sterilizer, organizing odd-angled instruments that cut and clamped and sewed the dog on the table. They glittered and clashed musically in the drawers. He wiped his hands and the counter and left the room.

Audrey's bandage looked unwieldy and impractical. Her exhalations were a quiet rasp. Her muzzle trembled. Susan ran her hand over the ribs. A drop from the nose ran onto the stainless steel. Her whiskers moved briefly, and she smelled of the anaesthesia and the medicated bandage.

Susan lifted her hand. The dog seemed dead but I wondered if there was some check we could do. She asked finally for the collar, and the license jingled weakly when I took it off. The boy went back in when we left, and behind us there was the flat sliding sound of Audrey being pulled from the table. In the car Susan's only words had to do with whether I needed a lift to the recital, and I rode with her all the way back with an overwhelming sense of what I could and couldn't do.

By the time of the recital it was raining. Susan's Opel, a sad mustard color in that weather, broke down. She sat beside me in the wings of the makeshift stage with her hair dripping. The collar of her new black blouse was floppy and soaked. The recital crowd was small and uncertainly enthusiastic, as if the rain might possibly have changed everything.

Susan was represented in the audience by Desmond, who looked apologetic, and an old boyfriend. The boyfriend's name was Kevin, and he looked more uncomfortable than I was. He looked at me with the unalloyed hatred of someone with no chance considering someone else in very much the same position.

Introduced, I walked to my piano, bowing unsteadily beside Mary Alice, her brown hair jumbled into an oversized pink bow. We sat down to our Minuet. Unhappy Kevin two rows back seemed to wish the piano would detonate. Mary Alice's parents projected sympathy.

Mary Alice stretched with a child's grace to reach the pedals, her polished black shoes gently toeing the brass. She could not look at me. She waited for the sound of my opening chord to begin.

My piano had not improved. Mary Alice's had not improved, and Susan's had perhaps deteriorated. We would work in concert with our instruments to order the sounds and give what we had to the music. Over the seats and before the mingy floor-to-ceiling divider I could see in the maroon linoleum wet with tracked-in rain an oscillating image of Susan coming to love me, of our raising wondrous children in a sunroomed house, with a Steinway and their growing young arms displaying a heartening gift for the instrument.

Susan would be unaware of the gift the future held for her: her life as a stirring solo across the harmonic map by Fatha Hines. Her life with the left-handed abandon of Oscar Peterson. Her life joined in mine and mine finding meaning in hers, if only I would have—and I knew I did—if only I would have the patience to wait.

Manslaughter

JOYCE CAROL OATES

E DDIE FARRELL, twenty-six, temporarily laid off from Lackawanna Steel, had been separated from his wife, Rose Ann, for several months, off and on, when the fatal stabbing occurred. This was on a January afternoon near dusk. Most of the day snow had been falling lightly and the sun appeared at the horizon for only a few minutes, the usual dull red sulfurous glow beyond the steel mills.

According to Eddie's sworn testimony, Rose Ann had telephoned him at his mother's house and demanded he come over, she had something to tell him. So he went over and picked her up—he was driving his brother's 1977 Falcon—they went to the County Line Tavern for a drink—then drove around, talking, or maybe quarreling. Suddenly Rose Ann took out a knife and went for him—no warning—but he fought her off—he tried to take the knife away—*she* was stabbed by accident—he panicked and drove like crazy for twenty, twenty-five minutes—until he was finally flagged down by a state trooper out on the highway, doing eighty-eight miles an hour in a fifty-five-mile zone. By then Rose Ann had bled to death in the passenger's seat— she'd been stabbed in the throat, chest, belly, thighs, thirty or more times.

"I guess I lost control," Eddie said repeatedly, referring to the drive in the "death car" (as the newspapers called it), not to stabbing his wife: he didn't remember stabbing his wife. It seemed to him he had only defended himself against her attack, somehow she had managed to stab herself. Maybe to punish him. She was always criticizing him, always finding fault. She called up his mother, too, and bitched over the telephone—*that* really got to him.

When asked by police officers how his wife had come into possession of a hunting knife belonging to his brother, Eddie replied at first that he didn't have any idea, then he said she must have stolen it and hidden it away in the apartment. He really didn't know. She did crazy things. She threatened all kinds of crazy things. The knife was German-made, with an eight-inch stainless steel blade and a black sealed wood handle, a beautiful thing, expensive. Lying on a little table at the front of the courtroom, beneath the judge's high bench, it looked like it might be for sale—the last of its kind, after everything else had been bought.

At first Eddie Farrell was booked for second-degree murder, with $45,000 bail (which meant 10 percent bond); then the charges were lowered to third, with $15,000 bail. Midway in the trial the charges would be lowered further to manslaughter, voluntary.

It was Beatrice Grazia's bad luck to happen to see the death car as it sped along Second Avenue in her direction. She was on her way home from work, crossing the street, when the car approached. She jumped back onto the curb, she said. The driver was a goddamned maniac and she didn't want to get killed.

Sure, she told police, she recognized Eddie Farrell driving—she got a clear view of his face as he drove past. But it all happened so quickly, she just stood on the curb staring after the car. Her coat was splashed with slush and dirt, he'd come that close to running her down.

At the trial five months later Beatrice swore to tell the truth, the whole truth, and nothing but the truth, but it all seemed remote now—insignificant. Her voice was so breathless it could barely be heard by the spectators in the first row. She was the tenth witness for the prosecution, out of twenty-seven, and her testimony seemed to add little to what had already been said. She hadn't wanted to appear—the district attorney's office had issued her a subpoena. Yes, she'd seen Eddie Farrell that day. Yes, he was driving east along Second. Yes, he was speeding. Yes, she had recognized him. Yes, he was in the courtroom today. Yes, she could point him out. Yes, she had seen someone in the passenger's seat beside him. No, she hadn't recognized the person. She believed it was a woman—she was fairly certain it was a woman—but the car passed by so quickly, she couldn't see.

Her voice was low, rapid, sullen, as if she were testifying against her will. Both the district attorney's assistant and the defense lawyer repeatedly asked her to speak up. The defense lawyer grew visibly irritated, his questions were edged with malice: How could she be certain she recognized the driver of the car?—wasn't it almost dark?—did she have *perfect* vision?

Blood rushed into her cheeks; she stammered a few words and went silent.

Eddie Farrell was sitting only a few yards away, staring dully into a corner of the courtroom—he didn't appear to be listening. His hair was slickly combed and parted on the side. He wore a pin-striped suit that fitted his skinny body loosely, as if he had put it on by mistake. His eyes were deep-set, shadowed; there was a queer oily sheen to his skin. Beatrice wasn't sure she would have recognized him, now.

Though everyone waited for Eddie to take the stand, to testify for himself, it wasn't his lawyer's strategy to allow him to speak: this disappointed many of the spectators. In all, the defense called only six people, four of them character witnesses. They spoke of Eddie Farrell as if they didn't realize he was in the courtroom with them; they didn't seem to have a great deal to say.

The most articulate witness was a young man named Ron Boci who had known Eddie, he said, for ten, twelve years, since grade school. He spoke rapidly and fluently, with a faint jeering edge to his voice; his swarthy skin had flushed darker. Yeah, he was a friend of Eddie's, they went places together—yeah, Eddie'd told him there was trouble with his wife—but it wasn't ever serious trouble, not from Eddie's side. He loved his wife, Ron Boci said, looking out over the courtroom, he wouldn't ever hurt her, he put up with a lot from her. Rose Ann was the one, he said. Rose Ann was always going on how she'd maybe kill herself, cut her throat, take an overdose or something, just to get back at Eddie, but Eddie never thought she meant it, nobody did—that was just Rose Ann shooting off her mouth. Yeah, Ron Boci said, moving his narrow shoulders, he knew her, kind of. But not like he knew Eddie.

Ron warmed as he spoke; he crossed his legs, resting one high-polished black boot lightly on his knee. He had a handsome beakish face, quick-darting eyes, hair parted in the center of his head so that it could flow thick and wavy to the sides, where it brushed against his collar. His hair was so black it looked polished. He too was wearing a suit—a beige checked suit with brass buttons—but it fitted his slender body snugly. His necktie was a queer part-luminous silver that might have been metallic.

During one of the recesses, when Beatrice went to the drinking fountain, Ron Boci appeared beside her and offered to turn on the water for her. It was a joke but Beatrice didn't think it was funny. "No thank you," she said, her eyes sliding away from his, struck by how white the whites were, how heavy the eyebrows. "No thank you, I can turn it on myself," Beatrice said, but he didn't seem to hear. She saw, stooping, lowering her pursed lips to the tepid stream of water, that there was a sprinkling of small warts on the back of Ron Boci's big-knuckled hand.

It was shortly after the New Year that Beatrice's husband, Tony, drove down to Port Arthur, Texas, on the Gulf, to work for an offshore oil drilling company. He'd be calling her, he said. He'd write, he'd send back money as soon as he could.

A postcard came in mid-February, another at the end of March. Each showed the same Kodacolor photograph of a brilliant orange-red sunset on the Gulf of Mexico, with palm trees in languid silhouette. Not much news, Tony wrote, things weren't working out quite right, he'd be telephoning soon. No snow down here, he said, all winter. If it snows it melts right away.

Where is Tony? people asked, neighbors in the building, Beatrice's parents, her girlfriends, and she said with a childlike lifting of her chin, "Down in Texas where there's work." Then she tried to change the subject. Sometimes they persisted, asking if she was going to join him, if he had an apartment or anything, what their plans were. "He's supposed to call this weekend," Beatrice said. Her narrow face seemed to thicken in obstinacy; the muscles of her jaws went hard.

He did call, one Sunday night. She had to turn the television volume down but, at the other end of the line, there was a great deal of noise—as if a television were turned up high. A voice that resembled Tony's lifted incoherently. Beatrice said, "Yes? Tony? Is that you? What?" but the line crackled and went dead. She hung up. She waited awhile, then turned the television back up and sat staring at the screen until the phone rang again. This time, she thought, I know better than to answer.

"What are you doing about the rent for July?—and you still owe for June, don't you?" Beatrice's father asked.

Beatrice was filing her long angular nails briskly with an emery board. Her face went hot with blood but she didn't look up.

"I better pay it," Beatrice's father said. "And you and the baby better move back with us."

"Who told you what we owe?" Beatrice asked.

She spoke in a flat neutral voice though her blood pulsed with anger. People were talking about them—her and Tony—it was an open secret now that Tony seemed to have moved out.

"Tony won't like it if I give this place up," Beatrice said, easing the emery board carefully around her thumbnail, which had grown to an unusual length. To provoke her father a little she said, "He'll maybe be mad if he comes back and somebody else is living here and he's got to go over to our house to find me and Danny. You know how his temper is."

Beatrice's father surprised her by laughing. Or maybe it was a kind of grunt—he rose from his chair, a big fleshy man, hands pushing on his thighs as if he needed extra leverage. "I can take care of your wop husband," he said.

It was a joke—it really *was* a joke because Beatrice's mother was Italian—but Beatrice hunched over the emery board and refused even to smile. "You wouldn't talk like that if Tony was here," she said.

"I wouldn't need to talk like this if Tony was here," her father said. "But the point is, he isn't here. That's what we're talking about."

"That's what you're talking about," Beatrice said.

When her father was leaving Beatrice followed after him on the stairs, pulling at his arm, saying, "Momma wants Danny with her and that's okay, Momma is wonderful with him, but, you know, this was supposed to be . . ." She made a clumsy pleading gesture indicating the stairs, the apartment on the landing, the building itself. She swallowed hard so that she wouldn't start to cry. "This was supposed to be a new place, a different place," she said, "that's why we came here. That's why we got married."

"I already talked to the guy downstairs," her father said, rattling his car keys. "He said you can move any time up to the fifteenth. I'll rent one of them U-Hauls and we'll do it in the morning."

"I don't think I can," Beatrice said, wiping angrily at her eyes. "I'm not going to do that."

"Next time he calls," Beatrice's father said, "tell him the news. Tell him your old man paid the rent for him. Tell him to look me up, he wants to cause trouble."

"I'm not going to do any of that," Beatrice said, starting to cry.

"It's already halfway done," her father said.

One night around ten o'clock Beatrice was leaving the Seven-Eleven store up the street when she heard someone approach her. As she glanced back an arm circled her shoulders, which were almost bare— she was wearing a red halter top—and a guy played at hugging her as if they were old pals. She screamed and pushed him away—jabbed at him with her elbow.

It was Ron Boci, Eddie Farrell's friend. He was wearing a T-shirt and jeans, no shoes. No belt, the waist of the jeans was loose and frayed, you could see how lean he was—not skinny exactly but lean, small-hipped. His hair was a little longer than it had been in the courtroom but it was still parted carefully in the center of his head; he had a habit of shaking it back, loosening it, when he knew people were watching.

"Hey, you knew who it was," he said. "Come on."

"You scared the hell out of me," Beatrice said. Her heart was knocking so hard she could feel her entire body rock. But she stooped and picked up the quart of milk she'd dropped, and the carton of cigarettes, and Ron Boci stood there with his knuckles on his hips, watching. He meant to keep the same kidding tone but she heard an edge of apology in his voice, or maybe it was something else.

"You knew who it was," he said, smiling, lifting one corner of his mouth, "you saw me in there but you wouldn't say hello."

"Saw you in where?" Beatrice asked. "There wasn't anybody in there but the salesclerk."

"I was in there, I stood right in the center of the aisle, where the soda pop and stuff is, but you pretended not to see me, you looked right through me," Ron Boci said. "But I bet you remember my name."

"I don't remember any name," Beatrice said. Her voice sounded so harsh and frightened, she added quickly, "It's just a good thing I wasn't carrying any bottles or anything, it'd all be broke now." She said, "Well, I know the name Boci. Your sister Marian."

"Yeah, Marian," Ron Boci said.

Beatrice started to walk away and Ron Boci followed close beside her. He was perhaps six inches taller than Beatrice and walked with his thumbs hooked into the waist of his jeans, an easy sidling walk, self-conscious, springy. His smell was tart and dry like tobacco mixed with something moist: hair oil, shaving lotion. Beatrice knew he was watching her but she pretended not to notice.

He was a little high, elated. He laughed softly to himself.

"Your telephone got disconnected or something," Ron Boci said after a pause. He spoke with an air of slight reproach.

"I don't live there anymore," Beatrice said quickly.

She saw a sprinkling of glass on the sidewalk ahead but she didn't intend to warn him: let him walk through it and slice up his filthy feet.

"Where do you live, then, Beatrice?" he asked casually. "I know Tony is in Texas."

"He's coming back in a few weeks," Beatrice said. "Or I might fly down."

"I used to know Tony," Ron Boci said. "The Grazias over on Market

Street—? Mrs. Grazia and my mother used to be good friends."

Beatrice said nothing. Ron Boci's elbow brushed against her bare arm and all the fine brown hairs lifted in goose bumps.

"Where are you living now, if you moved?" Ron Boci asked.

"It doesn't matter where I live," Beatrice said.

"I mean, what's their name? You with somebody, or alone?"

"Why do you want to know?"

"I'm just asking. Where are you headed now?"

"My parents' place, I'm staying overnight. My mother helps out sometimes with the baby," Beatrice said. She heard her voice becoming quick, light, detached, as if it were a stranger's voice, overheard by accident. She was watching as Ron Boci walked through the broken glass—saw his left foot come down hard on a sliver at least four inches long—but he seemed not to notice, didn't even flinch. His elbow brushed against her again.

He was watching her, smiling. He said, in a slow, easy voice, "I didn't know Tony Grazia had a kid, how long ago was that? *You* don't look like you ever had any baby."

Beatrice said stiffly, "There's lots of things you don't know."

"I saw you last night at the Hi-Lo but you sure as hell didn't see me," Beatrice's father told her across the supper table. His face was beefy and damp with perspiration. "Ten, ten-thirty. You sure as hell didn't notice *me.*"

It was late July and very hot. They'd had a heat spell for almost a week. Beatrice and her mother had set up a table in the living room, where it was cooler, but the effort hadn't made much difference. Beatrice's arms stuck unpleasantly to the surface of the table and her thighs stuck against her chair. She could see that her father was angry—his face was red and mottled with anger—but he didn't intend to say much in front of Beatrice's mother.

"I wasn't at the Hi-Lo very long," Beatrice said. "I don't even remember."

"Wearing sunglasses in the dark, *dark* glasses," Beatrice's father said with a snort of laughter, "like a movie star or something."

"That was just a joke," Beatrice said. "For five minutes. I had them on for five minutes and then I took them off."

"Okay," her father said, chewing his food. "Just wanted you to know."

"I just went out with some friends," she said.

"Okay," her father said.

After a while Beatrice said, "I don't need anybody spying on me, I'm not a kid. I'm twenty years old."

"You're a married woman," Beatrice's father said.

Beatrice's mother tried to interrupt but neither of them paid her any attention.

"If I want to go out with some friends," Beatrice said, her voice rising, "that's my business."

"I didn't see any *friends*, I saw only that one guy," Beatrice's father said. "As long as you know what you're doing."

Beatrice had stopped eating. She said nothing. She sat with her elbows on the table, staring and staring until her vision slipped out of focus. She could look at something—a glass saltshaker, a jar of mustard—until finally she wasn't seeing it and she wasn't thinking of anything and she wasn't aware of her surroundings either. In the past, when she lived at home, lapsing into one of these spells at the supper table could be dangerous—her father had slapped her awake more than once. But now he wouldn't. Now he probably wouldn't even touch her.

"Do you like this?" Ron Boci was saying.

Beatrice woke slowly. "No," she said. "Wait."

"Do you like *this*?" Ron said, laughing.

"No. Please. Wait." Her voice was muffled, groggy, she had dreamed she was suffocating and now she couldn't breathe. "Wait," she said.

After a while he said, "Christ, are you crying?"—and she said no. She was sobbing a little, or maybe laughing. Her head spun, Jesus she was hung over, at first she almost didn't know where she was, only that she didn't ever want to leave.

At work in the post office those long hours—waiting for the Clinton Street bus—changing the baby's diaper, her fingers so swift and practiced my God you'd think she had been doing this all her life—she found herself thinking of him. Of him and of it, what he did to her. That was it. That was the only thing. Sometimes the thought of him hit her so hard she felt a stabbing sensation in the pit of the belly, between her legs. She never thought of her husband, sometimes she went for hours without thinking of her baby. Once, changing his diaper, she pricked him and he began to cry angrily, red-faced, astonished, furious; she picked him up she held him in her arms she buried her face against him begging to be forgiven but the baby just kept crying: hot and wriggling and kicking and crying. Like he doesn't know who I am, Beatrice thought. Like he doesn't trust me.

Ron Boci's driver's license had been suspended for a year but in his line of work, as he explained, he had to use a car fairly often, especially for short distances in the city. He needed to make deliveries and he couldn't always trust his buddies.

He made his deliveries at night, he told Beatrice. During the day there was too much risk, his face was too well known in certain neighborhoods.

He usually borrowed his brother's '84 Dodge. Not in the best condition, it'd been around, Ron said, had taken some hard use. His own car, a new Century, white, red leather inside, wire wheels, vinyl roof, stereo—he'd totaled it last January out on the highway. Hit some ice, went into a skid, it all happened pretty fast. Totaled, Ron said with a soft whistle, smiling at Beatrice. He'd walked away from the crash, though, just a few scratches, bloody nose—"Not like the poor fuckers in the other car."

Beatrice stared. "So you were almost killed," she said.

"Hell no," Ron said, "didn't I just tell you? I walked away on my own two feet."

(Once Beatrice had happened to remark to Tony that he was lucky, real lucky about something. The precise reason for the remark she no longer remembered but she remembered Tony's quick reply: "Shit," he said, "you make your own luck.")

Manslaughter should have meant—how many years in prison? Not very many compared to a sentence for first-degree murder, or even second-degree murder, but, still, people in the neighborhood were astonished to hear that a governing board called the state appeals court had overturned Eddie Farrell's conviction. Like that!—"overturned" his conviction on a technicality that had to do with the judge's remarks while the jury was in the courtroom!

"Christ, I can't believe it," Beatrice's father said, tapping the newspaper with a forefinger. "I mean—*Jesus.* How do those asshole lawyers do it?"

So Eddie Farrell was free, suddenly. Released from the county house of detention and back home.

It was no secret that Eddie had killed his wife but people had been saying all along she'd asked for it, she'd asked for it for years, knowing

Eddie had a nasty temper (like all the Farrells). Beatrice was stunned, didn't know what to think. And didn't want to talk about it. Her father said, laughing angrily, "It says here that Eddie Farrell told a reporter 'I was innocent before, and I'm innocent now.'"

Word got around the neighborhood: Eddie hadn't any hard feelings toward people who'd testified against him at the trial. He guessed they had to tell the truth as they saw it, they'd been subpoenaed and all. He guessed they didn't mean him any personal injury.

Now, he said, he hoped everybody would forget. *He* wasn't the kind of guy to nurse a grudge.

Beatrice's mother heard from a woman friend that Tony was back in town—someone had seen him with one of his brothers over on Holland Avenue. One day, pushing Danny in the stroller, Beatrice thought she heard someone come up behind her, she had a feeling it was Tony, but she didn't look around: just kept pushing the stroller. In Woolworth's window she saw the reflection of a young kid in a T-shirt striding past her. It wasn't Tony and she was happy with herself for not being frightened. You don't have any claim on me, she would tell him. I'm twenty years old. I have my own life.

The rumor that Tony Grazia was back in town must have been a lie, because Beatrice received another postcard from him at the beginning of August. He'd written only hello, asked how she and Danny were, how the weather was up north—it was hot as hell, he said, down there. *Hot as hell* was underscored. Since there was no return address Beatrice couldn't reply to the card. I have my own life, she was going to tell him, all her anger gone quiet and smooth.

It was meant to be a joke in the household, Tony's three postcards Scotch-taped on the back of the bathroom door, each the same photo of a Gulf of Mexico sunset.

"You're getting a strange sense of humor," Beatrice's father told her.

"Maybe I always had one," Beatrice said.

Later that week Beatrice was in the shower at Ron Boci's, lathering herself vigorously under her arms, between her legs, between her toes, when she felt a draft of cooler air—she heard the bathroom door open and close. "Hey," she called out, "don't come in here. I don't want you in here."

He'd said he was going out for a pack of cigarettes but now he yanked open the scummy glass door to the stall and stepped inside, naked, grinning. He clapped his hands over his eyes and said, "Don't you look at me, honey, and I won't look at you." Beatrice laughed wildly. They were so close she couldn't see him anyway—the skinny length of him, the hard fleshy rod erect between his legs, the way coarse black hairs grew on his thighs and legs, even on the backs of his pale toes.

They struggled together, they nipped and bit at each other's lips, still a little high from the joint they'd shared, and the bottle of dago wine. Beatrice wanted to work up a soapy lather on Ron Boci's chest but he knocked the bar of soap out of her hands. He gripped her hard by the buttocks, lifted her toward him, pushed and poked against her until he entered her, already thrusting, pumping, hard. Beatrice clutched at him, her arms around his neck, around his shoulders, her eyes shut tight in pain. It was the posture, the angle, that hurt. The rough tile wall of the shower stall against her back. "Hold still," he said, and she did. She locked herself against him in terror of falling. "Hold still," he said, grunting, his voice edged with impatience.

Later they shared another joint, and Beatrice cut slices of a melon, a rich seedy overripe cantaloupe she'd bought him from the open-air market. Though it was on the edge of being rotten it still tasted delicious; juice ran down their chins. Beatrice stared at herself in Ron Boci's bread knife, which must have been newly purchased, it was so sharp, the blade so shiny.

"I can see myself in it," Beatrice said softly, staring. "Like a mirror."

One Saturday night in the fall Ron Boci played a sly little trick on Beatrice.

They were going out, they were going on a double date with another couple, and who should come by to Ron's apartment to pick them up but Eddie Farrell? He was driving a new green Chevy Camaro; his girlfriend was a slight acquaintance of Beatrice's from high school, named Iris O'Mara.

Beatrice's expression must have been comical because both Eddie and Ron burst out laughing at her. Eddie stuck out his hand, grinning, and said, "Hey Beatrice, no hard feelings, okay? Not on *my* side." Ron nudged her forward, whispered something in her ear she didn't catch. She saw her hand go out and she saw Eddie Farrell take it, as if they were characters in a movie. Was this happening? Was she doing this? She didn't even know if, beneath her shock, she was surprised.

"No hard feelings, honey: not on *my* side," Eddie repeated.

He was cheery, expansive, his old self. Grateful to be out, he said, and to be *alive*.

The focus of attention, however, was Eddie's new Camaro. He demonstrated, along lower Tice, how powerfully it accelerated—from zero to forty miles an hour *in under twenty seconds.* Hell, these were only city streets, traffic lights and all that shit, he'd really cut loose when they got out on the highway.

Ron and Beatrice were sitting in the back seat of the speeding car but Ron and Eddie carried on a conversation in quick staccato exchanges. Iris shifted around to smile back at Beatrice. She was a redhead, petite, startlingly pretty, Beatrice's age though she looked younger. Her eyelids were dusted with something silvery and glittering and her long, beautifully shaped fingernails were painted frosty pink. To be friendly she asked Beatrice a few questions—about Beatrice's baby, about her parents—*not* about Tony—but with all the windows down and the wind rushing in it was impossible to talk.

Eddie drove out of town by the quickest route, using his brakes at the intersections, careful about running red lights: he wasn't going to take any chances ever again, he said. It was a warm muggy autumn night but Beatrice had begun to shiver and couldn't seem to stop. She wore stylish white nylon trousers that flared at the ankle, a light-textured maroon top, open-toed sandals with a two-inch heel, she looked good but the goddamned wind was whipping her hair like crazy and it seemed to be getting colder every minute. Ron Boci noticed her shivering finally and laid his arm warm and heavy and hard around her shoulders, pulling her against him in a gesture that was playful, but loving: "Hey honey," he said, "is this a little better?"

True Romance

RON HANSEN

I T WAS STILL NIGHT OUT and my husband was shaving at the kitchen sink so he could hear the morning farm report and I was peeling bacon into the skillet. I hardly slept a wink with Gina acting up, and that croupy cough of hers. I must've walked five miles. Half of Ivan's face was hanging in the circle mirror, the razor was scraping the soap from his cheek, and pigs weren't dollaring like they ought to. And that was when the phone rang and it was Annette, my very best friend, giving me the woeful news.

Ivan squeaked his thumb on the glass to spy the temperature—still cold—then wiped his face with a paper towel, staring at me with puzzlement as I made known my shock and surprise. I took the phone away from my ear and said, "Honey? Something's killed one of the cows!"

He rushed over to the phone and got to talking to Annette's husband, Slick. Slick saw it coming from work—Slick's mainly on night shift; the Caterpillar plant. Our section of the county is on a party line: the snoops were getting their usual earful. I turned out the fire under the skillet. His appetite would be spoiled. Ivan and Slick went over the same ground again; I poured coffee and sugar and stirred a spoon around in a cup, just as blue as I could be, and when Ivan hung up I handed the cup to him.

He said, "I could almost understand it if they took the meat, but Slick says it looked like it was just plain ripped apart."

I walked the telephone back to the living room and switched on every single light. Ivan wasn't saying anything. I opened my robe and gave Gina the left nipple, which wasn't so standing-out and sore, and I sat in the big chair under a shawl. I got the feeling that eyes were on me.

Ivan stood in the doorway in his underpants and Nebraska sweatshirt, looking just like he did in high school. I said, "I'm just sick about the cow."

He said, "You pay your bills, you try and live simple, you pray to the Lord for guidance, but Satan can still find a loophole, can't he? He'll trip you up every time."

"Just the idea of it is giving me the willies," I said.

Ivan put his coffee cup on the floor and snapped on his gray coveralls. He sat against the high chair. "I guess I'll give the sheriff a call and then go look at the damage."

"I want to go with you, okay?"

The man from the rendering plant swerved a winch truck up the pasture until the swinging chain cradle was over the cow. His tires skidded green swipes on grass that was otherwise white with frost. I scrunched up in the pickup with the heater going to beat the band and Gina asleep on the seat. Ivan slumped in the sheriff's car and swore out a complaint. The man from the rendering plant threw some hydraulic levers and the engine revved to unspool some cable, making the cradle clang against the bumper.

I'd never seen the fields so pretty in March. Every acre was green winter wheat or plowed earth or sandhills the color of camels. The lagoon was as black and sleek as a grand piano.

Gina squinched her face up and then discovered a knuckle to chew as the truck engine raced again; and when the renderer hoisted the cow up, a whole stream of stuff poured out of her and dumped on the ground like boots. I slaughtered one or two in my time. I could tell which organs were missing.

Ivan made his weary way up the hill on grass that was greasy with blood, then squatted to look at footprints that were all walked over by cattle. The man from the plant said something and Ivan said something back, calling him Dale, and then Ivan slammed the pickup door behind him. He wiped the fog from inside the windshield with his softball cap. "You didn't bring coffee, did you?"

I shook my head as he blew on his fingers. He asked, "What good are ya then?" but he was smiling. He said, "I'm glad our insurance is paid up."

"I'm just sick about it," I said.

Ivan put the truck in gear and drove it past the feeding cattle, giving them a look-over. "I gotta get my sugar beets in."

I thought: the cow's heart, and the female things.

* * *

Around noon Annette came over in Slick's Trans Am and we ate pecan rolls hot from the oven as she got the romance magazines out of her grocery bag and began reading me the really good stories. Gina played on the carpet next to my chair. You have to watch the little booger every second because she'll put in her mouth what most people wouldn't step on. Annette was four months pregnant but it hardly showed—just the top snap of her jeans was undone—and I was full of uncertainty about the outcome. Our daytime visits give us the opportunity to speak candidly about things like miscarriages or the ways in which we are ironing out our problems with our husbands, but on this occasion Annette was giggling about some goofy woman who couldn't figure out why marriage turned good men into monsters, and I got the ugly feeling that I was being looked at by a peeping tom.

Annette put the magazine in her lap and rapidly flipped pages to get to the part where the story was continued and I gingerly picked up Gina and, without saying a peep to Annette, walked across the carpet and spun around. Annette giggled again and said, "Do you suppose this actually happened?" and I said yes, pulling my little girl tight against me. Annette said, "Doesn't she just crack you *up*?" and I simply kept peering out the window. I couldn't stop myself.

That night I took another stroll around the property and then poured diet cola into a glass at the kitchen sink, satisfying my thirst. I could see the light of the sixty-watt bulb in the barn and the cows standing up to the fence and rubbing their throats and chins. The wire gets shaggy with the stuff; looks just like orange doll hair. Ivan got on the intercom and his voice was puny, like it was trapped in a paper cup. "Come on out and help me, will you, Riva?"

"Right out," is what I said.

I tucked another blanket around Gina in the baby crib and clomped outside in Ivan's rubber boots. They jingled as I crossed the barnyard. The cattle stared at me. One of the steers got up on a lady and triumphed for a while but she walked away and he dropped. My flashlight speared whenever I bumped it.

Ivan was kneeling on straw, shoving his arm in a rubber glove. An alarm clock was on the sill. His softball cap was off and his long brown hair was flying wild as he squatted beside the side-laying cow. Her tail whisked a board so he tied it to her leg with twine. She was swollen wide with the calf. My husband reached up inside her and the cow lifted her head indignantly, then settled down and chewed her tongue. Ivan said, "P.U., cow! You stink!" He was in her up to his biceps, seemed like.

"You going to cut her?"

He shook his head as he snagged the glove off and plunked it down in a water bucket. "Dang calf's kaput!" He glared at his medicine box and said, "How many is that? Four out of eight? I might as well give it up."

I swayed the flashlight beam along the barn. Window. Apron. Pitchfork. Rope. Lug wrench. Sickle. Baling wire. And another four-paned window that was so streaked with pigeon goop it might as well've been slats. But it was there that the light caught a glint of an eye and my heart stopped. I stepped closer to persuade myself it wasn't just an apparition and what I saw abruptly disappeared.

Ivan grinded the tractor ignition and got the thing going, then raced it backwards into the barn, not shutting the engine down but slapping it out of gear and hopping down to the ground. He said, "Swing that flashlight down on this cow's contraption, will ya, Riva?" and there was some messy tugging and wrestling as he yanked the calf's legs out and attached them to the tractor hitch with wire. He jumped up to the spring seat and jerked into granny, creeping forward with his gaze on the cow. She groaned with agony and more leg appeared and then the shut-eyed calf head. My husband crawled the tractor forward more and the calf came out in a surge. I suctioned gunk out of its throat with a bulb syringe and squirted it into the straw but the calf didn't quiver or pant; she was patient as meat and her tongue spilled onto the paint tarp.

Ivan scowled and sank to his knees by the calf. The mother cow struggled up and sniffed the calf and began licking off its nose in the way she'd been taught, but even she gave up in a second or two and hung her head low with grief.

"Do you know what killed it?"

Ivan just gaped and said, "You explain it." He got up and plunged his arms into the bucket. He smeared water on his face.

I crouched down and saw that the calf was somehow split open and all her insides were pulled out.

After the sheriff and the man from the rendering plant paid their visits, the night was just about shot. Ivan completed his cold weather chores, upsetting the cattle with his earliness, and I pored over Annette's romance magazines, gaining support from each disappointment.

Ivan and I got some sleep and even Gina cooperated by being good as can be. Ivan arose at noon but he was cranky and understandably depressed about our calamities, so I switched off *All My Children* and suggested we go over to Slick's place and wake him up and party.

Annette saw I was out of sorts right away and she generously agreed to make our supper. She could see through me like glass. At two we watched *General Hospital*, which was getting crazier by the week according to Annette—she thought they'd be off in outer space next, but I said they were just keeping up with this wild and woolly world we live in. Once our story was over we made a pork roast and boiled potatoes with chives and garlic butter, which proved to be a big hit. Our husbands worked through the remaining light of day, crawling over Slick's farm machinery, each with wrenches in his pockets and grease on his skin like warpaint.

Annette said, "You're doing all right for yourself, aren't you, Riva."

"I could say the same for you, you know."

Here I ought to explain that Annette went steady with Ivan in our sophomore year, and I suspect she's always regretted giving him to me. If I'm any judge of character, her thoughts were on that subject as we stood at the counter and Slick and Ivan came in for supper and cleaned up in the washroom that's off the kitchen. Annette then had the gall to say, "Slick and me are going through what you and Ivan were a couple of months ago."

Oh, no you're not! I wanted to say, but I didn't even give her the courtesy of a reply.

"You got everything straightened out, though, didn't you."

I said, "Our problems were a blessing in disguise."

"I know exactly what you mean," she said.

"Our marriage is as full of love and vitality as any girl could wish for."

Her eyes were even a little misty. "I'm so happy for you, Riva!"

And she was; you could tell she wasn't pretending like she was during some of our rocky spots in the past.

Slick dipped his tongue in a spoon that he lifted from a saucepan and went out of his way to compliment Annette—unlike at least one husband I could mention. Ivan pushed down the spring gizmo on the toaster and got the feeling back in his fingers by working them over the toaster slots. My husband said in that put-down way of his, "Slick was saying it could be UFOs."

"I got an open mind on the subject," said Slick, and Ivan did his snickering thing.

I asked if we could please change the topic of conversation to something a little more pleasant.

Ivan gave me his angry smile. "Such as what? Relationships?"

Slick and Annette were in rare form that night but Ivan was pretty much of a poop until Slick gave him a number. Ivan bogarted the joint and Slick rolled up another and by the time Annette and I got the dishes into the sink, the men were swapping a roach on the living room floor and tooling Gina's playthings around. Annette opened the newspaper to the place that showed which dopey program was on the TV that evening. Slick asked if Ivan planted the marijuana seeds he gave us and Ivan shrugged. Which meant no. Slick commenced tickling Annette. She scooched back against the sofa and fought him off, slapping at his paws and pleading for help. She screamed, "Slick! You're gonna make me pee on myself!"

Ivan clicked through the channels but he was so stoned all he could say was, "What *is* that?"

Annette giggled but got out, "*Creature from the Black Lagoon!*"

I plopped Gina on top of her daddy's stomach and passed around a roach that was pinched with a hairpin. I asked Ivan, "Are you really ripped?" and Ivan shrugged. Which meant yes.

The movie was a real shot in the arm for our crew. My husband rested his pestered head in my lap and I rearranged his long hair. There was a close-up of the creature and I got such a case of the stares from looking at it you'd think I was making a photograph.

Ivan shifted to frown at me. "How come you're not saying anything?"

And I could only reply, "I'm just really ripped."

Days passed without event and I could persuade myself that the creature had gone off to greener pastures. However, one evening when Ivan was attending a meeting of the parish council, my consternation only grew stronger. Gina and I got home from the grocery store and I parked the pickup close by the feed lot so I could hear if she squalled as I was forking out silage. Hunger was making the cattle ornery. They straggled over and jostled each other, resting their long jaws on each other's shoulders, bawling *mom* in the night. The calves lurched and stared as I closed the gate behind me. I collared my face from the cold and as I was getting into the truck, a cry like you hear at a slaughterhouse flew up from the lagoon.

I thought, I ought to ignore it; or I ought to go to the phone; but I figured what I really ought to do is make certain that I was seeing everything right, that I wasn't making things up.

Famous last words!

I snuggled Gina in the baby crib and went out along the pasture road, looking at the eight o'clock night that was closing in all around me. I glided down over a hill and a stray calf flung its tail in my headlights as its tiny mind chugged through its options. A yard away its mother was on her side and swollen up big as two hay bales. I got out into the spring cold and inspected the cow even though I knew she was a goner, and then I looked at the woods and the moonlighted lagoon and I could make out just enough of a blacker image to put two and two together and see that it was the creature dragging cow guts through the grass.

The gun rack only carried fishing rods on it, but there was an angel food cake knife wedged behind the pickup's tool box and that was what I took with me on my quest, my scalp prickling with fright and goosebumps on every inch of me. The chill was mean, like you'd slapped your hand against gravel. The wind seemed to gnaw at the trees. You're making it up, I kept praying, and when I approached the lagoon and saw nothing I was pleased and full of hope.

The phone rang many times the next day, but I wouldn't get up to answer it. I stayed in the room upstairs, hugging a pillow like a body, aching for the beginning of some other life like a girl in a Rosemary Rogers book. Once again Annette provided an escape from my doldrums by speeding over in the orange Trans Am—her concern for me and her eternal spunk are always a great boost for my spirits.

I washed up and went outside with Gina, and Annette said, "What on earth is wrong with your phone?"

I only said, "I was hoping you'd come over," and Annette slammed the car door. She hugged me like a girlfriend and the plastic over the porch screens popped. The wind was making mincemeat of the open garbage can. And yet we sat outside on the porch steps with some of Slick's dope rolled in Zig-Zag papers. I zipped Gina into a parka with the wind so blustery. She was trying to walk. She'd throw her arms out and buck ahead a step or two and then plump down hard on her butt. The marijuana wasn't rolled tight enough and the paper was sticking all the time to my lip. I looked at the barn, the silo, the road, seeing nothing of the creature, seeing only my husband urging the tractor up out of a ditch with Slick straddling the gang plow's hook-ups and hoses. Slick's a master at hydraulics. The plow swung wide and banged as Ivan established his right to the road, then Ivan shifted the throttle up and mud flew from the tires. One gloved hand rested on a fender lamp and he looked past me to our daughter, scowling and acting put-out, then they turned into the yard and Annette waved. Ivan lifted his right index finger just a tad, his greeting, then turned the steering wheel hand-over-hand, bouncing high in the spring seat as Slick clung on for dear life.

Annette said, "My baby isn't Ivan's, you know."

I guess I sighed with the remembering of those painful times.

Annette said, "I'm glad we were able to stay friends."

"Me too," I said, and I scooched out to see my little girl with an angel food cake knife in her hands, waddling over to me. I yelled, "Gina! You little snot! Where'd you get that?"

She gave it to me and wiped her hands on her coat. "Dut," Gina said, and though my husband would probably have reprimanded her, I knelt down and told her how she mustn't play with knives and what a good girl she was to bring it right to me. She didn't listen for very long and I put the knife in my sweater pocket for the time being.

Annette was looking peculiar and I could tell she wanted an explanation, but then there was a commotion in the cattle pen and we looked to where Ivan and Slick were pushing cow rumps aside in order to get close to the trough. They glared at something on the ground out there, and I glanced at the cake knife again, seeing the unmistakable signs of blood.

"I'm going out to the cattle pen," I imparted. "You keep Gina with you."

Annette said, "I hope your stock is okay."

The day was on the wane as I proceeded across the yard and onto the cowpath inside the pen, the cake knife gripped in my right hand in my sweater pocket. The cattle were rubbing against the fence and ignorantly surging toward the silage in the feed trough. Slick was saying, "You oughta get a photograph, Ivan." My husband kept his eyes on one spot, his gloved hands on his hips, his left boot experimenting by moving something I couldn't see.

I got the cattle to part by tilting against them with all my weight. They were heavy as Cadillacs. And I made my toilsome way to my husband's side only to be greeted with a look of ill tidings and with an inquiry that was to justify all my grim forebodings. He asked, "Do you know how it happened, Riva?"

I regarded ground that was soggy with blood and saw the green creature that I'd so fervently prayed was long gone. He was lying on his scaly back and his yellow eyes were glowering as if the being were still enraged over the many stabbings into his heart. Death had been good for his general attractiveness, glossing over his many physical flaws and giving him a child-like quality that tugged at my sympathy.

Again Ivan nudged the being with his boot, acting like it was no more than a cow, and asking me with great dismay, "How'd the dang thing get killed, do ya think?"

And I said, "Love. Love killed it. Love as sharp as a knife."

Slick gazed upon me strangely and my husband looked at me with grief as I sank to the earth among the cattle, feeling the warmth of their breathing. I knew then that the anguish I'd experienced over those past many months was going to disappear, and that my life, over which I'd despaired for so long, was going to keep changing and improving with each minute of the day.

Sweet Talk

STEPHANIE VAUGHN

SOMETIMES SAM AND I loved each other more when we were angry. "Day," I called him, using the surname instead of Sam. "Day, Day, Day!" It drummed against the walls of the apartment like a distress signal.

"Ah, my beautiful lovebird," he said. "My sugar sweet bride."

For weeks I had been going through the trash trying to find out whether he had other women. Once I found half a ham sandwich with red marks that could have been lipstick. Or maybe catsup. This time I found five slender cigarette butts.

"Who smokes floral-embossed cigarettes?" I said. He had just come out of the shower, and droplets of water gleamed among the black hairs of his chest like tiny knife points. "Who's the heart-attack candidate you invite over when I'm out?" I held the butts beneath his nose like a small bouquet. He slapped them to the floor and we stopped speaking for three days. We moved through the apartment without touching, lay stiffly in separate furrows of the bed, desire blooming and withering between us like the invisible petals of a night-blooming cereus.

We finally made up while watching a chess tournament on television. Even though we wouldn't speak or make eye contact, we were sitting in front of the sofa moving pieces around a chess board as an announcer explained World Championship strategy to the viewing audience. Our shoulders touched but we pretended not to notice. Our knees touched, and our elbows. Then we both reached for the black bishop and our hands touched. We made love on the carpet and kept our eyes open so that we could look at each other defiantly.

We were living in California and had six university degrees between us and no employment. We lived on food stamps, job interviews and games.

"How many children did George Washington, the father of our country, have?"

"No white ones but lots of black ones."

"How much did he make when he was Commander of the Revolutionary Army?"

"He made a big to-do about refusing a salary but later presented the first Congress with a bill for a half million dollars."

"Who was the last slave-owning president?"

"Ulysses S. Grant."

We had always been good students.

It was a smoggy summer. I spent long hours in air-conditioned supermarkets, touching the cool cans, feeling the cold plastic stretched across packages of meat. Sam left the apartment for whole afternoons and evenings. He was in his car somewhere, opening it up on the freeway, or maybe just spending time with someone I didn't know. We were mysterious with each other about our absences. In August we decided to move east, where a friend said he could get us both jobs at an unaccredited community college. In the meantime, I had invented a lover. He was rich and wanted to take me to an Alpine hotel, where mauve flowers cascaded over the stone walls of a terrace. Sometimes we drank white wine and watched the icy peaks of mountains shimmer gold in the sunset. Sometimes we returned to our room carrying tiny ceramic mugs of schnapps which had been given to us, in the German fashion, as we paid for an expensive meal.

In the second week of August, I found a pair of red lace panties at the bottom of the kitchen trash.

I decided to tell Sam I had a lover. I made my lover into a tall, blue-eyed blond, a tennis player on the circuit, a Phi Beta Kappa from Stanford who had offers from the movies. It was the tall blond part that needled Sam, who was dark and stocky.

"Did you pick him up at the beach?" Sam said.

"Stop it," I said, knowing that was a sure way to get him to ask more questions.

"Did you have your diaphragm in your purse?"

We were wrapping cups and saucers in newspaper and nesting them in the slots of packing boxes. "He was taller than you," I said, "but not as handsome."

Sam held a blue and white Dresden cup, my favorite wedding present, in front of my eyes. "You slut," he said, and let the cup drop to the floor.

"Very articulate," I said. "Some professor. The man of reason gets into an argument and he talks with broken cups. Thank you Alexander Dope."

That afternoon I failed the California drivers' test again. I made four right turns and drove over three of the four curbs. The highway patrolman pointed out that if I made one more mistake I was finished. I drove through a red light.

On the way back to the apartment complex, Sam squinted into the flatness of the expressway and would not talk to me. I put my blue-eyed lover behind the wheel. He rested a hand on my knee and smiled as he drove. He was driving me west, away from the Vista View Apartments, across the thin spine of mountains which separated our suburb from the sea. At the shore there would be seals frolicking among the rocks and starfish resting in tidal pools.

"How come you never take me to the ocean?" I said. "How come every time I want to go to the beach I have to call up a woman friend?"

"If you think you're going to Virginia with me," he said, "you're dreaming." He eased the car into our numbered space and put his head against the wheel. "Why did you have to do it?"

"I do not like cars," I said. "You know I have always been afraid of cars."

"Why did you have to sleep with that fag tennis player?" His head was still against the wheel. I moved closer and put my arm around his shoulders.

"Sam, I didn't. I made it up."

"Don't try to get out of it."

"I didn't, Sam. I made it up." I tried to kiss him. He let me put my mouth against his, but his lips were unyielding. They felt like the skin of an orange. "I didn't, Sam. I made it up to hurt you." I kissed him again and his mouth warmed against mine. "I love you, Sam. Please let me go to Virginia."

"George Donner," I read from the guidebook, "was sixty-one years old and rich when he packed up his family and left Illinois to cross the Great Plains, the desert, and the mountains into California." We were driving through the Sierras, past steep slopes and the deep shade of an evergreen forest, toward the Donner Pass, where in 1846 the Donner family had been trapped by an early snowfall. Some of them died and the rest ate the corpses of their relatives and their Indian guides to survive.

"Where are the bones?" Sam said, as we strolled past glass cases at the Donner Pass Museum. The cases were full of wagon wheels and harnesses. Above us a recorded voice described the courageous and enterprising spirit of American pioneers. A man standing nearby with a young boy turned to scowl at Sam. Sam looked at him and said loudly, "Where are the bones of the people they ate?" The man took the boy by the hand and started for the door. Sam said, "You call this American history?" and the man turned and said, "Listen, mister, I can get your license number." We laughed about that as we descended into the plain of the Great Basin desert in Nevada. Every few miles one of us would say the line and the other one would chuckle, and I felt as if we had been married fifty years instead of five, and that everything had turned out okay.

Ten miles east of Reno I began to sneeze. My nose ran and my eyes watered, and I had to stop reading the guidebook.

"I can't do this anymore. I think I've got an allergy."

"You never had an allergy in your life." Sam's tone implied that I had purposefully got the allergy so that I could not read the guidebook. We were riding in a second-hand van, a lusterless, black shoebox of a vehicle, which Sam had bought for the trip with the money he got from the stereo, the TV, and his own beautifully overhauled and rebuilt little sports car.

"Turn on the radio," I said.

"The radio is broken."

It was a hot day, dry and gritty. On either side of the freeway, a sagebrush desert stretched toward the hunched profiles of brown mountains. The mountains were so far away—the only landmarks within three hundred miles—that they did not whap by the windows like signposts, they floated above the plain of dusty sage and gave us the sense that we were not going anywhere.

"Are you trying to kill us?" I said when the speedometer slid past ninety.

Sam looked at the dash surprised and, I think, a little pleased that the van could do that much. "I'm getting hypnotized," he said. He thought about it for another mile and said, "If you had managed to get your license, you could do something on this trip besides blow snot into your hand."

"Don't you think we should call ahead to Elko for a motel room?"

"I might not want to stop at Elko."

"Sam, look at the map. You'll be tired when we get to Elko."

"I'll let you know when I'm tired."

We reached Elko at sundown, and Sam was tired. In the office of the Shangrila Motor Lodge we watched another couple get the last room. "I suppose you're going to be mad because I was right," I said.

"Just get in the van." We bought a sack of hamburgers and set out for Utah. Ahead of us a full moon rose, flat and yellow like a fifty-dollar gold piece, then lost its color as it rose higher. We entered the Utah salt flats, the dead floor of a dead ocean. The salt crystals glittered like snow under the white moon. My nose stopped running, and I felt suddenly lucid and calm.

"Has he been in any movies?" Sam said.

"Has who been in any movies?"

"The fag tennis player."

I had to think a moment before I recalled my phantom lover.

"He's not a fag."

"I thought you made him up."

"I did make him up but I didn't make up any fag."

A few minutes later he said, "You might at least sing something. You might at least try to keep me awake." I sang a few Beatles tunes, then Simon and Garfunkel, the Everly Brothers, and Elvis Presley. I worked my way back through my youth to a Girl Scout song I remembered as "Eye, Eye, Eye, Icky, Eye, Kai, A-nah." It was supposed to be sung around a campfire to remind the girls of their Indian heritage and the pleasures of surviving in the wilderness. "Ah woo, ah woo. Ah woo knee key chee," I sang. "I am now five years old," I said, and then I sang, "Home, Home on the Range," the song I remembered singing when I was a child going cross-country with my parents to visit some relatives. The only thing I remembered about that trip besides a lot of going to the bathroom in gas stations was that there were rules which made the traveling life simple. One was: do not hang over the edge of the front seat to talk to your mother or father. The other was: if you have to throw up, do it in the blue coffee can, the red one is full of cookies.

"It's just the jobs and money," I said. "It isn't us, is it?"

"I don't know," he said.

A day and a half later we crossed from Wyoming into Nebraska, the western edge of the Louisiana Purchase, which Thomas Jefferson had made so that we could all live in white, classical houses and be farmers. Fifty miles later the corn began, hundreds of miles of it, singing green from horizon to horizon. We began to relax and I had the feeling that we had survived the test of American geography. I put away our guidebooks and took out the dictionary. Matachin, mastigophobia, matutolypea. I tried to find words Sam didn't know.

He guessed all the definitions and was smug and happy behind the wheel. I reached over and put a hand on his knee. He looked at me and smiled. "Ah, my little buttercup," he said. "My sweet cream pie." I thought of my Alpine lover for the first time in a long while, and he was nothing more than mist over a distant mountain.

In a motel lobby near Omaha, we had to wait in line for twenty minutes behind three families. Sam put his arm around me and pulled a tennis ball out of his jacket. He bounced it on the thin carpet, tentatively, and when he saw it had enough spring, he dropped into an exaggerated basketball player's crouch and ran across the lobby. He whirled in front of the cigarette machine and passed the ball to me. I laughed and threw it back. Several people had turned to stare at us. Sam winked at them and dunked the ball through an imaginary net by the wall clock, then passed the ball back to me. I dribbled around a stack of suitcases and went for a lay-up by a hanging fern. I misjudged and knocked the plant to the floor. What surprised me was that the fronds were plastic but the dirt was real. There was a huge mound of it on the carpet. At the registration desk, the clerk told us the motel was already full and that he could not find our name on the advance reservation list.

"Nebraska sucks eggs," Sam said loudly as we carried our luggage to the door. We spent the night curled up on the hard front seat of the van like boulders. The bony parts of our bodies kept bumping as we turned and rolled to avoid the steering wheel and dash. In the morning, my knees and elbows felt worn away, like the peaks of old mountains. We hadn't touched each other sexually since California.

"So she had big ta-ta's," I said. "She had huge ta-ta's and a bad-breath problem." We had pushed on through the corn, across Iowa, Illinois and Indiana, and the old arguments rattled along with us, like the pots and pans in the back of the van.

"She was a model," he said. He was describing the proprietress of the slender cigarettes and red panties.

"In a couple of years she'll have gum disease," I said.

"She was a model and she had a degree in literature from Oxford."

I didn't believe him, of course, but I felt the sting of his intention to hurt. "By the time she's forty she'll have emphysema."

"What would this trip be like without the melody of your voice," he said. It was dark, and taillights glowed on the road ahead of us like flecks of burning iron. I remembered how, when we were undergraduates attending different colleges, he used to write me letters which said: keep your skirts down and your knees together, don't let anyone get near your crunch. We always amused each other with our language.

"I want a divorce," I said in a motel room in Columbus, Ohio. We were propped against pillows on separate double beds watching a local program on Woody Hayes, the Ohio State football coach. The announcer was saying, "And here in front of the locker room is the blue and gold mat that every player must step on as he goes to and from the field. Those numbers are the score of last year's loss to Michigan." And I was saying, "Are you listening? I said I want a divorce when we get to Virginia."

"I'm listening."

"Don't you want to know why I want a divorce?"

"No."

"Well, do you think it's a good idea or a bad idea?"

"I think it's a good idea."

"You do?"

"Yes."

The announcer said, "And that is why the night before the big game Woody will be showing his boys reruns of the films *Patton* and *Bullitt*."

That night someone broke into the van and stole everything we owned except the suitcases we had with us in the motel room. They even stole the broken radio. We stood in front of the empty van and looked up and down the row of parked cars as if we expected to see another black van parked there, one with two pairs of skis and two tennis rackets slipped into the spaces between the boxes and the windows.

"I suppose you're going to say I'm the one who left the door unlocked," I said.

Sam sat on the curb. He sat on the curb and put his head into his hands. "No," he said. "It was probably me."

The policeman who filled out the report tried to write "Miscellaneous Household Goods" on the clipboarded form, but I made him list everything I could remember, as the three of us sat on the curb—the skis and rackets, the chess set, a baseball bat, twelve boxes of books, two rugs which I had braided, an oak bed frame Sam had refinished. I inventoried the kitchen items: two bread pans, two cake pans, three skillets. I mentioned every fork and every measuring cup and every

piece of bric-a-brac I could recall—the trash of our life, suddenly made
valuable by the theft. When the policeman had left without giving us
any hope of ever recovering our things, I told Sam I was going to
pack and shower. A half hour later when I came out with the suitcases,
he was still on the curb, sitting in the full sun, his cotton shirt beginning
to stain in wing shapes across his shoulder blades. I reached down
to touch him and he flinched. It was a shock—feeling the tremble of
his flesh, the vulnerability of it, and for the first time since California
I tried to imagine what it was like driving with a woman who said
she didn't want him, in a van he didn't like but had to buy in order
to travel to a possible job on the other side of the continent, which
might not be worth reaching.

On the last leg of the trip, Sam was agreeable and compliant. If I
wanted to stop for coffee, he stopped immediately. If I wanted him
to go slower in thick traffic, he eased his foot off the pedal without
a look of regret or annoyance. I got out the dictionary. Operose,
ophelimity, ophryitis. He said he'd never heard of any of those words.
Which president died in a bathtub? He couldn't remember. I tried to
sing to keep him company. He told me it wasn't necessary. I played
a few tunes on a comb. He gazed pleasantly at the freeway, so pleasantly that I could have made him up. I could have invented him and
put him on a mountainside terrace and set him going. "Sammy," I
said, "that stuff wasn't much. I won't miss it."
"Good," he said.

About three a.m. green exit signs began to appear announcing the
past and the future: Colonial Williamsburg, Jamestown, Yorktown,
Patrick Henry Airport. "Let's go to the beach," I said. "Let's just go
all the way to the edge of the continent." It was a ludicrous idea.
"Sure. Why not."
He drove on past Newport News and over an arching bridge towards Virginia Beach. We arrived there just at dawn and found our
way into a residential neighborhood full of small pastel houses and
sandy lawns. "Could we just stop right here?" I said. I had an idea.
I had a plan. He shrugged as if to say what the heck, I don't care,
and if you want to drive into the ocean that will be fine, too.
We were parked on a street that ran due east towards the water—I
could see just a glimmer of ocean between two hotels about a mile
away. "All right," I said, with the forced, brusque cheerfulness of a
high school coach. "Let's get out and do some stretching exercises."

Sam sat behind the wheel and watched me touch my toes. "Come on, Sammy. Let's get loose. We haven't done anything with our bodies since California." He yawned, got out of the van, and did a few arm rolls and toe touches. "All right now," I said. "Do you think a two-block handicap is about right?" He had always given me a two-block advantage during our foot races in California. He yawned again. "How about a one-and-a-half-block lead, then?" He crossed his arms and leaned against the van, watching me. I couldn't tell whether he had nodded, but I said anyway, "I'll give you a wave when I'm ready." I walked down the middle of the street past houses which had towels hanging over porch rails and toys lying on front walks. Even a mile from the water, I smelled the salt and seaweed in the air. It made me feel light-headed and for a moment I tried to picture Sam and myself in one of those houses with tricycles and toilet trainers and small latched gates. We had never discussed having a child. When I turned to wave, he was still leaning against the van.

I started out in a jog, then picked up the pace, and hit what seemed to be about the quarter-mile mark doing a fast easy run. Ahead of me the square of water between the two hotels was undulating with gold. I listened for the sound of Sam's footsteps but heard only the soft taps of my own tennis shoes. The square spread into a rectangle and the sky above it fanned out in ribs of orange and purple silk. I was afraid to look back. I was afraid that if I turned to see him, Sam might recede irretrievably into the merciless gray of the western sky. I slowed down in case I had gone too fast and he wanted to catch up. I concentrated on the water and listened to the still, heavy air. By the time I reached the three-quarters mark, I realized that I was probably running alone.

I hadn't wanted to lose him.

I wondered whether he had waited by the van or was already headed for Newport News. I imagined him at a phone booth calling another woman collect in California, and then I realized that I didn't actually know whether there was another woman or not, but I hoped there was and that she was rich and would send him money. I had caught my second wind and was breathing easily. I looked towards the shore without seeing it and was sorry I hadn't measured the distance and thought to clock it, since now I was running against time and myself, and then I heard him—the unmistakable sound of a sprint and the heavy, whooping intake of his breath. He passed me just as we crossed the main street in front of the hotels, and he reached the water twenty feet ahead of me.

Stephanie Vaughn

"Goddammit, Day," I said. "You were on the grass, weren't you?" We were walking along the hard, wet edge of the beach, breathing hard. "You were sneaking across those lawns. That's a form of cheating." I drummed his arm lightly with my fists pretending to beat him up. "I slowed down because I thought you weren't there." We leaned over from the waist, hands on our hips, breathing towards the sand. The water rolled up the berm near our feet and flickered like topaz.

"You were always a lousy loser," he said.

And I said, "You should talk."

Death Apples

MARY MORRIS

F OR REASONS that would never be clear to her, Rita Hoffman invited her mother to a Caribbean island to recover. Mrs. Hoffman had a lot to recover from. The divorce from her second husband being one. The death of her first husband being another. The death of her parents, of her firstborn in a car crash. In sum, Rita invited her mother to recover from her life.

Rita thought the island would be a perfect place. But there was nothing to do that Mrs. Hoffman liked to do. There was no shopping, no good restaurants, and not many white people. There were things about the island that Rita liked, though. She liked the lizards who blew up their red porous pouches and humped up and down when they seemed to be listening. She liked the little furry mongooses that slunk across the roads, bellies to the ground, and she liked to look at the bodies of the West Indian men. She liked swimming among the barracuda of Ginger Bay. And she liked the warning signs painted on the manchineel trees. Killer trees. Trees that if you touched them would take your life away. Rita liked all the things she discovered during their first three days while her mother slept.

Shortly after they arrived at the tiny island a few hundred miles east of Puerto Rico, Mrs. Hoffman said, "Honey, your mother needs her beauty rest," and she went to bed. Rita didn't know what to make of it. Her mother got up at noon, walked out to the patio, went back to bed, and slept until cocktails. Then she made it through dinner and went to bed again. Rita figured her mother was just tired, but by the third day this period of rest seemed to be getting a little long. It occurred to Rita that perhaps her mother had come here to die.

So the next day Rita rented a moped for her mother. "Mom," she said, waking her with a tray of coffee and rolls and fresh-squeezed orange juice, "it's time you tested your wings."

"My wings seem a bit weary," her mother replied. But then she said, "You're right. I suppose I should venture forth." Mrs. Hoffman got out of bed. She opened her striped cotton hospital robe, the only thing she'd kept—except for his name—that had belonged to Rita's father, whom she had nursed for the last six months of his life. At night, while her father lay upstairs, dying, Rita would go downstairs and in the darkened living room see just one red light, from a cigarette, glowing in the dark. Her mother would say, "Honey, is that you?" and Rita would sneak back up the stairs.

Mrs. Hoffman let the robe slip off her shoulders and onto the ground. Rita saw her mother, standing there, naked. Her thighs and hips were turning to flab; her breasts sagged. In her legs, thick blue veins like rivers twisted and ran. She had borne three children, and the oldest, James, had died in a car crash, speeding on an L.A. freeway, though the police said he wouldn't have had a scratch on him if he'd been wearing his seat belt. James had always been reckless, like their mother. Rita had her mother's body, she knew that, and now she could see what she'd look like in twenty-five years. Everything in Rita's life had thus far been directed toward one simple goal, the only real goal in Rita's life. She was determined not to grow up to be like her mother.

Mrs. Hoffman had never been on a moped before, but she was willing to try anything once. On their way to the moped place, Mrs. Hoffman glanced into all the windows of shops. She looked at the rose-colored shells and the T-shirts that read I'VE DONE IT AT THE BOTTOM OF THE SEA. She wore dark glasses with pale bule rims that winged up at the sides, and she lifted them from time to time, staring at her own reflection in the glass. "I don't look so bad, do I? For an old dame?"

Rita looked at her mother in the Bermuda shorts that didn't quite fit, the polo shirt that clung too tightly to her breasts. "You look terrific, Mom."

Mrs. Hoffman tucked her arm through her daughter's. "I needed to get away." As they walked, her mother looked at her reflection again. A group of Caribbean men on their way to the sugar cane fields watched them as they walked past. The men had dark skin and arms with thick working muscles. Their bellies were taut. They were accustomed to the white women who came down from the north. Sometimes they made love to them. Sometimes they married them. Rita looked at the men as they passed, and Rita supposed that the men had no right to look at her in that way. Rita supposed incorrectly. The men were not looking at her in that way. They were looking mostly at Rita's mother.

Just before they reached the moped place, her mother paused. "How could it have slipped my mind? I forgot to tell you. Did you hear about Russ Stapleton?" Rita couldn't help being stunned. Her mother hadn't mentioned Russ to her in ten years, perhaps more. Not since her father died. But Rita was certain, if she thought about it, that she hadn't spent a single day without thinking about him. And if Rita thought about it further, she knew there was no reason that her mother should even mention Russ Stapleton to her, yet her mother had said it in such a way that Rita had to assume her mother knew something about Rita that Rita didn't know her mother knew.

"He's getting divorced."

"Oh," Rita said. They had reached the moped place. Charlie, the huge fair-skinned man with fifteen tattoos—Rita had counted fifteen, up and down his arms—greeted them. He pointed to the moped Rita's mother was supposed to ride. Rita turned to her mother. "Is he really getting divorced? That's incredible."

"Oh." Her mother nodded. "That doesn't surprise me so much. I was more surprised when he didn't marry you."

Mrs. Hoffman took to the moped right away, after a brief lesson from Charlie. He sent them off on the ocean road, heading toward the ruins of Gustavberg, the old sugar cane plantation at the tip of the island. Rita checked to make sure her mother could drive the thing up the hill and use her brakes and not sail over the handlebars. And when Rita was sure of that, she took off.

Rita liked to fly. She liked to ride horses and bikes and motorcycles. She liked fast-moving trains and low-flying planes. When she'd been younger, she'd been reckless, like James. She'd liked riding on Russ Stapleton's Harley when he used to pick her up at night in the canyon and take her down to the sea.

It wasn't Russ who gave Rita her first kiss. It was some other boy, now faded into the memory of so many other nondescript boys who'd kissed her during spin the bottle or after movie dates. But it didn't matter who the others were or how old or when it happened, because for Rita there was only one night that mattered.

It was the night when Russ came over and said he wanted to talk, so they'd gone down to the ocean. But when they got there, he didn't seem to have anything to say. They'd been friends since they were children, and Leslie, Russ's girlfriend, was a good friend of Rita's. Rita asked him if anything was wrong with Leslie, and Russ had shaken his head. He'd taken her by the hand and walked in silence, the Pacific roaring at their feet. Then, suddenly, without a word, there on the beach with the warm breeze blowing off the ocean, he'd kissed her. She felt as if there were no world beyond the world of his lips on her lips. Nothing had prepared her for this. Nothing would ever be like it again. That kiss had wakened Rita as if she'd been sleeping her entire life.

She shuddered as the moped zipped along the ocean road. Rita had spent most of her life falling in or out of love with the wrong men. And not a single one of them had ever done for her what Russ did when he kissed her that night on the beach. And not a single one had ever done to her what Russ did when he married Leslie.

Black men grinned at Rita and her mother as they took the curves on their mopeds. Mrs. Hoffman waved and laughed. Defiantly she passed Rita. Most of the black people of the island were descendants of the slaves who had worked that plantation, and the sugar cane industry had declined since the slaves were freed. Mrs. Hoffman and Rita zipped along, waving at descendants of slaves, until they came near the ruins of the sugar cane plantation.

At the plantation they parked their mopeds and walked. They walked past beautiful trees named flamboyant, the frangipani, the genip, the sugar pear. And the manchineel. When they got to the manchineel, Mrs. Hoffman stopped. She stopped at the big red spot on the trees and the sign beneath them, the warning. These trees are fatal, the sign said. You cannot eat their fruit. On the trees Mrs. Hoffman and Rita saw little reddish-yellow apples, like crab apples, and another sign told them that these were called death apples. That Columbus, the great discoverer of America, had named them death apples because his men, thinking they were in paradise, had eaten of them and died.

That evening for dinner they went to a beach bar and ordered piña coladas and sea turtle steaks. Mrs. Hoffman talked about the breakup of her second marriage. She told Rita how she almost died of boredom with Ben. "Golf and gin rummy; that's all he ever talked about. In all of L.A., he'd only eat in three restaurants, and two of them were his private clubs." Rita laughed and her mother ordered another piña colada and a bottle of white wine. "But, you know, even when you want out," Mrs. Hoffman said, "it's always difficult to break up with somebody. Ben used to fix all the appliances in the house. He'd fix the dishwasher, the dryer, whatever. Do you know what I did when he left me? I showed up one day at his office with the toaster."

As Mrs. Hoffman poured Rita a glass of wine, they both laughed at the thought of Mrs. Hoffman arriving at Ben's office with a broken toaster. Mrs. Hoffman patted her daughter's hand. "I want you to marry a good man. Are you seeing anybody now?"

Rita had been seeing somebody for the past three years, but she didn't want to tell her mother about him. He was the lawyer she worked for as a paralegal. After hours, they made love on the red vinyl sofa in his office. He was supposed to leave his wife and sometimes he got closer to it than other times. "What about Russ?" Mrs. Hoffman asked. "Maybe you should call him. After a while, of course."

Rita turned her wine glass in her hands. "Mom, I didn't know you knew anything about it."

"You'd be surprised what I know," Mrs. Hoffman said. Then she added softly, "I'm your mother."

"Anyway, it was over ten years ago."

"Go for it," Mrs. Hoffman said, "while you still can."

Just then a group of boys, young men really, came into the beach bar. They wore Bermuda shorts and T-shirts and were drinking beer out of bottles. Rita counted thirteen of them. They formed a line and said they were called the Baker's Dozen from Yale University and they were going to sing. First they sang, "There ain't nobody here but us chickens." They tucked their thumbs into their armpits and clucked like chickens. And then they sang "Mammy" in a good Al Jolson rendition.

Rita and her mother were laughing and enjoying themselves. Then, for the next number, a young man with a head of auburn curls and blue eyes stepped forward. The beach bar was filling up, with tourists milling around. The young man glanced around.

Rita noticed her mother looking intensely at the young man, and the young man suddenly fixed his eyes on Rita's mother. He stared at her with a deep look of longing as he began to sing, in a beautiful tenor voice, "Oh, ye take the high road and I'll take the low road, and I'll be in Scotland afore ye." Rita put down her fork and her glass of wine. Her mother stared deep into the eyes of the young man, and the young man stared at her. "But me and my true love will never meet again, on the bonnie, bonnie banks of Loch Lomond."

After he finished singing, he stepped back into the crowd and disappeared. But Mrs. Hoffman continued to stare at the place where he'd been. "Your father," she mumbled, rubbing her eyes, "he used to sing to me like that when he was that boy's age."

Rita motioned for the waiter to get them their check. Mrs. Hoffman continued to scan the restaurant, searching for the boy who'd sung

"Loch Lomond." When she was convinced that the boy had left, she shook her head as if waking up. Then she caught Rita by the hand. "Listen," she said, "I'm going to tell you something. I don't know if you want to hear this, but I'm going to tell you. I loved your father more than I've ever loved anything. More than I loved you and your brothers."

Rita didn't think she wanted to hear more. She was eager to leave. "You don't have to tell me any of this, Mom." She knew her mother was drunk, and she wanted to get out of the restaurant before they embarrassed themselves.

But her mother went on. "If there's a kind of love that kills, I've had it. It eats away. It wants too much. That's not good love." Rita started to get up, but her mother pulled her down. "When he died, I buried myself. I dug a deep hole and I went in. And now this is what's left and I'm going to make the most of it." And she clasped her daughter by the wrist.

Rita paid the bill and helped her mother up. She lifted her mother and took her by the arm. Rita's mother leaned on Rita as she led her slowly along the beach, back to their room. In their room Rita undressed her mother. She took off her blouse and her skirt. She helped her mother into a nightgown. Her mother pulled her knees to her chest, the way she always slept, and curled into a fetal position. Then Rita kissed her mother as Mrs. Hoffman drifted to sleep.

Rita lay in her bed by the window with the view of the sea and the full moon. Mrs. Hoffman began to snore. Often Rita had to poke or kick her mother in the middle of the night to keep her from snoring so loud. Rita had shared rooms with her mother before. When her mother was married to Ben, and Rita would come to visit, Ben always went to sleep on the sofa bed and Rita slept with her mother.

Rita never liked Ben. He was a cardboard box entrepreneur. When he was courting Rita's mother, he came over one afternoon with a sample of each of his cardboard boxes. He made Rita, who was already in her late teens, crawl under one of the boxes and he'd crawled under another. He wanted to surprise Mrs. Hoffman when she came home from work. Rita never knew what her mother saw in anyone but her father.

When her father was dying, Rita's mother often got in bed with her. Rita remembered how her mother would wrap her arms tightly around Rita's shoulders and curl herself up against Rita's back and how Rita would want to push her away, not feel her breasts pointed against her back, not smell her stale, cigarette breath. And sometimes as her father lay dying in the next room, Rita could hear him calling her mother, and her mother in her sleep would clasp Rita tighter, not wanting to hear or let go of Rita. Rita felt like the log a drowning person clings to.

Rita knew now that her mother had probably heard her father calling in the night and that her mother had clung to Rita while she pretended not to hear. Rita knew now that her mother had come into Rita's bed not because she felt alone and wanted Rita's company. She had come because she was weaning Rita's father of this world.

In the morning they got on their mopeds and went to Ginger Bay. Rita asked her mother if she wanted to go snorkeling and her mother said no. She said, "I've lived all these years without putting my face in water except to wash it, so why should I put it in now."

"I thought you'd try anything once, Mom."

Her mother nodded. "Except get more wrinkles," she said as she rubbed Coppertone #4 all over her face and put on a sun visor. Then Mrs. Hoffman stretched out on their blankets. "Besides, what's to see at the bottom of the sea?" She laughed and pointed in the direction of some West Indian men on the beach. "I've got plenty to look at right here."

Rita got into the water and put on her fins, her snorkel, her mask. She saw her mother, propped up on her elbows, scanning the beach. Rita swam. She followed the signs put up by the Department of the Interior. This is coral. This is fire coral; do not touch. This is healthy coral. This is unhealthy coral. Dying coral. Dead coral. This Is Destruction: Coral being destroyed by boring organisms.

As Rita swam, she thought about Russ and what it would be like when she talked to him. What she would say. She wondered if it would be possible to go back again, and she thought it probably would not. When Rita finished her swim, she walked, stumbling in her flippers, back to where her mother lay. She plopped down beside her. "You should go in. It's beautiful."

"I like the land," her mother said.

"There're these funny signs in the water," Rita said, thinking about the little signs put there by the Department of the Interior. "One says, 'Coral being destroyed by boring organisms.'"

Mrs. Hoffman laughed. "Just like my second marriage." She flipped over. "Honey, put some cream on my back, will you?"

"You think you'll ever marry again, Mom?" Rita asked, wiping her hands and face with the towel.

"Naw." Her mother sighed. "Who'd have me now?"

Rita took the Coppertone and squirted it on her hand. She hesitated at her mother's back. She didn't want to feel the texture of sand and cream and her mother's skin, but she took a deep breath and rubbed.

In the evening they went to a fish fry in the town, and later Mrs. Hoffman wanted to go dancing. She wanted Rita to take her to the reggae bar near the harbor, and Rita said, Why not? In the bar the moon hung over the yachts in the harbor, and white women drank rum. The band set up and slowly began to play their drums. Mrs. Hoffman kept the beat with her hand on the bar. Then she began to tap her feet, and her body started to sway.

Her mother looked old to Rita. Her blond hair was bleached and her wrinkles more pronounced because of the afternoon at Ginger Bay. Her nail polish was chipping. Mrs. Hoffman looked like a secretary who doesn't bother with her appearance any longer.

Her mother wanted to dance. She turned to Rita and said, "I'm going to dance." Rita told her mother she should do whatever made her happy.

Black men were clustered in the corners. Since the native women didn't go to the reggae bars, several men danced by themselves. Rita's mother swayed and twisted at the bar almost, but not quite, in time to the music. It wasn't long before someone asked her to dance. Her mother winked at Rita, and Rita winked back. The man put his hand on Mrs. Hoffman's hip, and Mrs. Hoffman started to move. The man put his hand more firmly on Mrs. Hoffman's hip and began guiding her along the dance floor.

Rita watched her mother. Her mother didn't have the beat yet, but she tossed her head back and laughed, and so did the West Indian man. Then another man cut in and the first man disappeared. The second man who danced with Rita's mother was taller and more assured. The first man came to the bar and asked Rita to dance, but Rita said no.

Mrs. Hoffman motioned for Rita to join her, but Rita shook her head and smiled. The first man who danced with Rita's mother was insistent, and finally Rita agreed to dance with him. He pulled Rita close and sang into her ear, "I am the conqueror. I am the master of my race." He sang very loud. It was the song the band was singing, but the words had a harshness inside Rita's ear.

Rita looked at her mother. She waved her hands and rocked. The woman who'd slept for three days was suddenly a bundle of energy. Rita saw her mother's flesh shining through her slacks. She saw the line of her mother's underpants, visible through Mrs. Hoffman's white slacks. She watched the flab of her mother's thighs, her breasts, as her mother danced. She watched the fat that hung from her arms as her mother moved. "Your sister is a good dancer," said the man who danced with Rita.

Rita was shocked. "That's my mother," she said.

But the man opened his mouth wide and laughed, his white teeth shimmering. "That's no mother," he replied.

Suddenly Mrs. Hoffman was surrounded by men who wanted to dance with her. Sweat poured from her brow; her polo shirt clung to her breasts. Her slacks were damp with wet spots that clung to her flesh. Her smile grew coy and girlish. Her laughter was carefree. What if she goes home with one of them, Rita thought.

The music picked up, and Rita wanted to leave, but she couldn't. She tried to follow the man dancing with her, but her eyes were now suddenly fixed on her mother. She couldn't stop staring. Rita watched her mother, sweating, hair stuck to her skull, nipples erect under her polo shirt, white slacks clinging to her thighs, dancing for her life.

The next morning Rita wouldn't get out of bed. Her mother tried to wake her three or four times, but Rita just told her mother to leave her alone. Then Mrs. Hoffman went down to the beach bar without her. She ordered bacon and eggs, grits and coffee, juice, and she brought a tray back to Rita. "You had too much rum," her mother said.

Rita wanted to be left alone, but her mother made her sit up and eat. "Darling," Mrs. Hoffman said, running her hand over her daughter's brow. Rita pulled away. "Don't be angry about last night. I just wanted to dance."

"Leave me alone. Why won't you let me sleep?" Rita groaned. This vacation had been a terrible idea. She didn't know what had made her think of it in the first place. But in a few days they'd be home, and she'd never again plan another trip like this.

"Come on," her mother said, handing her two Bufferins. "Let's get out. I want to go to Ginger Bay."

They decided to take the long way, past the sugar cane plantation. They followed the coast road, overlooking the turquoise sea, little islands dotting it. Watermelon Island, Fat Virgin Island, Smuggler's Island, Pirate's Cove. They rode fast, Mrs. Hoffman ahead most of the time, and then they came to the manchineel trees again. And as she'd done the time before, Mrs. Hoffman stopped. She stared at the trees, their branches laden with death apples.

Then she reached her hand into the sky and plucked one from the tree. She plucked it and held it up as if she'd just caught it out of the sky. Then she pretended to take a bite. Rita waited for her mother's hand to burn. Mrs. Hoffman held the death apple in her hand and pretended to take another bite. "Honey," her mother said, "you've got no idea. I've had the time of my life."

Rita kicked the kick stand on her bike and walked over to her mother. Age lines were deep on her face. The sun made her skin look dry, her hair frizzy. Mrs. Hoffman stared at her own reflection in Rita's glasses. "You are my daughter," Mrs. Hoffman said, offering her the apple. Rita took the apple from her mother's hand and wrapped her arm around her mother. "You are my beautiful, beautiful daughter," Mrs. Hoffman said, "and I never taught you how to live."

When they reached Ginger Bay, Mrs. Hoffman's hand was turning red and so was Rita's, only less so. "I can't believe it," Mrs. Hoffman said. "Columbus was right." Rita looked at her mother's hand and told her it was a dumb thing to do, but that she thought a little salt water would do them both good.

"Yes," Mrs. Hoffman said, "I thought I'd try snorkeling today. Why don't you show me what to do, dear?" So Rita put on her own gear and showed her mother how to put on her snorkel, her mask, her flippers. Rita showed her mother how to breathe through the tube. Rita watched as her mother's eyes darted inside her mask, looking to Rita for guidance. The distortion of the mask hid the harshness of Rita's mother's face. The lines around the eyes softened. The face assumed the gentleness of the water around them. Her eyes blended in with the green sea. Years seemed to drift away or mean nothing.

Rita stuffed the snorkel into her mother's mouth. "Now breathe, Mom. Like this. Through your mouth." Rita breathed and her mother watched. Then her mother breathed and Rita watched. At first her breath sputtered forth. Rita laughed and so did her mother. Then her mother breathed a deeper breath.

They thrust their faces into the water, and Mrs. Hoffman looked to Rita for directions, her eyes wide, expectant. They pushed off into the warm, resilient water. Her mother followed in Rita's wake. Rita felt her mother at the back of her flippers as she moved toward the reefs. Mrs. Hoffman had been a housewife all her life and had never seen the bottom of the sea.

They followed the trail the Department of the Interior had marked with little blue signs. They saw angelfish and black fish with iridescent blue spots and bright yellow tails. They swam along the reef where parrot fish and small barracuda fed.

When they completed the trail, her mother said she wanted to find another reef, but this time she wanted to go where there were no signs. Rita had found one across the bay while her mother slept, so she knew which way to go. They moved in unison. They moved like twins on their way, preparing to greet the light of the new world.

Feathers

RAYMOND CARVER

T HIS FRIEND OF MINE from work, Bud, he asked Fran and me to
supper. I didn't know his wife and he didn't know Fran. That
made us even. But Bud and I were friends. And I knew there was a
little baby at Bud's house. That baby must have been eight months old
when Bud asked us to supper. Where'd those eight months go? Hell,
where's the time gone since? I remember the day Bud came to work
with a box of cigars. He handed them out in the lunchroom. They were
drugstore cigars. Dutch Masters. But each cigar had a red sticker on
it and a wrapper that said IT'S A BOY! I didn't smoke cigars, but I took
one anyway. "Take a couple," Bud said. He shook the box. "I don't
like cigars either. This is her idea." He was talking about his wife. Olla.

I'd never met Bud's wife, but once I'd heard her voice over the
telephone. It was a Saturday afternoon, and I didn't have anything I
wanted to do. So I called Bud to see if he wanted to do anything.
This woman picked up the phone and said, "Hello." I blanked and
couldn't remember her name. Bud's wife. Bud had said her name to
me any number of times. But it went in one ear and out the other.
"Hello!" the woman said again. I could hear a TV going. Then the
woman said, "Who is this?" I heard a baby start up. "Bud!" the woman
called. "What?" I heard Bud say. I still couldn't remember her name.
So I hung up. The next time I saw Bud at work I sure as hell didn't
tell him I'd called. But I made a point of getting him to mention his
wife's name. "Olla," he said. Olla, I said to myself. *Olla.*

"No big deal," Bud said. We were in the lunchroom drinking coffee.
"Just the four of us. You and your missus, and me and Olla. Nothing
fancy. Come around seven. She feeds the baby at six. She'll put him
down after that, and then we'll eat. Our place isn't hard to find. But
here's a map." He gave me a sheet of paper with all kinds of lines
indicating major and minor roads, lanes and such, with arrows pointing to the four poles of the compass. A large X marked the location
of his house. I said, "We're looking forward to it." But Fran wasn't
too thrilled.

That evening, watching TV, I asked her if we should take anything to Bud's.

"Like what?" Fran said. "Did he say to bring something? How should I know? I don't have any idea." She shrugged and gave me this look. She'd heard me before on the subject of Bud. But she didn't know him and she wasn't interested in knowing him. "We could take a bottle of wine," she said. "But I don't care. Why don't you take some wine?" She shook her head. Her long hair swung back and forth over her shoulders. Why do we need other people? she seemed to be saying. We have each other. "Come here," I said. She moved a little closer so I could hug her. Fran's a big tall drink of water. She has this blond hair that hangs down her back. I picked up some of her hair and sniffed it. I wound my hand in her hair. She let me hug her. I put my face right up in her hair and hugged her some more.

Sometimes when her hair gets in her way she has to pick it up and push it over her shoulder. She gets mad at it. "This hair," she says. "Nothing but trouble." Fran works in a creamery and has to wear her hair up when she goes to work. She has to wash it every night and take a brush to it when we're sitting in front of the TV. Now and then she threatens to cut it off. But I don't think she'd do that. She knows I like it too much. She knows I'm crazy about it. I tell her I fell in love with her because of her hair. I tell her I might stop loving her if she cut it. Sometimes I call her "Swede." She could pass for a Swede. Those times together in the evening she'd brush her hair and we'd wish out loud for things we didn't have. We wished for a new car, that's one of the things we wished for. And we wished we could spend a couple of weeks in Canada. But one thing we didn't wish for was kids. The reason we didn't have kids was that we didn't want kids. Maybe sometime, we said to each other. But right then, we were waiting. We thought we might keep on waiting. Some nights we went to a movie. Other nights we just stayed in and watched TV. Sometimes Fran baked things for me and we'd eat whatever it was all in a sitting.

"Maybe they don't drink wine," I said.

"Take some wine anyway," Fran said. "If they don't drink it, we'll drink it."

"White or red?" I said.

"We'll take something sweet," she said, not paying me any attention. "But I don't care if we take anything. This is your show. Let's not make a production out of it, or else I don't want to go. I can make a raspberry coffee ring. Or else some cupcakes."

"They'll have dessert," I said. "You don't invite people to supper without fixing a dessert."

"They might have rice pudding. Or Jell-O! Something we don't like," she said. "I don't know anything about the woman. How do we know what she'll have? What if she gives us Jell-O?" Fran shook her head. I shrugged. But she was right. "Those old cigars he gave you," she said. "Take them. Then you and him can go off to the parlor after supper and smoke cigars and drink port wine, or whatever those people in movies drink."

"Okay, we'll just take ourselves," I said.

Fran said, "We'll take a loaf of my bread."

Bud and Olla lived twenty miles or so from town. We'd lived in that town for three years, but, damn it, Fran and I hadn't so much as taken a spin in the country. It felt good driving those winding little roads. It was early evening, nice and warm, and we saw pastures, rail fences, milk cows moving slowly toward old barns. We saw red-winged blackbirds on the fences, and pigeons circling around haylofts. There were gardens and such, wildflowers in bloom, and little houses set back from the road. I said, "I wish we had us a place out here." It was just an idle thought, another wish that wouldn't amount to anything. Fran didn't answer. She was busy looking at Bud's map. We came to the four-way stop he'd marked. We turned right like the map said and drove exactly three and three-tenths miles. On the left side of the road, I saw a field of corn, a mailbox, and a long, graveled driveway. At the end of the driveway, back in some trees, stood a house with a front porch. There was a chimney on the house. But it was summer, so, of course, no smoke rose from the chimney. But I thought it was a pretty picture, and I said so to Fran.

"It's the sticks out here," she said.

I turned into the drive. Corn rose up on both sides of the drive. Corn stood higher than the car. I could hear gravel crunching under the tires. As we got up close to the house, we could see a garden with green things the size of baseballs hanging from the vines.

"What's that?" I said.

"How should I know?" she said. "Squash, maybe. I don't have a clue."

"Hey, Fran," I said. "Take it easy."

She didn't say anything. She drew in her lower lip and let it go. She turned off the radio as we got close to the house.

A baby's swing-set stood in the front yard and some toys lay on the porch. I pulled up in front and stopped the car. It was then that we heard this awful squall. There was a baby in the house, right, but this cry was too loud for a baby.

"What's that sound?" Fran said.

Then something as big as a vulture flapped heavily down from one of the trees and landed just in front of the car. It shook itself. It turned its long neck toward the car, raised its head, and regarded us.

"Goddamn it," I said. I sat there with my hands on the wheel and stared at the thing.

"Can you believe it?" Fran said. "I never saw a real one before."

We both knew it was a peacock, sure, but we didn't say the word out loud. We just watched it. The bird turned its head up in the air and made this harsh cry again. It had fluffed itself out and looked about twice the size it'd been when it landed.

"Goddamn," I said again. We stayed where we were in the front seat.

The bird moved forward a little. Then it turned its head to the side and braced itself. It kept its bright, wild eye right on us. Its tail was raised, and it was like a big fan folding in and out. There was every color in the rainbow shining from that tail.

"My God," Fran said quietly. She moved her hand over to my knee.

"Goddamn," I said. There was nothing else to say.

The bird made this strange wailing sound once more. "*May-awe, may-awe!*" it went. If it'd been something I was hearing late at night and for the first time, I'd have thought it was somebody dying, or else something wild and dangerous.

The front door opened and Bud came out on the porch. He was buttoning his shirt. His hair was wet. It looked like he'd just come from the shower.

"Shut yourself up, Joey!" he said to the peacock. He clapped his hands at the bird, and the thing moved back a little. "That's enough now. That's right, shut up! You shut up, you old devil!" Bud came down the steps. He tucked in his shirt as he came over to the car. He was wearing what he always wore to work—blue jeans and a denim shirt. I had on my slacks and a short-sleeved sport shirt. My good loafers. When I saw what Bud was wearing, I didn't like it that I was dressed up.

"Glad you could make it," Bud said as he came over beside the car. "Come on inside."

"Hey, Bud," I said.

Fran and I got out of the car. The peacock stood off a little to one side, dodging its mean-looking head this way and that. We were careful to keep some distance between it and us.

"Any trouble finding the place?" Bud said to me. He hadn't looked at Fran. He was waiting to be introduced.

"Good directions," I said. "Hey, Bud, this is Fran. Fran, Bud. She's got the word on you, Bud."

He laughed and they shook hands. Fran was taller than Bud. Bud had to look up.

"He talks about you," Fran said. She took her hand back. "Bud this, Bud that. You're about the only person down there he talks about. I feel like I know you." She was keeping an eye on the peacock. It had moved over near the porch.

"This here's my friend," Bud said. "He *ought* to talk about me." Bud said this and then he grinned and gave me a little punch on the arm.

Fran went on holding her loaf of bread. She didn't know what to do with it. She gave it to Bud. "We brought you something."

Bud took the loaf. He turned it over and looked at it as if it was the first loaf of bread he'd ever seen. "This is real nice of you." He brought the loaf up to his face and sniffed it.

"Fran baked that bread," I told Bud.

Bud nodded. Then he said, "Let's go inside and meet the wife and mother."

He was talking about Olla, sure. Olla was the only mother around. Bud had told me his own mother was dead and that his dad had pulled out when Bud was a kid.

The peacock scuttled ahead of us, then hopped onto the porch when Bud opened the door. It was trying to get inside the house.

"Oh," said Fran as the peacock pressed itself against her leg.

"Joey, goddamn it," Bud said. He thumped the bird on the top of its head. The peacock backed up on the porch and shook itself. The quills in its train rattled as it shook. Bud made as if to kick it, and the peacock backed up some more. Then Bud held the door for us. "She lets the goddamn thing in the house. Before long, it'll be wanting to eat at the goddamn table and sleep in the goddamn bed."

Fran stopped just inside the door. She looked back at the cornfield. "You have a nice place," she said. Bud was still holding the door. "Don't they, Jack?"

"You bet," I said. I was surprised to hear her say it.

"A place like this is not all it's cracked up to be," Bud said, still holding the door. He made a threatening move toward the peacock. "Keeps you going. Never a dull moment." Then he said, "Step on inside, folks."

I said, "Hey, Bud, what's that growing there?"

"Them's tomatoes," Bud said.

"Some farmer I got," Fran said, and shook her head.

Bud laughed. We went inside. This plump little woman with her hair done up in a bun was waiting for us in the living room. She had her hands rolled up in her apron. The cheeks of her face were bright red. I thought at first she might be out of breath, or else mad at something. She gave me the once-over, and then her eyes went to Fran. Not unfriendly, just looking. She stared at Fran and continued to blush.

Bud said, "Olla, this is Fran. And this is my friend Jack. You know all about Jack. Folks, this is Olla." He handed Olla the bread.

"What's this?" she said. "Oh, it's homemade bread. Well, thanks. Sit down anywhere. Make yourselves at home. Bud, why don't you ask them what they'd like to drink. I've got something on the stove." Olla said that and went back into the kitchen with the bread.

"Have a seat," Bud said. Fran and I plunked ourselves down on the sofa. I reached for my cigarettes. Bud said, "Here's an ashtray." He picked up something heavy from the top of the TV. "Use this," he said, and he put the thing down on the coffee table in front of me. It was one of those glass ashtrays made to look like a swan. I lit up and dropped the match into the opening in the swan's back. I watched a little wisp of smoke drift out of the swan.

The color TV was going, so we looked at that for a minute. On the screen, stock cars were tearing around a track. The announcer talked in a grave voice. But it was like he was holding back some excitement, too. "We're still waiting to have official confirmation," the announcer said.

"You want to watch this?" Bud said. He was still standing.

I said I didn't care. And I didn't. Fran shrugged. What difference could it make to her? she seemed to say. The day was shot anyway.

"There's only about twenty laps left," Bud said. "It's close now. There was a big pile-up earlier. Knocked out half-a-dozen cars. Some drivers got hurt. They haven't said yet how bad."

"Leave it on," I said. "Let's watch it."

"Maybe one of those damn cars will explode right in front of us," Fran said. "Or else maybe one'll run up into the grandstand and smash the guy selling the crummy hot dogs." She took a strand of hair between her fingers and kept her eyes fixed on the TV.

Bud looked at Fran to see if she was kidding. "That other business, that pile-up, was something. One thing led to another. Cars, parts of cars, people all over the place. Well, what can I get you? We have ale, and there's a bottle of Old Crow."

"What are you drinking?" I said to Bud.

"Ale," Bud said. "It's good and cold."

"I'll have ale," I said.

"I'll have some of that Old Crow and a little water," Fran said. "In a tall glass, please. With some ice. Thank you, Bud."

"Can do," Bud said. He threw another look at the TV and moved off to the kitchen.

Fran nudged me and nodded in the direction of the TV. "Look up on top," she whispered. "Do you see what I see?" I looked at where she was looking. There was a slender red vase into which somebody had stuck a few garden daisies. Next to the vase, on the doily, sat an old plaster-of-Paris cast of the most crooked, jaggedy teeth in the world. There were no lips to the awful-looking thing, and no jaw either, just these old plaster teeth packed into something that resembled thick yellow gums.

Just then Olla came back with a can of mixed nuts and a bottle of root beer. She had her apron off now. She put the can of nuts onto the coffee table next to the swan. She said, "Help yourselves. Bud's getting your drinks." Olla's face came on red again as she said this. She sat down in an old cane rocking chair and set it in motion. She drank from her root beer and looked at the TV. Bud came back carrying a little wooden tray with Fran's glass of whiskey and water and my bottle of ale. He had a bottle of ale on the tray for himself.

"You want a glass?" he asked me.

I shook my head. He tapped me on the knee and turned to Fran.

She took her glass from Bud and said, "Thanks." Her eyes went to the teeth again. Bud saw where she was looking. The cars screamed around the track. I took the ale and gave my attention to the screen. The teeth were none of my business. "Them's what Olla's teeth looked like before she had her braces put on," Bud said to Fran. "I've got used to them. But I guess they look funny up there. For the life of me, I don't know why she keeps them around." He looked over at Olla. Then he looked at me and winked. He sat down in his La-Z-Boy and crossed one leg over the other. He drank from his ale and gazed at Olla.

Olla turned red once more. She was holding her bottle of root beer. She took a drink of it. Then she said, "They're to remind me how much I owe Bud."

"What was that?" Fran said. She was picking through the can of nuts, helping herself to the cashews. Fran stopped what she was doing and looked at Olla. "Sorry, but I missed that." Fran stared at the woman and waited for whatever thing it was she'd say next.

Olla's face turned red again. "I've got lots of things to be thankful for," she said. "That's one of the things I'm thankful for. I keep them around to remind me how much I owe Bud." She drank from her root beer. Then she lowered the bottle and said, "You've got pretty teeth, Fran. I noticed right away. But these teeth of mine, they came in crooked when I was a kid." With her fingernail, she tapped a couple of her front teeth. She said, "My folks couldn't afford to fix teeth. These teeth of mine came in just any which way. My first husband didn't care what I looked like. No, he didn't! He didn't care about anything except where his next drink was coming from. He had one friend only in the world, and that was his bottle." She shook her head. "Then Bud came along and got me out of that mess. After we were together, the first thing Bud said was, 'We're going to have them teeth fixed.' That mold was made right after Bud and I met, on the occasion of my second visit to the orthodontist. Right before the braces went on."

Olla's face stayed red. She looked at the picture on the screen. She drank from her root beer and didn't seem to have any more to say.

"That orthodontist must have been a whiz," Fran said. She looked back at the horror-show teeth on top of the TV.

"He was great," Olla said. She turned in her chair and said, "See?" She opened her mouth and showed us her teeth once more, not a bit shy now.

Bud had gone to the TV and picked up the teeth. He walked over to Olla and held them up against Olla's cheek. "Before and after," Bud said.

Olla reached up and took the mold from Bud. "You know something?" That orthodontist wanted to keep this." She was holding it in her lap while she talked. "I said nothing doing. I pointed out to him they were *my* teeth. So he took pictures of the mold instead. He told me he was going to put the pictures in a magazine."

Bud said, "Imagine what kind of magazine that'd be. Not much call for that kind of publication, I don't think," he said, and we all laughed.

"After I got the braces off, I kept putting my hand up to my mouth when I laughed. Like this," she said. "Sometimes I still do it. Habit. One day Bud said, 'You can stop doing that anytime, Olla. You don't have to hide teeth as pretty as that. You have nice teeth now.'" Olla looked over at Bud. Bud winked at her. She grinned and lowered her eyes.

Fran drank from her glass. I took some of my ale. I didn't know what to say to this. Neither did Fran. But I knew Fran would have plenty to say about it later.

I said, "Olla, I called here once. You answered the phone. But I hung up. I don't know why I hung up." I said that and then sipped my ale. I didn't know why I'd brought it up now.

"I don't remember," Olla said. "When was that?"

"A while back."

"I don't remember," she said and shook her head. She fingered the plaster teeth in her lap. She looked at the race and went back to rocking.

Fran turned her eyes to me. She drew her lip under. But she didn't say anything.

Bud said, "Well, what else is new?"

"Have some more nuts," Olla said. "Supper'll be ready in a little while."

There was a cry from a room in the back of the house.

"Not him," Olla said to Bud, and made a face.

"Old Junior boy," Bud said. He leaned back in his chair, and we watched the rest of the race, three or four laps, no sound.

Once or twice we heard the baby again, little fretful cries coming from the room in the back of the house.

"I don't know," Olla said. She got up from her chair. "Everything's about ready for us to sit down. I just have to take up the gravy. But I'd better look in on him first. Why don't you folks go out and sit down at the table? I'll just be a minute."

"I'd like to see the baby," Fran said.

Olla was still holding the teeth. She went over and put them back on top of the TV. "It might upset him just now," she said. "He's not used to strangers. Wait and see if I can get him back to sleep. Then you can peek in. While he's asleep." She said this and then she went down the hall to a room, where she opened a door. She eased in and shut the door behind her. The baby stopped crying.

Bud killed the picture and we went in to sit at the table. Bud and I talked about things at work. Fran listened. Now and then she even asked a question. But I could tell she was bored, and maybe feeling put out with Olla for not letting her see the baby. She looked around Olla's kitchen. She wrapped a strand of hair around her fingers and checked out Olla's things.

Olla came back into the kitchen and said, "I changed him and gave him his rubber duck. Maybe he'll let us eat now. But don't bet on it." She raised a lid and took a pan off the stove. She poured red gravy into a bowl and put the bowl on the table. She took lids off some other pots and looked to see that everything was ready. On the table were baked ham, sweet potatoes, mashed potatoes, lima beans, corn on the cob, salad greens. Fran's loaf of bread was in a prominent place next to the ham.

"I forgot the napkins," Olla said. "You all get started. Who wants what to drink? Bud drinks milk with all of his meals."

"Milk's fine," I said.

"Water for me," Fran said. "But I can get it. I don't want you waiting on me. You have enough to do." She made as if to get up from her chair.

Olla said, "Please. You're company. Sit still. Let me get it." She was blushing again.

We sat with our hands in our laps and waited. I thought about those plaster teeth. Olla came back with napkins, big glasses of milk for Bud and me, and a glass of ice water for Fran. Fran said, "Thanks."

"You're welcome," Olla said. Then she seated herself. Bud cleared his throat. He bowed his head and said a few words of grace. He talked in a voice so low I could hardly make out the words. But I got the drift of things—he was thanking the Higher Power for the food we were about to put away.

"Amen," Olla said when he'd finished.

Bud passed me the platter of ham and helped himself to some mashed potatoes. We got down to it then. We didn't say much except now and then Bud or I would say, "This is real good ham." Or, "This sweet corn is the best sweet corn I ever ate."

"This bread is what's special," Olla said.

"I'll have more salad, please, Olla," Fran said, softening up maybe a little.

"Have more of this," Bud would say as he passed me the platter of ham, or else the bowl of red gravy.

From time to time, we heard the baby make its noise. Olla would turn her head to listen, then, satisfied it was just fussing, she would give her attention back to her food.

"The baby's out of sorts tonight," Olla said to Bud.

"I'd still like to see him," Fran said. "My sister has a little baby. But she and the baby live in Denver. When will I ever get to Denver? I have a niece I haven't even seen." Fran thought about this for a minute, and then she went back to eating.

Olla forked some ham into her mouth. "Let's hope he'll drop off to sleep," she said.

Bud said, "There's a lot more of everything. Have some more ham and sweet potatoes, everybody."

"I can't eat another bite," Fran said. She laid her fork on her plate. "It's great, but I can't eat any more."

"Save room," Bud said. "Olla's made rhubarb pie."

Fran said, "I guess I could eat a little piece of that. When everybody else is ready."

"Me, too," I said. But I said it to be polite. I'd hated rhubarb pie since I was thirteen years old and had got sick on it, eating it with strawberry ice cream.

We finished what was on our plates. Then we heard that damn peacock again. The thing was on the roof this time. We could hear it over our heads. It made a ticking sound as it walked back and forth on the shingles.

Bud shook his head. "Joey will knock it off in a minute. He'll get tired and turn in pretty soon," Bud said. "He sleeps in one of them trees."

The bird let go with its cry once more. "*May-awe!*" it went. Nobody said anything. What was there to say?

Then Olla said, "He wants in, Bud."

"Well, he can't come in," Bud said. "We got company, in case you hadn't noticed. These people don't want a goddamn old bird in the house. That dirty bird and your old pair of teeth! What're people going to think?" He shook his head. He laughed. We all laughed. Fran laughed along with the rest of us.

"He's not *dirty*, Bud," Olla said. "What's gotten into you? You like Joey. Since when did you start calling him dirty?"

"Since he shit on the rug that time," Bud said. "Pardon the French," he said to Fran. "But, I'll tell you, sometimes I could wring that old bird's neck for him. He's not even worth killing, is he, Olla? Sometimes, in the middle of the night, he'll bring me up out of bed with that cry of his. He's not worth a nickel—right, Olla?"

Olla shook her head at Bud's nonsense. She moved a few lima beans around on her plate.

"How'd you get a peacock in the first place?" Fran wanted to know.

Olla looked up from her plate. She said, "I always dreamed of having me a peacock. Since I was a girl and found a picture of one in a magazine. I thought it was the most beautiful thing I ever saw. I cut the picture out and put it over my bed. I kept that picture for the longest time. Then when Bud and I got this place, I saw my chance. I said, 'Bud, I want a peacock.' Bud laughed at the idea."

"I finally asked around," Bud said. "I heard tell of an old boy who raised them over in the next county. Birds of paradise, he called them.

We paid a hundred bucks for that bird of paradise," he said. He smacked his forehead. "God Almighty, I got me a woman with expensive tastes." He grinned at Olla.

"Bud," Olla said, "you know that isn't true. Besides everything else, Joey's a good watchdog," she said to Fran. "We don't need a watchdog with Joey. He can hear just about anything."

"If times get tough, as they might, I'll put Joey in a pot," Bud said. "Feathers and all."

"Bud! That's not funny," Olla said. But she laughed and we got a good look at her teeth again.

The baby started up once more. It was serious crying this time. Olla put down her napkin and got up from the table.

Bud said, "If it's not one thing, it's another. Bring him on out here, Olla."

"I'm going to," Olla said, and went to get the baby.

The peacock wailed again, and I could feel the hair on the back of my neck. I looked at Fran. She picked up her napkin and then put it down. I looked toward the kitchen window. It was dark outside. The window was raised, and there was a screen in the frame. I thought I heard the bird on the front porch.

Fran turned her eyes to look down the hall. She was watching for Olla and the baby.

After a time, Olla came back with it. I looked at the baby and drew a breath. Olla sat down at the table with the baby. She held it up under its arms so it could stand on her lap and face us. She looked at Fran and then at me. She wasn't blushing now. She waited for one of us to comment.

"Ah!" said Fran.

"What is it?" Olla said quickly.

"Nothing," Fran said. "I thought I saw something at the window. I thought I saw a bat."

"We don't have any bats around here," Olla said.

"Maybe it was a moth," Fran said. "It was something. Well," she said, "isn't that some baby."

Bud was looking at the baby. Then he looked over at Fran. He tipped his chair onto its back legs and nodded. He nodded again, and said, "That's all right, don't worry any. We know he wouldn't win no beauty contests right now. He's no Clark Gable. But give him time. With any luck, you know, he'll grow up to look like his old man."

The baby stood in Olla's lap, looking around the table at us. Olla had moved her hands down to its middle so that the baby could rock back and forth on its fat legs. Bar none, it was the ugliest baby I'd ever seen. It was so ugly I couldn't say anything. No words would come out of my mouth. I don't mean it was diseased or disfigured. Nothing like that. It was just ugly. It had a big red face, pop eyes, a broad forehead, and these big fat lips. It had no neck to speak of, and it had three or four fat chins. Its chins rolled right up under its ears, and its ears stuck out from its bald head. Fat hung over its wrists. Its arms and fingers were fat. Even calling it ugly does it credit.

The ugly baby made its noise and jumped up and down on its mother's lap. Then it stopped jumping. It leaned forward and tried to reach its fat hand into Olla's plate.

I've seen babies. When I was growing up, my two sisters had a total of six babies. I was around babies a lot when I was a kid. I've seen babies in stores and so on. But this baby beat anything. Fran stared at it, too. I guess she didn't know what to say either.

"He's a big fellow, isn't he?" I said.

Bud said, "He'll by God be turning out for football before long. He sure as hell won't go without meals around this house."

As if to make sure of this, Olla plunged her fork into some sweet potatoes and brought the fork up to the baby's mouth. "He's my baby, isn't he?" she said to the fat thing, ignoring us.

The baby leaned forward and opened up for the sweet potatoes. It reached for Olla's fork as she guided the sweet potatoes into its mouth, then clamped down. The baby chewed the stuff and rocked some more on Olla's lap. It was so pop-eyed, it was like it was plugged into something.

Fran said, "He's some baby, Olla."

The baby's face screwed up. It began to fuss all over again.

"Let Joey in," Olla said to Bud.

Bud let the legs of his chair come down on the floor. "I think we should at least ask these people if they mind," Bud said.

Olla looked at Fran and then she looked at me. Her face had gone red again. The baby kept prancing in her lap, squirming to get down.

"We're friends here," I said. "Do whatever you want."

Bud said, "Maybe they don't want a big old bird like Joey in the house. Did you ever think of that, Olla?"

"Do you folks mind?" Olla said to us. "If Joey comes inside? Things got headed in the wrong direction with that bird tonight. The baby, too, I think. He's used to having Joey come in and fool around with him a little before his bedtime. Neither of them can settle down tonight."

"Don't ask us," Fran said. "I don't mind if he comes in. I've never been up close to one before. But I don't mind." She looked at me. I suppose I could tell she wanted me to say something.

"Hell, no," I said. "Let him in." I picked up my glass and finished the milk.

Bud got up from his chair. He went to the front door and opened it. He flicked on the yard lights.

"What's your baby's name?" Fran wanted to know.

"Harold," Olla said. She gave Harold some more sweet potatoes from her plate. "He's real smart. Sharp as a tack. Always knows what you're saying to him. Don't you, Harold? You wait until you get your own baby, Fran. You'll see."

Fran just looked at her. I heard the front door open and then close.

"He's smart, all right," Bud said as he came back into the kitchen. "He takes after Olla's dad. Now there was one smart old boy for you."

I looked around behind Bud and could see that peacock hanging back in the living room, turning its head this way and that, like you'd turn a hand mirror. It shook itself, and the sound was like a deck of cards being shuffled in the other room.

It moved forward a step. Then another step.

"Can I hold the baby?" Fran said. She said it like it would be a favor if Olla would let her.

Olla handed the baby across the table to her.

Fran tried to get the baby settled in her lap. But the baby began to squirm and make its noises.

"Harold," Fran said.

Olla watched Fran with the baby. She said, "When Harold's grandpa was sixteen years old, he set out to read the encyclopedia from A to Z. He did it, too. He finished when he was twenty. Just before he met my mama."

"Where's he now?" I asked. "What's he do?" I wanted to know what had become of a man who'd set himself a goal like that.

"He's dead," Olla said. She was watching Fran, who by now had the baby down on its back and across her knees. Fran chucked the baby under one of its chins. She started to talk baby talk to it.

"He worked in the woods," Bud said. "Loggers dropped a tree on him."

"Mama got some insurance money," Olla said. "But she spent that.

Bud sends her something every month."

"Not much," Bud said. "Don't have much ourselves. But she's Olla's mother."

By this time, the peacock had gathered its courage and was beginning to move slowly, with little swaying and jerking motions, into the kitchen. Its head was erect but at an angle, its red eyes fixed on us. Its crest, a little sprig of feathers, stood a few inches over its head. Plumes rose from its tail. The bird stopped a few feet away from the table and looked us over.

"They don't call them birds of paradise for nothing," Bud said.

Fran didn't look up. She was giving all her attention to the baby. She'd begun to patty-cake with it, which pleased the baby somewhat. I mean, at least the thing had stopped fussing. She brought it up to her neck and whispered something into its ear.

"Now," she said, "don't tell anyone what I said."

The baby stared at her with its pop eyes. Then it reached and got itself a baby handful of Fran's blond hair. The peacock stepped closer to the table. None of us said anything. We just sat still. Baby Harold saw the bird. It let go of Fran's hair and stood up on her lap. It pointed its fat fingers at the bird. It jumped up and down and made noises.

The peacock walked quickly around the table and went for the baby. It ran its long neck across the baby's legs. It pushed its beak in under the baby's pajama top and shook its stiff head back and forth. The baby laughed and kicked its feet. Scooting onto its back, the baby worked its way over Fran's knees and down onto the floor. The peacock kept pushing against the baby, as if it was a game they were playing. Fran held the baby against her legs while the baby strained forward.

"I just don't believe this," she said.

"That peacock is crazy, that's what," Bud said. "Damn bird doesn't know it's a bird, that's its major trouble."

Olla grinned and showed her teeth again. She looked over at Bud. Bud pushed his chair away from the table and nodded.

It *was* an ugly baby. But, for all I know, I guess it didn't matter that much to Bud and Olla. Or if it did, maybe they simply thought, So okay if it's ugly. It's our baby. And this is just a stage. Pretty soon there'll be another stage. There is this stage and then there is the next stage. Things will be okay in the long run, once all the stages have been gone through. They might have thought something like that.

Bud picked up the baby and swung him over his head until Harold shrieked. The peacock ruffled its feathers and watched.

Fran shook her head again. She smoothed out her dress where the baby had been. Olla picked up her fork and was working at some lima beans on her plate.

Bud shifted the baby onto his hip and said, "There's pie and coffee yet."

That evening at Bud and Olla's was special. I knew it was special. That evening I felt good about almost everything in my life. I couldn't wait to be alone with Fran to talk to her about what I was feeling. I made a wish that evening. Sitting there at the table, I closed my eyes for a minute and thought hard. What I wished for was that I'd never forget or otherwise let go of that evening. That's one wish of mine that came true. And it was bad luck for me that it did. But, of course, I couldn't know that then.

"What are you thinking about, Jack?" Bud said to me.

"I'm just thinking," I said. I grinned at him.

"A penny," Olla said.

I just grinned some more and shook my head.

After we got home from Bud and Olla's that night, and we were under the covers, Fran said, "Honey, fill me up with your seed!" When she said that, I heard her all the way down to my toes, and I hollered and let go.

Later, after things had changed for us, and the kid had come along, all of that, Fran would look back on that evening at Bud's place as the beginning of the change. But she's wrong. The change came later—and when it came, it was like something that happened to other people, not something that could have happened to us.

"Goddamn those people and their ugly baby," Fran will say, for no apparent reason, while we're watching TV late at night. "And that smelly bird," she'll say. "Christ, who needs it!" Fran will say. She says this kind of stuff a lot, even though she hasn't seen Bud and Olla since that one time.

Fran doesn't work at the creamery anymore, and she cut her hair a long time ago. She's gotten fat on me, too. We don't talk about it. What's to say?

I still see Bud at the plant. We work together and we open our lunch pails together. If I ask, he tells me about Olla and Harold. Joey's out of the picture. He flew into his tree one night and that was it for him. He didn't come down. Old age, maybe, Bud says. Then the owls took over. Bud shrugs. He eats his sandwich and says Harold's going to be a linebacker someday. "You ought to see that kid," Bud says. I nod. We're still friends. That hasn't changed any. But I've gotten careful with what I say to him. And I know he feels that and wishes it could be different. I wish it could be, too.

Once in a blue moon, he asks about my family. When he does, I tell him everybody's fine. "Everybody's fine," I say. I close the lunch pail and take out my cigarettes. Bud nods and sips his coffee. The truth is, my kid has a conniving streak in him. But I don't talk about it. Not even with his mother. Especially her. She and I talk less and less as it is. Mostly it's just the TV. But I remember that night. I recall the way the peacock picked up its gray feet and inched around the table. And then my friend and his wife saying goodnight to us on the porch. Olla giving Fran some peacock feathers to take home. I remember all of us shaking hands, hugging each other, saying things. In the car, Fran sat close to me as we drove away. She kept her hand on my leg. We drove home like that from my friend's house.

The Sex Maniac

HILMA WOLITZER

E VERYBODY SAID that there was a sex maniac loose in the complex and I thought, It's about time. It had been a long asexual winter. The steam heat seemed to dry all of the body's moistures and shrivel the fantasies of the mind. From the nineteenth floor of Building A, I watched snow fall on the deserted geometry of the playground. The colors of the world were lustless, forbidding. White fell on gray. Gray shadows drew over the white.

He was first seen in the laundry room of Building C, but it was not clear just how he had presented himself. Was his attack verbal, physical, visual? The police came and they wrote down in books the fiction of the housewives. He was next seen near the incinerator shaft on the sixth floor of our building. He was seen twice by elderly widows, whose thin shrieks seemed to pierce the brain. There had been an invasion of those widows lately as if old men were dying off in job lots. The widows marched behind the moving men, fluttering, birdlike. Their sons and daughters were there to supervise, looking sleek and modern next to the belongings, chairs with curved legs, massive headboards of marriage beds trembling on the backs of the movers. The widows smiled shyly as if their survival embarrassed them.

Now two of them had encountered a sex maniac. Help, they had shrilled. Help and help, and he had been frightened off by their cries. I wondered where he waited now in ambush and if I would meet him on a loveless February night.

There were plenty of men in my life that winter, not one of them a sex maniac. The children developed coughs that made them sound like seals barking and the health plan sent a doctor. He was thin, mustachioed, and bowed with the burden of house calls. Bad boys in bad neighborhoods slashed his tires and snapped his aerial in two. Angry children bit his fingers as he pried open the hinges of their jaws. I clasped a flower pin to the bosom of my best housedress, the children jumped on the bed intoning nursery rhymes, but the doctor snapped his bag shut with the finality of the last word. His mustache thin and mean, he looked just like the doctors of my childhood. We trailed after him to the door but he didn't turn around. Never mind. There were policemen to ask us leading questions. There was the usual parade of repairmen and plumbers.

There was the delivery boy from the market. His name is Earl. We coaxed him into the apartment. Just put it there, Earl. Just wait a minute while I get my purse, Earl. Is it still as cold out there? we asked. Is it going to snow again? Do you think the price-level index will rise? Will I meet the man of my dreams? Will I take a long voyage? But he was a boy without vision or imagination. He counted out the change and hurried to leave.

That night I said to Howard, "Love has left this land." When the children were tucked in behind veils of steam from the vaporizer, he tried to disprove it. We turned to each other in that chorus of coughing and whispering radiators. The smell of Vick's was there, eaten into my hand, into the bedclothes, and the lovemaking was only ritual. It was no one's fault. It was the fault of the atmosphere, the barometric pressure, the wind velocity. We comforted each other in the winter night.

The next day the whole complex was thrumming with excitement. The sex maniac had been seen by a very reliable source. The superintendent's wife came from a mining area in Pennsylvania, a place not noted for frivolity. She had gazed at a constant landscape and she had known men who had suffocated in sealed mines. Her word was to be honored; she had no more imagination than the grocer's boy. After the police were finished, the women of the building fell on her with questions. Did he just—you know—show himself? Did he touch her? What did he say?

She answered with humorless patience. Contrary to rumor, he was merely a white man, not very tall, and young, like her own son. But not really like her own son, she was quick to add. He had said terrible, filthy things to her in a funny, quiet way, as if he were praying, and I saw him in my mind's eye, reedy and pale, saying his string of obscenities like a litany in a reverent and quaking voice.

I wondered who he was, after all, and why he had chosen us. Had he known instinctively that we needed him, that winter had chilled us in our hearts and our beds?

But the superintendent's wife said that he hadn't touched at all, only longed to touch, promised, threatened to touch.

Ahhhhh, cried the women. Ahhhhhh. The old widows ran to the locksmith for new bolts and chains.

The men in the building began to do the laundry for their wives. They went in groups with their friends. Did the sound of their voices diminishing in the elevators remind the superintendent's wife of men going down to the mines?

Did you see him? the wives asked later, and, flinging the laundry bags down, some of the husbands laughed and said, Yes, he asked for you, he told me to give you this and *this*, and the wives shrieked with pleasure.

Howard ruined our clothes, mixing dark and white things, using too much bleach. But when he came back from the laundry room it was as if he had returned from a crusade.

"Have you heard anything?" I asked, and he smiled and said, "*You* don't need a sex maniac."

But you *were*, I thought. Your eyes and your hands used to be wild and your breath came in desperate gulps. You used to mumble your own tender obscenities against my skin and tell me that I drove you crazy. I looked at Howard, his hand poised now on the rim of the laundry basket, and I knew that I was being unfair. But whose love is not unfair? When is it ever reasonable?

Perhaps whatever I needed was outside the confines of the building, farther than the outer edges of the complex where I could see the grocer's boy on his bicycle turning in concentric circles toward our building. Artfully, he raised the front wheel as he rode on the rear one, and then the bicycle became level again like a prancing pony. "Whoa," I said against the window pane, and then I waited for him to come up.

His ears were red from the cold wind. He snuffled and put the bag of groceries on the kitchen counter. He is the sort of boy who won't meet your eyes. His own, half-lidded and secret, seemed to look at my feet. And because I didn't want him to go yet and didn't know what else to do, I said, "Have you heard about the sex maniac, Earl?"

The red of his ears flamed to his face and I thought he would be consumed by his own heat. He answered from the depths of his throat in a voice that might have been silent for weeks. "Whaaa?" he asked.

There was no way to retreat. "The sex maniac," I said. "He stays in the complex. He molests women. *You* know."

Perhaps he did. But, if he didn't, then a match had been set to his fantasy. His eyes opened wide and for the first time I saw that they were a bovine brown. Sex maniac, he was thinking, and I watched his face change as the pictures rolled inside his head. Sex maniac! A grocery bag slid across the counter and into the bowl of the sink. But he stood there, his hand paused at the pocket of his vinyl jacket. Half-nude housewives lay in stairwells pleading for their release. Please don't, they begged. For God's sake, have mercy. His lips were moving, shaping melodies.

I pulled on the sleeve of his jacket. "Listen, did you bring the chow-chow?" I asked. "Look, Earl, the oranges are all in the sink."

Slowly the light dimmed in his face. He looked at me with new recognition. "I always take good care of you, don't I?" he asked.

"Yes, you do," I assured him. "You're a very reliable person."

"What does this here guy do?"

"Who?"

"The whachamacallit—the maniac."

I began to put the oranges back into the bag. "Oh, gosh, I don't know. I never saw him. Who knows? Rumors build up. You know how they snowball."

"Yeah," he said, dreamy, distant.

"Well, so long," I said. I pressed the money into his relaxed hand.

"Yeah," he said again.

I guided him down the hallway and out through the door.

That evening the superintendent came to fix the leaking faucet in the bathtub. "Keeping to yourself?" he asked as he knelt on the bathroom tile.

I was surprised. He usually avoided conversation. "More or less," I said cautiously.

"You women better stick close to home," he advised.

"Oh, I *do*, I *do*," I said.

"You know what that guy said to the Mrs.? You know the kind of language he used?" His eyes were a cruel and burning blue. He unscrewed a washer and let it fall into the tub. He raised his hand. "Do you know what I'll do if I catch that guy? Whop! Whop!" His hand became a honed razor, a machete, a cleaver. "Whop! Whop!"

I blinked, feeling slightly faint. I sat down on the edge of the closed toilet seat.

The superintendent replaced the washer and stood up. "You ever see him?" he asked.

I shook my head.

His long horny forefinger shot out and pushed against my left nipple as if he were ringing a doorbell. "Maybe he don't go for a big woman," he said, and lumbered through the doorway.

I sat there for a few minutes and then I went into the kitchen to start supper.

Several days went by and gradually people stopped talking about the sex maniac. He seemed to have abandoned the complex. It was as if he hadn't been potent enough to penetrate the icy crusts of our hearts. Poor harmless thing, I thought, but at least he had tried.

The children's coughs abated and I took them to the doctor's office for a final checkup. He examined them and scribbled something on their health records. "Did they ever catch that fellow?" he asked suddenly.

"I don't think so," I said.

"Did he actually attempt *assault*? the doctor asked. I must have seemed surprised because he poked at his mustache and said, "I've always had an interest in crimes of a sexual nature."

I dropped my eyes.

"I'm concerned with the psychodynamic origin of their obsession," he persisted.

Aha, I said to myself. I stood up, smoothing the skirt of my dress. His eyes followed my gesture, lingering, and I thought, So here's my chance if I want one. Here's unlicensed desire. Was this where the sex maniac had led me?

"Oedipal complex, all that jazz," said the doctor, but his gaze stayed on my hips and his hands became restless on the desk.

But this wasn't what I had meant at all, not those clinical hands that tapped, tapped their nervous message. I could see the cool competence in his eyes, the first-class mechanic at home in his element, but it wasn't what I needed. He had nothing to do with old longings and the adolescent rise and plunge of the heart. He had no remedies for the madness of dreams or the wistful sanity of what was familiar and dear.

"I once considered a residency in psychiatry," he said, and he laughed nervously and glanced up at his wall of diplomas as if for reassurance.

Nothing doing, I thought, not a chance. But I laughed back just to show no hard feelings. I walked to the door and the doctor followed. "So long," I told him in a voice as firm and friendly as a handshake.

"Keep an eye on those tonsils," he said, just to change the subject.

The children and I went out into the pale sunshine. Filthy patches of snow melted into the pavement.

Home, I thought, home, as if it were my life's goal to get there. We walked toward the bus stop. Everywhere color was beginning to bleed through the grayness and I felt a little sadness. I had never seen him. Not once crouched in the corner of the laundry room, not once moaning his demands on the basement ramp, not once cutting footprints across the fresh snow in the courtyard. It was as if he had never existed. The winter was almost over and I was willing to wait for summer to come again.

Pulling the children along, although there was no one waiting for me, I began to run.

The Priest's Wife

*Thirteen Ways of Looking
at a Blackbird*

JOHN L'HEUREUX

1

THE PRIEST AND HIS WIFE were seen skiing together before they were married; or, rather, she was seen skiing and he was around, somewhere.

She took the lift to the slope reserved for advanced skiers. She was wearing a black parka and formfitting ski pants, also black. Her blond hair hung loose and straight.

Those who watched with binoculars from the deck of the lodge said it was an exercise in discipline. She allowed herself none of the indulgences of the advanced skiers. She plunged straight down vertical slopes, shooting off at an angle over horizontal ones, slaloming between invisible poles even when her momentum would have seemed to indicate certain disaster. She never shifted weight suddenly from one leg to the other. She never skidded, never fell. She crouched, swerved, straightened, her body always completely in control.

An exercise in grace, someone said. No one could take eyes off her and so no one was sure who said it. It may have been the priest.

Snow had begun to fall, so they all went indoors for hot buttered rum and a little fooling around by the fireplace. Every now and then somebody would look out the window and see her mounting once more that precipitous slope, and then the lightning descent, the perfect turn around the invisible poles.

Among twenty snowy mountains she was the only moving thing.

2

After he met her the priest was of three minds regarding what he ought to do. After he watched her skiing on the slopes he was of one mind. He wanted to be a poet and write perfect love songs. For God, naturally. And then eventually perhaps for publication. And finally just to create a good thing. To make something. He was of one mind about that.

With such an attitude, it was inevitable that in time he got out and left behind him the order, the priesthood, and—he sometimes thought—common sense. Burdened with an artist's drive and a priest's training, he did what anyone would do. He married her and became a teacher of high school English.

3

She had a face like a woman in a novel. Her grandfather said that to her once when she was nine or ten, and it pleased her. It gave her an existence out there, in the real world, in a book.

She was Katharine Stone, age nine or perhaps ten, and she was called Kate. Her father was a psychiatrist and her mother was a psychiatric nurse; they employed a cleaning woman, a part-time gardener, and a part-time cook. These people, and her German shepherd, Heidi, were her serious world. Her play world was at school where nothing was serious, really, not for a girl who had a face like a woman in a novel.

When Kate grew up she scrutinized novels, old ones particularly, in an effort to discover what her grandfather had meant. When she grew up some more, she turned to psychology in an effort to discover which woman in which novel she might be. In time she came to know certain women well, in and out of novels.

Even though she knew she was not beautiful, she worried that she might be Anna Karenina, a woman she knew by instinct, a woman she feared. Anna, with her red leather bag, getting on the train at the beginning; Anna, with that same red leather bag, plunging beneath the train's wheels at the end. Why the red leather bag? Why the train? Surely Anna's fate was in some way connected to the fact of her face. Surely one day she would unravel what that mysterious connection might be.

Perhaps she should write a novel of her own, as Cora had told her to. Perhaps she would someday. In the meanwhile she entered the convent. It was autumn, and as the sisters walked in twos from chapel to school, the wind caught their veils and whirled them about so that they flapped like the wings of blackbirds.

4

Cora Kelleher had been the cleaning lady for the Stones ever since Kate's birth. She had seen Kate Stone grow up plain and skinny, she had seen her enter the convent, and she had seen her come out ten years later, blond and beautiful. In jig time Kate had gotten herself a husband, a job with IBM, and had taken up skiing, would you believe. There was no sign Kate was pregnant or about to be. Cora herself had had seven.

"I don't see she's pregnant," Cora said to Eunice, the part-time cook.

"Who would that be, now?" Eunice said, moony as ever.

"Kate Stone that was." She snorted. "The priest's wife."

"A lot of them today use the pill."

"A lot of them today use a lot of things."

"She's a beautiful girl, though." Eunice stopped peeling potatoes and gazed out the window dreamily. "And her a nun once."

"Her a nun and now that marriage. There's no luck on that marriage, let me tell you that."

"He teaches school," Eunice said, peeling again.

"Only high school. For all his priest education, he only teaches high school."

"She's a beautiful girl, though."

"Well, she was a plain stick of a thing when she was little. I remember once when she was no bigger than this, she says to me, giving herself airs, she says, 'Grandpa said I have the face of a woman in a novel.' 'And why is he telling you grand things like that?' I says. 'Because I asked him if he thought I was pretty,' she says. So I told her, I says to her, 'Well then, you'll have to write it yourself. There are no novels about skinny little things like yourself,' I says."

"Beautiful hair she has," Eunice said, peeling.

"She was always uppity. Another time, after her grandpa died it was, she said to me, all serious and with her eyes big, she says, 'I'm going to practice dying. Like Grandpa. I'm going to spend my whole life getting ready.' 'Are you, now!' I says to her. I says, 'Well, you're going to die anyway, ready or not, once it's your time.' Uppity she was and uppity she is."

"And her a nun once," Eunice said. "I could have been a nun once. Of course it's too late now." And she ran the water loudly, so Cora Kelleher had to shout.

"There'll be no luck to that marriage, you mark my words! A man and a woman are one thing. But a priest and a woman? It's like having a buzzard sitting right square on your tombstone."

5

It had been one hell of a day for him at school. The kids had been maliciously thickheaded and they had talked all through his exposition of Yeats's "Second Coming." So what was the use? And in the two hours before Kate got home from her office, he had accomplished absolutely nothing. The poem simply wouldn't come right, he just didn't have it, he wasn't a poet.

"You are a poet," she said, "you're a wonderful poet. Why don't you let me take a poet to dinner? Anywhere you want. Or you take me. Either way I get to dine with a poet. Bewitching."

So they went out to dinner and afterward to a movie and by then he'd cheered up and they made love. Kate had office work to do but she kept quiet about it and, for his sake, pinched and poked him until he felt like doing it again. After the second time they lay, exhausted, staring at the ceiling.

"I'm going to take one more try at that poem," he said.

"Good for you," she said. "And I'm going to take a shower and fix you a nice drink—I won't disturb you—and then I'll go do a little work too."

He heard the water come on and the glass doors slide closed. She was being awfully good; she always was. And he knew what a bore he must be, what a pain in the ass about being a failed poet. And God knows, he didn't mean to rage; he just couldn't help it. He'd make it up to her and surprise her in the shower.

He opened the bathroom door softly, though there was no need for stealth since the water was running wildly. He was about to slide open the glass doors to the shower when he saw—as if in a film—the long line of her body, complete, perfect. She had her head back so that the water struck her full in the face. He traced the long neck to where it disappeared in the rise of her small breasts. And then the rib cage and her little belly and the long severe thighs. Perfection.

He sat down on the toilet seat, his head in this hands.

"Will I ever know her?" he whispered, and then again, "Will I ever know her?" He had folded that body so completely into his own so many times now during these past three years, and still he had never seen her . . . he could not find the words . . . her naked face. "I will never know her," he whispered, but already he was thinking something else. He was thinking, I will never be a poet. Never.

He left the bathroom, angry, and went to his little study off the kitchen. Kate had shopped everywhere to get him just the right desk and she had decorated the study according to his instructions, but still he never used it. His desk was heaped with books and papers, so there was no room to write. He wrote either at the dining table, which he also kept heaped with books, or sitting in his easy chair. "You don't need a study if you can't write anyhow," he had told her, though it was he who had insisted on the study in the first place.

He could hear her tiptoeing around the kitchen as she got his drink ready. How could he concentrate knowing she might interrupt him at any second? "I don't want to bother you but . . . " He sat there, daring her. She glided into the room on her soft slippers and placed the drink on a coaster near him, patting him twice on the shoulder.

"God dammit," he shouted, "I'm trying to write. Is there no place in this goddamned apartment I can work in peace?"

"I didn't say anything," she said, defensive, used by now to these outbursts. "I just gave you your drink."

"You bumped me on the shoulder. You poked me twice. I was just getting it right and you interrupted and now it's gone." He looked at her with hatred and then took a good slug of his drink. "I'm sorry. I hate to sound like a bastard, but Jesus Christ!" He had been penitent for a second and now he was furious all over again. He slammed down the glass and the liquor sloshed onto his papers. "You always do this! You always ruin it! You always . . . " But she had gone. He followed her into the bedroom where she had her papers spread on the bed. She bent over the papers, not looking at him.

"Don't," she said. "Not again. I can't take it."

"Sometimes I detest you," he said. "Sometimes I curse the day I ever laid eyes on you."

She stared back at him in silence. And then she said, "Someday you'll say one thing too many. I give you warning. Now."

He backed out of the room. Several drinks later he woke her up. "Forgive me, sweet. Katie, forgive me, please," he said, and buried his head in her breasts.

"I know," she said. "It's all right. I love you."

"Friends?" he said.

"Friends," she said.

And so it was over, this time.

6

They had been married five years now, and it was winter. Icicles filled the long window that looked out over the ruined garden. It was evening and shadows in the garden and shadows in the living room flickered as Kate moved back and forth in front of the light, watering the indoor plants. She wore a red gown, knotted at the neck and waist, and it created for her a mood in which she could feel withdrawn but not unpleasant. Her husband sat with his chin in his hands, watching her, watching the shadows she cast. He had just despaired, yet again, of ever being a poet. And besides, he had a terrible sore throat. And so they had their last fight.

It was about her habit of visiting her widower father, that bastard, every Saturday, and about her job at IBM. And it was about her way of being vague with him, as if what he said required only half her attention, as if he didn't really matter. And it was about his failure as a writer.

Five years of this and now, at last, she had had enough.

"I can't live your life for you," she said. "There are some things you've got to do for yourself. You've got to breathe, you've got to eat, you've got to crap, and god dammit, you've got to live. And if you hate your job, then do something about it. And if you resent mine, which you do, then why don't you . . . "

"Go ahead, say it! Say it! You've been wanting to."

But she didn't say it. She went to bed and he went to the kitchen for a drink. He had a second and a third and then he went in to wake her but she wasn't asleep yet anyhow. He apologized and she apologized and it was almost over.

Deliberately he looked at her hand. He had had a sort of vision once of who she was and how she loved him and it had split him down the middle. He had thought at the time that he had become two people, both of them crazy. And all because of her hand. She had placed it on his knee during a quarrel—afterward he could not remember what the quarrel was about—and he had watched it crumple and break like an autumn leaf, while his words continued angry and smooth and satisfying. In those days he had had all the words. And then, as the hand fell from his knee, he stopped and said to her, "I'm not a good person. I'm not like you." He cried then, and he had not cried in fifteen years. That was during the first week of their marriage.

Now, five years later, he sat on the edge of the bed looking at her hand, white and small with long tapered fingers, trying to make it happen again, that vision.

But nothing happened.

"Friends?" he said.

"Friends," she said.

In bed, they both pretended to sleep. After a long while she got up and poured herself a drink and sat in the dark living room. She finished it and poured herself another. Then, not really knowing what she was going to do, she put on the light and got out a pencil and a legal pad and wrote, "I want out. I want a divorce." She stared at the words for a long time, and then she wrote them again. And then again. She found a peculiar satisfaction in forming the letters, in putting down on paper those words that finally said the unsayable. "I hate him. I hate what he turns me into. I hate the way he hates himself." She made a list of the things she could not say, and she said them. She wrote out their most violent quarrels, including in parentheses the words she had not said because they might kill him. ("You'll never be a poet." "You have a gift for words but no gift for poetry." "You're wrecking your life and you're trying to wreck mine, but I'm not going to let you." "Why didn't you stay in the priesthood and just drink yourself to death?") And it was astonishing. Words did not kill, at least not on paper. Rather, they gave her a wonderful feeling of release, of freedom. She got herself another drink and went on writing until, hours later, she had run out of things she was angry at. Without a pause she moved into a description of how she had first met him, her husband now, in the train station. The strap had broken on her red leather tote bag and he had offered to help her with it. But the bag was square, and with his hands occupied with skis and his own suitcase, he hadn't been able to get a good grip on it; he dropped it and it opened and spilled out keys and makeup and God knows what else. She had laughed at him then and he had laughed too.

She stopped writing—these notes, in time, would find their way into her first novel—and looked out at the garden where the sun was just touching the silver branches of the trees. A single blackbird lit on the end of a branch, making it bend, sending down a thin sifting of snow. Smiling to herself, she recited the Magnificat, as she had done every morning for the past twenty years.

And so the divorce was put off for eleven months.

7

During those eleven months they often walked by the river together. And they often dined out. He appeared to be the more talkative but in public she did most of the talking. If the marriage was not a happy one, they at least put a good face on it, and five years is a long time to put a good face on anything.

Acquaintances who had known them off and on for years said that marriage made them both merely conventional. His wild imagination and flights of whimsy disappeared altogether, replaced by a kind of watchfulness and a mildly sardonic humor. She talked politics a lot and, when the conversation turned to religion, she avoided discussion of how much she still believed, dismissing the topic with a remark about how bored she was with Sunday sermons.

Friends of hers who visited from the convent said the couple was supremely happy. She had taken to wearing high-fashion clothes, finding it necessary to be more feminine now that she had so many males directly responsible to her. She had a big job with big obligations. Friends of his who visited from the monastery said she had done wonders for him. He had put on weight and he was no longer so volatile. He had settled down to being a high school teacher; her big job with IBM obviously posed no ego problems for him.

They had private jokes and sometimes on the street they were caught laughing immoderately. They held hands at these times. They also held hands in restaurants, though not so frequently as on their walks. This was not natural in people married so long; it was probably a cover-up for something.

After eleven endless months they separated.

8

In the two years of their separation he had seven job promotions with his ad agency and she wrote two novels, both of them flops.

He had moved to New York, and by some fluke, or by talent, managed to put together a trendy portfolio. In no time he was making as much money as Kate, and by the end of the two years he was making a great deal more. He was happy and fulfilled, except of course that he missed her. He was a different man now. It was the writing that had made him so miserable. She'd see. Would she take him back? Would she agree to drop the divorce business and give the marriage another try? And, ahem, would IBM be willing to transfer her from her new job in Gaithersburg to a newer one in New York?

She smiled. She would think about it. But he'd better be clear on one thing: she was fiddling around with a novel and she didn't intend to give it up for anybody. Got that?

The first two novels were mistakes, no doubt about it. She had begun with a description of their meeting in the train station, a nice, tightly written scene, but when read aloud it sounded so like a murder mystery that she decided to turn it into one. She killed herself off in the first chapter and then . . . well, it didn't work out. Her murders were clumsy and her murderers uninteresting; she was more preoccupied with pyschoanalyzing the bereaved than with moving the damned plot along. Five publishers turned it down before she realized that it was a mistake, that she just didn't know anything about murders and she didn't care much either.

With the second novel she decided to stick to what she knew: life in a convent. She put in the mistress of novices and her more colorful teachers and her eager and ambitious nun friends, all of them meticulously drawn. She had gotten down every revealing gesture, every idiosyncrasy of speech and behavior, and yet somehow nobody came alive. The book was a jumble of real people rather than fictional characters, and it was rejected everywhere.

Her next novel, the one she wouldn't give up for anybody, would be different. She would write about what she knew as if she didn't really know it. And she would put herself in it. One thing was certain: whatever it was that she knew and was able to get down on paper, she herself was involved in it.

Meanwhile she would think about dropping the divorce suit. She might even think about requesting a transfer.

9

In Utica, New York, the priest's mother heard the following established facts at the Ladies' Guild:

1. Katharine Stone had grown up in Utica and moved to Boston when she was five. She was an airline stewardess for seven years and often flew back and forth between Boston and upper New York State. Now that she was separated she had gone back to United. She had been seen in her uniform only last week. In Utica. Many people in Utica knew her well.

2. Kate Stone was a staff editor of *Ms.* magazine and had formerly been a fashion model. She was six feet tall and beautiful. She dated married men.

3. Katharine Stone was a former nun who grew up in D.C. but who lived, at the time of her marriage, in Baltimore. She was from a distinguished family of doctors in which all the men went to Harvard and all the women to Radcliffe. She was, despite this, not the least bit snobbish and was quite content teaching high school English. Her family would never permit a divorce.

4. A friend of the guild's president's daughter had gone to Noroton with Kate Stone and there they had both known the Ford girls, Anne and Charlotte. They, the four, had not been close since she entered the convent. Kate Stone, of course. Anne Ford had not entered the convent and neither had Charlotte.

5. Kate Stone had been a dancer until she broke her foot. Since then she had worked for IBM and spent all her free time skiing. She was going to get a divorce and then marry her ski instructor.

The priest's mother went home and cried until ten, when "Kojak" came on.

10

In the spring of that year they both got transfers to Boston, where they bought a house and took up where they left off, only a lot better. Kate was involved in writing her novel and her husband was all worked up over a new ad campaign, and so they were happy. They even put in their names to adopt a child.

That summer they drove to Baltimore to visit Kate's friends in the convent. Kate was all in white and very tanned though it was still only the end of June. He was wearing his white suit and his white shoes, too summery perhaps, just this side of affectation. They knew they looked good.

Kate's friends came to the visiting parlor in twos and threes. Visits were not so exciting as they had been years ago, before the cloister had moved into the world. These days a visit from outside meant little. Still, everybody was curious to see the couple now that they were reconciled. How long would it last? Kate looked wonderful, but he was putting on weight. He was polite, said very little. Whenever they asked about him, he answered briefly and directed the conversation back to Kate and her friends. There was no telling from the way he acted whether or not he'd take off again for New York. Poor Kate.

At noon some of the sisters went to chapel for midday meditation. Kate and her husband went for a walk around the grounds. Hand in hand they walked down the long slope of grass to the lake. A small dirt path ran around the lake and they followed it for a while, disappearing among the overhanging willows and high swamp grass. There were pine needles everywhere. He wanted to lie down on them but she said no, it was time to turn back. They lay down for a little while anyway.

As they came out from under the trees, they paused and looked across the lake. The sun turned the water green and cast a green reflection on their faces and clothes.

The sisters, coming out of chapel, paused on the cloister walk to gaze out over the lake. The sisters saw the man and woman, their hands joined together, their clothes of dazzling white drenched green in the reflection from the lake. Just those two white figures, joined, against the world of green.

Someone cried out in disbelief.

11

And so she finished the damned book, as she said, and got a publisher, and sold 1,600 copies of it. *The New York Times* said it was a promising start and *The New Republic* said it was witty and disturbing. Nobody else said anything about it.

What she wrote was, in actuality, a pack of lies about her friends at IBM and about her husband and—in a peculiar way—about herself. The characters numbered thirteen and they were as diverse in their morals and desires and preoccupations as even God or nature would have made them. There was a man who was so insecure he dared to communicate with his employees only when he had worked himself into a rage. There was a man whose sole love was for machines and who had cut himself off from human intercourse completely. There was a housewife whose loneliness and vulnerability drove her into affairs with any man who presented himself. And another who wanted to write poetry and instead was drinking herself to death. And a woman executive who made passionate love to her husband each night, moaning and tearing at his flesh, and then went to the bathroom where she calmly and coldly masturbated before the full-length mirror. They were unscrupulous people and hateful people and pitiful people. And all of them, so her husband recognized, understanding at last, were Kate Stone. In some way, at some moment in the story, they all wore her face.

He was grateful for the book. She existed now, in reality, for him.

She was grateful too. The book was done, some kind of awful duty was discharged, and she felt no desire to write another. All she wanted to do now was to take up skiing once again and to conquer at last the dark fear of hers that plunging down that slope was somehow entering the valley of the shadow of death.

12

It was their anniversary and she gave him a card she had made herself. Inside it she had written, "This river that carries us with it, out of control, out of any control, at least carries us together."

He did not know what she meant, he never knew what she meant, but it no longer mattered because he had seen her naked face and loved her.

13

Time passed for them. There may have been children, a boy and a girl, adopted. There may have been a dog. There may have been . . . but the snow falls and everything recedes into uncertainty, except that we die and we do not wish to die.

"It's snowing," she said.

"And it's going to snow," he said.

The light on the snow had been pale purple all afternoon and, though it continued to snow, she insisted nonetheless on going skiing.

They were seen leaving the lodge where everyone was sitting around drinking hot buttered rum by the fireplace and they were seen again later taking the lift to the highest slope. Slowly at first, and then with lightning speed, they descended, two black figures against the white snow, darting across one another's path, plunging straight down and then veering off at an angle, dodging invisible poles. For a long while people from the lodge watched them, but then the sun dipped behind the trees. Nonetheless they went on ascending and descending that hill.

In the first dark an owl hooted and some winter bird shifted on his perch in the cedar limbs.

The Consolation of Philosophy

NICHOLAS DELBANCO

W HEN HE HEARD his first lover was getting divorced, Robert
Lewin panicked. He had not seen her in ten years; they had
not been together for fifteen. They had few friends in common; her
world was not his world. She was an actress of sufficient fame for her
private life to seem public; she smiled at him from newsstands or in the
supermarket checkout display. He read about her husband's drinking
problem, her near-fatal car crash in Topanga Canyon and their second
son's kidney malfunction. The photographs in gossip magazines had
captions like "Sally Smiles to Hide the Tears," or "Tragedy Offstage!"

Robert disapproved. But in a way that was not casual he had loved
her all his life; he dreamed that they grew old together, laughing in
their sixties at the passion they shared when eighteen. He was thirty-
eight years old, an architect; he, his wife and daughter lived on the
Connecticut and Massachusetts border. Sally would purchase a house
near their village. Knowing that he lived there, she would hire him
to remodel her country retreat. She would want the silo to have two
bedrooms and a bathroom, and the barn to be a studio. She would
dam the stream and have him build a sauna and a free-form swimming
pool. All this would be accomplished at long distance, and via inter-
mediaries. She would buy the property sight unseen, and with all its
furniture; Samantha, his wife, would not know. One bright autumn
morning, Sally would fly in from the Coast to check on her dream's
progress. He would receive her smiling, wearing dark glasses, not
old. She would fold herself into his arms. She would say nothing,
since nothing could improve the silence they shared.

At other times he gave her lines. "I never loved another man," she
said. "Not the way that I loved you. It never does happen again."

"I know."

"It happens differently," she said. "I won't pretend I didn't love Bill.
Our marriage was—well, workable. But no other man in my life . . ."

"We don't have to discuss it."

"We do. No other man in my life was ever quite as—what shall I call it, *protective* as you were. Considerate. You *did* take me under your wing."

Her diction had grown formal. "Is this a performance?" he asked.

"No. You took care of me. You helped with my homework, remember?"

At this point inventiveness stopped. Robert pictured them in bed but using their twenty-year-previous bodies; he had not seen her in the flesh to judge how flesh had changed. His own had thickened, some; his hair had thinned. Her consorts were the beautiful people, and he would not fit. His clothes were out of date. He passed for fashionable in the Berkshires, still, but felt less and less at ease in cities or with the gaudy young. He designed doctors' offices and banks. His clients all distrusted what they called the avant-garde. They wanted renovation work and, where possible, restoration. They wanted contemporary styling with a Colonial theme.

He worked alone. He had a large, illuminated globe on a teak stand by his desk. When drinking coffee, or in the intervals when concentration failed, his habit was to spin the globe and shut his eyes and stop its spinning with his finger. There, where the rotation ceased, he would embark on a new life. He landed in Afghanistan and northern Italy and the Atlantic Ocean and near Singapore. With disconcerting frequency, he landed on the Yucatán peninsula; once he pinpointed Mérida four times in a row.

The phone rang. "Are you coming home for lunch?" Samantha asked.

"I wasn't planning to."

"All right."

"Has something happened?"

"No. It's just I've got some errands, and you said you might come home this morning. And I wanted to be here if you did."

"If you're coming into town," he offered, "we could meet."

"No, darling, really. I've got forty things to do and might as well start doing them."

"I'll work right through," said Robert. "And I'll be home by five. Five-thirty at the latest."

"See you then."

Something in her manner troubled him, as if she called to know his plans rather than meet him for lunch. He lifted the receiver in order to return the call, to find her at the house and tell her he was coming home; his plans had changed. It was eleven o'clock. He did not dial. The prospect of a day without appointments was satisfying, nearly; he shut his eyes and spun and landed in Zagreb.

As the years passed, his years with Sally grew abstract; they both had been beginners, he would say. He forgot the reasons why they grew apart, the bitterness and boredom, and remembered only love. His memory was made up of amorous scenes. He remembered singing with her on a moonlit night in Tanglewood, standing by their blanket in the intermission, drinking rum from his initialed flask and harmonizing on the chorus of "Old Devil Moon." It was 1963; they both played the guitar. Their parents approved. She told him her last boyfriend drove a Thunderbird and wanted to be an astronaut; he probably would be, she said, he understood machines and thought the human body was just another machine. He didn't understand the finer things, spiritual things; by comparison with her last boyfriend— by comparison with everybody—Robert was a prince. Each night when he left her she whispered, " 'Good-night, sweet prince.' " He said, " 'And flights of angels sing thee to thy rest.' " She said, "Drive carefully," and he walked backward to the car so as not to lose the imprint of her face. She blinked the house lights three times in farewell; he flashed his car lights also and, for her sake, did drive carefully.

Sally wore her dark hair long. She had a Roman nose and large brown eyes. He called her "almond-eyes" and "beauty" and "love." They took each other's virginity. He remembered how she came to him in her parents' house in Weston, wearing a white negligee and carrying a towel. They spent their college weekends together; he attended Amherst and she, Smith. They embraced in pine lots and in barns and on the rear seat of his Impala and, later, in hotels. They intended to marry as soon as he got his degree. A hollowed-out tree trunk, he said, with a view of the sky would be plenty; it doesn't matter what we do so long as we do it together.

While Robert studied architecture, she applied to and was accepted by the Yale Drama School. They shared an apartment in New Haven, but her schedule and his schedule did not coincide. She performed when he came home from class, and he could not rouse her in the mornings. She dressed in black. They struggled with fidelity; she said she was attracted to Mercutio in her scene-study class. He did not confess to it but slept with a girl in Design; their afternoon encounters increased his passion for Sally at night. When she discovered his affair, she broke their stoneware plates and slammed the cutting board so hard against the counter that it broke.

He could remember how he watched her in rehearsal and saw a gifted stranger. Even then she had the quality of apartness, that silent holding-back the critics came to praise. Her first reviews were raves. They called it "presence," "power in reserve," and when she went to Hollywood, they said that Broadway lost a rising star. Robert lost control. All that fall he called her nightly, running up a telephone bill he had to borrow to pay. He drank too much and worked too little and flew round trip to Los Angeles just to have a cup of coffee with her at the airport. She was living with another man, she said, and would not take him home.

He completed architecture school and elected to practice in Stockbridge, not Manhattan. At twenty-six he married a girl from Springfield; they bought property southwest of town. He modernized the farmhouse and converted the barns. Samantha played the violin and formed a local string quartet; on their sixth anniversary, Helen, their daughter, was born. He prospered; they spent summers on the Cape.

He could have been an actor, people said; his voice was so mellifluous. He could have been associated with such men as I.M. Pei or Edward Larrabee Barnes. Once a friend had said to him, "Don't sweat the small stuff. I see you with a beggar's cup. Saffron robes. That's the kind of change you ought to contemplate, that's the way to get in touch with universal flux. I *see* it . . ." Robert failed to, but he had been flattered. He carried with him, always, a sense of alternative possibility; his dreams were of escape.

"What's wrong?" Samantha asked.

"Nothing. Why?"

"You're sure?"

He had been splitting wood. He brought in an armload of logs. "It's cold out there," he said. "It feels like snow."

"Is something bothering you?"

"No."

"Do you want to talk about it?"

"I told you," Robert said. "It's only I'm restless. That's all."

"Would you rather I take her?"

"No."

Helen studied ballet. She was plump and unenthusiastic; he had promised to drive her, that afternoon, to see *The Nutcracker* in Springfield. Helen had wanted to go with a friend. "Why can't we take Jessie?" she asked.

"There aren't any seats left."

"How do you know?"

"It's sold out," he said. "I heard it on the radio."

"Jessie's busy anyhow," Samantha said. "Her grandparents are visiting."

"Would *you* come, Mommy?"

Samantha looked at Robert, and he shook his head. He would have liked nothing better than an afternoon of silence, but he had committed himself. He showered and shaved; the forecast was for flurries, so he took the Jeep. "Be careful," said Samantha.

"Yes."

He called her Sam. They were happily married, he said; she had the kind of resilience he lacked. She lived in the present, he said; if she had an emotion she showed it. If she was angry she expressed it, and the anger disappeared; when she was happy she sang. Helen slept beside him, her seat belt cinching her coat. Beleaguered by desire, he watched the women in the cars he passed, and in oncoming cars. He was, he told himself, just facing middle age, the loss of prowess and mobility that torments every man. This did not help.

He had last seen Sally at a party in Hyannis Port. They had been eating baked stuffed clams and drinking spritzers; his host was saying that he never ate an uncooked clam these days. There had been a hepatitis scare. "It's not as if," his host admitted, "cooking makes a difference. But I feel safer, understand, as if the odds are better when it's cooked." He offered Robert the tray. "It's a kind of roulette we play with our bellies," he said. "It's the bourgeois way of risking things." He discoursed on the difference between littlenecks and cherrystones and quahogs; they were standing on a lawn that sloped down to the shore. "Littlenecks grow up to be cherrystones," said his host. "You understand that, I suppose. And cherrystones to quahogs; it's just a question of when you harvest them. As Marx observes, a sufficient change in quantity means a qualitative change." He lit a pipe. "I always ask myself at what point such change is enforced."

"Enforced?"

"Yes. Decided on. Agreed on, if you'd prefer. When does someone somewhere say, 'Enough. Thou shalt be no more Mr. Littleneck. I dub thee Cherrystone'?" His host laughed and flourished the pipe. "The trial by fire. Sir Clam."

Sally approached. She was wearing white. He felt his stomach tighten and release. "Ah," said his host. "The guest of honor. How *are* you, my darling? Do you know each other? This is Robert . . ."

"Lewin," Robert said. "Yes. We've met."

She had been as shocked as he, she confessed, but had seen him from the patio. She had been in the area for summer stock, a one-week stint, and was leaving; why is it always like this, she asked, why do we have to go just when we want to remain? He was looking wonderful; his beard made him look like a badger. Was his marriage working out; was his wife at the party?

They made their way to the beach. A rowboat and a Sunfish were pulled up past the tide line, and she settled in the rowboat. He also sat, facing her, facing the house.

"I miss you," Sally said.

"Yes."

"It doesn't change, does it?"

"Not really. No."

"This is horrible," she said. "I wish you wouldn't look like that. I wish I'd come here by myself."

"Who's with you?"

"Everybody. I hide it better, that's all. You should have seen your face—oh, Robert, when that man said, 'Do you know each other?' How *are* you, anyway?"

He scanned the lawn, then patio, then porch.

"All right."

"You mean it?"

He nodded.

"We've wrecked each other's lives, you know."

"No."

"Yes."

"That's overstating it."

With one of those reversals that had made her, always, his equal adversary, Sally said, "Of course. I know I'm overstating it. I'm being theatrical, darling. That's what I do best."

"Other things also," he said.

"But I'm not lying. You lied. You said you were all right."

She shifted weight in the boat. In a movement he could picture clearly, ten years thereafter, she stripped off her white tights. It was a practiced motion, neither suggestive nor coy; she crossed her long, bare legs. She leaned back on her seat. He asked himself—and would, repeatedly—if she were proposing sex or getting ready to walk on the sand. Her clothing was intact, her sandals and her tights placed neatly by her side. He looked away. Samantha appeared on the porch. Men stood with her, gesticulating. He could hear her laughter. "I hate this," Robert said. He rose; the rowboat rocked. He put one foot over the gunwale. "I want what's best for you," he lied. "And that was never me."

"I'll stay here, thanks," she said. "Goodnight."

"How did it go?" Samantha asked, when he and Helen returned. He hung up his coat. He kicked off his boots. "Terrific," Robert said. "Twenty dollars so she gets to see the bottom of the chair. The part you look at from the floor."

"I closed my eyes, Mommy," she said.

"But what about the Christmas tree? The celebration?"

"I liked *that* part," said Helen.

"And the dance of the Sugar Plum Fairy?"

"He was horrible," she said. "He had big teeth and this enormous tail and his sword was all bloody. He looked like a *rat*."

"The Nutcracker kills him," Robert said. "You should have watched that part."

"I *told* you," she said, stamping. She turned from him.

"Well, maybe next year," offered Samantha. "Maybe this year was too early for you."

"Let's have a drink," Robert said. "Two vodka Martinis and one hot chocolate for our famous ballerina here."

"All right."

"You do the hot chocolate," he said. "And I'll do the vodka."

They entered the kitchen. Light from the kitchen fireplace played off the copper pots. "Next year," Helen asserted, "I'll be the Sugar Plum Fairy. I will be. You'll see."

Outside, the first snow continued. He had spotlights in the tamarack and maple trees; he turned them on. The garden appeared to leap forward and the kitchen's cage recede. He watched with genuine attention while the fall increased. The grass above the septic tank retained a warmth that melted snow, making a rectangle of bare land on the lawn; it looked like a lap rug thrown over a sheet.

"I don't know what you want from me," Samantha said. "It feels like it's never enough. No matter how much I give, it feels like there's always this one thing left over—this way that we fail you."

"What is it now?" Robert asked.

"She's scared of the Mouse King." Helen was drinking her cocoa in the television room. "So you make it seem *my* fault . . ."

"It isn't your fault."

"I'm not saying that. I'm saying you *think* so; I'm saying you've blamed me all day. As if no child of yours could ever hide under a chair." Samantha exhaled. "As if her sensitivity is something we should apologize for—as if there's something, oh, shameful in a child who has feelings."

"It isn't shameful," he said. He set himself to placate her; he poured another drink. "Control yourself" had been his mother's injunction. Whenever he was greedy, loud or frightened, she would say, "Control yourself. A gentleman has self-control. He doesn't make a fuss about the things he doesn't understand. And if he understands them, there's no need to fuss."

"I love you," Sally said again. She would have purchased Sevenoaks Farm; they would be forty-five. "These barns, that view of the mountains."

"And I love you," he said.

"What have you been up to, baby?" She lit a cigarette. She offered him one; he declined.

"I didn't know you smoked," he said.

"Only when I'm happy. This house makes me happy. And how's your family?"

"They're good," he said. "We live a quiet life."

"You have a daughter, don't you?"

"Helen. Yes."

Sally examined the bay window. "Will you move in with me?" she asked.

"Right now?"

"No. Tomorrow," she said.

His most recent client had been a family therapy center. They had wanted picture windows in the waiting rooms. This had violated Robert's sense of decorum. He said so; they disagreed. There was a village graveyard in the adjoining lot, and he situated the pentagonal structure so the picture windows overlooked the graveyard. "It's tempting," Robert said.

"Be tempted."

"You're serious?"

"Yes. Never more so."

"We've got twenty years," he said. "With luck. Twenty good years, anyhow."

"I'm ready to quit," Sally said. She was emphatic. "I've done enough acting."

"You'll miss it."

"No way. Not for a minute."

He knew enough to know this was not likely. "It's a hard habit to kick," Robert said. "I'm sure it must be difficult. All that applause."

"Those flowers," she would tease him. "Those parties at Sardi's, those feet in Grauman's Theater. Baby, it's nothing like that. It's sons of bitches, ego trips and cameos from here on in."

"You're sure?"

"I'm sure. I've never been more certain in my life."

They would sit in peaceable silence; there were no telephones. They would not bicker as they'd bickered when young; they understood the value of a gentle reticence. The sunset would be doubled by the clear reflecting mirror in the pond and, beneath it, the pool. He dreamed of this in winter while he sluiced down his own pond and scraped it for skating; he dreamed of it that early spring while the ice cracked and thawed. He filled the pool in May. Brian Dennis, after his annual checkup and the lab results, pronounced Robert fit. He redesigned the railroad station, making it a restaurant. Samantha started to jog. She was a natural athlete and soon attained four miles a day. She looked radiant; he wondered what she pictured as she ran.

Their village had a harpsichord maker. He had a shop in West Street, with a sign saying "Master Craftsman" in the window and a harpsichord-in-progress on display. There were marble steps and lintels in the shop, and ornamental handcarved treble clefs on the door. Samantha knew him, apparently; she mentioned him in passing as a person Robert might enjoy, an adequate instrument maker. He sometimes joined their string quartet to add a piano part. The shop had an apartment on the second floor. Robert, walking to the bank or on his way from lunch or driving home from work, would slow down at the door. He was prepared to ask the price of harpsichords and, perhaps, to commission a lute. The door was never open. There were signs of life, however—fresh piles of sawdust at the workbench, or coffee mugs, or a wastepaper basket filled with what he recognized as that week's Sunday *Times*.

The upstairs apartment, too, seemed untenanted. One day Robert noticed its windows were open, and a woman with her back to him was brushing her brown hair. He stopped. He stood on the opposite side of the street, staring up. There were white lace curtains that obscured his view. He half crouched by a pickup truck; he put his feet on the bumper, one after the other, and pretended to adjust the laces of his boots. He felt exposed, aroused, but could not leave. Her body was supple. She wore a white brassiere that emphasized the pallor of her back. The light was on. She brushed her hair with metronomic regularity, stopping to shift angles every twenty strokes. She was looking at a mirror; he could not see her face. He wondered, was there someone in the room? Her attitude suggested readiness, a knowledge that she might be watched, a sense of self-display. She was familiar, somehow, yet he thought he did not know her: the mistress of the man who made the harpsichords. Her arms were lean. Robert shook his head to clear it, and in that unfocused instant the woman in the window disappeared. Yet he thought he heard her voice. He waited for some minutes, then continued home. Samantha was not there.

He turned thirty-nine in March, and they invited friends for dinner. There were jokes about Jack Benny and the wheelchair he would get next year. "If you think *this* one was bad," said Brian Dennis, "wait till you're forty." Richard Beale had been studying Baba Ram Dass. "'Doing your own being,'" he said. "That's what it's all about, really. Just being here in the here and now. Your health, amigo," he said. "May you be here with joy."

Samantha served poached salmon, and then a rack of lamb. This repeated the menu they shared on their first night as man and wife; Robert was touched. "It's better now," he told her. "You're a better cook than those restaurant chefs."

"You're paying more attention to your food these days."

"All right. I meant it as a compliment."

"I take it that way."

"I'm grateful," he said. "When I said things were better, I didn't mean only the food."

"Happy birthday. Many happy returns of the day."

"'After forty,'" Ellen Dennis said, "'I hold a man's face against him.' Who said that, anyway? I think it was Abraham Lincoln."

"Winston Churchill," Brian said. "It must have been Churchill, not Lincoln."

So they argued over eloquence, and whether Lincoln or Churchill had been the better native speaker, more in touch with the language and times. Jim and Patty Rosenfield had just returned from England, from his sabbatical semester; they contended that the English had a greater native eloquence. "The problem is, however," Jim said, "they all speak so well that you never know who's *saying* something. And who's just making sentences. Even the dumb ones sound smart."

"Another thing," said Patty. "Inflation. You can't imagine how bad it is over there. How expensive everything has gotten. We entertained a little less. Maybe we ate out more often. But at the end of every week we filled two garbage cans."

Richard drank. "What does all this have to do with Lincoln or with Churchill?"

"Waste," she said. "That's what I'm discussing. We throw away more food than all Australia eats."

"I'll drink to that," Robert said. He shut his eyes. The image of Sally assailed him again—some taste or word or smell or sight inciting memory. They were near a sandbar in a salt-water inlet, making love. He lay on his back in the warm shallows, and she sat on top of him. There was a thick fog. Sailors glided in the distance; he propped himself up on his elbows so as not to swallow salt. It was the start of the fall. The cranberries were purple already, and the bench-heather was brown. Gulls watched, incurious. She bounced and settled on him, smiling, her eyes wide. They rented a bungalow called Peony; it stood in a strip of bungalows named after flowers; their neighbors were Tulip and Rose. The fog felt palpable. He saw himself the sailor now, seeing from the channel how the complicated obscure shape of youth is jointed at the waist; he watched how fleetingly they fused and broke apart. He toasted his guests and his wife.

They kept in touch, but distantly; a friend of friends said, "Sally sends regards." Her telephone number was unlisted; she sent it to him in April and wrote, "Hope to hear from you." By the time he did call, from his office, a recorded voice pronounced, "We're sorry. We cannot complete your call as dialed." He was not sorry, he decided, he would not have known what to say. Panic is the fear engendered by the great god Pan. He comes to the party unannounced and over-turns the chairs and spills his drink on the rug. He will attempt his magic trick with the tablecloth. He scratches his beard , paws the floor.

Promising the cutlery and plate and crystal will remain in place, he whisks the white linen away. He is clumsy, however; things crash and tumble all over. The girl at the head of the table gets wine on her jumpsuit. She scrambles to her feet and scampers down the hall. He follows her, apologetic. There are remedies. They huddle together. There are dry cleaners, other parties, prospects of the sea. There is time.

Wind rattled at the pantry door when she opened the door to the mud room. She settled her handbag and two paper bags on the bench.

"You're having an affair," he said.

Samantha took off her gloves. She placed them on the shelf. "Was that a question?"

"No."

"Good." She shrugged out of her coat. "It didn't sound like a question."

"Are you having an affair?"

"In any case"—she selected a hook—"I don't think I'll bother to answer."

"His harpsichord. How quickly can he build one?"

"That depends," she said.

"He's careful?"

"Yes."

"Attentive?"

"Very."

"A master craftsman," Robert said.

"I've been downtown, master. Shopping." She opened the mud-room door again. "In case you're curious."

"Yes."

"Be careful with the eggs," she said. "They're in the bag in the Jeep."

In June the local ballet school offered a performance. It ran for three successive nights, and each was sold out in advance; the children came home from rehearsal with their allocated tickets. Helen was in the school's youngest class, but there were students all the way through high school. The program was immense. Its theme was that of "The Magic Garden," and children were divided, according to age and experience, into several units: there were butterflies and inchworms, bumblebees and bunny rabbits, a group of birds and flowers and scarecrows. The soloists were labeled Spring, Summer, Autumn, Winter; there were twelve such soloists, with four to perform on each night. The owner of the ballet school was, as she put it, *bouleversée*; she made a speech before the performance and said she was just so excitable because of these wonderful wonderful students that *bouleversée* was her only expression; we are enraptured to see you all here.

Helen was a Black-Eyed Susan; she wore a bright green tutu and brown leotard and fitted orange cap. There were twenty other Black-Eyed Susans, and they skipped onstage, then curtsied and circled and whirled. Helen did so by herself. Then they all joined hands and did what looked like the Virginia Reel; fathers filled the aisles and, using flash attachments, photographed their girls. Robert had not brought his camera. He had had a long afternoon. He had come directly from the office to the auditorium; there were problems with the railroad ties he'd used for decorative beams.

During intermission, he could not find Samantha in the sea of women and daughters waiting in the hall. He pushed through swinging doors to what would be backstage; the Rhododendrons and the Owls were doing warm-ups by the barre. There were belly dancers also, waiting for their turn in "The Magic Garden"; they wore veils and diaphanous skirts. Mothers were removing rouge and lipstick from their daughters' upturned faces. Helen said, "Hi, Daddy."

He looked for her.

"Hi. Here we are."

Samantha closed her makeup kit. She stood.

"Well, look at you," said Robert. "You look beautiful."

"Thank you, Daddy." Helen pursed her lips, demure.

"Doesn't she?" Samantha said. "How do you like these sequins?"

"Very much," he said.

"The ponytail?" asked Helen.

"Yes. You'll be a star."

All around him, Robert knew, fathers were thinking the same of their daughters; all around him the girls were transformed. She was, he said, his precious ballerina, his precocious soloist. A belly dancer brushed past. "Do you want to watch the second half?" he asked.

"I'm tired, Daddy."

"You?" he asked Samantha.

"I'll tell the Cartwrights we're leaving. We got a ride down here with them, so we could all go home together."

She was, he told Samantha, wonderful. Helen wore eye-liner and mascara and had not smudged her lipstick or her rouge. Samantha turned and, bending, began to scrub at the upturned face. "Leave it," he said to his ladies. Helen wore her tutu to the car.

A Father's Story

ANDRE DUBUS

M Y NAME IS Luke Ripley, and here is what I call my life: I own a
stable of thirty horses, and I have young people who teach
riding, and we board some horses too. This is in northeastern Massachusetts. I have a barn with an indoor ring, and outside I've got two
fenced-in rings and a pasture that ends at a woods with trails. I call
it my life because it looks like it is, and people I know call it that, but
it's a life I can get away from when I hunt and fish, and some nights
after dinner when I sit in the dark in the front room and listen to
opera. The room faces the lawn and the road, a two-lane country
road. When cars come around the curve northwest of the house, they
light up the lawn for an instant, the leaves of the maple out by the
road and the hemlock closer to the window. Then I'm alone again,
or I'd appear to be if someone crept up to the house and looked
through a window: a big-gutted gray-haired guy, drinking tea and
smoking cigarettes, staring out at the dark woods across the road,
listening to a grieving soprano.

My real life is the one nobody talks about anymore, except Father
Paul LeBoeuf, another old buck. He has a decade on me: he's sixty-
four, a big man, bald on top with gray at the sides; when he had hair,
it was black. His face is ruddy, and he jokes about being a whiskey
priest, though he's not. He gets outdoors as much as he can, goes
for a long walk every morning, and hunts and fishes with me. But I
can't get him on a horse anymore. Ten years ago I could badger him
into a trail ride; I had to give him a western saddle, and he'd hold
the pommel and bounce through the woods with me, and be sore for
days. He's looking at seventy with eyes that are younger than many
I've seen in people in their twenties. I do not remember ever feeling
the way they seem to; but I was lucky, because even as a child I knew
that life would try me, and I must be strong to endure, though in
those early days I expected to be tortured and killed for my faith, like
the saints I learned about in school.

Father Paul's family came down from Canada, and he grew up speaking more French than English, so he is different from the Irish priests who abound up here. I do not like to make general statements, or even to hold general beliefs, about people's blood, but the Irish do seem happiest when they're dealing with misfortune or guilt, either their own or somebody else's, and if you think you're not a victim of either one, you can count on certain Irish priests to change your mind. On Wednesday nights Father Paul comes to dinner. Often he comes on other nights too, and once, in the old days when we couldn't eat meat on Fridays, we bagged our first ducks of the season on a Friday, and as we drove home from the marsh, he said: For the purposes of Holy Mother Church, I believe a duck is more a creature of water than land, and is not rightly meat. Sometimes he teases me about never putting anything in his Sunday collection, which he would not know about if I hadn't told him years ago. I would like to believe I told him so we could have philosophical talk at dinner, but probably the truth is I suspected he knew, and I did not want him to think I so loved money that I would not even give his church a coin on Sunday. Certainly the ushers who pass the baskets know me as a miser.

I don't feel right about giving money for buildings, places. This starts with the Pope, and I cannot respect one of them till he sells his house and everything in it, and that church too, and uses the money to feed the poor. I have rarely, and maybe never, come across saintliness, but I feel certain it cannot exist in such a place. But I admit, also, that I know very little, and maybe the popes live on a different plane and are tried in ways I don't know about. Father Paul says his own church, St. John's, is hardly the Vatican. I like his church: it is made of wood, and has a simple altar and crucifix, and no padding on the kneelers. He does not have to lock its doors at night. Still it is a place. He could say Mass in my barn. I know this is stubborn, but I can find no mention by Christ of maintaining buildings, much less erecting them of stone or brick, and decorating them with pieces of metal and mineral and elements that people still fight over like barbarians. We had a Maltese woman taking riding lessons, she came over on the boat when she was ten, and once she told me how the nuns in Malta used to tell the little girls that if they wore jewelry, rings and bracelets and necklaces, in purgatory snakes would coil around their fingers and wrists and throats. I do not believe in frightening children or telling them lies, but if those nuns saved a few girls from devotion to things, maybe they were right. That Maltese woman laughed about it, but I noticed she wore only a watch, and that with a leather strap.

The money I give to the church goes in people's stomachs, and on their backs, down in New York City. I have no delusions about the worth of what I do, but I feel it's better to feed somebody than not. There's a priest in Times Square giving shelter to runaway kids, and some Franciscans who run a bread line; actually it's a morning line for coffee and a roll, and Father Paul calls it the continental breakfast for winos and bag ladies. He is curious about how much I am sending, and I know why: he guesses I send a lot, he has said probably more than tithing, and he is right; he wants to know how much because he believes I'm generous and good, and he is wrong about that; he has never had much money and does not know how easy it is to write a check when you have every thing you will ever need, and the figures are mere numbers, and represent no sacrifice at all. Being a real Catholic is too hard; if I were one, I would do with my house and barn what I want the Pope to do with his. So I do not want to impress Father Paul, and when he asks me how much, I say I can't let my left hand know what my right is doing.

He came on Wednesday nights when Gloria and I were married, and the kids were young; Gloria was a very good cook (I assume she still is, but it is difficult to think of her in the present), and I liked sitting at the table with a friend who was also a priest. I was proud of my handsome and healthy children. This was long ago, and they were all very young and cheerful and often funny, and the three boys took care of their baby sister, and did not bully or tease her. Of course they did sometimes, with that excited cruelty children are prone to, but not enough so that it was part of her days. On the Wednesday after Gloria left with the kids and a U-Haul trailer, I was sitting on the front steps, it was summer, and I was watching cars go by on the road, when Father Paul drove around the curve and into the driveway. I was ashamed to see him because he is a priest and my family was gone, but I was relieved too. I went to the car to greet him. He got out smiling, with a bottle of wine, and shook my hand, then pulled me to him, gave me a quick hug, and said: "It's Wednesday, isn't it? Let's open some cans."

With arms about each other we walked to the house, and it was good to know he was doing his work but coming as a friend too, and I thought what good work he had. I have no calling. It is for me to keep horses.

In that other life, anyway. In my real one I go to bed early and sleep well and wake at four forty-five, for an hour of silence. I never want to get out of bed then, and every morning I know I can sleep for another four hours, and still not fail at any of my duties. But I get up, so have come to believe my life can be seen in miniature in that struggle in the dark of morning. While making the bed and boiling water for coffee, I talk to God: I offer Him my day, every act of my body and spirit, my thoughts and moods, as a prayer of thanksgiving, and for Gloria and my children and my friends and two women I made love with after Gloria left. This morning offertory is a habit from my boyhood in a Catholic school; or then it was a habit, but as I kept it and grew older it became a ritual. Then I say the Lord's Prayer, trying not to recite it, and one morning it occurred to me that a prayer, whether recited or said with concentration, is always an act of faith.

I sit in the kitchen at the rear of the house and drink coffee and smoke and watch the sky growing light before sunrise, the trees of the woods near the barn taking shape, becoming single pines and elms and oaks and maples. Sometimes a rabbit comes out of the treeline, or is already sitting there, invisible till the light finds him. The birds are awake in the trees and feeding on the ground, and the little ones, the purple finches and titmice and chickadees, are at the feeder I rigged outside the kitchen window; it is too small for pigeons to get a purchase. I sit and give myself to coffee and tobacco, that get me brisk again, and I watch and listen. In the first year or so after I lost my family, I played the radio in the mornings. But I overcame that, and now I rarely play it at all. Once in the mail I received a questionnaire asking me to write down everything I watched on television during the week they had chosen. At the end of those seven days I wrote in *The Wizard of Oz* and returned it. That was in winter and was actually a busy week for my television, which normally sits out the cold months without once warming up. Had they sent the questionnaire during baseball season, they would have found me at my set. People at the stables talk about shows and performers I have never heard of, but I cannot get interested; when I am in the mood to watch television, I go to a movie or read a detective novel. There are always good detective novels to be found, and I like remembering them next morning with my coffee.

I also think of baseball and hunting and fishing, and of my children. It is not painful to think about them anymore, because even if we had lived together, they would be gone now, grown into their own lives, except Jennifer. I think of death too, not sadly, or with fear, though something like excitement does run through me, something more quickening than the coffee and tobacco. I suppose it is an intense interest, and an outright distrust: I never feel certain that I'll be here watching birds eating at tomorrow's daylight. Sometimes I try to think of other things, like the rabbit that is warm and breathing but not there till twilight. I feel on the brink of something about the life of the senses, but either am not equipped to go further or am not interested enough to concentrate. I have called all of this thinking, but it is not, because it is unintentional; what I'm really doing is feeling the day, in silence, and that is what Father Paul is doing too on his five-to-ten-mile walks.

When the hour ends I take an apple or carrot and I go to the stable and tack up a horse. We take good care of these horses, and no one rides them but students, instructors, and me, and nobody rides the horses we board unless an owner asks me to. The barn is dark and I turn on lights and take some deep breaths, smelling the hay and horses and their manure, both fresh and dried, a combined odor that you either like or you don't. I walk down the wide space of dirt between stalls, greeting the horses, joking with them about their quirks, and choose one for no reason at all other than the way it looks at me that morning. I get my old English saddle that has smoothed and darkened through the years, and go into the stall, talking to this beautiful creature who'll swerve out of a canter if a piece of paper blows in front of him, and if the barn catches fire and you manage to get him out he will, if he can get away from you, run back into the fire, to his stall. Like the smells that surround them, you either like them or you don't. I love them, so am spared having to try to explain why. I feed one the carrot or apple and tack up and lead him outside, where I mount, and we go down the driveway to the road and cross it and turn northwest and walk then trot then canter to St. John's.

A few cars are on the road, their drivers looking serious about going to work. It is always strange for me to see a woman dressed for work so early in the morning. You know how long it takes them, with the makeup and hair and clothes, and I think of them waking in the dark of winter or early light of other seasons, and dressing as they might for an evening's entertainment. Probably this strikes me because I grew up seeing my father put on those suits he never wore on weekends or his two weeks off, and so am accustomed to the men, but when I see these women I think something went wrong, to send all those dressed-up people out on the road when the dew hasn't dried yet. Maybe it's because I so dislike getting up early, but am also doing what I choose to do, while they have no choice. At heart I am lazy, yet I find such peace and delight in it that I believe it is a natural state, and in what looks like my laziest periods I am closest to my center. The ride to St. John's is fifteen minutes. The horses and I do it in all weather; the road is well plowed in winter, and there are only a few days a year when ice makes me drive the pickup. People always look at someone on horseback, and for a moment their faces change and many drivers and I wave to each other. Then at St. John's, Father Paul and five or six regulars and I celebrate the Mass.

Do not think of me as a spiritual man whose every thought during those twenty-five minutes is at one with the words of the Mass. Each morning I try, each morning I fail, and know that always I will be a creature who, looking at Father Paul and the altar, and uttering prayers, will be distracted by scrambled eggs, horses, the weather, and memories and daydreams that have nothing to do with the sacrament I am about to receive. I can receive, though: the Eucharist, and also, at Mass and at other times, moments and even minutes of contemplation. But I cannot achieve contemplation, as some can; and so, having to face and forgive my own failures, I have learned from them both the necessity and wonder of ritual. For ritual allows those who cannot will themselves out of the secular to perform the spiritual, as dancing allows the tongue-tied man a ceremony of love. And, while my mind dwells on breakfast, or Major or Duchess tethered under the church eave, there is, as I take the Host from Father Paul and place it on my tongue and return to the pew, a feeling that I am thankful I have not lost in the forty-eight years since my first Communion. At its center is excitement; spreading out from it is the peace of certainty. Or the certainty of peace. One night Father Paul and I talked about faith. It was long ago, and all I remember is him saying: Belief is believing in God; faith is believing that God believes in you. That is the excitement, and the peace; then the Mass is over, and I go into the sacristy and we have a cigarette and chat, the mystery ends, we are two men talking like any two men on a morning in America, about baseball, plane crashes, presidents, governors, murders, the sun, the clouds. Then I go to the horse and ride back to the life people see, the one in which I move and talk, and most days I enjoy it.

It is late summer now, the time between fishing and hunting, but a good time for baseball. It has been two weeks since Jennifer left, to drive home to Gloria's after her summer visit. She is the only one who still visits; the boys are married and have children, and sometimes fly up for a holiday, or I fly down or west to visit one of them. Jennifer is twenty, and I worry about her the way fathers worry about daughters but not sons. I want to know what she's up to, and at the same time I don't. She looks athletic, and she is: she swims and runs and of course rides. All my children do. When she comes for six weeks in summer, the house is loud with girls, friends of hers since childhood, and new ones. I am glad she kept the girl friends. They have been young company for me and, being with them, I have been able to gauge her growth between summers. On their riding days, I'd take them back to the house when their lessons were over and they had walked the horses and put them back in the stalls, and we'd have lemonade or Coke, and cookies if I had some, and talk until their parents came to drive them home. One year their breasts grew, so I wasn't startled when I saw Jennifer in July. Then they were driving cars to the stable, and beginning to look like young women, and I was passing out beer and ashtrays and they were talking about college.

When Jennifer was here in summer, they were at the house most days. I would say generally that as they got older they became quieter, and though I enjoyed both, I sometimes missed the giggles and shouts. The quiet voices, just low enough for me not to hear from wherever I was, rising and falling in proportion to my distance from them, frightened me. Not that I believed they were planning or recounting anything really wicked, but there was a female seriousness about them, and it was secretive, and of course I thought: love, sex. But it was more than that: it was womanhood they were entering, the deep forest of it, and no matter how many women and men too are saying these days that there is little difference between us, the truth is that men find their way into that forest only on clearly marked trails, while women move about in it like birds. So hearing Jennifer and her friends talking so quietly, yet intensely, I wanted very much to have a wife.

But not as much as in the old days, when Gloria had left but her presence was still in the house as strongly as if she had only gone to visit her folks for a week. There were no clothes or cosmetics, but potted plants endured my neglectful care as long as they could, and slowly died; I did not kill them on purpose, to exorcise the house of her, but I could not remember to water them. For weeks, because I did not use it much, the house was as neat as she had kept it, though dust layered the order she had made. The kitchen went first: I got the dishes in and out of the dishwasher and wiped the top of the stove, but did not return cooking spoons and pot holders to their hooks on the wall, and soon the burners and oven were caked with spillings, the refrigerator had more space and was spotted with juices. The living room and my bedroom went next; I did not go into the children's rooms except on bad nights when I went from room to room and looked and touched and smelled, so they did not lose their order until a year later when the kids came for six weeks. It was three months before I ate the last of the food Gloria had cooked and frozen: I remember it was a beef stew, and very good. By then I had four cookbooks, and was boasting a bit, and talking about recipes with the women at the stables, and looking forward to cooking for Father Paul. But I never looked forward to cooking at night only for myself, though I made myself do it; on some nights I gave in to my daily temptation, and took a newspaper or detective novel to a restaurant. By the end of the second year, though, I had stopped turning on the radio as soon as I woke in the morning, and was able to be silent and alone in the evening too, and then I enjoyed my dinners.

It is not hard to live through a day, if you can live through a moment. What creates despair is the imagination, which pretends there is a future, and insists on predicting millions of moments, thousands of days, and so drains you that you cannot live the moment at hand. That is what Father Paul told me in those first two years, on some of the bad nights when I believed I could not bear what I had to: the most painful loss was my children, then the loss of Gloria, whom I still loved despite or maybe because of our long periods of sadness that rendered us helpless, so neither of us could break out of it to give a hand to the other. Twelve years later I believe ritual would have healed us more quickly than the repetitious talks we had, perhaps even kept us healed. Marriages have lost that, and I wish I had known then what I know now, and we had performed certain acts together every day, no matter how we felt, and perhaps then we could have subordinated feeling to action, for surely that is the essence of love. I know this from my distractions during Mass, and during everything else I do, so that my actions and feelings are seldom one. It does happen every day, but in proportion to everything else in a day, it is rare, like joy. The third most painful loss, which became second and sometimes first as months passed, was the knowledge that I could never marry again, and so dared not even keep company with a woman.

On some of the bad nights I was bitter about this with Father Paul, and I so pitied myself that I cried, or nearly did, speaking with damp eyes and breaking voice. I believe that celibacy is for him the same trial it is for me, not of the flesh, but the spirit: the heart longing to love. But the difference is he chose it, and did not wake one day to a life with thirty horses. In my anger I said I had done my service to love and chastity, and I told him of the actual physical and spiritual pain of practicing rhythm: nights of striking the mattress with a fist, two young animals lying side by side in heat, leaving the bed to pace, to smoke, to curse, and too passionate to question, for we were so angered and oppressed by our passion that we could see no further than our loins. So now I understand how people can be enslaved for generations before they throw down their tools or use them as weapons, the form of their slavery—the cotton fields, the shacks and puny cupboards and untended illnesses—absorbing their emotions and thoughts until finally they have little or none at all to direct with clarity and energy at the owners and legislators. And I told him of the trick of passion and its slaking: how during what we had to believe were safe periods, though all four children were conceived at those times, we were able with some coherence to question the tradition and reason and justice of the law against birth control, but not with enough conviction to soberly act against it, as though regular satisfaction in bed tempered our revolutionary as well as our erotic desires. Only when abstinence drove us hotly away from each other did we receive an urge so strong it lasted all the way to the drugstore and back; but always, after release, we threw away the remaining condoms; and after going through this a few times, we knew what would happen, and from then on we submitted to the calendar she so precisely marked on the bedroom wall. I told him that living two lives each month, one as celibates, one as lovers, made us tense and short-tempered, so we snapped at each other like dogs.

To have endured that, to have reached a time when we burned slowly and could gain from bed the comfort of lying down at night with one who loves you and whom you love, could for weeks on end go to bed tired and peacefully sleep after a kiss, a touch of the hands, and then to be thrown out of the marriage like a bundle from a moving freight car, was unjust, was intolerable, and I could not or would not muster the strength to endure it. But I did, a moment at a time, a day, a night, except twice, each time with a different woman and more than a year apart, and this was so long ago that I clearly see their faces in my memory, can hear the pitch of their voices, and the way they pronounced words, one with a Massachusetts accent, one midwestern, but I feel as though I only heard about them from someone else. Each rode at the stables and was with me for part of an evening; one was badly married, one divorced, so none of us was free. They did not understand this Catholic view, but they were understanding about my having it, and I remained friends with both of them until the married one left her husband and went to Boston, and the divorced one moved to Maine. After both these evenings, those good women, I went to Mass early while Father Paul was still in the confessional, and received his absolution. I did not tell him who I was, but of course he knew, though I never saw it in his eyes. Now my longing for a wife comes only once in a while, like a cold: on some late afternoons when I am alone in the barn, then I lock up and walk to the house, daydreaming, then suddenly look at it and see it empty, as though for the first time, and all at once I'm weary and feel I do not have the energy to broil meat, and I think of driving to a restaurant, then shake my head and go on to the house, the refrigerator, the oven; and some mornings when I wake in the dark and listen to the silence and run my hand over the cold sheet beside me; and some days in summer when Jennifer is here.

Gloria left first me, then the Church, and that was the end of religion for the children, though on visits they went to Sunday Mass with me, and still do, out of a respect for my life that they manage to keep free of patronage. Jennifer is an agnostic, though I doubt she would call herself that, any more than she would call herself any other name that implied she had made a decision, a choice, about existence, death, and God. In truth she tends to pantheism, a good sign, I think; but not wanting to be a father who tells his children what they ought to believe, I do not say to her that Catholicism includes pantheism, like onions in a stew. Besides, I have no missionary instincts and do not believe everyone should or even could live with the Catholic faith. It is Jennifer's womanhood that renders me awkward. And womanhood now is frank, not like when Gloria was twenty and there were symbols: high heels and cosmetics and dresses, a cigarette, a cocktail. I am glad that women are free now of false modesty and all its attention paid the flesh; but, still, it is difficult to see so much of your daughter, to hear her talk as only men and bawdy women used to, and most of all to see in her face the deep and unabashed sensuality of women, with no tricks of the eyes and mouth to hide the pleasure she feels at having a strong young body. I am certain, with the way things are now, that she has very happily not been a virgin for years. That does not bother me. What bothers me is my certainty about it, just from watching her walk across a room or light a cigarette or pour milk on cereal.

She told me all of it, waking me that night when I had gone to sleep listening to the wind in the trees and against the house, a wind so strong that I had to shut all but the lee windows, and still the house cooled; told it to me in such detail and so clearly that now, when she has driven the car to Florida, I remember it all as though I had been a passenger in the front seat, or even at the wheel. It started with a movie, then beer and driving to the sea to look at the waves in the night and the wind, Jennifer and Betsy and Liz. They drank beer on the beach and wanted to go in naked but were afraid they would drown in the high surf. They bought another six-pack at a grocery store in New Hampshire, and drove home. I can see it now, feel it: the three girls and the beer and the ride on country roads where pines curved in the wind and the big deciduous trees swayed and shook as if they might leap from the earth. They would have some windows partly open so they could feel the wind; Jennifer would be playing a cassette, the music stirring them, as it does the young, to memories of another time, other people and places in what is for them the past.

She took Betsy home, then Liz, and sang with her cassette as she left the town west of us and started home, a twenty-minute drive on the road that passes my house. They had each had four beers, but now there were twelve empty bottles in the bag on the floor at the passenger seat, and I keep focusing on their sound against each other when the car shifted speeds or changed directions. For I want to understand that one moment out of all her heart's time on earth, and whether her history had any bearing on it, or whether her heart was then isolated from all it had known, and the sound of those bottles urged it. She was just leaving the town, accelerating past a night club on the right, gaining speed to climb a long, gradual hill, then she went up it, singing, patting the beat on the steering wheel, the wind loud through her few inches of open window, blowing her hair as it did the high branches alongside the road, and she looked up at them and watched the top of the hill for someone drunk or heedless coming over it in part of her lane. She crested to an open black road, and there he was: a bulk, a blur, a thing running across her headlights, and she swerved left and her foot went for the brake and was stomping air above its pedal when she hit him, saw his legs and body in the air, flying out of her light, into the dark. Her brakes were screaming into the wind, bottles clinking in the fallen bag, and with the music and wind inside the car was his sound, already a memory but as real as an echo, that car-shuddering thump as though she had struck a tree. Her foot was back on the accelerator. Then she shifted gears and pushed it. She ejected the cassette and closed the window. She did not start to cry until she knocked on my bedroom door, then called: "Dad?"

Her voice, her tears, broke through my dream and the wind I heard in my sleep, and I stepped into jeans and hurried to the door, thinking harm, rape, death. All were in her face, and I hugged her and pressed her cheek to my chest and smoothed her blown hair, then led her, weeping, to the kitchen and sat her at the table where still she could not speak, nor look at me; when she raised her face it fell forward again, as of its own weight, into her palms. I offered tea and she shook her head, so I offered beer twice, then she shook her head, so I offered whiskey and she nodded. I had some rye that Father Paul and I had not finished last hunting season, and I poured some over ice and set it in front of her and was putting away the ice but stopped and got another glass and poured one for myself too, and brought the ice and bottle to the table where she was trying to get one of her long menthols out of the pack, but her fingers jerked like severed snakes, and I took the pack and lit one for her and took one for myself. I watched her shudder with her first swallow of rye, and push hair back from her face, it is auburn and gleamed in the overhead light, and I remembered how beautiful she looked riding a sorrel; she was smoking fast, then the sobs in her throat stopped, and she looked at me and said it, the words coming out with smoke: "I hit somebody. With the *car*."

Then she was crying and I was on my feet, moving back and forth, looking down at her, asking *Who? Where? Where?* She was pointing at the wall over the stove, jabbing her fingers and cigarette at it, her other hand at her eyes, and twice in horror I actually looked at the wall. She finished the whiskey in a swallow and I stopped pacing and asking and poured another, and either the drink or the exhaustion of tears quieted her, even the dry sobs, and she told me; not as I tell it now, for that was later as again and again we relived it in the kitchen or living room, and, if in daylight, fled it on horseback out on the trails through the woods and, if at night, walked quietly around in the moonlit pasture, walked around and around it, sweating through our clothes. She told it in bursts, like she was a child again, running to me, injured from play. I put on boots and a shirt and left her with the bottle and her streaked face and a cigarette twitching between her fingers, pushed the door open against the wind, and eased it shut. The wind squinted and watered my eyes as I leaned into it and went to the pickup.

When I passed St. John's I looked at it, and Father Paul's little white rectory in the rear, and wanted to stop, wished I could as I could if he were simply a friend who sold hardware or something. I had forgotten my watch but I always know the time within minutes, even when a sound or dream or my bladder wakes me in the night. It was nearly two; we had been in the kitchen about twenty minutes; she had hit him around one-fifteen. Or her. The road was empty and I drove between blowing trees; caught for an instant in my lights, they seemed to be in panic. I smoked and let hope play its tricks on me: it was neither man nor woman but an animal, a goat or calf or deer on the road; it was a man who had jumped away in time, the collision of metal and body glancing not direct, and he had limped home to nurse bruises and cuts. Then I threw the cigarette and hope both out the window and prayed that he was alive, while beneath that prayer, a reserve deeper in my heart, another one stirred: that if he were dead, they would not get Jennifer.

From our direction, east and a bit south, the road to that hill and the night club beyond it and finally the town is, for its last four or five miles, straight through farming country. When I reached that stretch I slowed the truck and opened my window for the fierce air; on both sides were scattered farmhouses and barns and sometimes a silo, looking not like shelters but like unsheltered things the wind would flatten. Corn bent toward the road from a field on my right, and always something blew in front of me: paper, leaves, dried weeds, branches. I slowed approaching the hill, and went up it in second, staring through my open window at the ditch on the left side of the road, its weeds alive, whipping, a mad dance with the trees above them. I went over the hill and down and, opposite the club, turned right onto a side street of houses, and parked there, in the leaping shadows of trees. I walked back across the road to the club's parking lot, the wind behind me, lifting me as I strode, and I could not hear my boots on pavement. I walked up the hill, on the shoulder, watching the branches above me, hearing their leaves and the creaking trunks and the wind. Then I was at the top, looking down the road and at the farms and fields; the night was clear, and I could see a long way; clouds scudded past the half-moon and stars, blown out to sea.

I started down, watching the tall grass under the trees to my right, glancing into the dark of the ditch, listening for cars behind me; but as soon as I cleared one tree, its sound was gone, its flapping leaves and rattling branches far behind me, as though the greatest distance I had at my back was a matter of feet, while ahead of me I could see a barn two miles off. Then I saw her skid marks: short, and going left and downhill, into the other lane. I stood at the ditch, its weeds blowing; across it were trees and their moving shadows, like the clouds. I stepped onto its slope, and it took me sliding on my feet, then rump, to the bottom, where I sat still, my body gathered to itself, lest a part of me should touch him. But there was only tall grass, and I stood, my shoulders reaching the sides of the ditch, and I walked uphill, wishing for the flashlight in the pickup, walking slowly, and down in the ditch I could hear my feet in the grass and on the earth, and kicking cans and bottles. At the top of the hill I turned and went down, watching the ground above the ditch on my right, praying my prayer from the truck again, the first one, the one I would admit, that he was not dead, was in fact home, and began to hope again, memory telling me of lost pheasants and grouse I had shot, but they were small and the colors of their home, while a man was either there or not; and from that memory I left where I was and while walking in the ditch under the wind was in the deceit of imagination with Jennifer in the kitchen, telling her she had hit no one, or at least had not badly hurt anyone, when I realized he could be in the hospital now and I would have to think of a way to check there, something to say on the phone. I see now that, once hope returned, I should have been certain what it prepared me for: ahead of me, in high grass and the shadows of trees, I saw his shirt. Or that is all my mind would allow itself: a shirt, and I stood looking at it for the moments it took my mind to admit the arm and head and the dark length covered by pants. He lay face down, the arm I could see near his side, his head turned from me, on its cheek.

"Fella?" I said. I had meant to call, but it came out quiet and high, lost inches from my face in the wind. Then I said, "Oh God," and felt Him in the wind and the sky moving past the stars and moon and the fields around me, but only watching me as He might have watched Cain or Job, I did not know which, and I said it again, and wanted to sink to the earth and weep till I slept there in the weeds. I climbed, scrambling up the side of the ditch, pulling at clutched grass, gained the top on hands and knees, and went to him like that, panting, moving through the grass as high and higher than my face, crawling under the sky, making sounds too, like some animal, there being no words to let him know I was here with him now. He was long; that is the word that came to me, not tall. I kneeled beside him, my hands on my legs. His right arm was by his side, his left arm straight out from the shoulder, but turned, so his palm was open to the tree above us. His left cheek was cleanshaven, his eye closed, and there was no blood. I leaned forward to look at his open mouth and saw the blood on it, going down into the grass. I straightened and looked ahead at the wind blowing past me through grass and trees to a distant light, and I stared at the light, imagining someone awake out there, wanting someone to be, a gathering of old friends, or someone alone listening to music or painting a picture, then I figured it was a night light at a farmyard whose house I couldn't see. *Going*, I thought. *Still going*. I leaned over again and looked at dripping blood.

So I had to touch his wrist, a thick one with a watch and expansion band that I pushed up his arm, thinking *he's left-handed*, my three fingers pressing his wrist, and all I felt was my tough fingertips on that smooth underside flesh and small bones, then relief, then certainty. But against my will, or only because of it, I still don't know, I touched his neck, ran my fingers down it as if petting, then pressed, and my hand sprang back as from fire. I lowered it again, held it there until it felt that faint beating that I could not believe. There was too much wind. Nothing could make a sound in it. A pulse could not be felt in it, nor could mere fingers in that wind feel the absolute silence of a dead man's artery. I was making sounds again; I grabbed his left arm and his waist, and pulled him toward me, and that side of him rose, turned, and I lowered him to his back, his face tilted up toward the tree that was groaning, the tree and I the only sounds in the wind. Turning my face from his, looking down the length of him at his sneakers, I placed my ear on his heart, and heard not that but something else, and I clamped a hand over my exposed ear, heard something liquid and alive, like when you pump a well and after a few strokes you hear air and water moving in the pipe, and I knew I must raise his legs and cover him and run to a phone, while still I listened to his chest, thinking *raise with what? cover with what?* and amid the liquid sound I heard the heart, then lost it, and pressed my ear against bone, but his chest was quiet, and I did not know when the liquid had stopped, and do not know now when I heard air, a faint rush of it, and whether under my ear or at his mouth or whether I heard it at all. I straightened and looked at the light, dim and yellow. Then I touched his throat, looking him full in the face. He was blond and young. He could have been sleeping in the shade of a tree, but for the smear of blood from his mouth to his hair, and the night sky, and the weeds blowing against his head, and the leaves shaking in the dark above us.

I stood. Then I kneeled again and prayed for his soul to join in peace and joy all the dead and living; and, doing so, confronted my first sin against him, not stopping for Father Paul, who could have given him the last rites, and immediately then my second one, or, I saw then, my first, not calling an ambulance to meet me there, and I stood and turned into the wind, slid down the ditch and crawled out of it, and went up the hill and down it, across the road to the street of houses whose people I had left behind forever, so that I moved with stealth in the shadows to my truck.

When I came around the bend near my house, I saw the kitchen light at the rear. She sat as I had left her, the ashtray filled, and I looked at the bottle, felt her eyes on me, felt what she was seeing too: the dirt from my crawling. She had not drunk much of the rye. I poured some in my glass, with the water from melted ice, and sat down and swallowed some and looked at her and swallowed some more, and said: "He's dead."

She rubbed her eyes with the heels of her hands, rubbed the cheeks under them, but she was dry now.

"He was probably dead when he hit the ground. I mean, that's probably what killed—"

"Where was he?"

"Across the ditch, under a tree."

"Was he—did you see his face?"

"No. Not really. I just felt. For life, pulse. I'm going out to the car."

"What for? Oh."

I finished the rye, and pushed back the chair, then she was standing too.

"I'll go with you."

"There's no need."

"I'll go."

I took a flashlight from a drawer and pushed open the door and held it while she went out. We turned our faces from the wind. It was like on the hill, when I was walking, and the wind closed the distance behind me: after three or four steps I felt there was no house back there. She took my hand, as I was reaching for hers. In the garage we let go, and squeezed between the pickup and her little car, to the front of it, where we had more room, and we stepped back from the grill and I shone the light on the fender, the smashed headlight turned into it, the concave chrome staring to the right, at the garage wall.

"We ought to get the bottles," I said.

She moved between the garage and the car, on the passenger side, and had room to open the door and lift the bag. I reached out, and she gave me the bag and backed up and shut the door and came around the car. We sidled to the doorway, and she put her arm around my waist and I hugged her shoulders.

"I thought you'd call the police," she said.

We crossed the yard, faces bowed from the wind, her hair blowing away from her neck, and in the kitchen I put the bag of bottles in the garbage basket. She was working at the table: capping the rye and putting it away, filling the ice tray, washing the glasses, emptying the ashtray, sponging the table.

"Try to sleep now," I said.

She nodded at the sponge circling under her hand, gathering ashes.

Then she dropped it in the sink and, looking me full in the face, as I had never seen her look, as perhaps she never had, being for so long a daughter on visits (or so it seemed to me and still does: that until then our eyes had never seriously met), she crossed to me from the sink and kissed my lips, then held me so tightly I lost balance, and would have stumbled forward had she not held me so hard.

I sat in the living room, the house darkened, and watched the maple and the hemlock. When I believed she was asleep I put on *La Boheme*, and kept it at the same volume as the wind so it would not wake her. Then I listened to *Madame Butterfly*, and in the third act had to rise quickly to lower the sound: the wind was gone. I looked at the still maple near the window, and thought of the wind leaving farms and towns and the coast, going out over the sea to die on the waves. I smoked and gazed out the window. The sky was darker, and at daybreak the rain came. I listened to *Tosca*, and at six-fifteen went to the kitchen where Jennifer's purse lay on the table, a leather shoulder purse crammed with the things of an adult woman, things she had begun accumulating only a few years back, and I nearly wept, thinking of what sandy foundations they were: driver's license, credit card, disposable lighter, cigarettes, checkbook, ballpoint pen, cash, cosmetics, comb, brush, Kleenex, these the rite of passage from childhood, and I took one of them—her keys—and went out, remembering a jacket and hat when the rain struck me, but I kept going to the car, and squeezed and lowered myself into it, pulled the seat belt over my shoulder and fastened it and backed out, turning in the drive, going forward into the road, toward St. John's and Father Paul.

Cars were on the road, the workers, and I did not worry about any of them noticing the fender and light. Only a horse distracted them from what they drove to. In front of St. John's is a parking lot; at its far side, past the church and at the edge of the lawn, is an old pine, taller than the steeple now. I shifted to third, left the road, and, aiming the right headlight at the tree, accelerated past the white blur of church, into the black trunk growing bigger till it was all I could see, then I rocked in that resonant thump she had heard, had felt, and when I turned off the ignition it was still in my ears, my blood, and I saw the boy flying in the wind. I lowered my forehead to the wheel. Father Paul opened the door, his face white in the rain.

"I'm all right."

"What happened?"

"I don't know. I fainted."

I got out and went around to the front of the car, looked at the smashed light, the crumpled and torn fender.

"Come to the house and lie down."

"I'm all right."

"When was your last physical?"

"I'm due for one. Let's get out of this rain."

"You'd better lie down."

"No. I want to receive."

That was the time to say I want to confess, but I have not and will not. Though I could now, for Jennifer is in Florida, and weeks have passed, and perhaps now Father Paul would not feel that he must tell me to go to the police. And, for that very reason, to confess now would be unfair. It is a world of secrets, and now I have one from my best, in truth my only, friend. I have one from Jennifer too, but that is the nature of fatherhood.

Most of that day it rained, so it was only in early evening, when the sky cleared, with a setting sun, that two little boys, leaving their confinement for some play before dinner, found him. Jennifer and I got that on the local news, which we listened to every hour, meeting at the radio, standing with cigarettes, until the one at eight o'clock; when she stopped crying, we went out and walked on the wet grass, around the pasture, the last of sunlight still in the air and trees. His name was Patrick Mitchell, he was nineteen years old, was employed by CETA, lived at home with his parents and brother and sister. The paper next day said he had been at a friend's house and was walking home, and I thought of that light I had seen, then knew it was not for him; he lived on one of the streets behind the club. The paper did not say then, or in the next few days, anything to make Jennifer think he was alive while she was with me in the kitchen. Nor do I know if we—I—could have saved him.

In keeping her secret from her friends, Jennifer had to perform so often, as I did with Father Paul and at the stables, that I believe the acting, which took more of her than our daylight trail rides and our night walks in the pasture, was her healing. Her friends teased me about wrecking her car. When I carried her luggage out to the car on that last morning, we spoke only of the weather for her trip—the day was clear, with a dry cool breeze—and hugged and kissed, and I stood watching as she started the car and turned it around. But then she shifted to neutral and put on the parking brake and unclasped the belt, looking at me all the while, then she was coming to me, as she had that night in the kitchen, and I opened my arms.

I have said I talk with God in the mornings, as I start my day, and sometimes as I sit with coffee, looking at the birds, and the woods. Of course He has never spoken to me, but that is not something I require. Nor does He need to. I know Him, as I know the part of myself that knows Him, that felt Him watching from the wind and the night as I kneeled over the dying boy. Lately I have taken to arguing with Him, as I can't with Father Paul, who, when he hears my monthly confession, has not heard and will not hear anything of failure to do all that one can to save an anonymous life, of injustice to a family in their grief, of deepening their pain at the chance and mystery of death by giving them nothing—no one—to hate. With Father Paul I feel lonely about this, but not with God. When I received the Eucharist while Jennifer's car sat twice-damaged, so redeemed, in the rain, I felt neither loneliness nor shame, but as though He were watching me, even from my tongue, intestines, blood, as I have watched my sons at times in their young lives when I was able to judge but without anger, and so keep silent while they, in the agony of their youth, decided how they must act; or found reasons, after their actions, for what they had done. Their reasons were never as good or as bad as their actions, but they needed to find them, to believe they were living by them, instead of the awful solitude of the heart.

I do not feel the peace I once did: not with God, nor the earth, or anyone on it. I have begun to prefer this state, to remember with fondness the other one as a period of peace I neither earned nor deserved. Now in the mornings while I watch purple finches driving larger titmice from the feeder, I say to Him: I would do it again. For when she knocked on my door, then called me, she woke what had flowed dormant in my blood since her birth, so that what rose from the bed was not a stable owner or a Catholic or any other Luke Ripley I had lived with for a long time, but the father of a girl.

And He says: I am a Father too.

Yes, I say, as You are a Son Whom this morning I will receive; unless You kill me on the way to church, then I trust You will receive me. And as a Son You made Your plea.

Yes, He says, but I would not lift the cup.

True, and I don't want You to lift it from me either. And if one of my sons had come to me that night, I would have phoned the police and told them to meet us with an ambulance at the top of the hill.

Why? Do you love them less?

I tell Him no, it is not that I love them less, but that I could bear the pain of watching and knowing my sons' pain, could bear it with pride as they took the whip and nails. But You never had a daughter and, if You had, You could not have borne her passion.

So, He says, you love her more than you love Me.

I love her more than I love truth.

Then you love in weakness, He says.

As You love me, I say, and I go with an apple or carrot out to the barn.

Weary Kingdom

JOHN IRVING

M INNA BARRETT, fifty-five, looks precisely as old as she is, and her figure suggests nothing of what she might have looked like "in her time." One would only assume that always she looked this way, slightly oblong, gently rounded, not puritanical but almost asexual. A pleasant old maid since grammar school, neat and silent; a not overly stern face, a not overly harsh mouth, but a total composure which now, at fifty-five, reflects the history of her many indifferences and the conservative going of her own way.

Minna has her own room in a dormitory of Fairchild Junior College for Young Women, where she is the matron of the dormitory's small dining hall, in charge of the small kitchen crew, responsible for the appropriate dress of the girls at mealtime. Minna's room has a private entrance and a private bath, is shaded in the mornings by the elms of the campus, and is several blocks from Boston Common—not too far for her to walk on a nice day. This room is remarkably uncluttered, remarkable because it's a very small room which shows very little of the nine years she has lived there. Not that there is, or should be, a great deal to show; it is only as permanent a residence as any other place Minna has lived since she left home. This room has a television and Minna stays up at night, watching the movies. She never watches the regular programs; she reads until the news at eleven. She likes biographies, prefers these to autobiographies, because someone's account of their own life embarrasses her in a way she doesn't understand. She is partial to the biographies of women, although she does read Ian Fleming. Once at a party for the alumnae and trustees of the school, someone, a lady in a soft lavender suit who wanted, she said, to meet *all* of the school's personnel, found out about Minna's interest in biographies. The lavender lady recommended a book by Gertrude Stein, which Minna bought and never finished. It wasn't anything Minna would have called a biography, but she wasn't offended by it. She just felt that nothing ever happened.

So Minna reads until eleven, then watches the news and a movie. The kitchen crew comes early in the morning, but Minna doesn't have to be in the dining hall until the girls come in. After breakfast she takes a cup of coffee to her room, then maybe naps until lunch. Her afternoons, too, are quiet. Some of the girls in the dormitory will visit her at eleven, to watch the evening news—there is an entrance to Minna's room from the dormitory corridor. The girls probably come to see the television more than they come to see Minna, although they are very pleasant and Minna is amused at the varying stages of their undress at this hour. Once they were interested in how long Minna's hair would be if she let it down. She obliged them, unwinding, unfurling the long gray hair—somewhat stiff, but falling to her hips. The girls were impressed with how thick and healthy it was; one of the girls, with hair almost that long, suggested to Minna that she wear it in a braid. The next evening the girls brought a deep orange ribbon and they braided Minna's hair. Minna was meekly pleased, but she said that she never could wear it that way. She still might be tempted, the girls were so impressed, but it is too much to think of changing her hair from the tightly wrapped bun it has been all these years.

After the girls leave, after the movie, Minna sits in her bed, thinking of her retirement. The farm where she grew up, in South Byfield, comes back to her mind. If she thinks of it with a certain nostalgia she is not aware of this; she thinks only how much more restful her work at the school is, how much easier than on the farm. Her younger brother lives there now, and in a few years she'll return, to live with her brother's family, taking her tidy nest egg with her, and relinquishing herself and her savings to the care of her brother. It was only last Christmas, when she was visiting his family, that they asked her when she would come to stay for good. By the time she feels it is right for her to come, in another year or so, not *all* of her brother's children will be grown up, and there will be things for her to do. Certainly, no one would think of Minna as an imposition.

She thinks of South Byfield, what past and what future—after the news, after the movie—and she feels, now, no resentment toward this present time. She has no memories of a painful loss or separation, or failure. There were friends in South Byfield, whom she simply saw married or who just remained there after she quietly moved the thirty miles to Boston; her mother and father died, almost shyly, but there is nothing that she misses with particular pain. She doesn't think of herself as very anxious to retire, although she does look ahead to being a part of her brother's healthy family. She wouldn't say that she has a lot of friends in Boston, but friends for Minna always have been the pleasant and familiar people connected with the regular episodes of her life; they never have been emotional dependents. Now, for example, there is Flynn, the cook, who is Irish with a large family in South Boston, who complains to Minna of Boston housing, Boston traffic, Boston corruption, Boston this-and-that. Minna knows little of this but she listens pleasantly to him; in his swearing Flynn reminds her of her father. Minna doesn't swear herself, but she doesn't find Flynn's swearing unpleasant. He has a way of coaxing things that makes her feel as if his swearing really *works*. The daily battles with the coffee urn are invariably won by Flynn, who after long and dark curses, heavy jostles and violent threats of dismantling the whole thing, emerges the victor; for Minna, Flynn's animated obscenities seem constructive, the way her father would shout the tractor into starting, during the winter months, and Minna thinks Flynn is nice.

Also, there is Mrs. Elwood, a widow, with deeper lines on her face than Minna has—lines which move like rubber bands when Mrs. Elwood talks, as if her chin were hinged to these lines. Mrs. Elwood is the housemother of the dormitory, and she speaks with a British accent; it is well known that Mrs. Elwood is a Bostonian, but she spent one summer in England, after her graduation from college. Apparently, she had a whale of a time there. Minna tells Mrs. Elwood whenever there's a movie with Alec Guinness on the late show, and Mrs. Elwood comes, discreetly after the news, after her girls have gone back to their rooms. It often takes a good half of the movie for Mrs. Elwood to remember if she's seen this one before.

"I must have seen them all, Minna," Mrs. Elwood says.

"I always miss the ones at Christmas time," Minna replies. "At my brother's we usually play cards or have folks in."

"Oh, Minna," Mrs. Elwood says, "you really should go out more."

And, too, there is Angelo Gianni. Angelo is pale and slight, a bewildered-looking man, or boy, gray eyes that are merely a deeper shade of the color of his face, and there is nothing about him, outside of his name, to suggest that he's Italian. If his name were Cuthbert, or Cadwallader, there would be nothing in his appearance to suggest that. If he were a Devereaux or a Hunt-Jones you would see nothing of that in his awkward, embarrassed body—anticipating, with awe, the most minor crisis, and reacting dumb-struck every time. Angelo could be twenty or thirty; he lives in the basement of the dormitory, next to his janitor's closet. Angelo empties ashtrays, washes dishes, sets and cleans tables, sweeps, does things like that wherever he is needed, and does other, more complicated things when he is asked, and when the problem has been thoroughly explained to him, more than once. He is exceptionally gentle, and he behaves toward Minna with a curious combination of the deepest respect—at times, calling her "Miss Minna"—and the odd, shy, flirtatious gestures of true affection. Minna likes Angelo, she is tender and cheerful with him as she is with her brother's children, and she is aware of even *worrying* about him. Angelo, she feels, stands on precarious ground, and at every moment of his simple, delicate life—unguarded, she thinks—he is prone to the cruelest of injuries. The injuries go unnamed, yet Minna can picture a hoard of sufferings lying in wait for Angelo, who lives fragilely, artlessly, in his isolated world of kindness and faith. Minna seeks to protect Angelo, seeks to instruct him, although these sufferings she envisions for him are quite nebulous to her; she can think of no great injury she has received, no great threatening and destructive force which ever has loomed over her. Yet, for Angelo, she fears this, and she tells him her instructive stories, inevitably ending in a proverb (one of those proverbs she cuts from the daily newspaper and pins with a small, uncolored tack to the thick, black pages of her photograph album, which contains only two photographs—one brownish print of her parents, stonily posed, and one color shot of her brother's children). Minna'a stories are her own, stripped of any prelude, stripped of time and place, even names of characters, and certainly stripped of any emotional involvement of her own, that might have existed at the time, might linger still—*might*, if Minna ever remembered anything in that way, or if anything could affect her, personally, in that way. The proverbs range from "A little knowledge is a dangerous thing!" to a whole assembly of mottoes urging compromise. The danger of trusting *too* much, of believing *too* much. Angelo nods to her advice; a frequent, awesome seriousness seems to fix his eyes, suspend his mouth, until Minna is bothered so much by Angelo's painful concentration that she tells him, as a footnote, not to take anything that *anyone* says too seriously. This only further puzzles Angelo, and seeing what effect she has had, Minna changes the subject to something lighter.

"Why the other day," she says, "some of the girls tried to get me to wear my hair in a braid, a long braid."

"I'll bet you looked nice," Angelo tells her.

"Oh, you know, Angelo, I just didn't see the good in changing my hair from what it's been so long."

"You should do what you think best, Miss Minna," Angelo says, and Minna is helpless to break the penetrating and dangerous kindness which Angelo bears to everyone, bringing them the burden of his exposed heart, to do with as they may. And, well, Minna thinks, it's time they were both back to work.

Minna has no complaints about her work. She has asked for another woman to help her, another matron for the dining hall—so that when Minna has her day off, on Mondays, the girls and the kitchen crew won't be alone. No one, apparently, regards this request as very important. Mrs. Elwood thought it would be a fine idea, said she'd speak to the Director of Housing. Then later, when Minna asked her about it, Mrs. Elwood said that she thought it might be better if Minna spoke to the Director, or to someone, herself. Minna wrote to the Director, weeks ago, and she has heard nothing. It's not really important, she thinks, and so there's nothing to complain about. It would just be nice to have another woman, an older woman, of course, and who's had some experience with young girls. There's even an extra room in the dormitory for her, if the college could find a woman like that, who'd like a room of her own—a free room, after all, and all the protection a woman living alone could ask for. It would be nice, to have someone like that, but Minna doesn't push it. She is content to wait.

The first, bored ducks were roaming about as Minna, on her day off, walked through Boston Common. She shawled and unshawled as she walked, warm and then shivering, regarded the optimists in their short-sleeved shirts, their chilly seersucker. Several worldly mallards strutted with the awkward and stunned dignity of someone who'd been conspicuously insulted at a large, unfamiliar party. Shopping, summery mothers with winter-bundled children, blustering in the short blasts of cold wind, paused to find something to feed the ducks. The children leaned out too far, got wet feet, were scolded, hurried and dragged along, looking over their shoulders at the floating pieces of bread and the indifferent ducks. The ducks would get better about this as the spring wore on, but now, in the early stages of their hopeless revolution for privacy, they refused to eat if they were watched. Old men in year-round overcoats, clutching papers and knobby loaves of Jewish bread, hurled heavy chunks to the ducks— the men looked cautiously about, to see if anyone noticed that the pieces were too big (intended to hit and sink the ducks). Minna was cooly aware of their feeble arms and their bad aim. She didn't stay long, but turned out of the Common to Boylston Street. She window-shopped at Shreve's, warming herself in the elegance of crystal and silver, thinking what would be the loveliest piece for her brother's table. Schraft's was around the corner and she ate a small lunch there. Outside of Schraft's she pondered what to do next: it was two o'clock and the weather was typically, indecisively March. Then Minna saw a girl come out of Shreve's, the girl smiled in Minna's direction—a denim skirt came above her knees, sandals, a green crew-neck sweater, obviously some boy's. The sweater hung low on her hips, the cuffs were rolled, and the stretched knobs on the sleeves, which would have been the boy's elbows, swung like goiters under the girl's slender wrists. She called, "Hi, Minna!" and Minna recognized her as one of the girls who came to watch the news in her room. Not remembering her name, names always bothered her, Minna called the girl "Dear." Dear was going to Cambridge, taking the MTA, wanted to know if Minna would like to come and browse the shops. They went together, Minna greatly pleased at this; she noticed how differently people watched her on the subway—did they think she was the girl's grandmother, or, even, her mother? The smiles were for having such a pretty companion, and Minna felt as if she was being congratulated. In Cambridge they stopped at an extraordinary little delicatessen, where Minna bought several cans of exotic food, the labels in some foreign language, sealed with precious-looking stamps. It was like receiving some gift package from an imaginary uncle, a world traveler, adventurer sort. In a dusty little shop of orange crates and awnings, a shop with a lot of dulled and dented pewter, Minna bought a silver hors d'oeuvre fork, with which, the girl called "Dear" told her, she could comfortably eat the exotic foods. The girl was very kind to Minna, so kind that Minna felt she must not be well-liked by the other girls. At four o'clock the day turned ragged and cold once more, and the two of them went to a foreign movie in Brattle Square. They had to sit quite close to the front because Minna had difficulty reading the subtitles. Minna was embarrassed that the girl should see this film, but later the girl spoke so knowingly and seriously about it that Minna was somewhat eased. They had a nice meal after the movie— dark beer, saurkraut and stuffed peppers, in a German restaurant that the girl knew well. The girl told Minna that they wouldn't have served her the beer if Minna hadn't been with her. It was well after dark when they returned to the dormitory, and Minna told the girl what a lovely time she'd had. With her little bag of funny foods and the hors d'oeuvre fork, and feeling pleasantly tired, Minna went to her room. Although it was only nine o'clock she felt she could go to bed right away, but on her desk where she gently set her bag, she saw a curious, beige folder with a note attached. The note was from Mrs. Elwood.

> Dear Minna, I dropped this in your room this afternoon. The Director of Housing called me this morning to say that he'd found you a helper, another matron for the dining hall, and *with* experience. The Director said he was sending her over here. Since you were out I showed her around, got her settled in her room—it's a bit of a shame that she has to share the bathroom with the girls on that floor, but she did seem quite pleased with everything. She's most attractive—Angelo seems rather taken with her—and I told her that you'd take care of her in the morning. If you want to go and meet her tonight, she said she was tired, she'll be in her room.

So, Minna thought, they really got someone. She couldn't imagine what might be in the folder, and opening it, delicately, she saw it was a duplicate of the woman's job application. She felt a little uncertain about looking at this, it appeared to be such a private thing, but her eye caught the little bag of worldly foods and this, somehow, gave her confidence to read the application. Celeste was her name and she was forty-one. She'd done a "lot of waiting-on table," had been a counselor at a summer camp for girls, and she was from Heron's Neck, Maine—where her brother-in-law now operated an inn for summer tourists. She had also worked there. The inn had been owned by her parents. It sounds very nice, Minna thought, and she forgot how tired she had been. She suddenly became organized— arranging, proudly, the little cans of the curious food on the overhanging shelf of her desk. Then she checked the TV bulletin to see if there was an Alec Guinness movie on the late show. Mrs. Elwood would like to know, and the new woman might be lonely. Indeed, on this most surprising day, there was an Alec Guinness movie. Minna opened the door to the dormitory corridor and walked humming to Celeste's room. She thought, what a wonderful day it's been. She only wished she knew that Dear Girl's name, but she could ask Mrs. Elwood about that.

Minna rapped lightly on Celeste's door and heard, or thought she heard a murmured "Come in." She opened the door, hesitating on the threshold because the room was dark—all dark, except for the wobbly-necked desk lamp which pointed its feeble light to the cushion of the desk chair. The room, like most end-rooms in dormitories, was

neither square nor rectangular. Any symmetry appeared as an accident; there were *five* corners where the ceiling sloped almost to the
floor, and several alcoves in juxtaposition to the corners. In one of
these low-ceilinged alcoves was the bed, a cot really, and Minna saw
that some attempt had been made to conceal the bed from the rest
of the room. A heavy, crimson blanket was draped from the molding
and hung in such a way as to wall-off the bed in the alcove. Minna
saw the blanket flap and she guessed there was a window open over
the bed. The whole room was somewhat windy in the early evening
cool, yet the room smelled of a heavy, animal musk, rich as coffee,
and reminded Minna—oddly, she thought—of one late evening last
summer when her brother had been in Boston and had taken her to
a show. They were riding back on the subway, alone in the car, when
a massive Negress in a gaudy, flowered dress came in and sat just a
few seats away. The Negress had stepped in from the steamy rain,
the damp underground, and suddenly the car was filled with this
rich scent—smells of a hot summer day in a dirt floor cellar, closed
all winter with its jams and pickled beans. Minna whispered,
"Celeste?"—heard another murmur from behind the crimson blanket,
was aware of the odor again, somehow arousing the malign. Minna
gently pulled back a corner of the blanket; the faint light from the
desk lamp dully illuminated the long, large body of Celeste in a weird
sleep. The pillow rested under her shoulder blades, tipping her head
back and stretching a long, graceful neck—graceful, despite a sinewy
muscled look, visible in the swollen cords which even in the poor
light Minna could trace to the high, arched collar bones and chest.
Her breasts were rigid, full and not sagging, not fallen to her armpits.
Minna saw, only with this observation of the breasts, that Celeste
was naked. Her hips were hugely broad, flat dents lay inside her
pelvis, neatly symmetrical, and despite a certain heaviness to every
part of her body—a forceful, pleasant weight to her ankles, a rounded
smoothness in her thighs—the length of Celeste's waist, the incredible
length of her legs, made her appear almost slender. Minna spoke to
her again, louder this time, and then, as soon as she heard her own
voice, wished she hadn't said anything—thinking, how awful it would
be if the poor woman woke up and saw *me* here. This terrible body—
terrible, in its intimate potential for strength and motion—fixed Minna
to the bedside. Now Celeste began to move, slightly, first her hands.
The broad, flat fingers curled, her hands cupped, as if to hold some
tiny, wounded animal. Then her hands turned palms-down on the
bed and her fingers picked at the folds and wrinkles in the sheet.

Minna wanted to reach out and calm the hands, fearing they would wake Celeste, but her own hands, her whole body, felt frozen. Celeste turned on one elbow, arched her back, and the hands fell with a soft plop on her wide, flat stomach. Slowly and lightly at first, then with more weight and force, pressing with the heels of her hands, Celeste rubbed her stomach. The hands moved into the flat hollows of her pelvis, rolled the loose, puppy-like skin; the hands pulled down on the hips, pulled away from the waist, turned under the thighs—up, beneath the buttocks, up, to the small of the back. Celeste lifted herself, arched her back again, higher; her great neck cords thickened, empurpled by this exertion, and her mouth—slack, only a moment ago—curled up at the corners to a senseless grin. Celeste opened her eyes, blinked, saw nothing (Minna saw nothing but whites), and then Celeste's eyes closed. Her whole body now softly relaxed, appeared to sink deeply into the bed, and into a truer sleep; the long, still hands rested lightly inside her thighs. Minna backed out of the alcove, noticed the desk lamp, turned it off. Then she left, careful not to let the door bang behind her.

Back in her room, the bright cans of happy food smiled at Minna from her desk. Minna sat and looked at them. She felt strangely exhausted, and it would have been so nice for Mrs. Elwood and Celeste to join her for the movie—dining, exquisitely, out of the gay cans. But then, there wouldn't have been enough hors d'oeuvre forks to go around. Even if Mrs. Elwood came alone there wouldn't be a fork for her—and, Minna thought, I don't have a can opener. She had to tell Mrs. Elwood about the movie, too, and she felt again the strange exhaustion, just sitting where she was. Celeste, Minna thought, certainly *looked* a lot younger than forty-one. Of course the light had been poor, and in sleep the crows-feet always are softened and smoothed. But, she hadn't been *really* asleep. It hadn't looked, to Minna, *quite* like a dream. And how black her hair was! Perhaps it was dyed. Poor thing, she must have been very tired, or upset. Still, Minna couldn't escape the embarrassment of it! It was a little like reading one of the autobiographies. Embarrassment for Minna, was a general feeling she experienced often for others, almost never for herself; there didn't seem to be different *kinds* of embarrassment, and the degree to which Minna felt embarrassed could be measured only by how long the feeling lasted.

Well, there were all these things to be done and she'd better get at them. First, Mrs. Elwood and the movie. Another fork and a can opener. She would ask Mrs. Elwood about that Dear Girl, find out her name. But Mrs. Elwood would surely ask Minna about Celeste, had Minna gone to meet her?—and *what* would she say? Why, yes she'd gone to meet her, but the poor woman was asleep. Then Celeste would know she'd been there; and the desk lamp, Minna shouldn't have turned it off. She should have left everything as it was. Minna thought, for one wild moment, that she could go back to Celeste's room, turn on the lamp. Then she thought, What nonsense! Celeste had been asleep—not aware, in her sleep, of anything Minna might have seen. Except, of course, that she was naked, and she would certainly know she'd been naked. Well, what of it? Celeste wouldn't care about that. And Minna suddenly realized that she was thinking she already *knew* Celeste; she couldn't get that idea out of her mind. It seemed that she *did* know her, and how silly that was. Knowing someone, for Minna, was a matter of long, slow familiarity. Why that girl, for instance, with whom she'd spent such a delightful afternoon—Minna didn't *know* her at all.

Again, cheerily, the cans on Minna's desk hailed her. But there came, too, the curious exhaustion. If she didn't tell Mrs. Elwood about the movie she could go to bed right now; of course, there would have to be a note on the door to tell the girls, No News Tonight. But the thought of bed seemed not quite what her exhaustion asked of her; in fact, going to bed was out of the question. Mrs. Elwood enjoys the Alec Guinness movies so much. Minna thought, How could I think of such a thing? She looked at the cans again, and there was something about the foreignness of the little colored labels that repulsed her. Then someone knocked on the door, two raps, and Minna was startled—as if, it struck her, she'd been caught doing something wrong.

"Minna? Minna are you in?" It was Mrs. Elwood. Minna opened the door, too slowly, too cautiously, and she saw Mrs. Elwood's puzzled face.

"My word, Minna, were you in bed?"

"Oh, no!" Minna cried.

Mrs. Elwood came in and said, "Lord, how dark it is in here!" and Minna noticed that she hadn't turned on the overheads. Only her desk lamp was on—a single, unsteady shaft of light which illuminated the gaudy foods.

"Oh, what are these?" Mrs. Elwood asked, moving warily to the desk.

"I had the nicest afternoon," Minna said. "I met one of the girls downtown and we went to Cambridge together, shopping, and we saw a movie and ate in a German place. I only got back a moment ago. Or, maybe, twenty minutes."

"I'd say it was more like twenty minutes," Mrs. Elwood said. "I saw you both come in."

"Oh, then you saw her. What *is* her name?"

"You spent the afternoon with her and you don't know her name?"

"I should have known it, really. She watches television. I just would have felt foolish to ask."

"Lord, Minna!" Mrs. Elwood said. "The girl is Molly Cabot, and she seems to spend more time shopping and movie-going than she does in her classes."

"Oh, she was so nice to me," Minna said. "I didn't think about her classes, she was such a sweet girl. I *did* think she was lonely. But she's not in any trouble, is she?"

"Well, trouble," Mrs. Elwood repeated, turning one of the strange cans in her hand, scrutinizing the label and setting the can back in the row with a disapproving scowl. "I should say she's in trouble if she doesn't start going to her classes."

"Oh, I'm so sorry," Minna said. "She was so nice. I had a lovely day."

"Well," Mrs. Elwood said toughly, "perhaps she'll pull herself together."

Minna nodded, feeling sad, wishing she could help. Mrs. Elwood was still looking at the cans, and Minna hoped that she wouldn't notice the extravagant hors d'oeuvre fork.

"What's *in* these things?" Mrs. Elwood asked, holding another can in her lumpy palm.

"They're delicacies from other countries. Molly said they were very good."

"I wouldn't buy anything to *eat* if I didn't know what it was," Mrs. Elwood said. "Lord, they might be *unclean*! They might be from *Italy*, or somewhere like that."

"Oh, I just thought they were pretty," Minna said, and the familiar exhaustion seemed to numb her whole body and her speech. "It was a pleasant way to spend the afternoon," she mumbled, and there was something bitter which came into her voice and surprised her, surprised Mrs. Elwood, too, and brought an unsettling quiet to the small room.

"I think you're very tired," Mrs. Elwood said. "Let me put a note up for the girls, and you go to bed." The authority of Mrs. Elwood's voice seemed to fill Minna's exhaustion, so perfectly, and it made unnecessary any protest. Minna didn't even mention the Alec Guinness movie.

But her sleep was bothered by vague phantoms, in conspiracy, it

seemed, with the occasional scratching in the dormitory corridor—
presumably the girls who came to see the news and shuffled, puzzled,
around the note on the door. Once Minna was sure that Celeste was
in the room, still awesomely naked and huge, surrounded by grotesque dwarfs—like those horrific snail-men and fish-people, sub-
human crustaceans, Silurian-old, dreamily emerged from a Breughel
or a Bosch. Once Minna woke, felt the warm weight of her tired hands
against her sides, and felt repelled by her own touch. She lay back
again, her arms outstretched to the sides of her bed, her fingers curled
beneath the mattress as if she were manacled to a rack. If Minna had
eaten one of the strange foods, which she had not, she would have
attributed her nightmares to this. But as it was, inexplicable, her
troubled sleep struck her as somewhat of an enigma.

If Minna had any recurrent flickers of embarrassment, any lasting
reservations regarding Celeste, nothing of the kind was at all apparent.
If she was envious of Celeste's easy vibrancy—her immediate intimacy
with the girls, with gruff Flynn, especially with Angelo—she wasn't
conscious of such an envy. In fact, it was not until several weeks after
the first, awful night that Minna recalled how Mrs. Elwood had not
even *asked* her if she'd gone to meet Celeste. Also, Minna had occasion
to see more of Molly Cabot, she felt obligated to see more of her, to
mother her, in some small, inoffensive way; but Minna's sense of
duty took none of the former pleasures away from Molly's company.
Minna enjoyed the shy, secretive closeness of her days with Molly.
As she saw more of Molly, she saw less of Angelo—not that she
stopped worrying about him. Angelo, as Mrs. Elwood had said, was
"rather taken with" Celeste. He brought her flowers—expensive,
gaudy and tasteless flowers, which he couldn't have stolen in the
Common but would have had to buy. And Celeste received other,
less open admiration. On Saturdays the girls were allowed to bring
their weekend dates to the dining hall for lunch, and Celeste certainly
was noticed. The looks which the boys gave her were seldom casual;
they were the penetrating weighted looks which Celeste, when her
head was turned, received from Flynn—darkly and stealthily watching her from behind various pots and counters. Minna, if she thought
anything of this, thought it rather unbecoming to Flynn, and simply
rude of the boys. If she worried about Angelo's adoration, she thought
of it as nothing more than another example of Angelo's tragic exposure
of himself. Celeste, certainly, offered no threat to Angelo. Angelo, as
before, simply was a threat to himself.

Minna was perfectly at ease with Celeste. In two months Celeste had made herself at home; she was gay, a little raucous, always pleasant. The girls were obviously impressed with (or envious of) what Molly called "her Modigliani allure," and Flynn appeared to get great pleasure from his dark observations. Mrs. Elwood thought Celeste was charming, even if a bit bold. Minna liked her.

In June, with only a few weeks of regular classes remaining, Celeste bought an old car—a dented relic of Boston traffic. Once she drove Minna and Molly Cabot to Cambridge, for an afternoon's shopping. The car smelled of sun-tan oil and cigarettes—and, Minna noticed—of the curious, heavy scent, coffee-rich, the musk of sheeted furniture in unattended summer homes. Celeste drove like a man, one arm out the window, forceful wrenches on the wheel, fond of shifting from third to second, fond of competing with taxis. The car labored and knocked with sudden acceleration; Celeste explained that the carburetor was dirty or ill-adjusted. Minna and Molly nodded their bewildered respect. Celeste took her days off at Revere Beach; she became deeply tanned but complained about the "pee-like" condition of the water. It was an eager and active time of year.

And June brought a certain impatience to the girls, an irritable quality to Flynn, who always was great at sweating but seemed to suffer most acutely from this in Boston's early and long summers. Minna had grown quite used to the heat, it didn't seem to bother her much, and she noticed that she rarely sweated anymore. Angelo, of course, was forever pale and dry, a completely aseasonal face and body. Celeste looked damply hot.

June was an almost-over time of year, when the girls were brighter and more often in handsome company, when the weekend dining hall was something like a restless, overly chaperoned party. In a while, there would be different girls in the dormitory for the summer session, and summer sessions were so different anyway, lighter, breezier—and from the kitchen's point of view, people ate less. Now there was a distinctly light-handed way about things. Angelo, during the presentation of one horrendous bouquet to Celeste, asked her to see a movie with him. Their heads struggled on either side of the flowers, Angelo peering for an answer, Celeste amused, both at the size of the bouquet and at Angelo's question.

"What movie is it, Angelo?" Her wide, strong mouth; her rich, good teeth.

"Oh, some movie. We'll have to find one close. I don't have a car."

"Then sometime let's go in mine," Celeste said. And then, looking at the ridiculous bouquet, "Where on earth shall we put this?—by the window, out of Flynn's way? I like flowers in a window."

And Angelo scurried to arrange the window sill. Flynn's following eyes, from somewhere out of the steam, found Celeste's long back and strong legs—her broad, taut buttocks laboring under the weight of crocuses and anonymous greens, lilac branches and unopened buds.

There were very few girls who came to see the news on this Friday night, the last Friday of the school year, the last weekend before the final exams. Presumably the girls were studying, and those who weren't had chosen to go out and *really* not study (rather than compromise with the news). It had rained that afternoon, a rain you could smell, steaming off the sidewalks and leaving the streets nearly dry— only a few tepid puddles remained, and the evening air resembled the damp stuffiness of a laundromat. The heat was of that sensuous, gluttonous kind that people in Boston imagine is like the swamp-surrounded porches of a Southern estate, complete with a woman lolling nude in a hammock. Minna felt pleasantly tired; she sat by the window, looking out to the circular driveway in front of the dormitory. It was a private, gravel driveway with a high curb, and from the window it appeared to be carved, almost etched through the rows of elms and the green, green lawn. Minna saw Celeste, arms akimbo, sitting with her back against a tree. Her legs were extended straight in front of her so that her ankles stuck out over the curb of the driveway. It would have been an entirely unbecoming posture for almost any woman, but somehow Celeste lent to it a kind of magnificence in repose; a figure in semi-recline that seemed not exactly sluggish but rather wantonly indisposed to any motion. She was somewhat arrogantly dressed; a sleeveless, high-necked jersey, untucked and fallen outside one of those wrap-around skirts—the kind that always had a slit somewhere, and the slit on Celeste fell to the side of, and a little behind her hard, round thigh. She might have been a splendid Chinese madame, languishing alongside some still canal, waiting to hail a likely sampan as it wound its way through the eucalyptus trees.

The girls stayed after the news to hear the weather report, and to see the dapper little man in the weather station at Logan Airport painfully interpret his complex map. The girls' plans for the weekend obviously hinged on the good weather, and they were all there, Minna still at the window, Celeste still at the tree, when a motorcycle, the gas tank painted British Green, neatly cornered the right-angled entrance to the driveway, leaned cautiously into the gravel circle, and stopped (sliding just a little) in front of the dormitory. The motorcyclist was a young man, very tanned and very blond, with a remarkably babyish face. His shoulders were almost pointed and his head seemed too small for the rest of him; long, thin arms and legs, snuggly fitted in a beige summer suit which sported a wild silk handkerchief in the breast pocket. He wore no tie, just a white shirt open at the throat. His passenger was Molly Cabot. Molly skipped lightly away from the cycle and the curb, then waited for the driver to step off his machine, which he did quite stiffly and slowly. He walked with Molly into the front lobby of the dormitory, walking in the manner of a stoically injured athlete. Minna turned, to see how the weather was progressing, and saw that all the girls were surrounding her at the window.

One of the girls said, "So she *did* get a date with him!"

"We'll never hear the end of this," another girl added.

Everyone sat or stooped rather gravely about the window, waiting for the cyclist to reappear. He wasn't long inside, and when he came out he looked all around him and fiddled with several screws on the motorcycle. His gestures seemed hurried and not really intended to fix anything; they were the gestures of one who was conscious of being watched—or one, perhaps, who did everything as if he were being watched. He rose up on the seat and came down heavily on the kick starter; the report which followed the first sucking sound was startling to those in the window. It even caught the attention of Celeste, who straightened up from her repose against the tree and sat a little further out on the curb. The motorcycle moved around the driveway in Celeste's direction and when it was a few feet past her the brake light flickered, the rear wheel slid gently sideways toward the curb, and the cyclist brought his right foot to the ground as the machine stopped. He then straightened up off the seat and walked the motorcycle backwards to where Celeste sat. One of the girls moved away from the window and shut off the television, then came quickly back to her position in the huddle. No one could hear what the boy was saying because he kept the engine running. Celeste didn't seem to be saying anything. She just smiled, engaged looks of practiced scrutiny at the motorcycle and the boy. Then she got up, moved in front of the cycle, moved her hand once or twice in front of the headlamp, touched one of the instrument dials mounted on the handlebars, and stood back from the boy and his machine—giving what appeared from the window to be one last appraisal of everything that met her eyes. At that moment, or so it seemed to the window-watchers, Molly Cabot knocked once on the door of Minna's room, entered and said, "Wow!" Everyone stood up and tried to be doing something, one girl made an awkward move to the television, but

Molly came directly to the window and looked out to the driveway, asking, "Has he gone?" She was in time to see Celeste offer her hand to the cyclist and deftly swing herself up behind him—executed with surprising agility for her long weight. The skirt was a slight problem, she had to twist it so that the slit was directly behind her. Then she gripped the seat and the driver with her strong legs, rolled her long arms completely around him—her head was a full two inches higher than his, her back and her shoulders seemed broader, stronger than his. The cyclist shifted all his weight to his left leg, held the motorcycle up with some difficulty, and with his right foot shifted the machine into gear. They pulled away slowly, weaving slightly to the end of the driveway; then, once free of the gravel, and with a minimum of fish-tailing from the rear wheel, the cycle lurched into the traffic of the broad street. From the window they were able to follow the sound through the first three gears; then the machine and its riders either stayed in that gear or were lost to the window-watchers and listeners in the random blaring of horns and the other sounds of traffic in the night.

"That bastard," Molly Cabot said, coolly, analytically—and from the faces of the other girls, expectedly.

"Maybe he's just taken her for a ride around the block," someone said, not too convincingly, not even too hopefully.

"Sure," Molly said, and she turned from the window and walked directly out of the room.

All the girls went back to the window. They sat for another twenty minutes, just looking into the night, and finally Minna said, "It's surely time for the movie. Will anyone stay and see it with me?" It was suddenly a night when something extraordinary was called for, Minna thought, and so she considered the extravagance of asking all of them to stay for the movie. If Mrs. Elwood came, as she might, she would not be pleased about it, would speak to Minna about it—after the girls were gone.

"Why not?" someone said.

The movie, as if things weren't cruel enough, was an old musical. The girls commented harshly on each new scene and song. During the commercials the girls went and sat by the window, and whenever there was a likely roar in the street they ran over, regardless of what new horror in song the movie then explored. When the movie was over the girls were unwilling to leave (some of them had rooms that didn't face the driveway), and they appeared bitterly resolved to a night-long vigil. Minna asked politely, shyly, if she might go to bed, and the girls straggled into the corridor, aimlessly bitching. They didn't seem angry at Celeste, or angry because they felt badly for Molly; on the contrary, it struck Minna that they were almost glad about it, and certainly excited. Their anger came from a feeling that they had been deeply cheated out of witnessing the climax to the show. They'll be up all night, Minna thought. How awful.

But Minna waited up herself. She occasionally dozed at the window, waking every time with a start—ashamed at the thought that someone might see her there, watching. It was after three when she went to bed, and she didn't sleep well. She was too tired to get up at every sound, but listened intently to them all. Finally she woke to a sound which was unmistakably the motorcycle, or at least *some* motorcycle. It was stopped at the beginning of the driveway, she could tell, still out on the street, the engine still running. It growled warily out there, making funny, laboring sounds. Then she heard it pull away, heard it pass through three gears again, and lost it as all of them had lost it before, many blocks or even miles away. She listened for the driveway itself now, for the little crunching sounds it makes while supporting feet. She heard the little pops and snaps of the stones, the grating sound of feet and stones on the cement steps. She heard the screen door open, the main door open (she had thought, horribly, intriguingly, that it might have been locked), and then she heard, sometime later, the door at the end of the corridor. It was light in her room and she saw that it was nearly five o'clock. Angelo and Flynn would be in the kitchen soon, perhaps they were already there. Then she heard other doors open along the corridor, and the hurried, bare feet of the girls padding from room to room. She heard whispering and then she fell asleep.

Saturday morning it rained. A fine, inadequate kind of summer rain that did nothing but fog the windows and leave tiny beads of sweat on everyone's upper lip. It might just as well have been sunny and dazzling for all the difference it made on the temperature, and on Flynn's disposition. Flynn remarked, shortly before lunch, that there hadn't been so few people to breakfast since the flu epidemic in December. It always irritated him to prepare a lot of food and have no one there to eat it. Also, he was bothered by the luncheon menu, angry that they were still serving soup when it was so damn hot (and no one did anything but spill it anyway). Despite the weather, there were a lot of boys and parents in the dining hall. Minna always thought this odd, that everyone spent a year talking about the final exams, and that the weekend before the exams was invariably most festive.

Minna watched Celeste rather carefully that morning, wishing she could say something, although she couldn't think of what on earth she even wanted to say. It hadn't, of course, been wrong of Celeste, but Minna had to confess that Celeste just hadn't *looked* very nice. It was only sad because everyone had to *see* it, had to be hurt or angry because of it. And there wasn't much you could say about that. A peculiar uneasiness passed over Minna—some warm remembrance of a pervasive scent, fecund and coffee-rich, which quickly evanesced.

There was lunch to get ready. Most of the girls had filled the dining hall before the soup was served on every table. Angelo looked sadly at the drooping flowers on the many window sills, and received angry commands from Flynn that he finish serving the soup. Celeste worked steadily, carrying trays of potato salad, tureens of soup; every time she returned to the kitchen from the dining hall she took one luxurious pull on her cigarette, left dangling over the counter during her exits. Minna neatly arranged the lettuce in pretty patterns around the rim of the salad trays, being careful to hide the wilted and brown parts under the potatoes.

Celeste was taking what had to be the last drag on her cigarette when Molly Cabot swung open the aluminum door to the kitchen; she stepped inside, biting her lip, and allowed the door to swing closed behind her. Angelo, with a handful of flowers, turned to see who'd come in. Flynn stared indifferently. And Minna felt a tremendous weight on her diaphragm, pushing in or pushing out—it was hard to tell where the force was coming from. Molly Cabot, unsteady and small, stepped a little forward and away from the door. She squinted painfully at Celeste, in what might have been an attempt to intimidate the long, calm woman.

"You bitch, you whore!" Molly shouted. A voice as shrill and delicate as a coffee spoon striking a saucer. "You *really* dirty whore!"

And Celeste just looked, smiling gently—an inquiring, still puzzled face which invited Molly to please continue.

Molly gained a certain composure, a practiced restraint of the kind suggested in Beginning Speech Class, and said, "I will not stoop so low as to compete on *your* level!" It was not haughty, it was still the spoon on the saucer.

Minna said, "Molly, dear. Don't." And Molly, without taking her eyes from Celeste, stepped gingerly backwards, feeling for the door with her hand, and when her weight rested against the door she leaned back and swung with it—revolved out of the kitchen. The door swung back, bringing no new horrors in its path, swung twice before it squeaked and closed. Minna looked apologetically at Celeste.

"Celeste, dear," she began, but Celeste turned to her with the same penetrating calm, the same inquiring face she had turned to Molly.

"It's all right, Minna," she said, soothingly, as if she spoke to a child.

Minna shook her head and looked away; it seemed she would cry at any second. Then Flynn shook and clamored against the aluminum shelves. "Christ!" he hollered. "What's going on?"

There was a long moment when no one spoke, and then there was Angelo; with a curiously studied fury that never could have been his own, but something mimicked from countless bad movies and college plays, he stepped awkwardly to the middle of the kitchen, throwing himself off balance as he flung his wilted flowers to the floor. "Who does she think she is?" he demanded. "Who does she think she's talking to? Who *is* she?"

"She's just a girl who thinks I stole her boy," Celeste said. "We went out for a ride last night, after he brought her back here."

"But she can't say that!" Angelo cried, and Minna saw that the consistently pale face of Angelo was deeply flushed.

"I got a daughter her age," Flynn said. "I'd wash her damn mouth out with soap if she ever pulled any of that stuff."

"Oh, that's really good, Flynn," Celeste snapped, "that's really good, coming from you! Why don't you just shut up?"

But Angelo, they should have known, had at last encountered the dark illogical fate which any one of them might have envisioned for him. He made some quick, secretive movement with his hands and walked to the aluminum door—like one who'd seen a specter of his potential self, beckon and bid him follow. He was gone before anyone could say anything, even before anyone could move, leaving the kitchen in ghoulish silence.

Then Flynn said, "He took the lye soap out of the sink. He took it with him!" And Celeste moved more quickly than Flynn and Minna, moved in front of them, out through the swinging door.

The dining hall was very crowded, but very quiet. The occasional tinkle of ice cubes in the tea, the nervous creakings of chairs. Mrs. Elwood sat at the Head Table, surrounded by well-dressed parents and children with napkins tucked into their collars. Minna looked helplessly at Mrs. Elwood, whose chin was twitching in random little spasms. Angelo stood in the aisle between two rows of tables at the far end of the dining hall, the yellow-green bar of lye soap in his right hand—held as if it were extremely heavy or dangerous, held like a shot-put or a grenade. He stood like Odysseus, come home to Penelope, come home to throw the rabble of suitors out of his house—

to hack and behead them all—come fiercely to do great violence. Molly Cabot peered into her soup, prodigiously counting the noodles or rice. Angelo leaned across the table until his nose was almost in her hair.

"You got to apologize to Miss Celeste. Girl," he said softly, "you got to get up and do it right now."

Molly didn't look up from her soup. She said, "No, Angelo." And then, very quietly, she added, "You go back to the kitchen. Right now."

Angelo put his hand on the edge of Molly's soup dish, palm up, and he let the bar of lye soap slide into her soup.

"Right now," Angelo softly commanded. "You apologize or I'll wash your mouth out good."

Molly pushed her chair back from the table and began to stand up, but Angelo caught her by the shoulders, pulled her across the table to him, and began to force her head down, down to the soup dish. The girl sitting next to Molly screamed—one shrill and aimless scream—and Angelo got his hand on the back of Molly's neck and shoved her face into the soup. He dunked her swiftly, just once, and then he caught her by one shoulder and pulled her to him, his right hand groping for the soap. There was a boy sitting across the aisle from Molly's table. He jumped up and shouted, "Hey!" But Celeste was the first to get to Angelo; she seized him around the waist and picked him off the floor, loosened his grip on Molly, and then tried to shift him over her hip, tried to carry him down the aisle to the kitchen. But Angelo wriggled free of her, wriggled into hairy Flynn. Flynn grabbed Angelo in a bear hug and everyone heard Angelo grunt. Flynn just turned and walked Angelo toward the kitchen, bending the thin body to a sharp curve at the spine; Celeste ran in front of them, got to the door first and held it open. Angelo kicked and clawed, snapping his head around to try and see where Molly had gone. "You whore!" Angelo screamed, his breath pinched out of him in thin soprano. And then they passed through the great door— Angelo peering madly over the shoulders of Flynn—Celeste hurrying after them, the door swinging heavily closed.

Minna caught one glimpse of Molly Cabot, leaving the dining hall with a napkin over her face, her blouse spattered with soup and clinging to her bird-like chest. Her scalded, offended, demure breasts seemed to point the way of her determined exit. Then Mrs. Elwood took Minna by the arm and whispered, confidingly, "I want to know what this is about. Whatever possessed him? He must leave at once. At once!"

In the kitchen Angelo sat in grand disorder on the floor, leaning against an aluminum cabinet. Flynn roughly dabbed at Angelo's mouth with a wet towel; Angelo was bleeding from his mouth, and he slumped, bespattered with soup, bleeding slowly down his chin. He moaned a high, complaining moan—the whine of an abandoned dog—and his eyes were closed.

"What did you do to him?" Celeste asked Flynn.

"He must have bit his tongue," Flynn mumbled.

"I did, I did," Angelo said, his voice muted by the towel which Flynn squeezed against his mouth.

"Christ, what a stupid Wop," Flynn grumbled.

Celeste took the towel from Flynn and shoved him away from Angelo. "Let me do that," she said. "You'll rub his whole face off."

"I should have hit her," Angelo blurted. "I should have just hit her a good one."

"Christ, listen to him!" Flynn shouted.

"Shut up, Flynn," Celeste said.

And Minna, silent all this time, moused in a corner of the kitchen. She said, "He'll have to leave. Mrs. Elwood said he'll have to leave at once."

"Christ, what'll he do?" Flynn asked. "Where in Hell can he go?"

"Don't worry about me," Angelo said. He blinked his eyes and smiled at Celeste. She knelt in front of him, made him open his mouth so that she could see his tongue; she had a clean handkerchief in the pocket of her dress and she gently touched his tongue with it, gently closed his mouth, took his hand and made him hold the wet towel to his lips. Angelo shut his eyes again, leaned forward, his head falling on Celeste's shoulder. Celeste settled back on her ankles, wrapped one great arm around Angelo and slowly rocked him, forward and backward, until he made himself into a little ball on her breast—his curious moan began again, only now it was more like someone making up a song.

"I'll lock the door," Flynn said, "so's no one can come in."

Minna watched, a dull ache in her throat, the prelude to great weeping and sorrow; and arising with the ache was a coldness in her hands and feet. This was hate—oddly enough, she thought—hate for Angelo's possessor, for Celeste, his captor, who now held him as if he were a wild, trapped rabbit. She calmed him, she would tame him; Angelo, dutifully, was her pet and her child, her charge—possessed by this vast, sensuous body, which now and forever would be his magnificent, unachievable goal. And he wouldn't even be aware of what it was that held him to her.

"Angelo," Celeste said softly, "my brother-in-law has an inn, in

Maine. It's very nice there, on the ocean, and there would be work for you—a free place to stay. In the winter it's quiet, just clean snow to be shoveled and things to be fixed. In the summer the tourists come to swim and sail; there's boats and beaches, and you'd like my family."

"No," Minna said. "It's too far. How could he get there?"

"I'll take him myself," Celeste told her. "I'll drive him there tonight. I'd only miss one day, just tomorrow."

"He's never been out of Boston," Minna said. "He wouldn't like it."

"Of course he'd like it!" Flynn shouted. "It'll be perfect."

"Celeste?" Angelo asked. "Will you be there?"

"On weekends, in the summer," she said. "And all my vacations."

"What's it called?" Angelo asked her. He sat up, back against the counter cabinet, and he touched her hair with his hand. His wondering, adoring eyes passed over her thick, black hair, her strong-boned face and wide mouth.

"It's called Heron's Neck," Celeste told him. "Everybody's very friendly. You'd get to know them all, right away."

"I'll bet you'd like it just fine, Angelo," Flynn said.

"We'll go tonight," Celeste prompted. "We'll go as soon as we put your things in my car."

"You can't do it," Minna said. "You can't take him there."

"She'll only miss one day!" Flynn shouted. "Christ, Minna, what's one day?"

Minna passed her hand over her face, the powder wet and clotted at the corners of her eyes. She looked at Celeste.

"You can't have the day off," Minna told her. "It's a busy time of year."

"Christ!" Flynn hollered. "Speak to Mrs. Elwood about it!"

"I'm in charge of this kitchen!" Minna cried. "I saw to getting her hired, and I'll see to this." Flynn evaded Minna's eyes, and it was very quiet in the kitchen.

"What if I just left with Angelo tonight?" Celeste asked.

"Then you just leave for good," Minna said.

"Put Angelo on a bus!" Flynn bellowed; great purple globes, welt-like, stood out on his cheeks.

"I don't want to go there alone!" Angelo cried. "I don't know anybody," he added meekly.

It was quiet again, and this time Flynn evaded Celeste's eyes. Celeste looked down at her knees, then she touched Angelo's damp head.

"I'll take you right now," Celeste told him slowly.

"We'll be there together," Angelo said, rapidly nodding his head. "You can show me around."

"It'll be nicer that way," Celeste told him. "We'll just do that."

"I should say good-by to Mrs. Elwood," Angelo said.

"Why don't we just send her a postcard when we get there," Celeste suggested.

"Yeah," Angelo said. "And we can send one to Flynn and to Minna. What kind of postcard do you want, Flynn?"

"Maybe one of the water and cliffs," he answered gently.

"Cliffs, huh?" Angelo asked Celeste.

"Sure," she said.

"What kind do you want, Minna?" Angelo asked, but she had turned away from them. She was stooping to pick up the flowers from the floor.

"Anything you'd like to send," she told him.

"Then let's get ready," Celeste said.

"Do you want to go out the other door?" Flynn asked. "To get some air." He opened the door which led to the campus yard. It had stopped raining. The grass was shiny and smelled very lush.

When they were gone, when Flynn had shut the door behind them, Minna said, "Well, it's going to be busy with just the two of us, but I guess we'll get on."

"Sure we'll get on," Flynn told her. Then he added, "I think that was a pretty stinking thing to do."

"I *am* sorry, Flynn," she said—a thin, breaking voice—and then she saw the tureens of soup, the trays of potato salad. God, she thought, have they been waiting out there all this time? But when she peeked into the dining hall, gingerly leaning on the door, she saw that everyone was gone. Mrs. Elwood must have shooed them all away.

"There's no one out there," she told Flynn.

"Just look at all this food," he said.

Before the news, before the movie. Minna sits in her room, waiting for it to be finally dark. A soft, gray light falls over the driveway and over the elms, and Minna listens for sounds from Celeste's room—she watches for Celeste's car in the driveway. They must have gone by now, she thinks. They probably loaded the car somewhere else; Celeste would think of that. It is dusky in Minna's room; the faint light of early evening touches what few bright articles are placed on Minna's desk and bedside table, on the chest of drawers and television, on the coffee table. Most striking are the uneaten, unopened cans of foreign food. The hors d'oeuvre fork throws a dull reflection of the evening light back to Minna at the window. Poor Molly, Minna thinks—How awful that she has to go on *being* here, in front of everyone. And suddenly she feels the same sympathy for herself. It is a most ephemeral pity, though, and she soon feels thankful that school is so nearly over.

The street lights go on, whole rows of them lining the campus, giving the same luster to the elms and lawn that Minna noticed a night ago—a Chinese landscape, with canal, missing only Celeste. Minna moves from the window, turns on her desk lamp, mechanically hunts for a book. Then she sits deeply in the plush of her leather chair. She just sits, listening for nothing now, not reading, not even thinking. The toys of her weary mind seem lost.

A moth catches her eye. It has come from somewhere, somewhere safe, come to flutter wildly about the single light in the room. What on earth can it be that lures a moth out of the safety of darkness and into the peril of light? Its wings flap excitedly, it beats against the hot bulb of the lamp—it surely must scorch itself. Clumsily, carelessly, it bangs into things in an aimless frenzy. Minna thinks for a moment of getting up and turning off the light, but she doesn't feel like sitting in the dark—she doesn't feel like finding a newspaper to swat the moth. She sits, it grows darker, the buzz of the moth becomes soothing and pleasant. Minna dozes peacefully, briefly.

She wakes, startled, and thinks she is not awake—only dreaming. Then she sees the persistent moth and she knows she is really awake. It is completely dark outside now and she hears the familiar, restless growl of a motorcycle. She gets up from her chair and from the window she sees it, the same one, British Green. The cycle waits at the beginning of the driveway. Minna thinks, If he is coming for Molly he'll come into the dormitory. The cyclist glances around him, turns the throttle up and down, looks at his watch, jounces lightly on the seat. He has come for Celeste, Minna knows, and she watches him, aware that other windows around her are open, other eyes watching him. No one comes out of the dormitory; Minna hears whispers pass from window screen to window screen, like a bird looking for a place to get in or out. The motorcyclist turns the throttle up again, holds the throttle there a moment, then lets the engine fall to its wary idle. Nothing happens, the cyclist jounces more heavily on the seat, looks again at his watch. Minna wonders, Do the girls know that Celeste is gone? Of course, the girls know everything; some of them probably knew that the motorcyclist would be back tonight, and not for Molly. But the cyclist is impatient now—sensing, perhaps, that Celeste isn't coming. Minna wishes she could see his face, but it is too dark. Only the pale blond hair flashes at her window, the lustrous green gas tank of the motorcycle shimmers like water; and then the throttle turns up again, the rear wheel skids sideways in the gravel, squeaks on the street. The whispering window screens are now silent, listening for the first three gears. Each gear seems to reach a little further than the night before.

Now Minna is alone with the moth. She wonders whether the girls will come for the news, wonders what time it is. And if the girls come, will Molly come with them? Oh, Minna hopes not, at least not tonight. The moth soothes her again, she dozes or half-dozes to the drone. She has a final, alarming thought before she falls to a deeper sleep. What will she ever say to Mrs. Elwood? But the moth manages to calm even this. The happy, smudge-mouthed faces of her brother's children flood Minna's tidy room, and Angelo is somewhere among them. The motorcycle comes by once more, stops, snarls, goes madly on, ushered away to its dark journey by the titters at the window screens. But Minna doesn't hear it this time. She sleeps—lulled by the whirring, furry music of the moth.

Love Life

BOBBIE ANN MASON

O PAL LOLLS IN HER RECLINER, wearing the Coors cap her niece
Jenny brought her from Colorado. She fumbles for the remote-
control paddle and fires a button. Her swollen knuckles hurt. On TV,
a boy is dancing in the street. Some other boys dressed in black are
banging guitars and drums. This is her favorite program. It is always
on, night or day. The show is songs, with accompanying stories. It's
the music channel. Opal never cared for stories—she detests those
soap operas her friends watch—but these fascinate her. The colors
and the costumes change and flow with the music, erratically, the
way her mind does these days. Now the TV is playing a song in
which all the boys are long-haired cops chasing a dangerous woman
in a tweed cap and a checked shirt. The woman's picture is in all their
billfolds. They chase her through a cold-storage room filled with sides
of beef. She hops on a motorcycle, and they set up a road block, but
she jumps it with her motorcycle. Finally, she slips onto a train and
glides away from them, waving a smiling goodbye.

On the table beside Opal is a Kleenex box, her glasses case, a glass
of Coke with ice, and a cut-glass decanter of clear liquid that could
be just water for the plants. Opal pours some of the liquid into the
Coke and sips slowly. It tastes like peppermint candy, and it feels
soothing. Her fingers tingle. She feels happy. Now that she is retired,
she doesn't have to sneak into the teachers' lounge for a little swig
from the jar in her pocketbook. She still dreams algebra problems,
complicated quadratic equations with shifting values and no solutions.
Now kids are using algebra to program computers. The kids in the
TV stories remind her of her students at Hopewell High. Old age
could have a grandeur about it, she thinks now as the music surges
through her, if only it weren't so scary.

But she doesn't feel lonely, especially now that her sister Alice's
girl, Jenny, has moved back here, to Kentucky. Jenny seems so confident, the way she sprawls on the couch, with that backpack she

carries everywhere. Alice was always so delicate and feminine, but Jenny is enough like Opal to be her own daughter. She has Opal's light, thin hair, her large shoulders and big bones and long legs. Jenny even has a way of laughing that reminds Opal of her own laughter, the boisterous scoff she always saved for certain company but never allowed herself in school. Now and then Jenny lets loose one of those laughs and Opal is pleased. It occurs to her that Jenny, who is already past thirty, has left behind a trail of men, like that girl in the song. Jenny has lived with a couple of men, here and there. Opal can't keep track of all of the men Jenny has mentioned. They have names like John and Skip and Michael. She's not in a hurry to get married, she says. She says she is going to buy a house trailer and live in the woods like a hermit. She's full of ideas, and she exaggerates. She uses the words "gorgeous," "adorable," and "wonderful" interchangeably and persistently.

Last night, Jenny was here, with her latest boyfriend, Randy Newcomb. Opal remembers when he sat in the back row in her geometry class. He was an ordinary kid, not especially smart, and often late with his lessons. Now he has a real-estate agency and drives a Cadillac. Jenny kissed him in front of Opal and told him he was gorgeous. She said the placemats were gorgeous, too.

Jenny was asking to see those old quilts again. "Why do you hide away your nice things, Aunt Opal?" she said. Opal doesn't think they're that nice, and she doesn't want to have to look at them all the time. Opal showed Jenny and Randy Newcomb the double-wedding-ring quilt, the star quilt, and some of the crazy quilts, but she wouldn't show them the craziest one—the burial quilt, the one Jenny kept asking about. Did Jenny come back home just to hunt up that old rag? The thought makes Opal shudder.

The doorbell rings. Opal has to rearrange her comforter and magazines in order to get up. Her joints are stiff. She leaves the TV blaring a song she knows, with balloons and bombs in it.

At the door is Velma Shaw, who lives in the duplex next to Opal. She has just come home from her job at Shop World. "Have you gone out of your mind, Opal?" cries Velma. She has on a plum-colored print blouse and a plum skirt and a little green scarf with a gold pin holding it down. Velma shouts, "You can hear that racket clear across the street!"

"Rock and roll is never too loud," says Opal. This is a line from a song she has heard.

Opal releases one of her saved-up laughs, and Velma backs away. Velma is still trying to be sexy, in those little color-coordinated outfits she wears, but it is hopeless, Opal thinks with a smile. She closes the door and scoots back to her chaise longue.

Opal is Jenny's favorite aunt. Jenny likes the way Opal ties her hair in a pony tail with a ribbon. She wears muumuus and socks. She is tall and only a little thick in the middle. She told Jenny that middle-age spread was caused by the ribs expanding and that it doesn't matter what you eat. Opal kids around about "old Arthur"—her arthritis, visiting her on damp days.

Jenny has been in town six months. She works at the courthouse, typing records—marriages, divorces, deaths, drunk-driving convictions. Frequently, the same names are on more than one list. Before she returned to Kentucky, Jenny was waitressing in Denver, but she was growing restless again, and the idea of going home seized her. Her old rebellion against small-town conventions gave way to curiosity.

In the South, the shimmer of the heat seems to distort everything, like old glass with impurities in it. During her first two days there, she saw two people with artificial legs, a blind man, a man with hooks for hands, and a man without an arm. It seemed unreal. In a parking lot, a pit bull terrier in a Camaro attacked her at the closed window. He barked viciously, his nose stabbing the window. She stood in the parking lot, letting the pit bull attack, imagining herself in an arena, with a crowd watching. The South makes her nervous. Randy Newcomb told her she had just been away too long. "We're not as countrified down here now as people think," he said.

Jenny has been going with Randy for three months. The first night she went out with him, he took her to a fancy place that served shrimp flown in from New Orleans, and then to a little bar over in Hopkinsville. They went with Kathy Steers, a friend from work, and Kathy's husband, Bob. Kathy and Bob weren't getting along and they carped at each other all evening. In the bar, an attractive, cheerful woman sang requests for tips, and her companion, a blind man, played the guitar. When she sang, she looked straight at him, singing to him, smiling at him reassuringly. In the background, men played pool with their girlfriends, and Jenny noticed the sharp creases in the men's jeans and imagined the women ironing them. When she mentioned it, Kathy said she took Bob's jeans to the laundromat to use the machine there that puts knifelike creases in them. The men in the bar had two kinds of women with them: innocent-looking women with pastel skirts and careful hairdos, and hard-looking women without makeup in T-shirts and jeans. Jenny imagined that each type could be either a girlfriend or a wife. She felt odd. She was neither type. The singer sang "Happy Birthday" to a popular regular named Will Ed, and after the set she danced with him, while the jukebox took over. She had a limp, as though one leg were shorter than the other. The leg was stiff under her jeans, and when the woman danced Jenny could see that the leg was not real.

"There, but for the grace of God, go I," Randy whispered to Jenny. He squeezed her hand, and his heavy turquoise ring dug into her knuckle.

"Those quilts would bring a good price at an estate auction," Randy says to Jenny as they leave her aunt's one evening and head for his real-estate office. They are in his burgundy Cadillac. "One of those star quilts used to bring twenty-five dollars. Now it might run three hundred."

"My aunt doesn't think they're worth anything. She hides all her nice stuff, like she's ashamed of it. She's got beautiful dresser scarves and starched doilies she made years ago. But she's getting a little weird. All she does is watch MTV."

"I think she misses the kids," Randy says. Then he bursts out laughing. "She used to put the fear of God in all her students! I never will forget the time she told me to stop watching so much television and read some books. It was like an order from God Almighty. I didn't dare not do what she said. I read *Crime and Punishment*. I never would have read it if she hadn't shamed me into it. But I appreciated that. I don't even remember what *Crime and Punishment* was about, except there was an axe murderer in it."

"That was basically it," Jenny says. "He got caught. Crime and punishment—just like any old TV show."

Randy touches some controls on the dashboard and Waylon Jennings starts singing. The sound system is remarkable. Everything Randy owns is quality. He has been looking for some land for Jenny to buy—a couple of acres of woods—but so far nothing on his listings has met with his approval. He is concerned about zoning and power lines and frontage. All Jenny wants is a remote place where she can have a dog and grow some tomatoes. She knows that what she really needs is a better car, but she doesn't want to go anywhere.

Later, at Randy's office, Jenny studies the photos of houses on display, while he talks on the telephone to someone about dividing up a sixty-acre farm into farmettes. His photograph is on several certificates on the wall. He has a full, well-fed face in the pictures, but he is thinner now and looks better. He has a boyish, endearing smile, like Dennis Quaid, Jenny's favorite actor. She likes his smile. It seems so innocent, as though he would do anything in the world for someone he cared about. He doesn't really want to sell her any land. He says he is afraid she will get raped if she lives alone in the woods.

"I'm impressed," she says when he slams down the telephone. She points to his new regional award for the fastest-growing agency of the year.

"Isn't that something? Three branch offices in a territory this size—I can't complain. There's a lot of turnover in real estate now. People are never satisfied. You know that? That's the truth about human nature." He laughs. "That's the secret of my success."

"It's been two years since Barbara divorced me," he says later, on the way to Jenny's apartment. "I can't say it hasn't been fun being free, but my kids are in college, and it's like starting over. I'm ready for a new life. The business has been so great, I couldn't really ask for more, but I've been thinking— Don't laugh, please, but what I was thinking was if you want to share it with me, I'll treat you good. I swear."

At a stoplight, he paws at her hand. On one corner is the Pepsi bottling plant, and across from it is the Broad Street House, a restaurant with an old-fashioned statue of a jockey out front. People are painting the black faces on those little statues white now, but this one has been painted bright green all over. Jenny can't keep from laughing at it.

"I wasn't laughing at you—honest!" she says apologetically. "That statue always cracks me up."

"You don't have to give me an answer now."

"I don't know what to say."

"I can get us a real good deal on a house," he says. "I can get any house I've got listed. I can even get us a farmette, if you want trees so bad. You won't have to spend your money on a piece of land."

"I'll have to think about it." Randy scares her. She likes him, but there is something strange about his energy and optimism. Everyone around her seems to be bursting at the seams, like that pit bull terrier.

"I'll let you think on it," he says, pulling up to her apartment. "Life has been good to me. Business is good, and my kids didn't turn out to be dope fiends. That's about all you can hope for in this day and time."

Jenny is having lunch with Kathy Steers at the Broad Street House. The iced tea is mixed with white grape juice. It took Jenny a long time to identify the flavor, and the Broad Street House won't admit it's grape juice. Their iced tea is supposed to have a mystique about it, probably because they can't sell drinks in this dry county. In the daylight, the statue out front is the color of the Jolly Green Giant.

People confide in Jenny, but Jenny doesn't always tell things back. It's an unfair exchange, though it often goes unnoticed. She is curious, eager to hear other people's stories, and she asks more questions than is appropriate. Kathy's life is a tangle of deceptions. Kathy stayed with her husband, Bob, because he had opened his own body shop and she didn't want him to start out a new business with a rocky marriage, but she acknowledges now it was a mistake.

"What about Jimmy and Willette?" Jenny asks. Jimmy and Willette are the other characters in Kathy's story.

"That mess went on for months. When you started work at the office, remember how nervous I was? I thought I was getting an ulcer." Kathy lights a cigarette and blows at the wall. "You see, I didn't know what Bob and Willette were up to, and they didn't know about me and Jimmy. That went on for two years before you came. And when it started to come apart—I mean, we had *hell*! I'd say things to Jimmy and then it would get back to Bob because Jimmy would tell Willette. It was an unreal circle. I was pregnant with Jason and you get real sensitive then. I thought Bob was screwing around on me, but it never dawned on me it was with Willette."

The fat waitress says, "Is everything all right?"

Kathy says, "No, but it's not your fault. Do you know what I'm going to do?" she asks Jenny.

"No, what?"

"I'm taking Jason and moving in with my sister. She has a sort of apartment upstairs. Bob can do what he wants to with the house. I've waited too long to do this, but it's time. My sister keeps the baby anyway, so why shouldn't I just live there?"

She puffs the cigarette again and levels her eyes at Jenny. "You know what I admire about you? You're so independent. You say what you think. When you started work at the office, I said to myself, 'I wish I could be like that.' I could tell you had been around. You've inspired me. That's how come I decided to move out."

Jenny plays with the lemon slice in the saucer holding her iced-tea glass. She picks a seed out of it. She can't bring herself to confide in Kathy about Randy Newcomb's offer. For some reason, she is embarrassed by it.

"I haven't spoken to Willette since September 3rd," says Kathy.

Kathy keeps talking, and Jenny listens, suspicious of her interest in

Kathy's problems. She notices how Kathy is enjoying herself. Kathy is looking forward to leaving her husband the same way she must have enjoyed her fling with Jimmy, the way she is enjoying not speaking to Willette.

"Let's go out and get drunk tonight," Kathy says cheerfully. "Let's celebrate my decision."

"I can't. I'm going to see my aunt this evening. I have to take her some booze. She gives me money to buy her vodka and peppermint schnapps, and she tells me not to stop at the same liquor store. She says she doesn't want me to get a reputation for drinking! I have to go all the way to Hopkinsville to get it."

"Your aunt tickles me. She's a pistol."

The waitress clears away the dishes and slaps down dessert menus. They order chocolate pecan pie, the day's special.

"You know the worst part of this whole deal?" Kathy says. "It's the years it takes to get smart. But I'm going to make up for lost time. You can bet on that. And there's not a thing Bob can do about it."

Opal's house has a veranda. Jenny thinks that verandas seem to imply a history of some sort—people in rocking chairs telling stories. But Opal doesn't tell any stories. It is exasperating, because Jenny wants to know about her aunt's past love life, but Opal won't reveal her secrets. They sit on the veranda and observe each other. They smile, and now and then roar with laughter over something ridiculous. In the bedroom, where she snoops after using the bathroom, Jenny notices the layers of old wallpaper in the closet, peeling back and spilling crumbs of gaudy ancient flower prints onto Opal's muumuus.

Downstairs, Opal asks, "Do you want some cake, Jenny?"

"Of course. I'm crazy about your cake, Aunt Opal."

"I didn't beat the egg whites long enough. Old Arthur's visiting again." Opal flexes her fingers and smiles. "That sounds like the curse. Girls used to say they had the curse. Or they had a visitor." She looks down at her knuckles shyly. "Nowadays, of course, they just say what they mean."

The cake is delicious—an old-fashioned lemon chiffon made from scratch. Jenny's cooking ranges from English-muffin mini-pizzas to brownie mixes. After gorging on the cake, Jenny blurts out, "Aunt Opal, aren't you sorry you never got married? Tell the truth, now."

Opal laughs, "I was talking to Ella Mae Smith the other day—she's a retired geography teacher?—and she said, 'I've got twelve great-great-grandchildren, and when we get together I say, "Law me, look what I started!"'" Opal mimics Ella Mae Smith, giving her a mindless, chirpy tone of voice. "Why, I'd have to use quadratic equations to count up all the people that woman has caused," she goes on. "All with a streak of her petty narrow-mindedness in them. I don't call that a contribution to the world." Opal laughs and sips from her glass of schnapps. "What about you, Jenny? Are you ever going to get married?"

"Marriage is outdated. I don't know anybody who's married and happy."

Opal names three schoolteachers she has known who have been married for decades.

"But are they really happy?"

"Oh, foot, Jenny! What you're saying is why are *you* not married and why are *you* not happy. What's wrong with little Randy Newcomb? Isn't that funny? I always think of him as little Randy."

"Show me those quilts again, Aunt Opal."

"I'll show you the crazies but not the one you keep after me about."

"O.K., show me the crazies."

Upstairs, her aunt lays crazy quilts on the bed. They are bright-colored patches of soft velvet and plaids and prints stitched together with silky embroidery. Several pieces have initials embroidered on them. The haphazard shapes make Jenny imagine odd, twisted lives represented in these quilts.

She says, "Mom gave me a quilt once, but I didn't appreciate the value of it and I washed it until it fell apart."

"I'll give you one of these crazies when you stop moving around," Opal says. "You couldn't fit it in that backpack of yours." She polishes her glasses thoughtfully. "Do you know what those quilts mean to me?"

"No, what?"

"A lot of desperate old women ruining their eyes. Do you know what I think I'll do?"

"No, what?"

"I think I'll take up aerobic dancing. Or maybe I'll learn to ride a motorcycle. I try to be modern."

"You're funny, Aunt Opal. You're hilarious."

"Am I gorgeous, too?"

"Adorable," says Jenny.

After her niece leaves, Opal hums a tune and dances a stiff little jig. She nestles among her books and punches her remote-control paddle. Years ago, she was allowed to paddle students who misbehaved. She used a wooden paddle from a butter churn, with holes drilled in it. The holes made a satisfying sting. On TV, a nineteen-fifties convertible is out of gas. This is one of her favorites. It has an adorable couple in it. The girl is wearing bobby socks and saddle oxfords, and the boy has on a basketball jacket. They look the way children looked before the hippie element took over. But the boy begins growing cat whiskers and big cat ears, and then his face gets furry and leathery, while the girl screams bloody murder. Opal sips some peppermint and watches his face change. The red and gold of his basketball jacket are the Hopewell school colors. He chases the girl. Now he has grown long claws.

The boy is dancing energetically with a bunch of ghouls who have escaped from their coffins. "Grisly ghouls are closing in to seal your doom," Vincent Price says in the background. The girl is very frightened. The ghouls are so old and ugly. That's how kids see us, Opal thinks. She loves this story. She even loves the credits: "Scary Music by Elmer Bernstein." This is a story with a meaning. It suggests all the feelings of terror and horror that must be hidden inside young people. And inside, deep down, there really are monsters. An old person waits, a nearly dead body that can still dance.

Opal pours another drink. She feels relaxed, her joints loose like a dancer's now.

Jenny is so nosy. Her questions are so blunt. Did Opal ever have a crush on a student? Only once or twice. She was in her twenties then, and it seemed scandalous. Nothing happened—just daydreams. When she was thirty, she had another attachment to a boy, and it seemed all right then, but it was worse again at thirty-five, when another pretty boy stayed after class to talk. After that, she kept her distance.

But Opal is not wholly without experience. There have been men, over the years, though nothing like the casual affairs Jenny has had. Opal remembers a certain motel room in Nashville. She was only forty. The man drove a gray Chrysler Imperial. When she was telling about him to a friend, who was sworn to secrecy, she called him "Imperial," in a joking way. She went with him because she knew he would take her somewhere, in such a fine car, and they would sleep together. She always remembered how clean and empty the room was, how devoid of history and association. In the mirror, she saw a scared woman with a pasty face and a shrimpy little man who needed a shave. In the morning he went out somewhere and brought back coffee and orange juice. They had bought some doughnuts at the new doughnut shop in town before they left. While he was out, she made up the bed and put her things in her bag, to make it as neat as if she had never been there. She was fully dressed when he returned, with her garter belt and stockings on, and when they finished the doughnuts she cleaned up all the paper and the cups and wiped the crumbs from the table by the bed. He said, "Come with me and I'll take you to Idaho." "Why Idaho?" she wanted to know, but his answer was vague. Idaho sounded cold, and she didn't want to tell him how she disliked his scratchy whiskers and the hard, powdery doughnuts. It seemed unkind of her, but if he had been nicer-looking, without such a demanding dark beard, she might have gone with him to Idaho in that shining Imperial. She hadn't even given him a chance, she thought later. She had been so scared. If anyone from school had seen her at that motel, she could have lost her job. "I need a woman," he had said. "A woman like you."

On a hot Saturday afternoon, with rain threatening, Jenny sits under a tent on a folding chair while Randy auctions off four hundred acres of woods on Lake Barkley. He had a road bulldozed into the property, and he divided it up into lots. The lakefront lots are going for as much as two thousand an acre, and the others are bringing up to a thousand. Randy has several assistants with him, and there is even a concession stand, offering hot dogs and cold drinks.

In the middle of the auction, they wait for a thundershower to pass. Sitting in her folding chair under a canopy reminds Jenny of graveside services. As soon as the rain slacks up, the auction continues. In his cowboy hat and blue blazer, Randy struts around with a microphone as proudly as a banty rooster. With his folksy chatter, he knows exactly how to work the crowd. "Y'all get yourselves a cold drink and relax now and just imagine the fishing you'll do in this dreamland. This land is good for vacation, second home, investment—heck, you can just park here in your camper and live. It's going to be paradise when that marina gets built on the lake there and we get some lots cleared."

The four-hundred-acre tract looks like a wilderness. Jenny loves the way the sun splashes on the water after the rain, and the way it comes through the trees, hitting the flickering leaves like lights on a disco ball. A marina here seems farfetched. She could pitch a tent here until she could afford to buy a used trailer. She could swim at dawn, the way she did on a camping trip out West, long ago. All of a sudden, she finds herself bidding on a lot. The bidding passes four hundred, and she sails on, bidding against a man from Missouri who tells the people around him that he's looking for a place to retire.

"Sold to the young lady with the backpack," Randy says when she bids six hundred. He gives her a crestfallen look, and she feels embarrassed.

As she waits for Randy to wind up his business after the auction, Jenny locates her acre from the map of the plots of land. It is along a gravel road and marked off with stakes tied with hot-pink survey tape. It is a small section of the woods—her block on the quilt, she thinks. These are her trees. The vines and underbrush are thick and spotted with raindrops. She notices a windfall leaning on a maple, like a lover dying in its arms. Maples are strong, she thinks, but she feels like getting an axe and chopping that windfall down, to save the maple. In the distance, the whining of a speedboat cuts into the day.

They meet afterward at Randy's van, his mobile real-estate office, with a little shingled roof raised in the center to look rustic. It looks like an outhouse on wheels. A painted message on the side says, "REALITY IS REAL ESTATE." As Randy plows through the mud on the new road, Jenny apologizes. Buying the lot was like laughing at the statue at the wrong moment—something he would take the wrong way, an insult to his attentions.

"I can't reach you," he says. "You say you want to live out in the wilderness and grow your own vegetables, but you act like you're somewhere in outer space. You can't grow vegetables in outer space. You can't even grow them in the woods unless you clear some ground."

"I'm looking for a place to land."

"What do I have to do to get through to you?"

"I don't know. I need more time."

He turns onto the highway, patterned with muddy tire tracks from the cars at the auction. "I said I'd wait, so I guess I'll have to," he says, flashing his Dennis Quaid smile. "You take as long as you want to, then. I learned my lesson with Barbara. You've got to be understanding with the women. That's the key to a successful relationship." Frowning, he slams his hand on the steering wheel. "That's what they tell me, anyhow."

Jenny is having coffee with Opal. She arrived unexpectedly. It's very early. She looks as though she has been up all night.

"Please show me your quilts," Jenny says. "I don't mean your crazy quilts. I want to see that special quilt. Mom said it had the family tree."

Opal spills coffee in her saucer. "What is wrong with young people today?" she asks.

"I want to know why it's called a burial quilt," Jenny says. "Are you planning to be buried in it?"

Opal wishes she had a shot of peppermint in her coffee. It sounds like a delicious idea. She starts toward the den with the coffee cup rattling in its saucer, and she splatters drops on the rug. Never mind it now, she thinks, turning back.

"It's just a family history," she says.

"Why's it called a burial quilt?" Jenny asks.

Jenny's face is pale. She has blue pouches under her eyes and blue eyeshadow on her eyelids. Her eyes are ringed like a raccoon's.

"See that closet in the hall?" Opal says. "Get a chair and we'll get the quilt down."

Jenny stands on a kitchen chair and removes the quilt from beneath several others. It's wrapped in blue plastic and Jenny hugs it closely as she steps down with it.

They spread it out on the couch, and the blue plastic floats off somewhere. Jenny looks like someone in love as she gazes at the quilt. "It's gorgeous," she murmurs. "How beautiful."

"Shoot!" says Opal. "It's ugly as homemade sin."

Jenny runs her fingers over the rough textures of the quilt. The quilt is dark and sombre. The backing is a heavy gray gabardine, and the nine-inch-square blocks are pieced of smaller blocks of varying shades of gray and brown and black. They are wools, apparently made from men's winter suits. On each block is an appliquéd off-white tombstone—a comical shape, like Casper the ghost. Each tombstone has a name and date on it.

Jenny recognizes some of the names. Myrtle Williams. Voris Williams. Thelma Lee Freeman. The oldest gravestone is "Eulalee Freeman 1857-1900." The shape is irregular, a rectangle with a clumsy foot sticking out from one corner. The quilt is knotted with yarn, and the edging is open, for more blocks to be added.

"Eulalee's daughter started it," says Opal. "But that thing has been carried through this family like a plague. Did you ever see such horrible old dark colors? I pieced on it some when I was younger, but it was too depressing. I think some of the kinfolks must have died without a square, so there may be several to catch up on."

"I'll do it," says Jenny. "I could learn to quilt."

"Traditionally, the quilt stops when the family name stops," Opal says. "And since my parents didn't have a boy, that was the end of the Freeman line on this particular branch of the tree. So the last old maids finish the quilt." She lets out a wild cackle. "Theoretically, a quilt like this could keep going till doomsday."

"Do you care if I have this quilt?" asks Jenny.

"What would you do with it? It's too ugly to put on a bed and too morbid to work on."

"I think it's kind of neat," says Jenny. She strokes the rough tweed. Already it is starting to decay, and it has moth holes. Jenny feels tears start to drip down her face.

"Don't you go putting my name on that thing," her aunt says.

Jenny has taken the quilt to her apartment. She explained that she is going to study the family tree, or that she is going to finish the quilt. If she's smart, Opal thinks, she will let Randy Newcomb auction it off. The way Jenny took it, cramming it into the blue plastic, was like snatching something that was free. Opal feels relieved, as though she has pushed the burden of that ratty old quilt onto her niece. All those miserable, cranky women, straining their eyes, stitching on those dark scraps of material.

For a long time, Jenny wouldn't tell why she was crying, and when she started to tell, Opal was uncomfortable, afraid she'd be required to tell something comparable of her own, but as she listened she found herself caught up in Jenny's story. Jenny said it was a man. That was always the case, Opal thought. It was five years ago. A man Jenny knew in a place by the sea. Opal imagined seagulls, pretty sand. There were no palm trees. It was up North. The young man worked with Jenny in a restaurant with glass walls facing the ocean. They waited on tables and collected enough tips to take a trip together near the end of the summer. Jenny made it sound like an idyllic time, waiting on tables by the sea. She started crying again when she told about the trip, but the trip sounded nice. Opal listened hungrily, imagining the young man, thinking that he would have had handsome, smooth cheeks, and hair that fell attractively over his forehead. He would have had good manners, being a waiter. Jenny and the man, whose name was Jim, flew to Denver, Colorado, and they rented a car and drove around out West. They visited the Grand Canyon and Yellowstone and other places Opal had heard about. They grilled salmon on the beach, on another ocean. They camped out in the redwoods, trees so big they hid the sky. Jenny described all these scenes, and the man sounded like a good man. His brother had died in Vietnam and he felt guilty that he had been the one spared, because his brother was a swimmer and could have gone to the Olympics. Jim wasn't athletic. He had a bad knee and hammertoes. He slept fitfully in the tent, and Jenny said soothing things to him, and she cared about him, but by the time they had curved northward and over to Yellowstone the trip was becoming unpleasant. The romance wore off. She loved him, but she couldn't deal with his needs. One of the last nights they spent together, it rained all night long. He told her not to touch the tent material, because somehow the pressure of a finger on the nylon would make it start to leak at that spot. Lying there in the rain, Jenny couldn't resist touching a spot where water was collecting in a little sag in the top of the tent. The drip started then, and it grew worse, until they got so wet they had to get in the car. Not long afterward, when they ran short of money, they parted. Jenny got a job in Denver. She never saw him again.

Opal listened eagerly to the details about grilling the fish together, about the zip-together sleeping bags and setting up the tent and washing themselves in the cold stream. But when Jenny brought the story up to the present, Opal was not prepared. She felt she had been dunked in the cold water and left gasping. Jenny said she had heard a couple of times through a mutual friend that Jim had spent some time in Mexico. And then, she said, this week she had begun thinking about him, because of all the trees at the lake, and she had an overwhelming desire to see him again. She had been unfair, she knew now. She telephoned the friend, who had worked with them in the restaurant by the sea. He hadn't known where to locate her, he said, and so he couldn't tell her that Jim had been killed in Colorado over a year ago. His four-wheel drive had plunged off a mountain curve.

"I feel some trick has been played on me. It seems so unreal." Jenny tugged at the old quilt, and her eyes darkened. "I was in Colorado, and I didn't even know he was there. If I still knew him, I would know how to mourn, but now I don't know how. And it was over a year ago. So I don't know what to feel."

"Don't look back, hon," Opal said, hugging her niece closely. But she was shaking, and Jenny shook with her.

Opal makes herself a snack, thinking it will pick up her strength. She is very tired. On the tray, she places an apple and a paring knife and some milk and cookies. She touches the remote-control button, and the picture blossoms. She was wise to buy a large TV, the one listed as the best in the consumer magazine. The color needs a little adjustment, though. She eases up the volume and starts peeling the apple. She has a little bump on one knuckle. In the old days, people would take the family Bible and bust a cyst like that with it. Just slam it hard.

On the screen, a Scoutmaster is telling a story to some Boy Scouts around a campfire. The campfire is only a fireplace, with electric logs. Opal loses track of time, and the songs flow together. A woman is lying on her stomach on a car hood in a desert full of gas pumps. TV sets crash. Smoke emerges from an eyeball. A page of sky turns like a page in a book. Then, at a desk in a classroom, a cocky blond kid with a pack of cigarettes rolled in the sleeve of his T-shirt is singing about a sexy girl with a tattoo on her back who is sitting on a commode and smoking a cigarette. In the classroom, all the kids are gyrating and snapping their fingers to wild music. The teacher at the blackboard with her white hair in a bun looks disapproving, but the kids in the class don't know what's on her mind. The teacher is thinking about how, when the bell rings, she will hit the road to Nashville.

My Man Bovanne

TONI CADE BAMBARA

B LIND PEOPLE got a hummin jones if you notice. Which is under-
standable completely once you been around one and notice what
no eyes will force you into to see people, and you get past the first time,
which seems to come out of nowhere, and it's like you in church again
with fat-chest ladies and old gents gruntin a hum low in the throat to
whatever the preacher be saying. Shakey Bee bottom lip all swole up
with Sweet Peach and me explainin how come the sweet-potato bread
was a dollar-quarter this time stead of dollar regular and he say uh
huh he understand, then he break into this *thizzin* kind of hum which
is quiet, but fiercesome just the same, if you ain't ready for it. Which
I wasn't. But I got used to it and the onliest time I had to say somethin
bout it was when he was playin checkers on the stoop one time and
he commenst to hummin quite churchy seem to me. So I says, "Look
here Shakey Bee, I can't beat you and Jesus too." He stop.

So that's how come I asked My Man Bovanne to dance. He ain't my
man mind you, just a nice ole gent from the block that we all know
cause he fixes things and the kids like him. Or used to fore Black Power
got hold their minds and mess em around till they can't be civil to ole
folks. So we at this benefit for my niece's cousin who's runnin for
somethin with this Black party somethin or other behind her. And I
press up close to dance with Bovanne who blind and I'm hummin and
he hummin, chest to chest like talkin. Not jammin my breasts into
the man. Wasn't bout tits. Was bout vibrations. And he dug it and
asked me what color dress I had on and how my hair was fixed and
how I was doin without a man, not nosy but nice-like, and who was
at this affair and was the canapés dainty-stingy or healthy enough to
get hold of proper. Comfy and cheery is what I'm tryin to get across.
Touch talkin like the heel of the hand on the tambourine or on a drum.

But right away Joe Lee come up on us and frown for dancin so close
to the man. My own son who knows what kind of warm I am about;
and don't grown men call me long distance and in the middle of the

night for a little Mama comfort? But he frown. Which ain't right since Bovanne can't see and defend himself. Just a nice old man who fixes toasters and busted irons and bicycles and things and changes the lock on my door when my men friends get messy. Nice man. Which is not why they invited him. Grass roots you see. Me and Sister Taylor and the woman who does heads at Mamies and the man from the barber shop, we all there on account of we grass roots. And I ain't never been souther than Brooklyn Battery and no more country than the window box on my fire escape. And just yesterday my kids tellin me to take them countrified rags off my head and be cool. And now can't get Black enough to suit em. So everybody passin sayin My Man Bovanne. Big deal, keep steppin and don't even stop a minute to get the man a drink or one of them cute sandwiches or tell him what's goin on. And him standin there with a smile ready case someone do speak he want to be ready. So that's how come I pull him on the dance floor and we dance squeezin past the tables and chairs and all them coats and people standin round up in each other face talkin bout this and that but got no use for this blind man who mostly fixed skates and scooters for all these folks when they was just kids. So I'm pressed up close and we touch talkin with the hum. And here come my daughter cuttin her eye at me like she do when she tell me about my "apolitical" self like I got hoof and mouf disease and there ain't no hope at all. And I don't pay her no mind and just look up in Bovanne shadow face and tell him his stomach like a drum and he laugh. Laugh real loud. And here come my youngest, Task, with a tap on my elbow like he the third-grade monitor and I'm cuttin up on the line to assembly.

"I was just talkin on the drums," I explained when they hauled me into the kitchen. I figured drums was my best defense. They can get ready for drums what with all this heritage business. And Bovanne stomach just like that drum Task give me when he come back from Africa. You just touch it and it hum thizzm, thizzm. So I stuck to the drum story. "Just drummin that's all."

"Mama, what are you talkin about?"

"She had too much to drink," say Elo to Task cause she don't hardly say nuthin to me direct no more since that ugly argument about my wigs.

"Look here Mama," say Task, the gentle one. "We just tryin to pull your coat. You were makin a spectacle of yourself out there dancing like that."

"Dancin like what?"

Task run a hand over his left ear like his father for the world and his father before that.

"Like a bitch in heat," say Elo.

"Well uhh, I was goin to say like one of them sex-starved ladies gettin on in years and not too discriminating. Know what I mean?"

I don't answer cause I'll cry. Terrible thing when your own children talk to you like that. Pullin me out the party and hustlin me into some stranger's kitchen in the back of a bar just like the damn police. And ain't like I'm old old. I can still wear me some sleeveless dresses without the meat hangin off my arm. And I keep up with some things through my kids. Who ain't kids no more. To hear them tell it. So I don't say nuthin.

"Dancin with that tom," say Elo to Joe Lee, who leanin on the folks' freezer. "His feet can smell a cracker a mile away and go into their shuffle number post haste. And them eyes. He could be a little considerate and put on some shades. Who wants to look into them blown-out fuses that—"

"Is this what they call the generation gap?" I say.

"Generation gap," spits Elo, like I suggested castor oil and fricassee possum in the milk-shakes or somethin. "That's a white concept for a white phenomenon. There's no generation gap among Black people. We are a col—"

"Yeh, well never mind," says Joe Lee. "The point is Mama . . . well, it's pride. You embarrass yourself and us too dancin like that."

"I wasn't shame." Then nobody say nuthin. Them standin there in they pretty clothes with drinks in they hands and gangin up on me, and me in the third-degree chair and nary a olive to my name. Felt just like the police got hold to me.

"First of all," Task say, holding up his hand and tickin off the offenses, "the dress. Now that dress is too short, Mama, and too low-cut for a woman your age. And Tamu's going to make a speech tonight to kick off the campaign and will be introducin you and expecting you to organize the council of elders—"

"Me? Didn nobody ask me nuthin. You mean Nisi? She change her name?"

"Well, Norton was supposed to tell you about it. Nisi wants to introduce you and then encourage the older folks ass. And people'll say, 'Ain't that the horny bitch that was to form a Council of the Elders to act as an advisory—'"

"And you going to be standing there with your boobs out and that wig on your head and that hem up to your grindin with the blind dude?"

"Elo, be cool a minute," say Task, gettin to the next finger. "And then there's the drinkin. Mama, you know you can't drink cause next thing you know you be laughin loud and carryin on," and he grab another finger for the loudness. "And then there's the dancin. You been tattooed on the man for four records straight and slow draggin even on the fast numbers. How you think that look for a woman your age?"

"What's my age?"

"What?"

"I'm axin you all a simple question. You keep talkin bout what's proper for a woman my age. How old am I anyhow?" And Joe Lee slams his eyes shut and squinches up his face to figure. And Task run a hand over his ear and stare into his glass like the ice cubes goin calculate for him. And Elo just starin at the top of my head like she goin rip the wig off any minute now.

"Is your hair braided up under that thing? If so, why don't you take it off? You always did do a neat cornroll."

"Uh huh," cause I'm thinkin how she couldn't undo her hair fast enough talking bout cornroll so countrified. None of which was the subject. "How old, I say?"

"Sixtee-one or—"

"You a damn lie Joe Lee Peoples."

"And that's another thing," say Task on the fingers.

"You know what you can all kiss," I said, gettin up and brushin the wrinkles out my lap.

"Oh, Mama," Elo say, puttin a hand on my shoulder like she hasn't done since she left home and the hand landin light and not sure it supposed to be there. Which hurt me to my heart. Cause this was the child in our happiness fore Mr. Peoples die. And I carried that child strapped to my chest till she was nearly two. We was close is what I'm tryin to tell you. Cause it was more me in the child than the others. And even after Task it was the girlchild I covered in the night and wept over for no reason at all less it was she was a chub-chub like me and not very pretty, but a warm child. And how did things get to this, that she can't put a sure hand on me and say Mama we love you and care about you and you entitled to enjoy yourself cause you a good woman?

"And then there's Reverend Trent," say Task, glancin from left to right like they hatchin a plot and just now lettin me in on it. "You were suppose to be talking with him tonight, Mama, about giving us his basement for campaign headquarters and—"

"Didn nobody tell me nuthin. If grass roots mean you kept in the dark I can't use it. I really can't. And Reven Trent a fool anyway the way he tore into the widow man up there on Edgecomb cause he wouldn't take in three of them foster children and the woman not even comfy in the ground yet and the man's mind messed up and—"

"Look here," say Task. "What we need is a family conference so we can get all this stuff cleared up and laid out on the table. In the meantime I think we better get back into the other room and tend to business. And in the meantime, Mama, see if you can't get to Reverend Trent and—"

"You want me to belly rub with the Reven, that it?"

"Oh damn," Elo say and go through the swingin door.

"We'll talk about all this at dinner. How's tomorrow night, Joe Lee?" While Joe Lee being self-important I'm wonderin who's doin the cookin and how come no body ax me if I'm free and do I get a corsage and things like that. Then Joe nod that it's O.K. and he go through the swingin door and just a little hubbub come through from the other room. Then Task smile his smile, lookin just like his daddy, and he leave. And it just me in this stranger's kitchen, which was a mess I wouldn't never let my kitchen look like. Poison you just to look at the pots. Then the door swing the other way and it's My Man Bovanne standin there sayin Miss Hazel but lookin at the deep fry and then at the steam table, and most surprised when I come up on him from the other direction and take him on out of there. Pass the folks pushin up towards the stage where Nisi and some other people settin and ready to talk, and folks gettin to the last of the sandwiches and the booze fore they settle down in one spot and listen serious. And I'm thinkin bout tellin Bovanne what a lovely long dress Nisi got on and the earrings and her hair piled up in a cone and the people bout to hear how we all gettin screwed and gotta form our own party and everybody there listenin and lookin. But instead I just haul the man on out of there, and Joe Lee and his wife look at me like I'm terrible, but they ain't said boo to the man yet. Cause he blind and old and don't nobody there need him since they grown up and don't need they skates fixed no more.

"Where we goin, Miss Hazel?" Him knowin all the time.

"First we gonna buy you some dark sunglasses. Then you comin with me to the supermarket so I can pick up tomorrow's dinner, which is goin to be a grand thing proper and you invited. Then we goin to my house."

"That be fine. I surely would like to rest my feet." Bein cute, but you got to let men play out they little show, blind or not. So he chat on bout how tired he is and how he appreciate me takin him in hand this way. And I'm thinkin I'll have him change the lock on my door first thing. Then I'll give the man a nice warm bath with jasmine leaves in the water and a little Epsom salt on the sponge to do his back. And then a good rubdown with rose water and olive oil. Then a cup of lemon tea with a taste in it. And a little talcum, some of that fancy stuff Nisi mother sent over last Christmas. And then a massage, a good face massage round the forehead which is the worryin part. Cause you gots to take care of the older folks. And let them know they still needed to run the mimeo machine and keep the spark plugs clean and fix the mailboxes for folks who might help us get the breakfast program goin, and the school for the little kids and the campaign and all. Cause old folks is the nation. That what Nisi was sayin and I mean to do my part.

"I imagine you are a very pretty woman, Miss Hazel."

"I surely am," I say just like the hussy my daughter always say I was.

Horace and Margaret's Fifty-second

CHARLES BAXTER

A FEW MONTHS AFTER she had put her husband, all memory gone, into the home, she herself woke one morning with an unfamiliar sun shining through a window she hadn't remembered was there. A new window! Pranksters were playing a shabby joke on her. She rose heavily from the bed, a groan bursting by accident out of her throat, and shuffled to the new window they had installed during the night. Through the dusty glass she saw the apartment's ragged backyard of cement and weeds. A puddle had formed in the alley, and a brown bird was flapping in it, making muddy waves as it bathed. Then she looked more closely and saw that the bird was lying on its side.

"I remember this view," she said to herself. "It's not a new window. I just forgot to pull down the shade." She did so now, blocking the sun, which seemed to her more grayish-blue than it had for years. She coughed rhythmically with every other step to the bathroom.

It was Tuesday, and their anniversary. He would forget, as usual. Now, in his vacancy, he had stopped using shaving cream and razor blades. He tore photographs out of their expensive frames, folded them into baskets, and used them as ashtrays. He took cigarette lighters to pieces to see how they worked and left their tiny wet parts scattered all over his nightstand. He refused to read, claiming that what she brought him was dull trash, but she had suspected for a long time that he had forgotten both the meaning of the words and how to read them from left to right across the page. She didn't want to buy him cigarettes (in his dotage, he had secretly and then quite openly taken up smoking Chesterfields again). He lost clothes or put them on backward or declared universal birthdays so he could give everything he owned to strangers. The previous Wednesday, she had asked him what he would want for their upcoming anniversary, their fifty-second. "Light bulbs," he said, giving her an unpleasantly sly look.

She glanced at his lamp and saw that the shade was pleated oddly. "They give you plenty of bulbs here," she said. "Ask them."

He shook his head for thirty seconds before he replied. "Wrong bulbs," he said. "It's the special ones I need, with the flames."

"Light bulbs don't have flames," she said. "It's filaments now."

"Don't argue with me. I know what I want. Light bulbs."

She was at the breakfast table reading the paper when she remembered that she had dropped an egg into the frypan, where, even at this moment, it must still be frying: hard, angry, and dry. She forgave herself, because she had been thinking about how to get to the First Christian Residence before lunch, and which purple bus she should take. She walked to the little four-burner stove with its cracked oven window, closed her eyes against the smoke, picked up the frypan using a worn potholder with a picture of a cow on it, and dropped her last egg into the wastebasket's brown paper bag. Now she had nothing to eat but toast. She was trying to remember what she had done with the bread when she heard the phone ring and she saw from the kitchen clock that it was 10:30, two hours later than she had thought.

She picked the receiver angrily off the wall. "Yes," she said. She no longer said "Hello"; she was tired of that.

"Hello?"

"Yes," she said. "Yes, yes, yes, who is it?"

"It's me," the voice said. "Happy anniversary."

Very familiar, this woman's voice. "Thank you," Margaret said. "It's our fifty-second."

"I know," the voice told her. "I just wish I could be there."

"So do I," Margaret said, a thin electrical charge of panic spreading over her. "I wish you could be here to keep me company. How are you?"

"Just fine. Jerry's out of town, but of course David's with me, and last night we roasted marshmallows and made a big bowl of popcorn."

David. Oh yes: her grandchild. This must be David's mother. "Penny," she said.

"What?"

"I just wanted to say your name."

"Why?"

"Because," Margaret said carelessly, "because I just thought of it."

"Mother, are you all right?"

"Just fine, dear. I'm going to take the bus to see your father in half an hour's time. I'm going to wish him a happy anniversary. I doubt he'll notice. He won't remember it's our anniversary, I don't think. Maybe he won't remember me. You can never tell." She laughed. "As he says, the moving men just come and take it all away. You can't tell about anything. For example, I thought they put a new window in my room last night, but I'd only forgotten to pull down the window shade." She noticed a list on the refrigerator, a list of things she must do today. It was getting late. "Good-bye, Penny," she said, before hanging up. She picked the list off the refrigerator and put it in her pocket. Then she stood in the middle of the room, her mind whirling and utterly blank, while she stared at the faucet on the right-hand side of the sink and, above it, attached to the cabinet, a faded color photograph of a brown-haired girl, looking away from the camera toward a tree. It was probably Penny, when young.

Once Margaret was on the bus, she was sure that everything would be fine. The sun was out and several children were playing their peculiar games on the sidewalk, smacking each other and rolling over to play dead. Why weren't they in school? She knew better than to ask children to explain their reasons for being in any one spot. If you asked such questions, they always had that look ready.

The bus was practically empty. All the passengers, thank God, seemed to be respectable taxpayers: a gentleman with several strands of attractive gray hair sat two rows in front of her, comforting her with his presence. The sun, now yellow, was shining fiercely on Margaret's side of the bus, its ferocity tempered by tinted glass.

Margaret felt the sun on her face and said, "Sweet sweet sweet sweet sweet tea." This, her one and only phrase to express joy, she had picked up in 1935, from a newspaper article that had tried to make fun of Gertrude Stein. The article had quoted one of her poems, and Margaret had remembered its first line ever since. "Sweet sweet sweet sweet sweet tea," she said again, gazing out the window at obscurely sinister trees, with far too many leaves, all of them the wrong shape.

Horace, before he had been deposited in the First Christian Residence, had been a great one for trees: after they had bought a house, he had planted them in the backyard, trimmed them, fed them, watered them when droughts dusted their leaves. "Trees," he liked to say, "give back more than they take. Fruit, oxygen, and shade. And for this they expect no gratitude." He would have been happy working in a nursery or greenhouse. As it was, he worked in a bank, and never talked about exactly what he did there. "It's boring," he would say. "You don't want to hear about it." Margaret agreed; she didn't. Only toward the end had he raged against the nature of his work. But he didn't shout at Margaret; he told the trees. He told them how money had gobbled up his life. He talked about waste and cash, and he wept into his hands. Margaret watched him from the kitchen window. She watched him as he lost his memory and began to give names to trees: Esther, Jonas, Ezekiel, Isaiah. He told Margaret that trees should have serious, adult names. For eighteen months now, he had confused the names of his trees with the names of his children. He wanted his trees to come visit him in the home. "Bring in Esther," he would say. "I want to see her."

Because of this, Margaret no longer gazed at trunks, branches, or leaves with any special pleasure.

She remembered where to get off the bus and was about to go into the residence when she realized that she had no anniversary present. She stood motionless on the sidewalk. "He won't remember," she said aloud. "What's the difference?" She waited a moment and found that she disagreed with her own assessment. "It does make a difference. He'll think I'm making it up if I don't bring him something." She looked around. At the corner there was a small grocery store with a large red Coca-Cola sign over its door. "I'll go down there," she said.

The store was darker than it should have been and was crowded with confusing teenagers. Margaret found herself looking at peanut-butter labels and long rows of lunch meat. Then she was in front of the cash register, holding two Hershey bars. "I'll buy these," she said to the coarse girl with the brown ponytail and the pimples. She was already far down the street when she realized that she hadn't waited for change, or a bag to put the chocolate in. It was the first time she had given him a present she hadn't wrapped.

Holding the candy bars and her purse in one hand, she opened the large front door of the First Christian Residence with the other. This was the worst moment, because of the smell. Margaret knew that oldsters couldn't always keep themselves clean and tidy, but their smell offended her nevertheless. Just inside, a man with wild hair and a bruise on his forehead, whose eyes were an angelic blue, smiled at her and followed her in his wheelchair as she walked to the elevator. A yellow Have-a-nice-day sticker, with a smile face, was glued to the back of the chair.

"Beautiful day, Margaret. Don't you agree?"

"Yes." This man had been pestering her for months. He was forward, and looked at her with an old man's dry yearning. "Yes," she repeated, inside the elevator, as she pressed the button for the third floor, wanting the door to close, "it is indeed a nice day. You should get outside into the sunshine for some fresh air and vitamin D, instead of staying in here all the time."

He wheeled himself onto the elevator and turned around so he was next to her. "I stayed," he said, "because I was hoping you'd come." The elevator doors closed, at last. "I can still walk, you know. This chair is a convenience."

Margaret tried to sound chilly. "I'm going to see Horace, my husband. I don't have time for you."

"Horace won't miss you. His memory's bad. He remembers the 1945 World Series better than he remembers you. Let's go for a walk."

"No, thank you." She remembered his name. "No, thank you, Mr. Bartlett."

"It's Jim. Not 'Mr. Bartlett.' Jim." He smiled. She noticed again his remarkable eyes. The numbers above the doors flashed. It was the slowest elevator she'd ever been on, slow to prevent shocks to the elderly.

"This is my stop," she said, backing out into the hallway once the doors opened. As they closed again, Mr. Bartlett leaned back in his wheelchair and gave her a bold look.

Horace was in his room, wearing a Wayne State University sweatshirt, gray corduroys, and tennis shoes. He was watching "The Price Is Right" and eagerly smoking a Chesterfield when Margaret came in. He glanced at her and then went back to the activity of the contestants. On screen, a woman in uniform was spinning a huge, multicolored wheel, and the studio audience was roaring, but Horace failed to share the excitement and watched the television set indifferently. Margaret picked up a newspaper from the chair by the window and arranged the flowerpots on the sill.

"Good morning, dear," she said. "How did you sleep?"

Horace didn't answer. Perhaps it would be one of those days. Lately he had been retreating into silence. Apparently he found it comforting. Margaret clucked, shook her head, and walked over to the television set, which she turned off.

"It's our anniversary," she said. "I don't want daytime television on our anniversary."

On the table next to Horace was a breakfast roll. A fly walked back and forth on it, as if on sentry duty. Margaret picked up the plate and took it out to the hallway, placing it on the floor next to the wall. When she came back, Horace was still staring at the dark television screen.

She gazed at him for a moment. Then she said brightly, "Do you remember Mrs. Silverman, two floors up in the building, Horace? The apartment building? Where we moved after we sold the house? Mrs. Silverman, whose husband was so terribly bald? I'm sure you do. Well, anyway, several nights ago there was a great commotion, and it seemed that Mrs. Silverman was reading the paper, probably just the want ads, as she did usually, when she had one of those seizures of hers. She knocked over a tall glass of ginger ale. It left a stain on the rug, I think. They came for her and took her to the hospital, but the word in the building is that it may be curtains for Mrs. Silverman."

"The moving men," Horace rasped.

"Yes, Horace, the moving men. Someone in the building called for them. Sometimes they can help and other times they can't. You are looking very scruffy today, Horace," she said. "Where did you get that awful sweatshirt?"

"Someone gave it to me," he said, avoiding eye contact.

"Who?" she asked. "Not that horrid little Mr. List?"

"Maybe." Horace shrugged.

"I'd think you'd be ashamed to be in that sweatshirt. You were never a student at Wayne State. Never. You went to Oberlin."

"It's warm," Horace said. "And it's green."

"Which reminds me," Margaret announced, "that I thought they had put a new window into our bedroom last night. But I just forgot to pull down the shade. Oh. Someone called this morning." She thought for a moment. "Penny." She waited for him to show recognition, but he kept his face turned away from hers. "She called to wish us a happy anniversary. It's our anniversary today, Horace."

"I know that," he said. "I know that very well."

"Well, I'm glad. I brought you something."

"Light bulbs?"

"No. Not light bulbs. I explained to you about the light bulbs. You don't need them. What do you need them for?"

"Bliss," Horace said.

"For bliss? I doubt it. No. Well, what I brought you was this." She handed him the Hershey bars. "Happy anniversary, dear. These were the best I could do. I am sorry. Age has brought us low. I would have presented you with a plant in the old days."

"These *are* the old days," Horace said. He gazed down at the dark-brown wrappers. "Thank you. Mr. List likes chocolate. So do I, but

Mr. List likes chocolate more than I do." Horace suddenly looked at her, and she flinched. "How's Penny? And where's Isaiah?"

"Penny's fine. She toasted marshmallows with David last night. And Isaiah's lost his leaves because it's late October."

Horace nodded. He appeared to think for a long time. Then he said, "I went out yesterday. I wanted to drop something on the ground the way the trees do. Dead leaves reactivate the soil, you know. They don't rake leaves in the forest, only in the suburbs. It's against nature and foolhardy to rake leaves. I pulled out a strand of my hair and left it in the grass. Why did we get married in October? Tell me again." He smirked at her. "I've forgotten. I've lost my memory."

"It was 1930, Horace. Times were hard. When you finally secured a job at the Farmers and Mechanics' Bank, I agreed to marry you."

"Yes."

Margaret knew she had made a serious mistake as soon as she saw the tears: she had mentioned the bank.

"When did you stop kissing me?" Horace asked.

"What?"

"After the war. You wouldn't kiss me after the war. Why not?"

"I think this is very unpleasant, Horace. I don't know what you're talking about."

"Of course you do. You wouldn't kiss me after the war. Why?"

"You know very well," she said.

"Tell me again," Horace said. "I've lost my memory."

"I didn't like it," she muttered, standing up to look out of the window.

"What didn't you like?"

"I didn't like the way you kissed me."

"We weren't old yet," Horace said. "It's what adults do. They have passions. You can't fool me about that."

Margaret felt tired and hungry. She wished she hadn't taken the breakfast roll out to the hallway."

"I'm not here to settle old scores," she said. "Do you want to split one of these candy bars?" Outside, a blue convertible with a white-canvas roof came to a stop at an intersection and seemed unable to move, and all around it the small pedestrians froze into timeless attitudes, and the sun blinked on and off, as if a boy were flipping a wall switch.

Horace struck a kitchen match on the zipper of his pants and lit up a cigarette. "I love cigarettes," he said. "I get ideas from the smoke. Call me crazy if you want to, but yesterday I was thinking about how few decisions in my life were truly important. I didn't decide about the war and I didn't decide to drop the bomb. They didn't ask me about nuclear generators, or, for that matter, about coal generators. I had opinions. They could have asked me. But they didn't. Mr. List and I were discussing this yesterday. The only thing they ever asked us was what we were going to do on the weekends. That's all. 'What are you doing Saturday night?' That's the only question I can remember."

Margaret tore the brown paper away from the candy bar, then crumpled up the inner wrapper before she snapped off four little squares of the chocolate. Someone seemed to be flicking lights inside the First Christian Residence as well. The taste of the chocolate rushed across her tongue, straight from heaven.

"Want any rum?" Horace asked. "I have some in the closet. Mr. List brought it for me. On days like this, I take to the rum with a fierce joy." This line sounded like, and was, one of his favorites.

"Horace, you can't have liquor in here! You'll be expelled!"

Suddenly he appeared not to hear her. His face lost its color, and she could tell he would probably not say another word for the rest of the morning. She took the opportunity to snap off one more piece of the chocolate and to straighten the room, to put smelly ashtrays, pens, shirts, and dulled pencils in their rightful place. There were pencil sketches of trees, which she stacked into a neat pile. In this mess she noticed a photograph of the two of them together, young, sitting under a large chandelier, smiling fixedly. Where was that? Margaret couldn't remember. Another photo showed Natwick, Horace's dog in the 1950s, under a tree, his mouth open and his dirty retriever's teeth prominent. Horace had trained him to smile on cue.

"Someday, Horace," Margaret said, "you'll remember to keep your valuables and to throw away the trash. You've got the whole thing backward." Seeing that he said nothing, she went on. "So often I myself have . . . so often I, too, have found that I have been myself in a place where I have found myself so often in a place where I have found myself." Standing there, squarely in the middle of the room, she felt herself tipping toward Horace's cigarette smoke, falling through it, tumbling as if off a building, end over end, floor after floor. Horace held his hand up. Margaret, whose mind was still plunging, walked toward him. He whirled his hand counterclockwise as an invitation to bring her ear down to his mouth.

"Don't tell me anything," he whispered. "That's for kids. And be quiet. Listen. There's a bird scratching in the tree outside. Hear it?"

She did not. Margaret bent down to kiss his forehead and made her way out of the room, sick with vertigo. The hallway stretched and shrank while she balanced herself like a tightrope walker in a forward progress to the elevator. Three floors down, Mr. Bartlett was waiting for her, wearing a cap and a jacket in his wheelchair, but she tottered past him, out into the sun, which she saw had turned a sickly blue.

There was something wrong with the bus.

She sat near the back. The bus would start, reach twenty-five miles an hour, then stop. Not slow down. Stop. In midair, as it were. When it stopped, so did the world. The trees, pedestrians, and birds froze in midair, the birds glued to the sky. And when this occurred, Margaret grabbed the top of the seat in front of her, pressing it hard with her thumbs, hoping she could restart the world again.

She looked up. In front of her a little girl was kneeling on the plastic seat next to her mother, facing the back, staring at Margaret. The little girl had two pigtails of brown hair, a bright-red coat, and round-rimmed glasses too large for her face. As the bus began to move, Margaret stared at the girl, frowning because she wanted the youngster to know that staring is rude, a sign of bad breeding. But as she scowled and frowned, and the bus passengers swayed like a chorus together, she was horrified to feel her own eyes producing tears, which would run partway down her cheeks and then stop, as the bus itself stopped, as time halted. The little girl reminded Margaret of someone, someone she would never exactly remember again.

The girl's mouth opened slightly. Her eyes widened, and now she, too, was crying. Her glasses magnified her tears, which were caught by the rims in tiny pools. Margaret gathered herself together. It was one thing to cry herself for no special reason. It was quite another to make a little girl cry. That was contagion, and a mistake in anyone's part of the world. So Margaret wiped her eyes with her coat sleeve and smiled fiercely at the girl, even laughing now, the laugh sounding like the yip of a small dog. *"Toujours gai, toujours gai,"* she said, louder than necessary, before she realized that little girls on buses don't speak French and would never have heard of archy and mehitabel even if they did. "There's a dance in the old dame yet," Margaret said, to finish the phrase, quietly and to herself. She drew herself up and looked serious, as if she were on her way to someplace. She was not about to be cried at on a public bus in broad daylight.

"What a nice day!" Margaret said aloud, but no one turned toward her. The little girl took off her glasses, wiped her eyes on her mother's coat, and gave Margaret a hostile look before turning around. "The old lady shows her mettle," Margaret continued, editorializing to herself, simultaneously making a mental note not to engage in private conversations where other people could hear her. It takes a minimum of sixty years' experience to recognize how useful and necessary talking to oneself actually is. When you're young, it just seems like a crazy habit. Margaret did not speak these thoughts aloud, as the bus whirled upside down and righted itself; she whispered them.

They went past a world of details. Sidewalks broke into spiderweb patterns. A green squirt gun was in a boy's hand, but the bus was moving too quickly for her to see the rest of the boy. In a tree that she noticed by accident, a brown bird flew out of a nest. Something redbreast. Robin redbreast. The bus driver's head, suddenly in the way of the sun, shone a fine gunmetal blue. On a jungle gym, a boy wearing a green sweatshirt, smaller than Horace's, hung down from a steel bar with only his legs, his knees, holding him there. Margaret stared at him. How was it possible for a human being to hang by his knees from a bar? More important, why would anyone want to do it? Before an answer came, the boy faded out and was replaced by another detail, of a sea gull standing proudly in someone's alley, an arrogant look on its face. The sea gull cheered Margaret. She admired its pluck. The other details she saw were less invigorating: an old man, very white in all respects, asleep in a doorway; two young people, across the street from the art institute, kissing underneath a tree (the tree and the kissing made her flesh crawl); and now, at last, a cumulating, bright-pink, puffing cloud of smoke exploding out of someone's back yard, someone's shed, on fire or dynamited, even the smell reaching her. The bus drove on and Margaret forgot about it.

She remembered her stop, however, and was halfway up the sidewalk when she remembered that she had forgotten to get out at Safeway to buy groceries. She counted all her canned goods, in her mind's eye. "I'll be all right," she said, "and besides, there are more buses going here and there. It's their fate in life." She trudged on into the building.

Skinny Mr. Fletcher, employee of the United States Postal Service, had already come and gone with his Santa's sack of bills and messages. Margaret unlocked her mailbox, hoping for a free sample of a new soap. Instead, there was a solitary postcard inside, showing on its picture side Buster Keaton walking squarely down the middle of a railroad track. On the other side was a message from Horace, written in his miserable script. Some letters had been crossed out, but he had not given up.

> Dear Margaret,
>   Happy ~~bitrh~~aniversery
>   today
>   from love Horace
>   ps remember lightbulbs

Where had he mailed the message? Where, more important, had he found the stamp? How had he remembered the address? It was all very mysterious. The postcard was, of course, simply one of his monstrously large postcard collection, which he had taken with him to the First Christian Residence, over two hundred of them. He had traded a few for cigarettes. Margaret looked at Buster Keaton as she went up the stairs, the stairway extending and shortening, like a human-sized accordion.

She opened her door and stepped into the living room. On the left was her pastel-blue sofa, next to her Emerson radio and Muntz television set, and on the right was her mother's harmonium, underneath a mirror. Behind the sofa were bookshelves, filled with books she and Horace had read to each other: Robert Benchley, Don Marquis, Brooks Atkinson. She could remember their names but not the character of their work. "Feels like I'm walking through Jell-O," she meant to say, but no sound could make its way out of her throat.

She stood stranded inside the door, waiting for something to happen. At last the invisible steel wires holding her feet loosened for a moment, and she managed to get as far as the harmonium. Then the movie came to a halt again. She hadn't taken her coat off, nor could she. She was forced to look at more details: the spiral pattern on her white rug; the legs of the harmonium; her own white surprised face in the mirror. "I know where I am," she said. "I'm home." But she didn't remember the mirror. Who had brought it here? Had it been delivered by Mr. Fletcher, from his sack?

"I should go to the kitchen," she said. "Or I should take a nap." Step by step, feeling the great work her progress required, she walked to the kitchen, weighted down by the thousands of details that were in her way. A nick in the floor, a jolly afternoon sun, a cookie crumb in the shape of an elf sleeping on the dinner table. A brown lamp with a tiny dial switch on its base, and hundreds of slits in its metal shade. And on the harmonium, photographs. Photographs of her three daughters, and one of herself, Margaret, and her husband, Horace, sitting down beneath a chandelier somewhere, and smiling. In the chandelier were eight light bulbs, their glass transparent, like Mazda bulbs, shaped from a broad base to a sharp tip, like a flame. "Well, I never noticed," she said. "You can't blame me for that."

In the kitchen, she was drinking water when she looked out the window and saw them. They were dressed in uniforms, and they had big arms and big faces. They had their truck in the alley and were carefully loading chairs, lamps, sofas, and tables into it. She noticed that they didn't joke as they took Mrs. Silverman's furniture away, that it was a solemn event, like running up a flag. Feeling foolish and annoyed, Margaret cranked open the window and began to shout. "Who told you boys to come here? Where do you think you're taking those things?" She noticed a lion painted on the side of the moving van and was momentarily disconcerted. "I hope you boys know what you're doing!" she shouted at last, down to the large, astonished faces. When they finally looked away from her, she lifted the glass of water to them, drank, then spilled out the rest into the sink.

She tried to remember what she had planned to eat for either lunch or dinner and found her way back into the living room, where she sat down in front of the television set. She saw, reflected in the dark screen, herself, in black-and-white, miniaturized. She smiled and laughed at the tricks television could play, whether on or off. And then, behind her, but also in the background of the set, she saw a tree, waiting for her. Horace had left his trees behind when she and he had moved out of the house. She stood up and went to the window again, and with the clatter of furniture being hauled away in the alley serving as a background, she began to stare at the branches and dried leaves of the one tree the management had planted, and then she began to talk. She told the tree about Horace. Then she laughed and said that she and he would probably sit together again, checking on the sun and the other tricks of light shining from odd directions on the open gulf lying radiant and bare between them.

RON HANSEN is the author of a collection of short stories, *Nebraska*, and of the novels *Desperadoes, The Assassination of Jesse James by the Coward Robert Ford, Mariette in Ecstasy,* and *Atticus*. His next novel, *Hitler's Niece*, will be published in September. He teaches in the English Department at Santa Clara University where he is the Gerard Manley Hopkins, S. J. Professor in the Arts and Humanities.